Measuring Transport Equity

Measuring Transport Equity

Karen Lucas
Karel Martens
Floridea Di Ciommo
Ariane Dupont-Kieffer

ELSEVIER

Elsevier
Radarweg 29, PO Box 211, 1000 AE Amsterdam, Netherlands
The Boulevard, Langford Lane, Kidlington, Oxford OX5 1GB, United Kingdom
50 Hampshire Street, 5th Floor, Cambridge, MA 02139, United States

Library of Congress Cataloging-in-Publication Data
A catalog record for this book is available from the Library of Congress

British Library Cataloguing-in-Publication Data
A catalogue record for this book is available from the British Library

ISBN: 978-0-12-814818-1

For information on all Elsevier publications
visit our website at https://www.elsevier.com/books-and-journals

Publisher: Joe Hayton
Acquisition Editor: Brian Romer
Editorial Project Manager: Michelle W. Fisher
Production Project Manager: Anitha Sivaraj
Cover Designer: Miles Hitchen

Typeset by SPi Global, India

Working together
to grow libraries in
developing countries

www.elsevier.com • www.bookaid.org

Contents

Editors biography

Karen Lucas

Karen Lucas is a Professor of Transport and Social Analysis at the Institute of Transport Studies, University of Leeds, and the Deputy Director of the Leeds Social Sciences Institute. She has 20 years of experience in social research in transport. She is a world's leading expert in the area of transport-related social exclusion in the Global North and South. She leads the International Network for Transport and Accessibility in Low Income Communities (INTALInC). In 2015, she won Edward L. Ullman Award by the Transport Geography Specialty Group of the Association of American Geographers and in 2016 the University of Leeds "Women of Achievement" Award, both awards for her significant contribution to transportation geography. Karen is a regular advisor to national governments in the United Kingdom and abroad. She is a recent adviser to the New Zealand Government for its new Social Assessment of Transport guidance, and she is currently seconded to Highways England in the United Kingdom to set up the methodology for a community impact assessment of the Lower Thames Crossing project. Karen is cochair of the Special Interest Group on Cultural and Social Issues in Transport for the World Conference on Transport and Society (WCTRS) and of the NECTAR Cluster 7: Social and Health Impacts of Transport and a member of the Editorial Boards for the Journal of Transport Geography, Springer's Transportation journal, and Urban Book Series.

Karel Martens

Karel Martens is an Associate Professor at the Faculty of Architecture and Town Planning, Technion-Israel Institute of Technology (Haifa, Israel), and at the Institute for Management Research, Radboud University (Nijmegen, the Netherlands). He is also the chair of the Graduate Program in Urban and Regional Planning at the Technion. Martens is an international expert on transport and justice. He has authored numerous publications on the topic, culminating in his recent book *Transport Justice: Designing Fair Transportation Systems*, which has been described by colleagues as "groundbreaking" and "a revolution." His work has resonated in the academy and in practice, as evidenced by numerous invitations for keynote lectures, among others, in the United Kingdom, Belgium, the Netherlands, Italy, South Africa, Canada, Israel, and Germany. In 2014, Martens was elected Transport Professional of the Year in the Netherlands, in part because of his inspiring work on transport and justice. Martens is a member of the Editorial Board of the journals *Transport Policy* and *Sustainability*.

Floridea Di Ciommo

Floridea Di Ciommo is a codirector of the cooperative cambiaMO-changing MObility. She has an extensive experience on transport demand modeling and Transport Equity Assessment. She coordinated the EU Cost Action Transport Equity Analysis (TU 1209). She has extensively worked on the nexus between Travel behavior, social variables, and equity issues. She is a member of Transportation Research Board (TRB) Committees on Travel Behavior and Value and Women's Issues in Transportation. She is chairing the Behavioral Processes: Qualitative and Quantitative Methods subcommittee. She also regularly teaches at universities in Spain and in France and supervises students for their PhD or masters MSc. Currently, she is cochairing the WP on Mobility for the Urban Innovative Action project Mares Madrid and chairing WG1 of EU COST Action Wider Impacts and Scenario Evaluation of Autonomous and Connected Transport (WISE-ACT) (CA16222). She is cooperating with international and national institutions and associations such as the Organization for Economic Cooperation and Development (OECD), the Spanish Transport Department (DGT) for gender and transport aspects, and Climate Change Foundation for modeling health impacts of transport. She is involved in the Advisory Board of H2020 project such as Mobility and Time Value (MOTIV).

Ariane Dupont-Kieffer

Ariane Dupont-Kieffer, PhD, is the Dean of the Sorbonne School of Economics at the Université Paris 1 Panthéon-Sorbonne. Her research focuses on the links between economic theory, modeling and policy making, and policy assessment. She has done extensive research in the area of Epistemology and History of Economic Thought and focused specifically on the history of econometrics and macroeconomics and the relationship between measurement issues, statistical analysis, and policy making. After 10 years of experience of investigating theoretical and methodological issues, she worked with Institut Français des Sciences et Technologies des Transports, de l'Aménagement et des Réseaux (IFSTTAR) (former INRETS) to contribute to the assessment of road externalities. Within the perspective of sustainable transportation, she has developed the understanding of determinants of sustainable mobility with a focus on gender and equity issues to be related to efficiency. An important part of her work is dedicated to enhance international comparison of data on gender and equity in mobility and to translate research findings into policy implementation. Ariane was cochair of the EU COST Action "Transport Equity Analysis," where she developed with colleagues a proxy measure to appraise equity in urban mobility policy. She is a key member of the TRB Scientific Committee on Women's Issues in Transportation.

Authors biography

Imuentinyan Aivinhenyo

Mr. Imuentinyan Aivinhenyo is a Carnegie Research Fellow currently completing his Doctoral (PhD) dissertation at the Centre for Transport Studies, University of Cape Town (UCT) in South Africa. He has also been actively involved in teaching of various transportation engineering topics both at the undergraduate and postgraduate masters' level in the Department of Civil Engineering, UCT, since 2014. His research interests include public transport accessibility analyses in the context of social exclusion and urban poverty in low-income societies, equity issues in transport, and land-use/transport integration strategies.

Philippe Apparicio

Philippe Apparicio is a full professor at the Urbanisation Culture Société Research Center at INRS. He is also the director of the Environmental Equity Laboratory (LAEQ). His research focuses on environmental justice, air pollution, quality of life, and spatial analysis.

Jeroen Bastiaanssen

Jeroen Bastiaanssen is a PhD candidate at the Institute for Transport Studies, University of Leeds. He holds a Master's degree in Urban Planning and Transport from the Radboud University (2013), the Netherlands. His PhD research (2016–19) is sponsored by West Yorkshire Combined Authority (WYCA) (the United Kingdom) and the City of Rotterdam (NL) and examines the extent to which young people's employment outcomes in the United Kingdom and the Netherlands can be explained from their accessibility to employment opportunities.

Frans van den Bosch

Frans van den Bosch studied informatics and has over 25 years of experience in applying Geographic Information Science for Urban related applications. He executes a variety of tasks in the field of education, research, and consultancy at the Department of Urban and Regional Planning and Geo-Information Management at ITC, University of Twente. His main research interests are in (transport) system modeling and analysis with advanced GIS-based spatial analytic methods, modeling techniques, and the development of collaborative spatial decision support systems in urban planning.

Mark Brussel

Mark Brussel is a senior lecturer on urban infrastructure planning at the Department of Urban and Regional Planning and Geo-Information Management at ITC, University of Twente. He specializes in the application of Geographic Information Science in urban infrastructure systems. His current research interests are in spatial and social equity of infrastructure systems, spatial decision support in infrastructure planning, and sustainable transport.

Juan Antonio Carrasco

Dr. Juan Antonio Carrasco is an Associate Professor of Transport Engineering and Planning at the Universidad de Concepcion in Chile. His research has mainly focused on the development of analytic methods for modeling and understanding travel behavior and its implications in the overall urban context. He is a pioneer studying the role of social networks in travel behavior, both in the development of new data collection techniques and in the analysis of the role of social structure in space and its travel implications. He is also codirector of the Chilean Center for Sustainable Urban Development (CEDEUS).

Mathieu Carrier

Mathieu Carrier is an urban planner and received a PhD in urban studies from the Centre Urbanisation Culture Société Research Center of the National Institute of Scientific Research (INRS) in 2015. He is also an associate professor at the INRS. His research focuses on environmental equity, land-use planning, and road traffic noise.

Giuseppe Costa

Giuseppe Costa is a Professor of Public Health at the Department of Clinical and Biological Sciences of the University of Turin and an Epidemiologist and head of the Regional Unit of Epidemiology and Health Promotion in the Piedmont Region since 1994. His research interests are in health inequalities and in particular social inequalities in health, health information systems, environmental and occupational health (occupational mortality, occupational injuries, and risk communication), migrants and health system, health impact assessment, and policy evaluation.

Adrian Davis

Dr. Adrian Davis is a Professor of Transport and Health (a global first), based at the Transport Research Institute, Edinburgh Napier University. He has an international reputation in the interdisciplinary field of road transport and health, which he has helped to shape for over 30 years. As designer and evidence adviser on road safety for Bristol City Council since 2008, including for the city-wide 20mph program, Adrian coauthored the Safe Systems Road Safety Plan for Bristol City Council in 2015.

Steven Farber

Steven Farber is an assistant professor in the Department of Human Geography at the University of Toronto Scarborough. He is the codirector of the Spatial Analysis of Urban Systems (SAUSy) Lab. His research focuses on the social and economic effects of transportation policy and travel behavior.

Koos Fransen

Koos Fransen is a postdoctoral fellow at the Cosmopolis research group at the Vrije Universiteit Brussel (Belgium). He has a background in Industrial Engineering—Land Surveying and Urbanism and Spatial Planning. His research focuses on accessibility and its link to spatial planning and transport policy, with a primary focus on aspects of social exclusion and transport poverty. In 2018, he received the Flemish Association for Geographic Information Systems (FLAGIS) and Automatic Mapping/Facility Management AM/FM-GIS BeGeo Geospatial Awards for his PhD thesis on the impact of temporal and personal restrictions on equitable access to opportunities.

Karst T. Geurs

Karst T. Geurs is a full Professor of Transport Planning at the Centre for Transport Studies, University of Twente. His research focuses on the dynamics in travel behavior, accessibility modeling, smartphone-based travel data collections, and new mobility services. In 2006, he received his PhD at the Faculty of Geosciences, Utrecht University, the Netherlands, on accessibility appraisal of land-use and transport policy strategies. He is chair of the Network on European Communications and Transport Activities Research (NECTAR) and the Editor in Chief of the European Transport Research Review (ETRR).

Aaron Golub

Dr. Golub is a director and associate professor in the Toulan School of Urban Studies and Planning at Portland State University (PSU). His work focuses on the social contexts of urban transportation systems, explored in three ways: (1) how people participate in transportation planning and who wins and loses from transportation plans; (2) planning, research, and advocacy in support of alternatives to the automobile (especially public transportation and bicycles); and (3) the historical roots of automobile dependence in the United States. At PSU, Dr. Golub teaches courses on urban transportation policy, planning research methods, transportation finance, and public transportation.

Wenbo Guo

Wenbo Guo is a DPh (PhD) candidate of Transport Studies Unit at the School of Geography and the Environment, University of Oxford. His research focuses on the interactions between mobility, subjective well-being, and air pollution in rapidly socioeconomic transitional Chinese cities.

Alvaro Guzman

Dr. Alvaro Guzman is the Executive Director of the National Transportation Agency in Ecuador. He gained his PhD at the University of Leeds studying the Role of Power during the Implementation of BRT Systems. Prior to this, he gained a wide range of experience in transport projects in Latin America. His work focuses on reducing transport inequality, increasing accessibility for the most vulnerable, and reducing road casualties.

Alex Karner

Alex Karner, PhD, is an assistant professor in the Graduate Program in Community and Regional Planning at The University of Texas at Austin. His work critically engages with the practice of transportation planning with the goal of achieving progress toward equity and sustainability. To this end, he develops innovative methods for analyzing the performance of integrated transportation/land-use systems in the areas of civil rights, environmental justice, public health, and climate change. He teaches classes in advanced GIS, demography, and transportation policy/planning.

Haneen Khreis

Haneen Khreis, PhD, is a cross-disciplinary expert in the health impacts of transport planning and policy. She has experience in transport planning and engineering, vehicle emissions, air quality, exposure assessment, health impact and burden of disease assessment, policy option generation, knowledge translation, cross-disciplinary collaboration, and science-policy link in transport and health. She has published broadly on the topic and has recently edited a book on *Integrating Human Health into Urban and Transport Planning*.

Tiffany Lam

Tiffany Lam is an urban policy researcher with expertise in gender, cycling and sustainable mobility, and urban climate action. She has done cycling advocacy in London, New York City, and Washington, DC, and recently created a zine, *Mind the Cycling*

Gender Gap, to elevate gender-inclusive urban cycling in public policy and debate. She holds an MSc in City Design and Social Science from LSE Cities and a BA in Women's Studies and Peace & Justice Studies from Tufts University.

Beatriz Mella Lira

Beatriz Mella Lira is a Research Assistant and PhD candidate at the Bartlett School of Planning, UCL. She is an Architect with a Master's degree in Urban Development from P. Universidad Catolica de Chile (2013). Her PhD research is sponsored by Becas Chile (2014–18) and examines transport and social equity in Santiago, Chile. She leads the Doctoral Research Group on Transport and Social Equity and guest lectures at UCL.

Francesc Magrinyá

Francesc Magrinyá is a director of strategically planning Barcelona Metropolitan Area. He used to be an assistant professor of urban planning at the Technical University of Catalonia (UPC). He worked at the Catalan Agency for Urban Ecology of Barcelona (2000–06), in which he participated, among others, in the project Octagonal Barcelona Bus Network and in the draft of the Superblock of Gracia. He has worked since 1988 in various jobs and transport planning consultancy. He has organized two expositions about urban planning in Barcelona: Cerdà. Urbs i Territori (1994) and 150 anys of Modernitat Cerdà (2009). His social activity has been performed in cooperation projects (American Securitization Forum (ASF) and European Securitization Forum (ESF)) and cultural (Idensitat and Collective Architectures), environmental (CST, PTP, BACC, and Som Energia), and social entities (RecreantCruïlles).

Lucy Mahoney

Lucy Mahoney leads the Mobility Management Network at C40 Cities Climate Leadership Group. She has worked for Transport for London (TfL) where she was in Road Safety, Public Transport Strategy and in the Road Strategy and Freight team. Lucy read Geography and the Environment for her DPh at the University of Oxford based within the Transport Studies Unit (TSU).

Martin van Maarseveen

Martin van Maarseveen is an Emeritus Professor of Management of Urban-Regional Dynamics at the University of Twente, faculty ITC. He started his career at TNO, the Netherlands Organization for Applied Scientific Research, and worked as a senior researcher and later Director of the Traffic and Transportation Research Centre in Delft. In 1995, he became a full Professor of Strategic Transport Planning and Sustainable Development, and Head of the Centre for Transport Studies at the University of Twente. He has been a lecturer in transport planning, transport modeling, travel demand analysis, traffic engineering, traffic flow theory, sustainable transport analysis, and traffic safety.

Giulia Melis

Giulia Melis is an Architect and MSc in History and Conservation of Architectural and Environmental Heritage. Since 2007, she is collaborating with Istituto Superiore sui Sistemi Territoriali per l'Innovazione (SiTI), where she holds a position as senior researcher at Environmental heritage and urban redevelopment Unit. She is involved in several projects on strategic planning and urban renewal, ranging from EU to local level. Her main research interests encompass participatory methods, spatial Decision Support System (sDSS), smart solutions for sustainability in urban areas, impacts of the built environment on citizens' health, and inequalities.

Talat Munshi

Talat Munshi is working as PostDoc at UNEP DTU partnership, Denmark Technical University, and is also an Associate Professor at the Faculty of Planning, CEPT University (CEPT), India. Prior to his current employment, he has worked as Lecturer in Transport at the Faculty of ITC (ITC), University of Twente in the Netherlands, and at The Energy and Resources Institute (TERI) University in India. An engineer by background, he has a PhD from ITC and has two master's degrees in planning from CEPT and in urban infrastructure management from ITC. His research interests cover areas including urban development planning, social equity, transport planning, and the use of geoinformation.

Tijs Neutens

Tijs Neutens has 10 years of academic experience in the field of transport and health geography, of which he served 5 years as a postdoctoral research fellow at the Research Foundation Flanders (FWO) in Belgium. He has coauthored over 55 papers in international peer-reviewed journals. From November 2014 till March 2018, Tijs was an adviser of Social Affairs and Public Health to the Deputy Prime Minister and the Minister of Public Health in Belgium. In April 2018, Tijs joined a pharmaceutical company as Government Affairs and Corporate Communication Senior Manager.

Mark J. Nieuwenhuijsen

Mark J Nieuwenhuijsen, PhD, is the Director of the Urban Planning, Environment and Health Initiative at ISGlobal in Barcelona. He is a world's leading expert in environmental exposure assessment, epidemiology, and health risk/impact assessment with a strong focus and interest on healthy urban living through better urban and transport planning.

Ian Philips

Dr. Ian Philips is a senior research fellow at the Institute for Transport Studies, University of Leeds. He has worked on projects using spatial data, GIS, and spatial analysis to understand social and environmental issues in transport in order to provide insights to policy makers.

Paul Pilkington

Dr. Paul Pilkington is a registered Public Health Specialist and Senior Lecturer in Public Health in the Faculty of Health and Applied Sciences, University of the West of England (UWE), Bristol. Taking a socioecological perspective, Paul's research centers on how the promotion of healthy and sustainable environments can impact on population health and well-being. Paul's particular interests include how to reduce danger in the road environment and better consideration of health in the development and spatial planning process. Paul has published widely in international peer-reviewed journals and presented at numerous national and international conferences.

John P. Pritchard

John P. Pritchard works as a researcher at the University of Twente. He holds a BS in Civil Engineering from Northwestern University and a PhD in Transportation Systems from the University of Lisbon, where he conducted his doctoral research as part of the MIT Portugal program.

Louise Reardon

Louise Reardon is a lecturer in Governance and Public Policy at the Institute of Local Government Studies (INLOGOV), University of Birmingham. Louise has authored a number of publications on public policy and well-being, including her recent book (coauthored with Ian Bache, University of Sheffield) *The Politics and Policy of Wellbeing: Understanding the Rise and Significance of a New Agenda* published with Edward Elgar.

Gianni Rondinella

Gianni Rondinella is an urban planner. In 2010, he cofounded the cooperative cambiaMO-changing MObility to provide a tool for urban mobility transformation. He is an expert in nonmotorized urban mobility and has more than 15 years of experience in the field of urban sustainability and alternatives to the current sociotechnical mobility system. He also works on conflicts and synergies between different modes and users of transport and public space and on their effects in terms of social equity, deepening knowledge, and strategies to make urban spaces more livable for citizens, in particular for walking, cycling, and public transport.

Yoram Shiftan

Yoram Shiftan is a Professor of Civil and Environmental Engineering in the Technion and the previous head of Technion Transportation Research Institute. Prof. Shiftan teaches and conducts research in travel behavior with a focus on activity-based modeling and response to policies and technology, transport economics, and project evaluation. Lately, his research focuses on activity and travel behavior implications of autonomous vehicles and new transportation services. Prof. Shiftan was the editor of Transport Policy and the previous chair of the International Association of Travel Behavior Research (IATBR). Prof. Shiftan received his PhD from MIT and since then has published dozens of papers and coedited four books.

Yamini Jain Singh

Yamini J. Singh (PhD) is an urban and transport planner, author, entrepreneur, and public speaker. Her research interests include sustainable mobility, social impacts of smart mobility/cities, and gendered mobility. During her work experience in India and the Netherlands, she has worked on projects funded by the World Bank and Asian Development Bank, published research articles, given lectures internationally, advised PhD students, and reviewed papers for journals. She recently gave a TEDx talk on gendered mobility at Amsterdam, the Netherlands, and her forthcoming book on "transit-oriented development for developing countries" will be published by Springer.

Marcin Stępniak

Marcin Stępniak is Marie Curie Postdoctoral fellow at the tGIS Transport, Infrastructure and Territory research group at the Complutense University of Madrid. He holds a PhD in Earth Sciences (2011, Institute of Geography and Spatial Organization, Polish Academy of Sciences). His research focuses on urban and transport geography, accessibility, and application of Geographic Information Science (GIS).

Morena Stroscia

Morena Stroscia is a Public Health MD. She works at the Turin Public Health Office—Urban and Environmental Hygiene Service—and collaborates with the ASL TO3 Epidemiology Unit in researches, which deal with health inequalities, environment and built environment impact on health, health-care system performance evaluation, and stakeholder engagement.

Matteo Tabasso

Matteo Tabasso holds a Master of Science degree in Architecture and Urban Planning of Politecnico di Torino. Since 1998, he developed an extended experience in transport and urban planning both working for public authorities and for research institutions. Since July 2006, he has coordinating researches and projects on urban redevelopment. The main recent experiences concern the land-use management, the redevelopment of brownfields, and the analysis of the link between urban environment and health. He also took part to several European networks and projects.

Tanu Priya Uteng

Tanu Priya Uteng (PhD), senior researcher at the Institute of Transport Economics in Oslo, has worked extensively across a host of crosscutting issues in the field of urban and transport planning. She is currently leading and participating in multiple long-term strategic research projects, funded by the Norwegian Research Council, Nordic Council of Ministers, and EU, studying green shift, shared mobilities, and inclusive public spaces. Her first book *Gendered Mobilities* was published in 2008, while her second book *Urban Mobilities* in the Global South came out in fall 2017. Her latest, *Gendering Smart Mobilities*, will be available in Spring 2019.

Mark Zuidgeest

Mark Zuidgeest is the South African National Roads Agency Limited (SANRAL) Chair in Transport Planning and Engineering at the University of Cape Town in South Africa since 2013. He is a civil engineer by training with degrees from the University of Twente in the Netherlands. His main research interest is in transport system modeling, analysis, and assessment, using GIS, Agent-Based Simulation, and travel demand models, particularly related to questions of transport-related social exclusion in the Global South.

Foreword

The society in the 21st century is becoming increasingly polarized between those that are wealthy and those that are poor. In the past, there has been an understanding that those in need would be supported by the state so that a sufficient quality of life could be guaranteed for all. But more recently, the state has substantially reduced its investment and levels of subsidy across many sectors of the economy (e.g., for housing and welfare), and many public services have been privatized. The society has moved away from a concern over the welfare of all its people to one than places a much stronger role on the individual to look after her(him)self. Nevertheless, there are still many people that cannot provide fully for themselves and they still need the support of their families, local communities, and the state to enjoy a reasonable quality of life, together with the opportunity to fully engage in the society.

Since 2008, these changes have become more pronounced as result of a combination of financial meltdown, globalization, and technological innovation. This "perfect storm" has led to lower wages, higher levels of debt, skilled job losses, cheap goods, and the substitution of technology for labor (automation). Individually, these effects are not necessarily problematical, but taken together it has meant that questions of fairness and justice have become even more important. These impacts have highlighted the increasing patterns of inequality that have now become entrenched. People have begun to feel disempowered, and this in turn has led to the rise in populism and the politics of discontentment.

Transport provides a fine example of such inequalities as there are many people (the rich) that do not need any subsidy or particular provision, as they have the freedom to do what they want, when they want, they have no constraints over how far they might travel, and perhaps little concern over the impact they may have on other people's mobility or quality of life. However, there are many others (perhaps the majority) that do not have that same freedoms. The equity debate is directed at these disadvantaged people that do not have the opportunities to get access to "needed" services and facilities (including jobs). Such a requirement might be seen as a right in a fair and just society. In addition, there are many groups within the society that are seen to be more vulnerable in the sense that the transport services available to them are not suited to their particular needs.

Together, these two forms of transport disadvantage mean that the inequalities are likely to be maintained or increased as a result of societal polarization. Measurement is central to our understanding of the scale and the nature of equity, and how it has changed over time. It is not just the measurement of the growing transport inequity between nations, but also a clear indication of the substantial variations that occur within nations. Transport inequity is both global and local.

Transport is also unique in that it is not usually seen as a basic right or even one of the fundamental needs, yet it impacts on all of them as it provides the connectivity between all activities. All societies require transport for the movement of people and goods, and the absence of suitable means to get around discriminates against those people with perhaps the greatest needs–transport must be available, accessible, and affordable for all.

To begin to breakdown these barriers so that transport provision becomes available, accessible, and affordable for all is not straightforward. A clear sequence is required that starts with problem identification, the assemblage of the evidence, and the measurement of the extent and scale of equity in transport. The sequence then moves onto the analysis of the problems identified, followed by the testing of possible solutions, and the recommendations to policy and decision makers.

The editors and authors contributing to this book provide such a framework for the measurement of transport equity. As acknowledged in the book, it is not just the direct effects of not being able to get to needed services and facilities, but also the implications on the individual well-being, and the health, employment, and educational opportunities available to the disadvantaged. The benefits of transport mobility and accessibility are addressed, together with the burdens created by highly mobile car-dependent lifestyles. The disadvantaged include those that travel less and create fewer externalities, yet they are the ones that are impacted more by pollution, noise, and danger created by the most mobile. This double injustice is also likely to have impacts on their health and well-being.

In a just society, the social outcomes from interventions in transport must form an integral part of evaluation. Too often the concern is primarily over whether the society as a whole benefits, and not over the question of who actually benefits. Perhaps, it is always the same people that benefit disproportionately at the expense of others, hence increasing rather than decreasing the levels of inequity. Measurement here should cover both the direct and indirect effects from the transport investment (or subsidy), and the indirect effects from the externalities (imposed by others), and the implications of not being able to fully engage in everyday activities.

Transport equity is not just about transport or just about equity, but it is a part of what we value in our society–whether it is fair and just and the rights that each person is entitled to. In more substantive terms, this would include well-being, opportunity, inclusivity, the quality of life, and the ability to engage and participate in decisions that have a direct or indirect effect on any individual. It is also about accepting the premise that transport can and should contribute to each of these societal values positively.

David Banister

Part One

Introduction

Introduction

Karen Lucas, Karel Martens, Floridea Di Ciommo, Ariane Dupont-Kieffer

1

1 Introduction to the book

This book aims to introduce the researchers and policymakers interested in the issue of transport equity to a range of approaches to evaluate what is a fair allocation of transport resources between different population groups and places. This is a thorny issue which has already been identified as an important policy problem for the 21st century within an array of academic and policy literatures. In this book, we do not attempt to directly revisit or review these wide-ranging discussions, except to say that many of them have helped to shape our own understandings of what transport inequity might be like, how it occurs, and its social consequences for the individuals and wider society.

What we do is to offer *a range of practical methods and evaluation tools* (without necessarily preferring one over the other) to allow readers to select approaches that best fit a specific line of inquiry or identified area of transport-related disparities. By employing various approaches in parallel, the analyst will be able to develop more systematic and deeper understandings of the underlying causal factors which drive inequities in transport. This will help to identify, and subsequently to evaluate, practical ways to direct transport decision making toward more socially and spatially equitable solutions that are inclusive for all.

Typically, the analyses presented in the book demonstrate that the *benefits* of the transport systems, such as mobility resources and the accessibility these provide to goods, services, and activity destinations, are not fairly distributed across different sectors of the population and the places where they live, work, and play. The various methods that we present in the chapters of this book seek to draw out differences in framings of these transport "problems," to identify who and where is most or least advantaged by the system of provision, and to evaluate how this can link to wider social problems, such as unemployment, poor healthcare uptake, and social isolation.

Perversely, the people who have the lowest access to vehicle ownership, less overall vehicle use, and poorer availability of other transport resources (e.g., physical infrastructures, online ticket booking and journey planner systems, etc.), are most often also the worst impacted by the *disbenefits* of the transport system. In the book, the authors analyzing the distribution of the exposure to these negative impacts identify how vulnerable population sectors, such as children, older people, and low-income households are often the most disproportionately affected by traffic-related injuries and fatalities, air and noise pollution, and attacks on their personal safety. Whilst all these negative transport impacts can create serious problems for the affected individuals, they are also a significant burden for the society as a whole in terms of increased health costs, reduced social cohesion, and diminished community well-being.

Measuring Transport Equity. https://doi.org/10.1016/B978-0-12-814818-1.00001-9

Transport decision makers, in different and diverse contexts worldwide, and in both the Global North and South, are increasingly recognizing these important transport inequities, as well as an increasingly urgent need to address them in the achievement of economically productive, environmentally sustainable, and socially inclusive cities. To do so, they require new evaluation tools that can readily signal the equity implications of their decision processes and policy options and to evaluate the success of their policy interventions in terms of reducing inequities of outcome. Simultaneously, more and more students in transport studies, and related fields such as environmental and public health sciences, urban geography, and planning, are turning their attention toward transport equity, as a fruitful topic for study and new research developments. The book aims to help them in this most important and rewarding journey.

2   Discussion of different concepts of equity and its measurement

How transport equity is defined can significantly influence the way that it is measured as well as the analytical outcome. A policy solution may seem equitable when evaluated one way but inequitable when evaluated another way, when using different datasets or metrics, or when conducting analyses at different spatial scales, and when considering various social factors.

In this book, we take the view that there is *no single correct approach to measuring transport equity*, and that it is possible to consider various positionings, perspectives, contexts, measures, and methodologies. In the main, however, the four key issues for transport equity analysis relate to the questions about:

(1) A *fair allocation* of transport resources, including infrastructures, services, and expenditures—it is recognized that additional resources or efforts may need to be targeted toward some groups in order to bring them into line with the rest of the population.
(2) A *fair opportunity* to be mobile in order to gain accessibility to key "life chance" activities—however, it is also recognized that providing accessibility opportunities may not necessarily involve the need to be mobile, in fact there are often tensions between increased mobility, especially for already highly mobile segments of the population, and increased travel burdens for the least mobile.
(3) The *reduction of adverse effects* of transport systems—including exposures to pollution, traffic-related risks, and personal safety, with particular emphasis on protecting the most vulnerable population groups.
(4) *Widening participation* in the decision-making process—it is recognized that the people and communities who are currently suffering inequities from the transport system should be given a (larger) say in how these problems are resolved as an integral part of the policy process.

An important issue in each of these four cases is where to set the benchmark in terms of the desired policy outcome. Is it the policy intention to create parity of opportunity, for instance that everyone has *equality of opportunity* to connect via public transit with key destinations such as employment, education, and health-care services? Or to adopt a policy of *zero tolerance* whereby no person should be exposed to unhealthy levels of

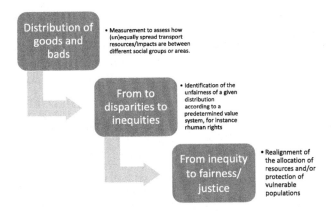

Fig. 1 Simple schema for measuring transport equity at different stages of its interpretation.

traffic pollutants? Or is it the intention to target those who are the worst off by ensuring that they have a sufficient level of access to given goods and services based on a benchmark of what is deemed to be an acceptable level within society?

Each benchmark or policy goal will require a different form of measurement and metric to determine "equity." What is most important in the interpretation of such analyses, is that a disparity in the distribution of goods and services does not necessarily denote an inequity and that noting an inequity is a long way from delivering fairness in terms of the realignment of the allocation of resources and/or protection of individuals (as shown in Fig. 1).

Because this issue of the type of comparison that is being made is such an important issue to consider in the determination of appropriate policy responses to transport inequities and to the chapters of this book, we next offer some further discussion of the separation between these different interpretations.

2.1 Observed differences or disparities

Uncovering, explaining, and understanding patterns in people's behaviors are one of the core missions of social research. It may, therefore, be no surprise that a substantial share of transport equity research (in its broadest definition) analyzes the differences between people in multiple dimensions, such as the number of trips, daily travel distances, the use of transport modes, traffic-related deaths and injuries, the share of public transport subsidies received, the transport-related tax burden, or the exposure to transport-related pollution. From studying patterns and differences, it is only a small step to the analysis of disparities.

The transport literature abounds with studies that primarily employ the word "disparities" in a descriptive sense. A large share of these transport studies goes further and employs the word disparities to implicitly or explicitly identify observed differences as "unfair or inequitable." Such studies often fall short in presenting an explicit standard for assessment, and fail to acknowledge that the mere observation of disparities does not, by itself, raise issues of equity. Hence, in this book, we use the word disparities merely in a descriptive sense and thus as a synonym for differences or dissimilarities. The aim of the chapters is then to go beyond the description of disparities toward an *explicit assessment of inequity, for which a directly stated evaluation standard* is needed to actually determine whether a disparity is fair or not.

2.2 Moving from disparities to inequality to inequity

One reason why disparity in behaviors and outcomes are often perceived as unfair, lies in the (implicit and often intuitive) use of the normative benchmark of equality. Against this background, the step between observing disparities and (implicitly) criticizing them because they imply a deviation from equality is then but a small one. This typically goes hand in hand with a concern for the protection of vulnerable population groups, for instance in terms of gender, socioeconomic position, age, ethnicity, disability, or disadvantaged residential location.

At the same time, it should be acknowledged that equality, like disparity, can also be used in a solely descriptive way. A descriptive use of the term would include statements like "rich and poor households spend an equal amount of money on transport." Such a statement, which is centered on the notion of equality, may implicitly equate the word "equal" with "fair," "just," or "equitable." However, such a descriptive statement does not point at an issue of justice or injustice, unless there is a clear and explicit benchmark. For example, a possible benchmark could be that spending an equal amount is fair (in which case the statement above points at a fair or just state of affairs) or that transport expenditures should be affordable for all households (in which case the statement above may point toward an injustice). The step from inequalities to inequities is but a small one, but it should be underscored that inequalities only become a matter of justice if equality is considered as the morally proper state of affairs.

2.3 From measured inequities to judgments about fairness and justice

The final, and perhaps most difficult step, is to move from the observation of inequities to policies and interventions addressing inequities so as to promote greater fairness and justice. This will often imply painful choices that maybe at odds with traditional and still dominant preconceptions regarding the primary economic purpose of transport planning and policy. While much of the current policy attention is directed toward solving congestion and reducing journey times, equity analyses may unveil a very different set of problems. Some of these are already on the agenda of many governments in both the Global North and South, such as the need to reduce traffic-related air pollution and traffic fatalities and injuries. Equity analyses may underscore the need to intensify these efforts and to direct them toward particularly vulnerable population groups. Other inequities, such as those related to improved accessibility to key life chances for the purposes of social inclusion, have received very little attention in most countries and its "treatment" may well require quite radical changes in investment priorities. For example, a move away from major roads and long-distance infrastructures, toward more localized investments in the transport options that are more readily available to transport poor populations, such as walking, cycling and road-safety infrastructures, and the subsidy of informal and formal transit services. The fundamental point is that such policies can only be justified on a proper understanding of inequity in transport. The explicit acknowledgment of inequities is a prerequisite to move toward the delivery of fairness and justice.

3 Equity, fairness, and justice

More than the notions of equity and fairness, the term justice is used in multiple contexts and multiple ways. The list is nearly endless and includes legal justice, social justice, environmental justice, spatial justice, distributive justice, procedural justice, and intergenerational justice. First of all, it is important to distinguish between *legal justice* and *social justice*. Legal justice refers to "the proper administration of the law," whereas social justice is typically applied to concerns about the moral acceptability of a situation, often irrespective of its formal legality. Obviously, in a "well-organized" society, legal justice is rooted in conceptions of social justice.

In this book, we are only concerned with social justice, not about the question whether transport systems have been provided in line with the letter of the law. Nevertheless, social justice is still a broad term, often defined as the "morally proper" distribution of benefits and burdens among members of a society. Given its focus on distribution, this conceptualization of social justice is often captured with the term distributive justice. Definitions of *distributive justice* highlight three key components relevant for measuring equity (see also Chapter 2 in this volume):

(1) What benefits and burdens should be the subject of analysis, for example, mobility, accessibility, traffic risks, traffic pollutions, etc.?
(2) By what social characteristics should different members of society be distinguished, for example, by age, gender, income, home location, etc.?
(3) Which yardstick or distributive principle should be used to determine whether a particular distribution is just, fair, or equitable, for example, should everyone get the same, or should those in most need get more, should most vulnerable be most protected or should there be zero tolerance, etc.?

In terms of transport, it is important to note that what is considered to be the general norm for the majority within a society is not necessarily fair for everyone living within it. For example, in the global north, it is the norm for people to own and drive a car; it does not follow that the best route for transport justice is to give everyone a car. For one reason, not everyone is able to drive, and for another vehicle ownership can be a considerable burden on household finances. There is also the conflicting issue that road traffic causes pedestrian and cyclist deaths, and pollution, which mostly adversely affects the most vulnerable in the society, who morally should be protected from harm.

There is also a distinction to be made here between *wants* and *needs*. Some people may want to travel further and faster than everyone else, but this doesn't necessarily mean that they should be able to, or that it is socially just for them to do so. This is why we have laws in place to make sure that people drive safely for the protection of others. Comparable laws exist to protect people from other damaging effects of road traffic, such as air and noise pollution, although the implementation of these laws is often lagging in spite of the proven detrimental effects on people's health and well-being. So, while the majority of people may want to drive, a more socially just transport system would restrict how much and where they use motor vehicles to protect the interests of those experiencing the adverse effect and in the wider interests of protecting public health.

There is also a difference between perceived and actual need here or in other words between *choice* and *necessity*. People who choose to live in a place which is remote from their place of employment or their children's school may need to travel more, but this is not the same as having a basic need to do so because they have made the choice to adopt this lifestyle. On the other hand, if households have little choice over where they live (e.g., because they are locked into social housing and cannot afford to relocate) and they reside in an inaccessible location with inadequate public transport services, they may need to own a car out of necessity. This can then place an unfair burden on their household, due to the costs of owning and maintaining a vehicle. In practice, it will be often difficult to determine whether people are responsible for their residential and other choices or whether they are induced to do so by the circumstances, implying that it may often be impossible to take people's responsibility into account when measuring and promoting transport equity.

4   Outline of contents

Following on from this introductory chapter, in Part 1, Chapter 2 *Martens, Lucas, and Bastiaanssen* offer a broad discussion of the key issues associated with the development of indicators and metrics for transport equity assessment. They then propose an overarching indicators framework for measuring the different factors associated with the distribution of transport benefits and burdens and offer some basic principles for determining what might be considered a "fair" or "proper" allocation of transport resources and negative burdens from the transport system in different places and across different populations.

The book is then separated into three parts according to the different topics that are covered and for ease of reference.

Part 2: Benefits of transport—mobility and accessibility comprises five chapters to demonstrate a variety of different ways in which measures of mobility and accessibility have been developed to determine transport equity. Each chapter focuses on different aspects of mobility and accessibility (e.g., journey distance, mode type, and affordability) and activity destinations (e.g., employment, health care, and education) and compares the disaggregated outcomes for different population groups (e.g., by age or gender or ethnicity) and/or different spatial areas (e.g., high- and low-income settlements). The authors also discuss the use of accessibility indicators in different geographical contexts, where the issues for transport equity might affect larger or smaller parts of the population, for example, in Europe, the United States, India, or Africa.

In Chapter 3, *Martens and Bastiaanssen* expand the initial indicator development ideas they identify in Chapter 2 to develop a place-based *accessibility poverty risk index* underpinned by the measurement of income poverty. The latter is bidimensional, taking into account both the intensity of accessibility poverty—how low is the general accessibility level experienced by a person—and the extent of accessibility poverty—how many people are affected by accessibility poverty? The index is applied to analyze the Rotterdam—The Hague region, showing surprising results, which underscore the need to develop existing public transportation in (sub)urban areas.

Following directly on from the previous chapter approach, in Chapter 4, *Fransen Farber and Neutens* follow in the traditions of Hägerstrand's time geography approaches to develop and apply a person-based metric of accessibility. The method allows for highly individualized analyses of people's time-space trajectories, which can be used to pinpoint the role of transport in their accessibility to key destinations, as well as their time and distance-based travel constraints. The authors discuss both the advantages and disadvantages of their method, including the tendency for data hungry tools and technologies. The approach is then applied to the US case study of Salt Lake City.

Next, in Chapter 5, *Pritchard, Geurs, and Stepniak* turn their attention to the measurement of bicycle and walking accessibility with particular attention to the notion of "bike and ride," the use of the bicycle and public transport for one trip, which can considerably enhance accessibility for people who depend on public transport for their mobility. They take adopt an egalitarian measure of equity to analyze national and city-level distributions of accessibility by mode and analyze how bike and ride can reduce the gaps between car-based and public transport-based accessibility.

Chapter 6 shifts our attention from the Global North to Ahmedabad in India where author *Brussel* evaluates the spatial and social equity of two urban transit systems–Bus Rapid Transit and Metro. He uses network systems modeling based on geographic information systems (GIS) to measure the levels of public transport accessibility to jobs. The focus of the case study analysis is to assess the accessibility impacts of, first, planned improvements in the public transport system, and, second, an evaluation of how well these improvements serve a housing relocation project, which removes low-income households to a peripheral locations. The results show that the public transport improvements will not be able to compensate for the enormous drop in accessibility for most of the relocated population. This latter issue is a repeated phenomenon for many rapidly urbanizing cities, where lower-income people are locating or being relocated to the urban periphery to live, remote from the economic opportunities the city has to offer.

Continuing with the focus on Global South cities but this time South Africa, *Aivinhenyo and Zuidgeest* use a gravity-based model to evaluate city-wide job accessibility via the multimodal transit options that are available in the City of Cape Town. In particular, they investigate the impact of household income and travel budget restrictions on people's place-based accessibility, showing which populations experience a particularly large drop in accessibility if concerns over affordability are considered. As the authors point out, this is a critical issue for many of the lowest-income households in development contexts, who often spend a disproportionately high proportion of their household budgets to meet their basic daily travel needs.

Part 3: *Burdens of Transport–health, environment, and other externalities* comprises five chapters that primarily focus on the burdens related to transport and how these are often unevenly distributed across different spatial locations and populations groups. These issues should not be seen separate from the one of mobility and accessibility because often the people who have the greatest allocation of mobility resources, particularly cars, are the ones who generate the greatest burdens for those with the least benefits and resources. This phenomenon is often referred to in the literatures as "transport injustice," and so many of the chapters in this section concentrate on the measurement of who is most affected by these burdens.

In Chapter 8, *Khreis and Nieuwenhuijsen* relate the negative externalities of road traffic, particularly traffic-related air pollutants (TRAP), to their direct and indirect impacts on human health. The authors provide a framework for policymakers to investigate this causal relationship and to identify the vulnerable groups who are most deeply impacted by pollution exposures. Their framework enables transport and public health policymakers to assess the more or less fair distribution of road projects in terms of health for the entire inhabitants of an area.

Continuing with a focus on health, in Chapter 9, *Melis and her coauthors* seek to identify the urban and transport determinants of mental ill-health and stress. It uses a longitudinal dataset, which was started in 1971 to describe the health status of the population to identify how different traffic externalities and urban structures can contribute to mortality and morbidity across different demographic profiles. Their approach is applied to a case study of the City of Turin where their results were used to involve local decision makers in a health audit process to reduce health inequalities city-wide.

In Chapter 8, *Davis and Pilkington* turn their attention to the issue of road safety where they propose an approach that aims to assess the full equity implications of road injury outcomes in a case study of Bristol in the United Kingdom. Their Road Safety Equity (RoSE) approach offers a set of guidance principles for the introduction of transport policies, such as 20 mph zones to reduce danger on the roads with a focus on vulnerable road users such as pedestrians and cyclists. The authors investigate the assumption that higher social classes tend to use travel modes which increase the exposure to road risk to other users, whilst poorer classes are disproportionately disadvantaged in this respect.

Next turning to the Canadian context, in Chapter 11, *Carrier and Apparicio* offer a framework to measure the socio-spatial distribution of environmental impacts of road traffic such as air and noise pollution and also road fatalities risk. They first measure the spatial concentrations of these burdens using GIS-based tools in a case study of the Island of Montréal and they then determine whether minority populations and low-income individuals are overrepresented as the residents of these locations. The authors then evaluate the potential of different policy interventions to tackle these environmental burdens for the most disadvantaged populations in the city.

The authors of the final chapter of this section adopt a female-centric approach to the issue of personal safety within the transport and urban realm with particular reference to Global South cities. Priya Uteng, Singh, and Lam argue the need for a gendered perspective within mainstream urban and transport planning agendas to make cities safe places for women to inhabit and be mobile. The chapter draws on the Indian context where there has been a considerable concern about the unsafe travel environments for women and the problems of "eve-teasing" whilst using the public transport system. Their chapter offers a number of safety audit tools for generating the information base to expose the inequities embedded in gendered urban landscapes and to create safer travel environments, specifically for women, but ultimately for all users of public streets and public transit systems.

Part 4: *Social Outcomes from Transport Interventions* contains six further chapters this time with the intention of revealing how different transport environments serve to affect wider social outcomes such as people's social well-being, economic inclusion, social interactions, and civic engagement and participation. What binds these chapters together is the authors' approaches to determine how disparities in transport can be measured in different ways so as to offer insights for other policy sectors to intervene to recognize and address these issues.

In Chapter 13, *Reardon, Mahoney, and Guo* turn their attention to the issue of the subjective well-being of travelers, based on the assessments of individuals self-reported positive and negative experiences of their surroundings and daily travel activities. They use the Day Reconstruction Method to identify how commuters use and experience their travel time, particularly focusing on inequalities in their subjective well-being whilst and directly after traveling. The added value of the method is twofold. First, it relies on people's own experiences and perceptions of the transport system rather than relying on predetermined proxy measures, which they may not personally value. Second, it provides direct insight into how (poor) travel experiences directly affect other domains of life, broadening the transport (equity) debate beyond traditional concerns of travel times and costs. Their case study is focused on the evaluation of a cycle and walking bridge in the city of Cardiff, Wales.

Chapter 14, by *Guzman Jaramillo, Philips, and Lucas,* switches to the Latin American context of Quito, the capital city of Ecuador, to develop a disparity index of the mismatch between the need for public transport and its supply. They use the Index of Unsatisfied Basic Needs, which is the Ecuadorian version of an index used in a range of Latin American countries, to map the geographical locations of deprived populations, which are mostly located in peripheral and informal settlements at the outskirts of the city. They then map the public transit network onto these areas to identify places with a shortage in the supply of public transport services, which are essential to connect people to jobs and other services and facilities located mostly in the city center. This is a common urban planning problem within many Latin American countries, as well as other large cities in the Global South, which the authors argue is not readily solved by extending bus rapid transit and metro systems on the main corridors, if the access to these systems from outlying and often poor neighborhoods is systematically ignored.

Chapter 15 retains the focus on Latin America but this time the City of Concepcion in Chile, to understand how people's self-reported transport constraints affect their ability to maintain their social networks and to seek social support. The method is based on a sample survey which was undertaken in four different locations of the city in order to compare the personal networks of low- and high-income households in central and peripheral locations. Authors *Carrasco and Lucas* combine the use of an activity disadvantage index and a transport disadvantage index to identify where and for whom a lack of transport resources reduces activity interactions with negative consequences for their economic and social participation.

Still focused on Chilean cities, Chapter 16 by *Mella Lira* adopts Sen's capabilities approach to identify how to reduce equity gaps in transport appraisal with a case study of the capital city of Santiago de Chile. The survey that was developed explores the perceptions and experiences of users to identify differences between social groups and income classes. The particular departure and novelty of the approach from mainstream methods is that it considers people's resources and abilities to appropriate different modes of transport and types of services and differentiates between choice and necessity in people's travel behaviors.

Chapter 17 follows with a focus on people's perceptions and their needs satisfaction when using the public transport system, this time tested in the European context of Barcelona. *Di Ciommo and colleagues* base their assessment on two components, one of travel time thresholds—which is based on the idea of an acceptable travel time to get from one destination to another, in light of the distance between them—and the second uses self-reported travel satisfaction data collected from a travel survey with public transport users. Where travel times are longer than the average for the area in which the respondent resides and they also indicate dissatisfaction with their travel, these individuals are determined to be in travel need. The case study demonstrated low-income women to be particularly marginalized by the transport system.

The final chapter in this section *by Karner and Golub* links the benefits and environmental burdens of transport in a methodology to assess the equity of transport investments. Rooted in the US tradition of environmental justice, they propose that population groups benefiting from enhanced mobility and accessibility from a new transport project should also be located closer to the project, so that they shoulder the majority of the environmental burdens. The application of the approach would avoid repeating the historic injustices, in which highways were built in close proximity to disadvantaged neighborhoods in terms of income and race, who enjoyed little benefits of these new infrastructures due to relatively low-car ownership while shouldering the majority of burdens. The authors show how their "balancing" approach can be applied to road and transit project and apply it to assess a large set of road projects in the greater Philadelphia area.

Part 5: Closure offers some overarching observations and comments on the contribution of the book by the editors, as well as identifying some topics for further research. The main takeaway here is that the measurement of transport equity is only in the early stages of its development and that further research and experimentation is necessary if equity assessment is to obtain the central role it deserves as a part of transport planning and policy making.

Measuring transport equity: Key components, framings and metrics

2

Karel Martens, Jeroen Bastiaanssen, Karen Lucas

1 Introduction and overview of the issues

A key issue for measuring transport equity resides in the question which framings, indicators, and metrics to use for the assessment. In this chapter, we start from the widely accepted definition of equity or justice as *the morally proper distribution of benefits and burdens over members of society*. While this distributive approach is certainly not the only dimension of equity, it is widely considered a *key dimension* of it.

Based on this broad definition, three key components of equity can be distinguished:

1. The benefits and burdens that are being distributed;
2. The populations and social groups over which they are distributed; and
3. The yardstick or distributive principle that determines whether or not a given distribution is considered "morally proper."

The challenge for any assessment of equity is, first, to present a coherent account that addresses all three components and their interrelationships, and second, to *operationalize* the resulting account using *appropriate measures or indicators*. This is a prerequisite for conducting an empirically robust assessment of equity, which (ideally) will serve to influence the *fairer redistribution* of a given resource, and/or to *protect vulnerable people* from a specified burden.

The operationalization of an equity measure thus requires a critical examination of each of the three components. It should:

1. Specify as precisely as possible the *benefit or burden* under consideration. Key is to ensure that the right metric is being used, so that *what is valued is being counted*. For example, when considering benefits, the question is whether we are most interested in mobility itself, in the access the transport system provides to destinations, or in actual activity outcomes? Comparable issues arise with burdens. For instance, if we are concerned about airborne pollutants generated by transport, we could measure air quality, actual exposure to air pollution, or the increased incidence of respiratory diseases.
2. Determine how to *differentiate population groups* from each other. For instance, if we are interested in the distribution of transit fare subsidies over different income groups, we have to operationalize how we will measure income (e.g., by household or person) and how we will distinguish the different income groups (e.g., by income decile or the "poor" vs the "rich," etc.).

Measuring Transport Equity. https://doi.org/10.1016/B978-0-12-814818-1.00002-0

3. Define the *equity standard* for the assessment of a particular distribution. For instance, should everyone get the same amount and be equally protected, or should those most in need get the most, or should the most vulnerable be most protected, and so forth. Equity standards or yardsticks can vary tremendously and determining the right yardstick is inevitably a normative question, which ultimately has to be answered by either society as a whole (e.g., through the ballot box, inclusive planning processes, consultation exercises, etc.) or by the (elected) representatives of that society (e.g., politicians, informed by "professionals" such as lobbyists, funders, developers, policymakers, etc., and some minimal level of participation).

Academics can play an important role in informing the underlying societal debate, both by providing empirical insights on disparities in society, and by developing systematic moral accounts of distributive issues.

2 Selection and specification of the indicators of benefits and burdens

The first step in the assessment of transport equity is to select and define the benefits and burdens that will serve as the main focus for the equity analysis. This is no simple matter, as transport has multiple dimensions and concerns about equity are relevant for virtually all of them. In what follows, we distinguish four key dimensions of transport-related equity: (i) mobility/accessibility, (ii) traffic-related pollution, (iii) traffic safety, and (iv) health.

For each of these dimensions, the benefits or burdens that are generated by transport can be defined in many ways. The decision what to measure is clearly a very important issue in the assessment of transport equity because each conceptualization may well show quite different disparities within society. This issue reflects a more general debate in the social justice literature about the proper "focal variable" of equity analyses. Based on that literature, four different focal variables can be distinguished: resources, opportunities or risks, outcomes, and well-being.

Resources refers to the (intangible) things being held by a person. For instance, vehicle ownership or proximity to public transport routes or local air quality in a neighborhood can all be seen as a resource, either directly owned by a person or indirectly conferred to persons through the environment they live in.

Opportunities and risks refer to the possible implications of holding a particular resource, as these may vary substantially. Transport-related benefits may bring varying levels of opportunity. For instance, car ownership can bring tremendous benefits to a person, but they may be of little value if a person loses the ability to drive or lives in a highly congested city where a car is slower than walking or public transport. Transport-related burdens, in turn, may imply various levels of risk. For instance, a particular level of air pollution may have little consequences for some, but may impose severe risks on someone suffering from a respiratory disease.

Outcomes describes what people have succeeded to obtain by using resources and opportunities or how burdens have actually affected their life. When talking about benefits, an example of an outcome is the number of trips a person makes a day. When talking about burdens, it may relate to the incidence of diseases across different populations. Outcomes can be measured in an "objective" way, in contrast to well-being.

Well-being in the most general sense relates to the subjective (i.e., mental) state a person has attained, as a result of the interplay between the allocation of resources, opportunities and objective outcomes on the one hand, and features of the persons and the wider context on the other. In contrast to outcomes, it relates to persons' subjective assessment of their situation. Well-being thus directs attention toward people's perceived or subjective well-being, which may sometimes be measured in response to the mere ownership of resources. It is more typically assessed in relation to the activities people are actually involved in and how they experience them or the particular states they have obtained (e.g., living in a location with a particular level of noise pollution).

We now turn to the four key dimensions of transport-related equity (mobility/accessibility; traffic-related pollution; traffic safety; and health), providing examples of possible focal variables for an equity analysis.

2.1 The mobility/accessibility dimension

The fundamental importance of transport as an enabler of movement and out-of-home activities is generally acknowledged. Yet, more movement does not always mean improved accessibility and having potential access to a service does not mean that it is necessarily valued or used or that it can be used. It is also clear that transport's contribution to movement and accessibility can be measured in multiple ways, and that people's situation may vary widely depending on the focal variable that is selected for analysis.

Resources: Equity in the mobility/accessibility dimension can first be understood in terms of differences in persons' resources, that is, access to different means of transport. This includes commonly collected data such as the ownership of various means of transport, and in particular cars. It can also include an analysis of people's access to public transport or to safe walking and cycling environments. The latter forms of access are often more difficult to measure because they are a resource in a more abstract sense than vehicle ownership. For instance, access to public transport can be understood in the most basic terms as proximity to public transport stations. A richer account of public transport as a resource would also consider the number of public transport routes, their frequencies, and hours and days of operation. A still more comprehensive assessment could account for the cost of various forms of transport and, as a result, might exclude high speed rail or taxis as unaffordable to lower income populations. The analysis of a safe walking environment could also go beyond an assessment of the quality of pavements, to include the negative impacts of busy roads in terms of barrier effects and the attractiveness of the walking environment.

Opportunities: Two possible conceptualizations of opportunities can be distinguished. In the first case, access to transport means translates into the potential for mobility, that is, a person's ease of movement, measured for instance as the area which a person can cover or reach within a given time by the transport modes that are available to that person. In the second case, access to transport means translates into a person's ability to reach important activity opportunities, such as employment, education, healthcare, shopping, or leisure facilities. This is typically referred to in the literature as accessibility and can be measured in multiple ways (see below). Persons' level of potential mobility and accessibility is highly dependent on their personal characteristics, including their financial resources, physical and cognitive abilities or impairments, and so forth. It may also include concerns about personal safety or comfort, which might prevent some people from using some parts of the transport system, or from using it at particular times of the day. The chapters in Part 2 of this volume use accessibility as the focal variable and thus belong to this category of opportunities.

Outcomes: Equity analyses can also focus on mobility/accessibility outcomes, for example, trips frequencies, journey distances, travel times, and transport expenses. Data on each of these outcomes are routinely collected through household travel surveys, often within the framework of transport planning and policymaking. "Big data" are also increasingly used to enable the collection of outcome-related data, on a more continuous basis and at much lower costs than traditional travel surveys. Even more than the transport-related benefits discussed earlier, outcome-related statistics always represent the result of the complex interplay between choice and constraint. For instance, long trip distances can be the result of either spatial mismatches or of a deliberate choice to access a well-paying job or cheaper housing in the far-flung suburbs. In spite of this inherent limitation, the analysis of mobility/accessibility-related outcomes can serve as an important indicator of disparities across different population groups. A more complex perspective on outcomes would assess to what extent the transport system enables or prevents people from actually participating in activities or even fulfilling their basic needs, thus critically reflecting on people's revealed trip patterns.

Well-being: The notion of well-being has entered the transport literature relatively recently and, with it, the multiple conceptualizations of this complex notion. Some of these interpretations are firmly in line with the common understanding of well-being as persons' subjective assessment of their situation. This includes, for instance, studies into people's satisfaction with trip making, or studies seeking to make a link between the experience of movement and more general feelings of happiness. The chapter by Reardon et al. in this volume employs well-being as the focal variable and provides more detail on the way in which well-being can be understood in relation to transport.

Table 1 illustrates the range of mobility- and accessibility-related benefits that could be the subject of an equity analysis and arranges them along the sequence of focal variables. The overview shows that there are multiple ways to understand equity in relation to the mobility/accessibility dimension. While some of the examples may be considered more "fundamental" in character than others, we argue that a comprehensive understanding of mobility-related and accessibility-related disparities in a population could benefit from the combination of a number of equity analyses.

Table 1 Examples of equity indicators for measuring mobility/accessibility

Focal variable	Possible equity measure	Possible operationalization	Possible disaggregation
Resources	Ownership of transport means	Average number of cars in household	By income group
		Average number of bicycles in household	By ethnic group
	Public transport availability	Number of bus stops within 400-m walking distance	By neighborhood By ethnic group
	Walkability	Area that can be reached within a 10 min walk	By age
Opportunities	Access to local parks	Number of parks that can be reached safely on foot within a 10 min walk	By age By gender
	Access to jobs	Number of jobs that can be reached within 30 min travel time	By mode availability By neighborhood
	Access to health care	Number of health clinics that can be reached within 15 min travel time	By age By neighborhood
Outcomes	Trip frequency	Average number of trips per day per person	By gender
	Trip distance	Total trip distance per week per household	By income By gender
	Transport costs	Percentage of income spend on travel per year	By income
	Number of activities	Average number of out-of-home activities per week per household	By income By ethnicity
Well-being	Satisfaction with vehicle ownership	Self-reported satisfaction with ownership of a motor vehicle	By income
	Enjoyment of travel	Self-reported satisfaction with travel	By primary mode of transport
	Enjoyment of activities	Self-reported satisfaction with participation in (out-of-home) activities	By gender

2.2 The traffic-related pollution dimension

A large body of research has provided evidence of how transport-related air pollutants (TRAPs) such as CO_2, NOx, and PM10s affect the environment and people's health. TRAPs have been associated with an increased risk of premature mortality and chronic diseases such as asthma and atopy, in particular in dense urban areas, as discussed by Khreis and Nieuwenhuijsen in their chapter on health impact assessment of transport systems (Chapter 8). Carrier also uses air quality as his focal variable for assessing children's exposures at the school in Chapter 11. Beyond TRAPs, transport is also the most pervasive source of noise in the daily environment and a major source of nuisance, causing stress and affecting attention, memory, and analytical abilities of people.

It is now well recognized that the negative externalities produced by transport may contribute to widening health inequalities. For example, research has shown that certain vulnerable population groups, such as children and young people experience significant deficits in cognition, memory, and executive functions when exposed to high levels of ambient noise pollution. Lower income populations are also more often adversely affected because they tend to be more exposed to these pollutants because they often live in dense urban locations close to busy roads, and for the same reason they are also more likely to walk in polluted environments. The pollution dimension of transport is thus of particular importance from an equity perspective, given its disproportionate impact on vulnerable social groups.

Resources: Equity analysis of the pollution dimension of transport is commonly associated with acceptable health thresholds for levels of air and noise pollution. Strictly speaking, pollutants are the inverse of a resource and what should be measured is the cleanliness of local air and the absence of noise nuisance based on the notion that everyone has the right to a healthy environment. Traffic-related pollutants can thus be seen as negative resources, which can significantly shape people's health outcomes, especially among more vulnerable and "at risk" populations such as children, older people, and people suffering from chronic-related diseases. While the exact level of pollution is sometimes difficult to measure, air quality modeling is increasingly able to consider the effect of complex variations in traffic levels and vehicle types, weather conditions, and topographies while accounting for distance from the source of pollution and the duration of people's exposures as depending on their actual travel behavior.

Risks: Exposure to traffic pollution creates substantial risks to people's physical or mental health, as well as their life expectancy. The severity of this risk will strongly depend on the person experiencing the exposure. For example, research shows that in particular older persons and young children have a reduced tolerance threshold to air and noise pollution because of their preexisting physical condition. The risks of negative externalities can be measured in multiple ways, ranging from simple comparisons across neighborhoods and population groups to more advanced source-oriented pollution and impact models.

Outcomes: Most of the research conducted on the equity outcomes of transport-related pollutants focuses on the actual health burden, in terms of increased morbidity (e.g., incidence of respiratory diseases) and premature mortality rates. As such, we discuss these outcomes in Section 2.4.

Well-being: The exposure to traffic-related pollutants also affects people's subjective well-being. Perceptions of high traffic-related air and noise pollution have been associated with lower probabilities of well-being; hence, interventions to reduce these transport burdens are likely to have a positive effect on people's perceptions of well-being. Combining (changes in) levels of air and noise pollution with the respective well-being probability for neighborhoods and population groups provides an indication of (changes in) well-being across the population.

Table 2 provides examples of the range of pollution variables that could be the subject of an equity analysis.

Table 2 Examples of equity indicators for measuring traffic-related pollution

Focal variable	Possible equity measure	Possible operationalization	Possible disaggregation
Resources	Exposure to air pollution	Level of NOx at neighborhood level	By neighborhood
		Experienced levels of air pollution as dependent on travel behavior by person	By primary transport mode
			By income
	Exposure to noise pollution	Level of dB(A) at level of neighborhood or residential units	By ethnicity
Risks	Increased risk of premature death due to exposure to air pollution	Number of life years lost	By neighborhood
			By ethnicity
	Increased risk of cardiovascular diseases due to exposure to noise pollution	Percentage increase in risk level, at street level	By street
			By ethnic composition of population in street
Outcomes	Increased morbidity	Incidence of respiratory diseases in the population	By neighborhood
	Increased morbidity among young children	Incidence of asthma attacks among children 0–12 years old	By neighborhood
			By household income
	Decreased life expectancy	Variation in average life expectancy	By neighborhood, according to long-term pollution levels
		Number of life years lost	By neighborhood, according to long-term pollution levels
Well-being	Satisfaction with quality of the local environment	Variation in self-reported satisfaction with local environmental quality	By objective level of air pollution
			By income
	Levels of stress	Self-reported stress levels	By ethnicity
			By objective levels of transport-related exposures at neighborhood level
		Prescriptions of stress-reducing medication	By objective levels of transport-related exposures at neighborhood level
	Health status	Variation in self-reported health status	By objective levels of transport-related exposures at neighborhood level
			By income

2.3 The traffic safety dimension

Although it is obviously also health-related, the issue of traffic safety deserves separate attention, in light of the severity of the issue in terms of the equity outcomes of transport systems. While traffic injuries and deaths have long been seen as "traffic accidents," implying a level of acceptance as a part of everyday life in traffic dominated environments, recently more serious attempts have been made to reduce their incidence, in part under the banner of "Vision Zero" (Johansson, 2009). In equity terms, traffic safety measures to protect people from traffic-related injuries and deaths cannot be seen as an "add-on" to the transport system, but should rather be understood as an integral part of its correct functioning. It is an issue of particular importance from an equity perspective, given the disparate impacts on differently positioned population groups. Research shows substantially differences in negative traffic safety impacts across age, income, and ethnicity. Despite falling levels of road casualties and fatalities in many (developed) countries over the past decades, serious inequalities in injuries and death rates remain, in particular among children and older people and for those traveling as pedestrian or cyclist. Perception of safety is also a relevant issue, as it may affect travel behavior (not traveling or avoiding certain modes) and psychosocial well-being.

Resources: Equity analysis of traffic safety as a resource could focus on transport resources in a narrow or broad sense. In a narrow sense, it could for instance map the type of vehicle(s) owned or used by different types of households, with vehicles distinguished by the level of protection they provide to their occupants. More broadly understood, it could map the urban environment around people's home locations, for instance in terms of permitted travel speeds, the width of streets, the quality and width of pavements, or the prevalence of safety features like zebra crossing, street bumps, chicanes, and so on. These can all be seen as resources that shape a person's (objective and subjective) traffic safety.

Risks: Persons differ substantially in the risk of being injured or killed while traveling. Their holding of resources, whether narrowly or broadly conceived, is but one factor explaining this risk level. Another key factor is people's actual travel behavior. Especially low-income groups and ethnic minorities tend to use the most vulnerable means of transport: walking and cycling. This mode reliance, combined with the often poor quality of the traffic environment in low income neighborhoods, leads to substantial disparities in exposure to traffic risks across income. The young and the old are also more vulnerable to traffic injuries and death, in part because of a higher incidence of walking (and in some countries cycling) and in part because of physical and mental abilities. The level of traffic risk can be measured in multiple ways, ranging from simple comparisons across users of different transport modes, to more comprehensive assessments of traffic risk exposure based on peoples actually travel behavior, including trip frequencies, trip distances and mode use, as well as the specific trajectories of trips.

Outcomes: Most of the research on traffic safety focuses on health-related outcomes. Indeed, regular data collection regarding traffic safety focuses on two key outcomes: the number of road deaths and the number of severely injured people.

These data have been criticized on a number of grounds, including data quality, but they do provide valuable insights regarding equity if analyzed across age, gender, income, ethnicity, and so on. In the academic literature, multiple other outcome measures have been developed and employed, such as number of life years lost or the financial costs of traffic risks. While studies often focus on aggregate statistics, such measures can provide key insights into equity if they are decomposed by population groups.

Well-being: People's well-being when traveling is directly affected by their concerns and feelings regarding traffic safety. These feelings have been shown to depend strongly on gender and age, with women and older people generally being more risk averse than men and younger people, which is reflected in their feelings regarding traffic safety. Clearly, it is often the perception of traffic safety rather than "objective" safety that shapes people's travel behaviors and mobility/accessibility choices. For instance, busy roads may sever residential communities from each other and from activity destinations, thereby hindering social contact, in particular for risk-sensitive people. Even if busy roads do not act as a barrier, the presence of busy motorized traffic inhibits residents from socializing in, and children from playing on, the street. This shows that the impacts of traffic unsafety reach beyond feelings of satisfaction with travel itself and potentially impact persons' mental health (see below). Here, too, the traffic safety and mobility dimensions directly touch upon each other.

Table 3 gives an illustration of possible safety-related variables that could be addressed in an equity analysis.

2.4 The health dimension

The literature on transport and health has drawn attention to the potentially positive health impacts generated by the physical exercise that is involved in active travel. The increasing knowledge about the transport and health nexus, and the uneven distribution of transport interventions to promote active travel, clearly suggests that this is a dimension that warrants equity analyses, either separately or in conjunction with the health effects related to negative externalities and traffic safety. In what follows, we discuss the health benefits related to active travel separately from these externalities and safety concerns, as they have already been discussed earlier. Active transport includes walking and cycling, as well as fringe modes, such as jogging, skating, and skateboarding. Public transport also includes an important active transport component, as access to the public transport system tends to require a (substantial) amount of walking or cycling. It is increasingly understood that active transport is one excellent way to achieve the internationally recommended levels of physical exercise because it can be integrated with relative ease in people's everyday activities.

Resources: People may be expected to differ substantially in terms of the resources they have available to engage in active transport. One key resource is obviously access to appropriate nonmotorized vehicles and in particular ownership of a bicycle or access to a bike-sharing facility. Just as important is the affordances provided by the built environment, in terms of safe walking and cycling routes. The availability of (high-quality) public transport within walking or cycling distance also substantially

Table 3 Examples of equity indicators for measuring traffic safety

Focal variable	Possible equity measure	Possible operationalization	Possible disaggregation
Resources	Level of protection when traveling by car	Average safety score of vehicles in a household	By income
	Available walking infrastructure	Walkability index	By neighborhood
	Available bicycle infrastructure	Distance to nearest separated bicycle lane	By ethnicity
Risks	Exposure to traffic risks	Level of traffic risk as dependent on primary mode of transport	By primary mode of transport By income
		Level of exposure as dependent on actual travel behavior	By income By neighborhood
Outcomes	Involvement in traffic accidents	Number of injuries and deaths	By age By ethnicity By primary mode use
	Reduction in life expectancy	Number of life years lost	By primary transport mode By ethnicity
	Costs of lack of traffic safety	Costs related to treatment of injuries and lost work days	By income group
Well-being	Satisfaction with traffic safety	Overall feeling of traffic safety	By neighborhood By age By mode use
	Satisfaction with traffic safety when cycling	Subjective assessment of traffic safety while cycling	By gender By ethnicity

enhances people's possibility to engage in active transport and can therefore be seen as an important resource. In other words, from a health perspective, neighborhoods can be seen as a unique resource, a rich one facilitating or a poor one limiting active transport.

Opportunities: The mere availability of safe walking and cycling routes is not sufficient for active transport. Walking and cycling only become feasible transport modes if destinations are within walking and cycling distance. This includes, for instance, schools, health clinics, shops, parks, as well as public transport stations and stops. How these opportunities are distributed over different population groups depends heavily on the local context. As already discussed, low-income population groups often live in dense urban environments. These offer multiple destinations in relatively proximity, but they also tend to be car-dominated environments that are not amenable to walking or cycling. How these two factors work out strongly depends on the transport policies vis-à-vis the car in these areas. Some low-income and ethnic minority groups also live in post-war housing estates that have often been designed around the car and often offer a low density of destinations. Many higher income groups may experience a comparable combination of a car-oriented environment and low destination density, albeit for different reasons. It is therefore by no means clear how opportunities for active travel are distributed across the population.

Outcomes: Research shows that the health benefits of active transport for both the individual and for society are tremendous, even when the negative impacts of increased exposure to pollutants and traffic risks are taken into account. Much of the research on the health benefits from travel habits is conducted by researchers with a background in health studies. This has clearly shaped the way in which the health benefits are measured. Typically, measures include mortality (deaths avoided), morbidity (incidence of diseases), and quality-of-life indices, with the former two often specified for particular types of diseases. These are all outcome measures, with health researchers typically using large-scale analysis to explain these outcomes based on characteristics of the physical environment, among others. An example of this approach is the more recent research on the significant increase of obesogenic life-styles among adults and children, and the physical environments and activity trends that contribute to this.

Well-being: The engagement in active travel does not only affect "objective" measures of health (i.e., "objective" outcomes as discussed earlier), but also may affect people's feelings of well-being. A growing body of literature shows that people's perceived well-being is strongly related to the question whether active travel is a matter of choice or necessity. As may be expected, more positive feelings are associated with choice. Furthermore, feelings of well-being are not only shaped by the amount of active travel, but as much by the quality of the physical environment within which it occurs. Here, well-designed, safe, and clean environments enhance people's enjoyment of active travel. Both factors—choice versus necessity and the quality of the physical environment—are strongly correlated with socioeconomic composition, underscoring the relevance of this focal variable for equity analysis.

Table 4 illustrates the range of health-related benefits that could be the subject of an equity analysis.

3 Distinguishing and defining population groups (disaggregation)

As we have already demonstrated in the earlier sections, the assessment of equity hinges on the identification of different population groups and their residential and activity locations, as equity analyses are essentially inspired by the questions whether every person receives his/her fair share of transport benefits and is sufficiently protected from the burdens of the transport system.

Table 4 Examples of equity indicators for measuring health

Focal variable	Possible equity measure	Possible operationalization	Possible disaggregation
Resources	Walkability	Length and quality of pavements and pedestrian paths	By income
	Bikeability	Length and quality of (dedicated) bicycle infrastructure	By ethnicity
	Public transport availability	Number of bus stops with high frequency service within walking distance	By neighborhood
Opportunities	Access to destinations by slow modes	Number of key destinations that can be reached within 15 min of walking or cycling	By neighborhood By ethnicity
	Access to destinations by public transport	Number of jobs that can be reached within 30 min travel time	By income
Outcomes	Frequency of walking as means of transport	Total kilometers walked per year	By income By ethnicity
	Frequency of cycling as means of transport	Average number of bicycle trips per day	By ethnicity By neighborhood
	Use of public transport	Share of trips made by public transport	By income
Well-being	Level of stress	Self-reported stress levels	By intensity of active mode use By neighborhood
		Prescriptions of stress-reducing medication	By intensity of active mode use By income
	Satisfaction with health	Variation in self-reported health status	By intensity of active mode use By income

Assessing whether the *benefits* of transport are fairly distributed invariably implies the identification of population sectors and social groups who are most likely to experience transport disadvantage. The academic literatures overwhelmingly agree that low-income households and people who cannot drive are most likely to experience disadvantage; within this, children, young people, and the elderly, single parent households, low-skilled workers, ethnic minority groups, people with physical or mental impairments, are usually identified as often most poorly served. Women are also likely to be more disadvantaged than men within each of these social groups and can be particularly affected by some issues such as sexual harassment while traveling, which can also affect other vulnerable groups such as lesbians, gay men, and bisexual and transgender people.

In the assessment of the *burdens* generated by the transport system, the challenge is to identify population groups that are most vulnerable to various kinds of burdens. In case of airborne pollutants, this will include children, elderly, and people with respiratory and cardiovascular diseases. The former two groups are also particularly at risk of traffic injuries and fatalities, as are population groups that rely substantially on non-motorized modes and public transport for their travel, including lower-income households, people who cannot drive, people with physical or mental impairments, and some (but not all) ethnic minority groups. Regarding both exposure to traffic pollutants and traffic safety, residential location is clearly an additional dimension to account for in equity analyses.

The delineation of population groups for the disaggregation component of an equity assessment thus shows considerable overlap, irrespective of whether the focus is on the benefits or burdens of transport. The literature shows a host of approaches to distinguish population groups in a systematic way but almost all recognize the importance of focusing equity assessments on socially disadvantaged population groups, who often face multiple forms of deprivation, and with which transport disadvantage is highly correlated, such as financial hardship and debt, work precarity, unemployment and underemployment, peripheral housing location (often in areas of high crime and incidence of anti-social behavior), ill-health, low skills, educational underachievement, and social exclusion. Note that particularly disadvantaged groups may fall in multiple of these categories and may experience the multiple adverse effects of deprived neighborhoods, in terms of lower employability, deterioration in the quality of social networks, and neighborhood stigmatization.

3.1 Distinction based on residential location

The residential location of people and households is a key factor in assessing differences in their access to transport and participation in key out-of-home activities. This relates to well-established and often difficult to change intrinsic characteristics of neighborhoods including residential segregation, peripheral location, and an adverse economic and (social) housing structure, which has direct negative impacts on its residents and often limits their access to opportunities. Disadvantaged social groups tend to be concentrated in the less desirable neighborhoods, where housing prices are lowest or driven by (social) housing policies. The resulting segregation in the housing market creates neighborhoods where residents are exposed, directly or indirectly, to social deprivation and the economic distress associated with deprivation.

The social disadvantage of residing in deprived neighborhoods strongly interacts with transport disadvantage, as these neighborhoods tend to be associated with low levels of overall car ownership, often combined with an inadequate supply of public transport services (as public transport services are often concentrated on the main corridors in many cities). They also experience the worst travel environments, as previously discussed. All of these factors make it difficult for the residents of these neighborhoods to access opportunities, thereby mutually reinforcing the social disadvantages of those residing in deprived neighborhoods. However, it should be noted that not all deprived areas are homogenous in their population profiles and so it cannot automatically be assumed that all residents in them will experience the same levels of transport disadvantages. Similarly, many of the people who do experience transport disadvantage may not be living in deprived areas.

Indices of multiple deprivation are commonly used as a background metric in the assessment of transport equity across space. They are useful because they combine a series of the attributes that are most associated with social disadvantage, for example, income, housing, health, education, crime, environment, etc., and allocate population groups a rank score, which can then be spatially coded and mapped using GIS tools for all kinds of policy assessments, including transport. As mobility and physical access is not always a feature of these indices, a number of studies explore ways to add this "transport domain" to these widely adopted policy decision tools.

However, an analysis across space alone is not a very accurate way to determine the distribution of transport resources, opportunities and risks, outcomes, and well-being for different individuals because it provides an aggregate measure of assessment for all the people living in a chosen area with no regard for the differences between the people living there, including differences within households. For example, even though overall car ownership in an area might be low, some households will own a car while others will not, and even in car owning-households some members might have access to the vehicle while others might not. As such, it is also important to consider other factors in the assessment of equity over and above disparities across space.

3.2 Mode-based distinctions

In current societies, access to a car provides multiple individual advantages. Furthermore, transport policies and investments are strongly organized around the various transport modes. The distinction of groups based on level of car access is thus of key importance to understand current differences between population groups, as well as the impact of policy interventions on different groups. It is important to note that car ownership is not a binary but a continuous variable, based on levels of personal access to the vehicle within households. While this is widely understood, many studies do represent car ownership as a binary variable, often due to a lack of adequate data or difficulty in operationalizing it as a continuous variable. Furthermore, it should be noted that car ownership alone is not a good proxy to distinguish between population groups, because many car-owning low income households experience an additional financial burden because of their car use, which is often referred to as car-related economic stress (see Mattioli, 2017 for more on how to measure this).

The highest level of car ownership encompasses the situation of a person who has his or her own car and experiences no (financial) limitation in the use of a car. The lowest level of access is perhaps represented by the situation in which a person cannot drive a car for lack of a driving license, or the case in which a person has a driving license but does not own a car and cannot afford to rent a car (and lacks the social network to incidentally borrow a car). A substantial share of people belongs to one of these extreme categories, but most people will be positioned somewhere between these two extremes. Clearly, people who are positioned more toward the bottom of the spectrum are likely to face greater difficulties in reaching destinations, which may limit their access to essential services, opportunities, and their social networks.

Lack of access to a car often translates into dependency on the public transport system that is (currently) much slower than the car-road system with many areas often poorly or not at all covered, and on walking and cycling. Access to cars (even within households who own them) can be limited due to financial difficulties (lack of money for repairs, insurance or fuel), legal reasons (lack of driver's license, which can also restrict the travel of nondriving members of households with cars), or mental and physical reasons (see disability below). Population groups who are identified as most often car-less include people on low incomes, young people and elderly, women and ethnic minorities.

It is important to stress that having a car within households does nothing to denote whether or not is actually usable, or equally available to all its members. This is largely based on factors of affordability and ability, which should also, therefore, be considered in the disaggregation process.

3.3 Distinction based on income

Income is strongly correlated with multiple dimensions of mobility and accessibility, such as vehicle ownership, trip frequency, trip distance, residential location, and so on. It is also strongly correlated with residential locations and, through it, with exposure to traffic-related pollution and noise. Income is thus a key dimension for distinguishing between population groups.

People and households in the lowest income quintile(s) are less likely to have access to a private car, which makes them more dependent on public transport to cover larger distances, in particular buses, and on walking and cycling. The travel costs associated with operating a car or using public transport can also present a barrier to travel for low-income groups.

In particular low-skilled people and the unemployed and underemployed (people in low-hour and low-pay jobs) are likely to be in the lowest income quintiles. This limits their access to a private car and reduces their financial ability to travel long distances. Since commuting often constitutes a large amount of the travel conducted by employed people, its partial absence means that the un(der)employed often have less travel experience and are therefore more likely to restrict their travel and job search horizons to their local area. Poor public transport services may further limit the spatial span of their job search area and impose difficulties when accessing job interviews and traveling to as well as maintaining jobs. As a result, people on low-income tend to make fewer journeys and travel shorter distances compared with higher-income households, which is both a symptom of, and cause for, restricted access to and participation in spatially dispersed activities.

3.4 Age

As already discussed, age is highly related to the incidence of transport benefits and burdens. Young people and the elderly are more dependent on public transport, walking, and cycling, as car-ownership and the share of youth and elderly with a driver's license is relatively low. As such, both ends of the age spectrum tend to travel less often than other age groups and are more likely to make local journeys. Transport problems may also be associated with being predominantly dependent on others for transport. In particular for young people, high fares for public transport services may prevent them from attending education or obtaining jobs. In terms of transport burdens, both the (very) young and the (very) old are particularly vulnerable to airborne pollution and also experience more difficulties in navigating a hostile traffic environment. The latter may lead to more traffic injuries and fatalities but may also limit the mobility and accessibility of some population groups. Children's independent mobility has been particularly affected by urban environments build for motorized traffic.

3.5 Gender

Gender plays a crucial role in shaping access to transport resources, travel needs, and revealed travel patterns. Women have been identified as a group that experiences transport disadvantage as a result of poor public transport services and because they are less likely than men to have a driving license or access to a car (Hine and Grieco, 2003), even though this is rapidly changing in some countries. This is especially the case in developing Global South contexts where the ratios of car ownership and use are much lower among the female population. Women tend to have different travel patterns, with multiple roles and often primary responsibilities for child care and domestic work, while their specific travel needs are not always catered for by public transport services. Also, personal safety while using (public) transport is a major consideration for this group.

Single parent households (of which approximately 95% are female heads of household), especially with younger children, can often be more disadvantaged because they make more daily trips than the average adult. This can be a particular problem if they are reliant on public transport. The frequency and reliability of public transport is important to parents of young children, as they are more likely to trip-chain, that is, combine commuting with trips to day care, school, shopping, etc. Since these trips are not always colocated, public transport services may lack the flexibility and regularity to meet the requirements of their personal schedules. Taking a buggy or a pram in a bus or tram may be a further difficultly and traveling with multiple children on public transport can also be expensive.

3.6 (Dis)ability

Persons experiencing various forms of physical or mental impairments, whether temporal or permanent, are more likely than others to face limitations on their mobility and, subsequently, on their access to activities. Although disabilities are predominantly experienced by the elderly, as the prevalence and severity of disability increases with age, they can also affect younger age groups. Transport is often cited as one of the most significant problems facing people with impairments, where the inaccessible design of the street environment and public transport vehicles, and attitudes of drivers and other passengers when boarding or alighting vehicles may severely restrict the ability of disabled people to travel. Transport costs are also usually higher for people with impairments due to their high dependence on expensive modes such as taxis.

3.7 Ethnicity

The distinction of population groups by ethnicity has been of particular importance in the United States, where concerns over race are high on the political agenda, also in the domain of transport. As in the United States, in most countries ethnic minority status tends to go hand in hand with multiple forms of disadvantage, but their differential share in transport-related benefits of burdens is often overlooked within equity assessment, largely due to the paucity of data. Some ethnic minority groups have lower levels of car ownership and driver's license than others, partly due to the level of household incomes and economic status. However, some ethnic groups place a higher reliance on car-based travel, for cultural reasons or for fears about personal safety or racial harassment. Some ethnic communities prefer to undertake their activities within the local neighborhood and can feel uncomfortable traveling outside of their cultural enclaves. A lack of knowledge about the availability of public transport services, language barriers with regard to travel information, a perception of a lack of safety, and cultural differences (e.g., women might feel restricted to talk with male bus drivers) means that ethnic minorities may (have to) restrict their travel to areas and modes they are familiar with.

4 Selection and specification of equity principles

Before presenting a number of possible equity principles, it is important to stress the fundamental difference between the assessment of the fairness of a *situation* and the assessment of the fairness of an *intervention*. In the ideal case, the latter is guided by the former. That is, the assessment of the fairness of interventions is to be based on their contribution to move toward the desirable distribution. This will often imply that two equity principles are needed for policy purposes: one that describes the ideal "end" state, and one that determines whether the intervention does enough to move toward that "end" state.

For instance, if equality is considered the proper equity standard regarding the end state, an equal distribution of the benefits of interventions may be very unfair as it will do nothing to address existing disparities. That is precisely why "winner and loser" analyses, which are also common in the transport literature, are highly problematic, as they de facto accept the status quo as their benchmark without raising the question whether the status quo is fair. The challenge to define equity principles relates first and foremost to the existing situation, not to the interventions, as it also shapes the assessment of the interventions. For this reason, in what follows we first focus on the equity principles regarding the existing situation and discuss the implications for the assessment of new interventions in relation to this current state.

4.1 Standards for assessing the existing situation

The intuitively appealing standard of equity to assess an existing situation is *equality*, that is, *an equal distribution* of a particular good or bad over people or population groups. Because of this "default" status, the standard of equality is often used as an implicit yardstick in the literature, often without further justification, to assess the fairness of an existing situation. The standard of equality has intuitive appeal, but it is clearly not a suitable principle for all benefits or burdens. For instance, a situation in which a part of the population enjoys zero pollution and a part of the population a very low, yet acceptable level of pollution, is probably preferable over the case of an equal distribution of the low level of pollution, even if the latter situation lives up to the standard of equality and the former does not. Thus, the standard of equality is by no means suitable as the benchmark for the assessment of all transport-related benefits and burdens.

Furthermore, the application of the equality principle is often problematic because transport-related benefits and burdens typically have an explicit spatial dimension. This often implies that equality can never be achieved, simply because it is practically infeasible to achieve an equal distribution over space. For instance, access to public transport will always show an uneven distribution across space because of the localized nature of public transport stops and lines, as does air and noise pollution. This spatial dimension has also consequences for the spatial resolution of measurement, as equality achieved at the neighborhood scale may go hand in hand with quite substantial disparities within a neighborhood. If two neighborhoods are served equally well by public transport (e.g., as measured by the number of bus lines and bus stops), this does not necessarily imply that everyone living in both neighborhoods has equal access to the service (because of geography) or is equally able to access it (because of differences in personal abilities and characteristics).

A variation on the standard of equality is the principle of *proportionality*. The proportionality standard requires that benefits or burdens are distributed over population groups roughly in proportion to the size of the groups, without requiring perfect equality in distribution. More precisely, the proportionality principle accepts deviations from the ideal of equality as long as these deviations remain within reasonable boundaries. Take, as an example, the case traffic injuries. The standard of equality would require that each population group, as distinguished along the lines of, for example, ethnicity, age, gender, and income, be exposed to the same level of risk of traffic injury per trip made (or per kilometer traveled, although there are strong arguments to use trips). It may be clear that equality will be difficult to achieve, simply for reasons of statistics in combination with some inevitable random effects in traffic injuries across space and time. In such a case, it is practically more attractive to employ the proportionality standard rather than the standard of equality, as it is actually possible to achieve the former (as it allows for some deviation from equality) but virtually impossible to achieve the latter. The proportionality standard may also be relevant for other benefits and burdens, such as health benefits or exposure to pollution. In all these cases, the proportionality principle may provide a suitable, and less demanding, standard compared to the principle of equality. Note that the proportionality standard has been extensively employed in US practice, especially in relation to environmental burdens.

A third possible equity principle regarding the ideal end state is a *maximum gap standard*. This principle accepts substantial inequality, as long as these inequalities remain within a certain predefined range. It differs from the proportionality standard in that it is not a pragmatic deviation from the principle of equality, but the explicit acceptance of inequality. The underlying reasoning here is not only that equality cannot be achieved for reasons of geometry, but also that disparities may in part be a result of differences in personal preferences. For instance, research has shown that many (middle-income) households accept a lower accessibility level in exchange for lower housing costs or higher housing quality in the suburbs. Low levels of accessibility may also be experienced by other (low-income) households, who have less choice in the housing market. The use of a maximum gap standard guarantees that the differences between households remain within reasonable boundaries, irrespective of the causes of the differences.

An even less demanding equity principle is *a minimum standards approach*. This standard directs the attention away from the overall distribution of goods and benefits toward the situation of those who are positioned at the bottom of the distributive spectrum (see Martens and Bastiaanssen, this volume). The idea here is that justice requires securing a certain minimum of a good or maximum of a bad. This standard is commonly used across the world in relation to pollution, as reflected in (legal) norms regarding maximum levels of exposure. While these norms are rarely explicitly framed in terms of equity, they de facto represent an equity principle stating that justice is done if no population group, irrespective of location of residence, race, income, and so on, receives a level of air or noise pollution that goes beyond the stipulated maximum. Minimum standards can of course also be used in relation to other goods, such as the provision of public transport, pedestrian or cycling infrastructure, or traffic safety.

The above standards do not explicitly relate to the characteristics of, and differences between, different population groups. They are in this sense "arithmetic" equity principles. A fundamentally different principle is the notion of *basic need*. This equity principle requires that each person's basic needs are fulfilled as a prerequisite for a flourishing life (see Chapter 17). Since people differ in their basic needs, the need principle cannot be applied without detailed knowledge of the characteristics of (groups within) a population. A needs-based approach can draw on the extremely large body of (philosophical) literature on basic needs, many of which are directly or indirectly related to transport. A fair distribution according to need may imply that some should receive more than others. For instance, in the case of transport, persons with travel-related impairments may require more financial resources to fulfill their mobility needs. Likewise, the basic needs approach could imply, at least in theory, that vulnerable populations, such as persons with respiratory diseases, receive an additional protection against airborne pollutants. The principle of need has been proposed by a number of authors in the transport literature, notably in relation to public transport provision. Here, the argument is that public transport should serve first and foremost population groups that *need* public transport, such as low-income populations who cannot reasonably afford the price of (private, motorized) transport or persons who cannot drive (or cycle) for health or legal reasons. Note that the need principle is closely related to the minimum standard principle, but that the latter principle does not (explicitly) require detailed knowledge of people's needs.

4.2 Standards for assessing interventions

The above-mentioned equity principles regarding the situation or desirable "end" state need to be complemented by equity principles to assess the impacts of proposed interventions. Here, we want to mention three equity principles that have been regularly mentioned in the literature to assess proposed interventions.

The first is again the principle of *equality*. This principle is only relevant for interventions if equality is considered the ideal end state and if the existing distribution already lives up that ideal. In all other cases, an intervention that distributes benefits or burdens equally is likely to perpetuate an injustice. Indeed, this is precisely the drawback of the equality principle in relation to interventions: it does nothing to address existing inequities because its application will lead to a positive evaluation of interventions that maintain or even strengthen the (inequitable) status quo. The same critique holds for "winner and loser" analyses, as mentioned above.

The second principle is the long-standing Aristotelian principle of "Do No Harm." This principle has been interpreted in multiple ways but is generally understood to mean that public initiatives should, insofar as possible, *leave no one worse off*. The principle is thus closely related to the more familiar Pareto-improvement criterion, where a policy or investment program is deemed to be socially beneficial (efficient, or welfare improving) if it improves the situation of at least one individual while not making any other individual worse off. The Do No Harm and Pareto principles do open the possibilities that existing disparities will be reduced, so that the situation moves toward the ideal "end" state (whether it is defined as equality, proportionality, maximum gap, or something else). However, the principles do not guarantee the selection of policies that lead to a move in that direction. Their application may actually go hand in hand with growing disparities, when policies are selected that do not harm any group yet provide most benefits to already well-off groups. Thus, both principles are hardly suited as assessment criteria if decision-makers want to select policies that move the existing situation toward a particular ideal.

The third principle we discuss here is the standard of *equalization*, as this standard has regularly been suggested in the (transport) literature. This equity principle can be formulated in two ways. In the first definition, equalization is inevitable related to equality and requires that interventions move a situation toward the ideal of equality. In the second definition, equalization merely requires that interventions reduce existing disparities. This latter interpretation is based on the understanding that equality is *not* necessarily the ultimate goal, nor the ultimate equity yardstick, but that existing disparities are clearly unfair, without an explicit agreement about what is the ideal, fair, situation. In this case, the question of what is "a morally proper distribution" is left to be answered in a later stage, when steps have been made toward equality and the question emerges whether equality should indeed be the ultimate goal or whether a less demanding ideal can be accepted (e.g., proportionality, maximum gap, and minimum standard).

This latter conceptualization of equalization could be applied for a broad range of transport-related benefits and burdens. It could, for instance, be applied to the distribution of accessibility, based on the argument that the existing disparities in accessibility between persons with and without access to a car are disproportionately large, even if no agreement exists about the morally proper distribution of accessibility. The principle of equalization is particularly suited as a criterion for the assessment of policy interventions, as it will lead to a clear ranking of these interventions. The standard of equalization, however, also has a drawback, as an intervention that only marginally reduces existing disparities already lives up the equalization standard, even if it does very little to fundamentally reduce these disparities over time. Without further specification, equalization may thus be no more than tokenism, while largely maintaining the status quo. This suggests that moving toward equity is not so much about setting a *standard* regarding the distribution of the benefits of interventions, but rather about agreeing upon a *timeline* to achieve the ideal end state, whether it is defined in terms of equality, proportionality, maximum gap, need fulfillment, or some other equity principle.

5 Policy relevance

It is rare across all sectors of public policy, but especially within the transport domain, that a systematic and explicit moral argument has been developed for a particular distributive principle of equity. Perhaps more remarkable is the fact that there is little agreement in the transport domain about the key equity principle(s) to guide the field. This stands in sharp contrast to fields like housing, education, or health care, where there is broad agreement about the equity principles underpinning the policy domains, even if there may be discussion about its precise implications or measurement. It is an open question whether this points at an immature stage or at the fundamentally contested nature of the domain of transport. We have not addressed this question here, but rather discussed some general equity principles and have briefly illustrated their possible application to various kinds of transport benefits and burdens. We leave it to the other chapters to illustrate how equity principles can be practically applied to transport analysis and subsequently feed decision-making in the transport domain.

We end with the general observation that the delineation of an equity principle, either regarding the ideal end state or regarding interventions, is fundamentally a political matter. It is not something that can be settled by normative reasoning or empirical evidence alone. Academic research along both these lines can feed societal debates about the equitable distribution of a range of goods, including transport, but it cannot provide the final answers. Equity is ultimately intrinsically related to the vision about a good society and about seeking a balance between individual freedoms and collective goals. What is perhaps most striking is that these debates tend to be at best secondary in the domain of transport, given the dominant technical and economic discourse in the field. It is precisely the framing of transport in these terms that hinders explicit debate about the inevitable normative underpinnings of transport policies and interventions. One of the key aims of this edited volume is to change that discourse.

6 Further reading

This chapter has discussed the key dimensions that need to be addressed in the development of equity indicators. For the actual specification of a particular equity indicator, researchers and practitioners can draw on the extensive literature on the development of indicators in a general sense, and equity indicators in particular. This is a valuable resource, because even when the key dimensions of an equity analysis are clearly defined, the measurement of equity is still a complex and sensitive issue that requires careful consideration.

Since equity measurement is in the relatively early stages of development in the domain of transport, researchers and practitioners may find inspiration in other policy domains. Examples of areas in which a host of equity indicators have been developed include income poverty (see the recent volume edited by Klasen (2018) for key contributions), health inequities (e.g., Asada, 2007; Eyal et al., 2013; Alonge and Peters, 2015), education (e.g., Holsinger and Jacob, 2009), or equality of opportunity (e.g., Rodríguez, 2011). Note that in these latter three domains, inequities are typically equated with inequalities. This obviously has implications for the type of indicators that are developed and proposed. Some of these inequality indicators may be transposed with relative ease to the measurement of transport inequities, certainly when also in transport inequities are identical to inequalities. In other cases, indicators and measures can serve as a source of inspiration and much may be learned from the extensive analysis of the advantages and disadvantages of the various equity indicators.

Clearly, also in the transport domain advances have been made in the development of equity indicators, as evidenced by the chapters in this volume. However, most efforts in indicator development have focused on the assessment of particular benefits or burdens, without explicit attention for concerns of equity (e.g., Pronello and Camusso, 2012 for noise; Hakkert et al., 2007 for road safety; or the host of literature on accessibility measurement). Several researchers have discussed indicators for the broad notion of sustainable transport, sometimes touching on issues of equity (e.g., Zegras, 2006; Litman, 2007), but typically without a systematic exploration of the three dimensions discussed in this chapter. Yet, these papers do provide directions on how to develop composite indicators, which is particularly relevant for equity, given the multiple dimensions of the phenomenon. The work by Miller et al. (2013) is especially useful in this respect.

Examples of thorough indicator development based on a careful answer to the three questions posed at the outset of the chapter are relatively scarce in the transport domain. Lucas et al. (2016) provide a thoughtful discussion of the ethical theories and related equity yardsticks and then propose concrete equity indicators for use in practice that link to these yardsticks. Several studies into transport affordability work in part along the lines proposed here. For instance, Fan and Huang (2011) present a detailed discussion of the factors shaping household's transport needs and propose a contextualized transport affordability analysis framework that differentiates population groups based upon their sociodemographics, the built environment, and the policy environment. This approach is particularly thoughtful in its delineation of population groups and the related equity yardstick. Falavigna and Hernandez (2016), in turn, present a thoughtful discussion of the good that is at stake in the analysis of transport affordability, by distinguishing observed mobility versus potential mobility as the focal variable for the analysis and analyzing the possible implications of using either variable. Sider et al. (2015) engage in a comparable discussion regarding traffic-related air pollution, suggesting that an adequate equity analysis of air pollution should incorporate multiple focal variables: exposure to pollution, generation of pollution, and the relationship between the two.

These examples underscore that the field of measuring transport equity is developing rapidly and is becoming more systematic in its treatment of equity along the way. It is the ambition of this book to further strengthen and support this development. The measurement of equity is an inevitably normative activity; equity indicators inevitably represent a particular perspective on justice and fairness. A careful consideration of the three dimensions discussed in this chapter is a prerequisite to make progress in the field.

References

Alonge, O., Peters, D.H., 2015. Utility and limitations of measures of health inequities: a theoretical perspective. Glob. Health Action 8 (1), 27591.

Asada, Y., 2007. Health Inequality: Morality and Measurement. University of Toronto Press, Toronto.

Eyal, N., et al., 2013. Inequalities in Health: Concepts, Measures, and Ethics. Oxford University Press, Oxford.

Falavigna, C., Hernandez, D., 2016. Assessing inequalities on public transport affordability in two latin American cities: Montevideo (Uruguay) and Córdoba (Argentina). Transp. Policy 45, 145–155.

Fan, Y., Huang, A., 2011. How affordable is transportation? A context-sensitive framework. In: Center for Transportation Studies, University of Minnesota.

Hakkert, A., et al., 2007. Road Safety Performance Indicators: Theory. Deliverable D3 6: 164.

Hine, J.P., Grieco, M.S., 2003. Scatters and clusters in time and space: implications for delivering integrated and inclusive transport. Transp. Policy 10 (4), 299–306.

Holsinger, D.B., Jacob, W.J., 2009. Inequality in Education: Comparative and International Perspectives. Springer Science & Business Media, Hong Kong.

Johansson, R., 2009. Vision zero–implementing a policy for traffic safety. Saf. Sci. 47 (6), 826–831.

Klasen, S. (Ed.), 2018. Measuring Poverty. The International Library of Critical Writings in Economics Series. Edward Elgar.

Litman, T., 2007. Developing indicators for comprehensive and sustainable transport planning. Transp. Res. Rec.: J. Transp. Res. Board 2017, 10–15.

Lucas, K., et al., 2016. A method to evaluate equitable accessibility: combining ethical theories and accessibility-based approaches. Transportation 43 (3), 473–490.

Mattioli, G., 2017. 'Forced Car Ownership' in the UK and Germany: socio-spatial patterns and potential economic stress impacts. Soc. Incl. 5 (4), 147–160.

Miller, H.J., et al., 2013. Developing context-sensitive livability indicators for transportation planning: a measurement framework. J. Transp. Geogr. 26, 51–64.

Pronello, C., Camusso, C., 2012. A review of transport noise indicators. Transp. Rev. 32 (5), 599–628.

Rodríguez, J.G., 2011. Inequality of Opportunity: Theory and Measurement. Emerald Group Publishing.

Sider, T., et al., 2015. Smog and socioeconomics: an evaluation of equity in traffic-related air pollution generation and exposure. Environ. Plann. B. Plann. Des. 42 (5), 870–887.

Zegras, C., 2006. Sustainable transport indicators and assessment methodologies. In: Biannual Conference and Exhibit of the Clean Air Initiative for Latin American Cities.

Part Two

Benefits of transport: Accessibility

An index to measure accessibility poverty risk

Karel Martens, Jeroen Bastiaanssen

1 Introduction

A key purpose of transport systems is to provide people with access to destinations. A growing body of academic literature has delivered extensive evidence of the, sometimes large, disparities in accessibility between population groups. This chapter aims to add to this extensive body of literature in two ways. First, we will propose an explicit normative yardstick, an explicit principle of justice, to evaluate and assess the observed patterns of accessibility. Second, we will propose an approach and an index to systematically assess the equity performance of a regional transport system.

The index we propose is intended as an equity-based parallel, or even alternative, to the widely used measures of congestion on the road network, such as the amount of lost hours in traffic. This and other measures of congestion are widely employed in transport planning to identify and prioritize "failures" in a region's transport system. The widespread use of these congestion measures has had far-reaching implications for the level of accessibility experienced by differently positioned people, as the application of congestion measures has led to continuous road investments and a lack of attention for the accessibility levels enjoyed by, and accessibility problems encountered by, people who cannot benefit (fully) from that network. To address these flaws, the index we propose focuses on (groups of) people rather than on transport modes and analyzes the level-of-service differently positioned *persons* receive from the transport system, taking into account their access to various modes of transport.

We first present our normative yardstick to assess patterns of accessibility and by translating this yardstick into an index that can be applied in the various stages of transport planning (Section 2). We subsequently describe how we have applied our index to the Rotterdam-The Hague metropolitan region. In Section 4 we present the results of the analysis. We end with a brief discussion on the policy relevance of the proposed index (Section 5) and some suggestions for further reading (Section 6).

2 Methodology

2.1 A normative yardstick for evaluating accessibility

What is a fair pattern of accessibility? This question can be answered in multiple ways, as evidenced by the burgeoning body of literature on this topic. Here, we propose to use the standard of *sufficiency* as the yardstick for fairness in accessibility

Measuring Transport Equity. https://doi.org/10.1016/B978-0-12-814818-1.00003-2

(see Martens, 2017). In other words, we argue that people are treated fairly if they experience a sufficient level of accessibility to destinations within the city.

In line with the literature, we define accessibility as the ease with which a person can reach a range of destinations from a given location in space. Accessibility thus captures the range of places people can reach, or activities they can potentially deploy, as dependent on time, money, comfort, and so on, irrespective of whether people are *actually* engaging in these activities. From an equity perspective, measuring accessibility is of key importance, because it provides insight into the range of possibilities people have at their disposal, and thus provides an understanding of the level of freedom a transport system confers to people, which in turn is an important measure of a person's quality of life and potential inclusion in the society.

Drawing inspiration from the literature on income poverty, we use the term *accessibility poverty line* to describe the sufficiency threshold regarding accessibility. As in the case of income, we cannot be entirely certain that people below the accessibility poverty line will encounter transport problems, or that people slightly above the accessibility poverty line will not encounter problems. Yet, we argue that, like in the case of income, it is inevitable to draw a line somewhere for policy reasons. By explicitly setting a standard, it becomes possible to systematically and regularly assess the equity performance of a transport system against this standard and thus to systematically assess the equity impacts of proposed policy interventions. In what follows, we use the term accessibility poverty *risk* to underscore that low levels of accessibility do not necessarily translate into severe transport problems or transport-related social exclusion.

2.2 An index to measure accessibility poverty risk

The adoption of a sufficiency threshold sets clear standards for the equity assessment of a transport system. From an equity perspective, a transport system performs well against this standard if it provides everybody with a sufficient level of accessibility. A transport system performs poorly if it fails to do so. More generally, two dimensions should be considered in the equity assessment of transport systems:

- The *number of people* experiencing an accessibility level below an agreed-upon accessibility poverty line. The more people below the accessibility poverty line, the less fair a transport system.
- The *accessibility shortfall* as experienced by those people, that is, the difference between the accessibility level they enjoy and the accessibility poverty line. The lower the level of accessibility experienced by people below the accessibility poverty line, the less fair a transport system.

Drawing on literature from the domain of income, we have developed an accessibility poverty index (API) that combines these two dimensions. The higher a region's API score, the more inequitable that region's transport system. A region's API score is dependent on three components: the accessibility sufficiency threshold or accessibility poverty line; the share of the population below the poverty line; and the exact level of accessibility experienced by persons below the poverty line. Fig. 1 depicts the three components of the assessment. The vertical axes in the figure depict a continuum of

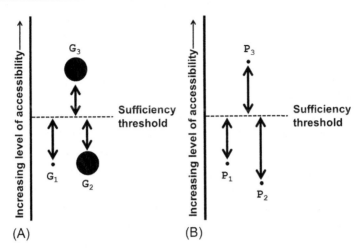

Fig. 1 Visual representation of (A) the prevalence of accessibility shortfalls and (B) the intensity of accessibility shortfalls. Taken together, they determine the severity of the accessibility deficiency in a study area.
Based on Martens, K., 2017. Transport Justice: Designing Fair Transportation Systems. Routledge, New York/London.

accessibility levels experienced by different persons or population groups in a region. Each figure also features an accessibility poverty line. Note that the index can be employed irrespective of the exact accessibility measure that is used (such as a cumulative opportunity measure or gravity-based measure).

Fig. 1A represents the prevalence of accessibility shortfalls, that is, the number of persons below the accessibility poverty line. In the figure, groups G_1 and G_2 experience an identical level of accessibility. Both are positioned below the poverty line, but the number of persons belonging to group G_2 is larger than the number belonging to group G_1, as depicted by the size of the circles. All else being equal, a study area with a larger population group below the accessibility poverty line provides a less fair transport system to the area's residents. The size of group G_3 does not directly influence the prevalence of accessibility shortfalls, but it does influence the severity of accessibility deficiency: the larger the share of the total population that is located above the accessibility poverty line, the lower the accessibility deficiency and the fairer a transport system.

Fig. 1B represents the intensity or depth of accessibility shortfalls: person P_2 is farther removed from the accessibility poverty line than person P_1 and thus faces a more intense accessibility shortfall than person P_1. Person P_3 has an accessibility level above the poverty line and thus faces no accessibility shortfall at all. Her situation should, therefore, not be taken into account in the assessment of the fairness of a transport system, except indirectly, as noted above.

The API integrates both the prevalence and the intensity of accessibility shortfalls across a population, to generate a measure of equity delivered by a transport system in a region.

For purposes of the equity assessment of a transport system, the API has two important properties. First, it generates an overall score for the entire transport system in a region (across all modes). This score can vary between 0 and 1, with 0 indicating a situation in which everybody in a region is above the accessibility poverty line, and 1 indicating the situation in which all residents fall below the accessibility poverty line. This overall score makes it possible to trace changes overtime and to compare regions with one another.

Second, the API delivers insight into the relative contribution of each population group to overall accessibility poverty in a region. This is so, because the index has two important technical properties: it is totally decomposable and subgroup consistent. This means that the contribution of each population group to overall accessibility poverty can be expressed as a percentage, with the contributions of all subgroups adding up to exactly 100%. This is an important property from a policy perspective, as it implies that it is possible to rank subgroups. This, in turn, provides valuable input for the setting of priorities and the design of policy interventions.

To summarize, the API has two important properties from the perspective of equity. First, it allows a systematic tracking of the equity performance of a region's entire transport system over time or vis-à-vis peer regions. Second, it provides valuable information for prioritizing interventions that can move the transport system toward equity. For a formal specification of the index, we refer to Martens (2017).

2.3 Measuring accessibility and setting a poverty line

Before presenting our case study, we first address three key issues that need to be answered before the index can be employed: the measurement of accessibility; the setting of an accessibility poverty line; and the contribution of the transport system to accessibility levels.

2.3.1 Accessibility measurement

The accessibility enjoyed by a person depends on a multitude of factors, including a person's residential location, access to transport modes, enjoyment of traveling, income level, travel-related impairments, as well as constraints and preferences regarding participation in out-of-home activities. Since people differ from each other along all these dimensions, there can be no single accessibility measure that can adequately capture the situation of all persons in a population. Whatever accessibility measure is used, it is important to understand that the measure can only provide an *indication* of a person's experienced level of accessibility.

This does not limit a meaningful use of accessibility measurement. From an equity perspective, it is key to understand that accessibility measurement is intended to identify *differences* between population groups. The purpose is thus not to capture accessibility in an exact sense (an elusive goal in any case), but to reveal the *patterns of accessibility* across groups. This purpose requires the incorporation of factors that fundamentally structure persons' accessibility levels. In what follows, we account for two key structuring factors: residential location and access to transport modes.

Clearly, these are not the only structuring factors, but they do fundamentally shape accessibility patterns. We therefore expect that the results may provide a reasonable proxy of the relative position of persons or population groups vis-à-vis each other. In other words, we suggest that even this relatively simple distinction between persons may provide an understanding about who is clearly well-off and who is clearly less well-off in terms of accessibility.

In the Rotterdam-The Hague case study presented below, we will employ a rather straightforward measure of accessibility to jobs. We focus on jobs not merely because of concerns about employment, but also because an analysis of job accessibility may provide insight into levels of accessibility in a more general sense. This is so, because jobs tend to be distributed over an urban area and measuring access to jobs can thus give an indication, even if only a rough one, of the differences between population groups in their ability to access various parts of a region. Clearly, additional analysis of accessibility to key destinations, like health care services or leisure and social activities, could provide additional information about the population groups at risk of accessibility poverty. The API allows for such applications.

2.3.2   Establishing an accessibility poverty line

The setting of an accessibility poverty line is clearly not a straightforward matter, for at least two reasons. First, there is hardly any empirical evidence about the impact of low accessibility–however measured–on activity participation and social exclusion. Second, the setting of an accessibility poverty line is obviously a normative matter, certainly in light of the cost related to providing sufficient accessibility to each and every person. The setting of an accessibility poverty line can be informed by academic research, but ultimately needs to be determined in a proper political process. In our case study, we will therefore adopt a range of accessibility poverty lines, to show how the height of the line influences the pattern of accessibility poverty.

2.3.3   Transport's role in delivering accessibility

Accessibility is a resultant of the quality of the transport system and of land use patterns. The measurement of accessibility thus provides no direct information on the contribution of the transport system to accessibility. For the assessment of the equity performance of transport systems, it is thus important to explicitly analyze the contribution of that system to accessibility. For this purpose, we use an index that provides insight into the quality-of-service provided by a transport system to differently positioned individuals: the potential mobility index (PMI). In general terms, at the level of one origin-destination pair, the PMI is defined as the quotient of the aerial distance ("as the crow flies") and the travel time on the transport network between that origin and that destination. The PMI value thus represents the aerial speed between an origin and a destination and may obviously differ by transport mode. By calculating the PMI between a person's residential location and all relevant destinations, a single PMI value can be obtained indicating the quality-of-service that person is receiving from the transport system, given her residential location and the available (set of) transport mode(s). For the formal notation of the PMI, we again refer to Martens (2017).

It is important to underscore that, like accessibility, the PMI has to be measured at the level of individuals or groups of people. This implies that personal characteristics, and in particular mode availability, need to be considered. It also implies that potential mobility will not only vary between (residential) locations, but also inevitably between persons.

By juxtaposing potential mobility and accessibility on a set of axes, it is possible to systematically determine whether a low level of accessibility is caused, at least in part, by a poorly functioning transport system or by a low density of destinations. In the analysis that follows, we will only focus on the population groups that are experiencing *both* accessibility poverty and a below-average level of potential mobility, as their situation can clearly be improved through interventions in the transport system. In contrast, the situation of the population groups with a substandard accessibility level but an above-average potential mobility level may be better addressed through interventions in the land use system.

3 Introduction to the Rotterdam—The Hague case

Our case study encompasses the Rotterdam–The Hague metropolitan region, situated in the Randstad, the main economic area of the Netherlands in the west of the country (Fig. 2). In 2009, the region had ∼2.2 mln residents. The region is divided in 316 four-digit postal code areas, which are used as the basis for our analyses.

3.1 Measuring accessibility

In the measurement of accessibility, we distinguish between people with and without access to a private car, given the considerable differences in car-based and public transport-based accessibility. Considering the phenomenon of forced car ownership and voluntarily car-free lifestyles, we do not use car ownership but income level as a criterion to determine whether someone has, or could have, affordable access to a car. Data from the Netherlands show that while 72% of all households own one or more cars, only 38% of households in the lowest income quintile own a car, compared to 95% in the highest income quintile (CBS, 2010). In the analyses that follow, we have assumed that persons belonging to the lowest income quintile do not own, or would prefer to avoid the costs of owning, a car and thus rely on public transport for their accessibility to destinations beyond walking or cycling distance. Persons who belong to the four highest quintiles are assumed to have access to a car and therefore to the extensive road system in the region. Note that for lack of data we do not account for the bicycle, either as an independent mode or as a feeder mode to public transport. Based on mode availability and residential location, a total of 2 * 316 = 632 population groups are distinguished in our analysis. The groups belonging to the lowest income quintile account for 13% of the population in the region (287,091 residents in 2008).

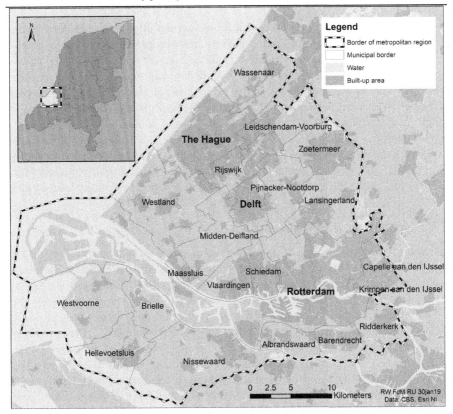

Fig. 2 The municipalities composing the Rotterdam-The Hague metropolitan region.

For these 632 population groups, we have measured accessibility to employment in multiple ways. We have conducted accessibility analyses for three travel time thresholds (20, 30, and 45 minutes), for two periods of the day (peak and off-peak), and for two types of accessibility measures (a cumulative opportunity measure and a gravity-based measure). Here, we present only a part of the results: accessibility in peak and off-peak hours, for a 30 minutes travel time threshold, and employing a cumulative opportunity measure. Clearly, if our approach would be employed in practice, the analyses should include multiple types of destinations as well as multiple ways of measuring accessibility, in order to obtain a more solid information base for policy making.

3.2 Setting the accessibility poverty line

As mentioned above, the setting of an accessibility poverty line is partly a matter of empirical evidence and partly a matter of political decision making. Lacking input on both dimensions, we have adopted a mathematical approach for setting the accessibility poverty line, which is also common in the domain of income poverty.

This approach starts from the observed levels of accessibility in the case study area, and subsequently sets the accessibility poverty line as a percentage of that average.

For this purpose, we have calculated car-based and public transport-based accessibility levels for each of the 316 zones in order to determine a weighted average accessibility level by mode for the entire region. As may be expected, and in spite of the relatively well-developed public transport system in the region, the average weighted accessibility by car in morning peak hours is substantially higher than by public transport ($\sim$655,000 vs $\sim$235,000 jobs). We have used the population-weighted average accessibility by car in peak hours as the benchmark for setting accessibility poverty lines. Subsequently, we have set the accessibility poverty lines as 50%, 40%, 30%, 20%, and 10% of this regional average accessibility level by car.

3.3 Measuring potential mobility

The measurement of the potential mobility level as experienced by the 632 population groups follows the way of measuring accessibility. The PMI is calculated for each population group separately. This implies that for each zone in the case study region, it is necessary to obtain mode-specific travel times to all zones located within the travel time threshold of 30 minutes (note that we include zones outside the case study region in the measurement of accessibility and potential mobility). The aerial distances between the centroid of each zone and the centroids of all zones within 30 minutes are obtained from geographic information system (GIS) data. The group-specific PMI is simply an arithmetic average of the zone-to-zone aerial speeds for the particular zone and transport mode. No weighting of the zone-to-zone aerial speeds is applied.

3.4 Data sources

For the analyses, we have made use of zone-specific data on the total population, the population belonging to the lowest income quintile, the urbanization level, the number of jobs accessible by car or public transport within a 30 minutes travel time threshold, and the mode-specific travel times between all relevant zones. Data on the population and urbanization level are obtained from the Dutch Central Bureau of Statistics (CBS). The CBS defines urbanization level as the number of addresses per square kilometer and distinguishes between five levels of urbanization (from "very highly urbanized" to "not urbanized"). All data obtained from the CBS relate to the year 2008. Data on accessibility by car and public transport and mode-specific travel times to all zones relate to the year 2008 and were provided by the Dutch consultancy Goudappel Coffeng.

4 Analysis

The first step in our analysis encompasses the positioning of the different population groups in the Rotterdam-The Hague region in a diagram representing the groups' potential mobility levels (horizontal axis) and accessibility levels (vertical axis) (Fig. 3).

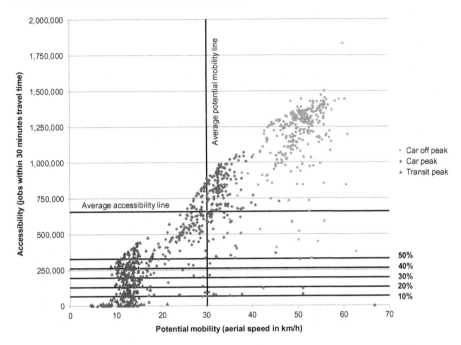

Fig. 3 Potential mobility and accessibility levels for population groups with and without access to a car, in peak and off-peak hours, for the Rotterdam-The Hague metropolitan region.

The dots in the diagram represent the population groups based on residential location (by postal code zones) and mode availability. The population groups with access to a car (the four highest income quintiles, as explained above) are depicted twice in the diagram, reflecting their situation in peak and off-peak hours. The population groups dependent on public transport (the lowest income quintile) are depicted just once, for the peak hour situation, as no data were available on their situation in off-peak hours (so the total number of dots in the diagram is 3 * 316 zones = 948). Since during rush hours, public transport frequency tends to be better but speeds may be lower, it is assumed that the position of the low-income groups during off-peak hours will be roughly comparable to their position in the peak hours.

Fig. 3 clearly shows the vast disparities in potential mobility and accessibility between persons with and without access to a car, despite the relatively well-developed public transport system in the region. The average weighted potential mobility of the public transport-dependent groups is 43% of the average car-based level in peak hours, and only 26% of the average car-based potential mobility in off-peak hours. The disparities in accessibility are even larger: the average weighted accessibility level of the public transport-dependent groups is only 36% of the average car-based accessibility level in peak hours and 19% in off-peak hours. In what follows, we employ our approach to determine the fairness of the transport system in the Rotterdam-The Hague region.

4.1   Accessibility poverty among people with access to a car

The preliminary analysis shows that people with access to a car tend to be served quite well by the transport system. Still, some part of this population group does suffer from a substandard accessibility level in peak hours. For the highest accessibility poverty line (50% of the weighted average accessibility level in peak hours by car), 20 zones accounting for less than 6% of the population with access to a car experiences a substandard accessibility level (note that only part of these zones also experience a below-average potential mobility level). This share drops to only one zone and less than 1% of the car-owning population for the harshest accessibility poverty line. Obviously, the situation of these car groups is much better during off-peak hours. During these hours, only one group experiences a minimal accessibility shortfall when the highest accessibility poverty line is employed. For all other accessibility poverty lines, no group with access to a car experiences accessibility poverty during off-peak hours. Given the fact that only a small share of people with access to car experience accessibility poverty and that they only experience this poverty for a relatively small (albeit important) part of the day, in the remainder of this case study we focus on the population dependent on public transport, as a substantial share of this population is at risk of accessibility poverty during the entire day and across all days of the year.

4.2   Accessibility poverty among people who rely on public transport

In line with our expectations, accessibility poverty is substantially higher among the population dependent on public transport. For the 50% accessibility poverty line, 268 zones accounting for 73% of the public transport-dependent population experiences accessibility poverty (Table 1). This share drops gradually when adopting lower sufficiency thresholds, to 81 zones and 12% of the public transport-dependent population for the lowest 10% poverty line.

Table 1 Accessibility poverty in the Rotterdam-The Hague metropolitan region for population groups that rely on public transport, for five accessibility poverty lines, and for a 30-min travel time threshold

AP-line	Zones below AP-line and PMI-line		Affected people in lowest income quintile		Average weighted shortfall	Minimum shortfall	Maximum shortfall
	Abs.	%	Abs.	%	Abs.	Abs.	Abs.
50%	268	85%	210,265	73%	172,992	996	329,667
40%	213	67%	141,951	49%	143,668	1,336	263,726
30%	169	53%	94,824	33%	114,515	805	197,786
20%	124	39%	64,593	22%	83,281	1,085	131,845
10%	81	26%	35,511	12%	45,166	2,795	65,904

The spatial pattern of accessibility poverty gives insight into which areas (and thus which population groups) experience substandard accessibility levels. The results show, first, that the spatial pattern of accessibility poverty changes fundamentally with a decrease in the accessibility poverty line (Fig. 4). For the 50% threshold, only the public transport-dependent population groups residing directly in and around the city centers of Rotterdam, The Hague and Delft have a sufficient level of accessibility (48 zones, i.e., 15% of all zones in the region). These population groups obviously benefit from the high number of jobs in the direct vicinity, as well as from the excellent public transport connections to key employment areas, including the city centers of the other cities. The small core of zones enjoying a sufficient level of public transport accessibility expands, in a nearly exemplary way, outward with each drop in the accessibility poverty line. Note that this pattern emerges in spite of the fact that *all* jobs within a

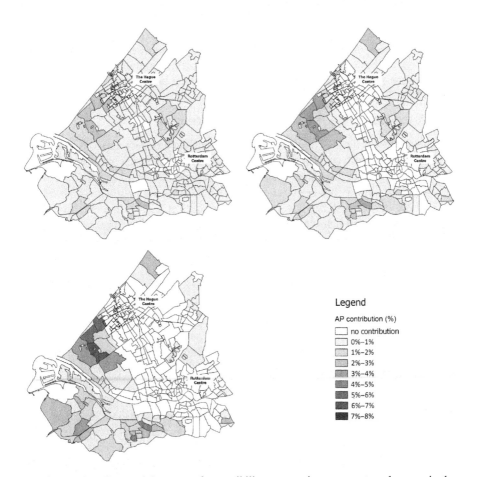

Legend

AP contribution (%)
- no contribution
- 0%–1%
- 1%–2%
- 2%–3%
- 3%–4%
- 4%–5%
- 5%–6%
- 6%–7%
- 7%–8%

Fig. 4 The changing spatial pattern of accessibility poverty in response to a decrease in the accessibility poverty line.

30 minutes travel time threshold are taken into account in measuring accessibility, also those located outside the case study region.

The analysis of the spatial pattern seems to suggest that accessibility poverty is mostly a rural phenomenon for low levels of the accessibility poverty line. This impression is misleading, however. The vast share of the zones that contribute to accessibility poverty is in fact highly and moderately urbanized, underscoring that accessibility poverty is a primarily (sub)urban phenomenon in the Rotterdam-The Hague region. Despite the more substantial accessibility shortfalls in the more rural zones, their contribution to accessibility poverty remains low, irrespective of the poverty line, which is obviously the consequence of the small size of the population in these zones.

This observation is confirmed if we focus on the zones with the most severe accessibility poverty in the region (see Table 2 and Fig. 5). This "top-10" is composed of the zones with the highest overall contribution across the five accessibility poverty lines. The top-10 only includes zones that are "very highly urbanized" (represented in the table as "urban level" 1), "highly urbanized" (urban level 2), or "moderately urbanized" (urban level 3). Their contribution to overall accessibility poverty is high both because of the size of the public transport-dependent population in the zones and because of the size of the accessibility shortfall in each case.

4.3 Rotterdam-The Hague versus Amsterdam

As discussed above, the API does not only deliver insight into the relative contribution of different population groups to overall accessibility poverty. It also provides an overall score signifying the level of equity of a region's transport system. Theoretically, this score can vary between 0 and 1, with 0 indicating a situation in which everybody is above the accessibility poverty line, and a score of 1 indicating the situation in which all residents fall below the accessibility poverty line. However, since the API takes into account both the prevalence and the intensity of accessibility shortfalls across a population, the API scores actually tend toward 0, certainly if the entire population is used as the benchmark (as most people with access to a car experience accessibility levels well above any accessibility poverty line). While this seems to suggest that accessibility poverty is rather limited, it would be a mistake to interpret the scores in this way, as a low score can go hand in hand with quite a substantial share of the population experiencing a substandard level of accessibility, as was shown above. The API scores should thus be interpreted with care and should always be assessed in comparison, either over time or across regions.

For this reason, we compare the API scores for our case study area Rotterdam–The Hague with those for the Amsterdam metropolitan region. Table 3 presents the API scores of both regions. The results show that the Amsterdam region has lower API scores than the Rotterdam–The Hague region, suggesting that Amsterdam's transport system is (slightly) more equitable than the system in Rotterdam-The Hague. This difference is remarkably consistent across the accessibility poverty lines, implying that the inevitably political decision regarding the appropriate accessibility poverty line would not affect the relative positive of the two regions vis-à-vis each other.

Table 2 Top-10 zones with highest contribution to accessibility poverty in the Rotterdam-The Hague region

Rank	Name of zone and postcode	Urban level	Accessibility shortfalls as dependent on AP-line		Affected people in lowest income quintile	Contribution to accessibility poverty as dependent on AP-line					AP-contribution overall
			50% AP-line	10% AP-line		50%	40%	30%	20%	10%	%
			Abs.	Abs.	Abs.	%	%	%	%	%	%
1	NAALDWIJK (2671)	3	325,960	62,197	1400	2.3	2.8	3.5	4.5	6.1	19.1%
2	HOOGVLIET RT (3192)	1	316,203	52,440	1560	2.4	2.9	3.5	4.3	4.8	17.8%
3	S GRAVENHAGE (2553)	1	327,961	64,198	1220	2.0	2.5	3.1	4.0	5.6	17.3%
4	MONSTER (2681)	3	321,364	57,601	1370	2.2	2.6	3.2	4.1	5.1	17.2%
5	S GRAVENZANDE (2691)	3	317,663	53,900	1080	1.7	2.0	2.5	3.0	3.5	12.7%
6	SPYKENISSE (3206)	2	327,699	63,936	870	1.4	1.8	2.2	2.9	4.0	12.2%
7	DE LIER (2678)	3	321,557	57,794	960	1.5	1.9	2.3	2.9	3.6	12.1%
8	WASSENAAR (2242)	3	315,404	51,641	920	1.4	1.7	2.0	2.5	2.8	10.4%
9	HELLEVOETSLUIS (3223)	2	322,824	59,061	780	1.2	1.5	1.9	2.4	3.1	10.1%
10	HELLEVOETSLUIS (3225)	2	322,824	59,061	750	1.2	1.5	1.8	2.3	2.9	9.7%

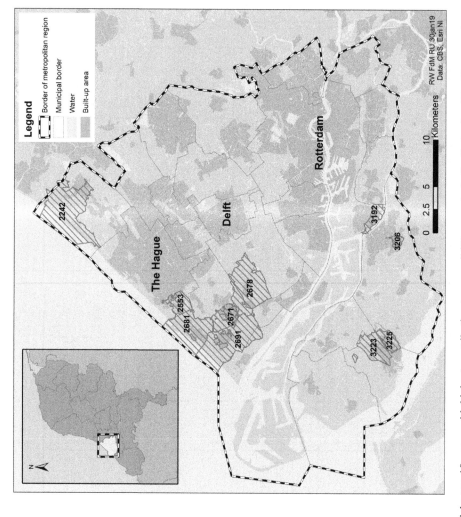

Fig. 5 Location of the top-10 zones with highest contribution to accessibility poverty in the Rotterdam-The Hague region.

Table 3 Overall accessibility poverty level in the Rotterdam-The Hague and Amsterdam metropolitan regions

Accessibility poverty line	API-score		
	Rotterdam-The Hague	**Amsterdam**	**Difference**
50%	0.21	0.19	0.02
40%	0.17	0.14	0.03
30%	0.14	0.11	0.03
20%	0.10	0.08	0.02
10%	0.07	0.05	0.03

Obviously, it is by no means certain whether this would also be the case if more regions would be compared with each other. Equity assessment can never be only a technical exercise, but will always contain an inevitably normative component.

5 Policy relevance

In what ways can the API be used in the practice of transport planning? We have already suggested some directions, which we bring here together in a discussion of two key applications.

First, the index can play a key role in the development of strategic transport plans at the regional level. The preparation of these plans usually encompasses a systematic assessment of the functioning of the transport system. Typically, a core input for the planning effort is an assessment of the functioning of the road system based on the level-of-service standard, resulting in a mapping of congestion levels across the road network. While this analysis may still be relevant from other perspectives, it fails to provide any insight into the accessibility level provided by the road system to people and even less in the accessibility level provided to people who cannot make use of that system. The analysis we propose can fill this crucial void.

The information delivered by the application of the API can provide a systematic understanding of the extent to which the available transport infrastructures and services, taken together, serve the population in the region. At the aggregate level, it provides one single number which can be used to assess whether the system is moving in the right direction or not. At the disaggregate level, and of key importance for planning purposes and the design of possible interventions, the index enables the identification of population groups, and the related areas, that are currently inadequately served by the transport system. The latter information can provide an excellent starting point for the generation of alternative investment proposals, which can subsequently be assessed based on their contribution to the reduction in accessibility poverty risk in (specific areas within) the region.

Second, the API can be used at the project level, to explicitly assess a project's contribution to the alleviation of accessibility poverty as experienced by different groups of people. Currently, projects are typically evaluated based on their contribution to congestion reduction, although broader concerns such as road safety and air pollution are increasingly taken into account. The API can be readily used as an additional key performance indicator (KPI), to be presented alongside these other KPIs. If more weight is given to equity considerations, the API can even serve as a selection criterion, employed to differentiate between projects that are worth considering and those that are not, because they do not contribute to a reduction in accessibility poverty. Since persons with accessibility levels below the accessibility poverty line are at risk of social exclusion, it could be argued that these persons are particularly entitled to improvements in their situation and that public investments cannot ignore their plight but should explicitly seek to alleviate their situation. The use of the API as such a selection criterion for projects would certainly be in line with the demands of equity, but it would clearly require a major change in the practice of transport planning before such an approach would be adopted.

6 Further reading

The analysis of disparities in accessibility dates back to at least the early 1970s (Wachs and Kumagai, 1973; Black and Conroy, 1977). Much of this work has had an empirical focus, typically with a critical angle, but virtually always without an explicit equity or justice standard to assess observed patterns of accessibility. Páez et al. (2012) provide a detailed discussion of the differences between positive and normative implementations of accessibility measurement. The accessibility indicator proposed in this chapter is normative in nature. It is a direct adaptation of the poverty index developed by Foster et al. (1984). This poverty index is discussed in detail by Ravallion (1992) and by Foster and Sen (2008 [1997]), who both compare the properties of a range of poverty and inequality measures, and both underscore the powerful properties of the Foster-Greer-Thorbecke index that served as the basis for the API presented in this chapter. The index of potential mobility (PMI) was first developed by Martens in a study for the Israeli Ministry of Transport (Martens, 2007) and is currently a part of the Israeli cost-benefit analysis guidelines. A variation of the PMI index can be found in Gutierrez et al. (1998), although they have developed their index for quite a different purpose. The PMI, its underlying rationale, and its possible application in transport planning and urban planning has been discussed in more detail by Martens (2015). The link between accessibility, activity participation, and social exclusion, which lies at the basis of the proposed accessibility poverty risk index, has been extensively studied, in particular in the United Kingdom. Lucas (2012) and Lucas et al. (2016) provide an excellent review of the social exclusion literature, while Martens discusses the interrelationships between accessibility and activity participation in a conceptual sense (Martens, 2017). The mathematical specification of the API and PMI can also be found in Martens (2017, Chapter 8).

Acknowledgments

We would like to thank Dirk Bussche of Goudappel Coffeng for providing us with data on accessibility and potential mobility for the Rotterdam-The Hague region and Ron Wunderink of the Institute for Management Research at Radboud University for preparing two of the maps.

References

Black, J., Conroy, M., 1977. Accessibility measures and the social evaluation of urban structure. Environ Plan A 9, 1013–1031.

CBS, 2010. Personenautobezit van huishoudens en personen. Den Haag, Centraal Bureau voor de Statistiek.

Foster, J., Greer, J., Thorbecke, E., 1984. A class of decomposable poverty measures. Econometrica, 761–766.

Foster, J., Sen, A.K., 2008 [1997]. On economic inequality after a quarter century. In: Sen, A. (Ed.), On Economic Equality. Clarendon Press, Oxford.

Gutierrez, J., Monzon, A., Pinero, J.M., 1998. Accessibility, network efficiency, and transport infrastructure planning. Environ. Plan. A 30, 1337–1350.

Lucas, K., 2012. Transport and social exclusion: Where are we now? Transp. Policy 20, 105–113.

Lucas, K., Mattioli, G., Verlinghieri, E., Guzman, A., 2016. In: Transport poverty and its adverse social consequences, Proceedings of the Institution of Civil Engineers—Transport.

Martens, K., 2007. Integrating Equity Considerations Into the Israeli Cost-Benefit Analysis: Guidelines for Practice. Israeli Ministry of Transport, Tel Aviv/Nijmegen, p. 33.

Martens, K., 2015. Accessibility and potential mobility as a guide for policy action. Transp. Res. Rec. 2499, 18–24.

Martens, K., 2017. Transport Justice: Designing Fair Transportation Systems. Routledge, New York/London.

Páez, A., Scott, D.M., Morency, C., 2012. Measuring accessibility: positive and normative implementations of various accessibility indicators. J. Transp. Geogr. 25, 141–153.

Ravallion, M., 1992. Poverty comparisons. In: Living Standard Measurement Study Working Paper. 88.

Wachs, M., Kumagai, T.G., 1973. Physical accessibility as a social indicator. Socioecon. Plann. Sci. 6, 357–379.

Using person-based accessibility measures to assess the equity of transport systems

4

Koos Fransen, Steven Farber

1 Introduction

1.1 Introducing temporal and individual aspects into accessibility analysis

Research, especially in the domain of transportation, often seeks to find the relation between place-based contextual variables and place-based outcomes. Transport systems play an important role in defining accessibility as the relative ease by which the locations of activities (e.g., work, recreation, or shopping) can be reached from a certain location. An insufficient level of accessibility results in an inequitable distribution of transport benefits, as certain people are unable to reach the desired activities and, therefore, are unable to fully participate in our society. Herein, accessibility varies over space, related to where people (demand) and activities or services (supply) are located, as well as overtime, because of the time dependability of demand, supply, and the transport system. Although simplistic, this general definition of accessibility provides a rather useful starting point to show the possible implications related to place-based methods that associate proximity and accessibility with a location and fail to address contextual or individual factors not fixed in space. The structural simplicity of these place-based analysis measures that define accessibility as physical separation opens room for more complex embellishments. The main strategies for counteracting the negative effects of sprawl on accessibility involve increasing mobility–the ease with which people can travel–and increasing the density and diversity of land-use patterns. However, these are supply-side concepts that fail to address individual preferences and constraints and, consequently, strongly rely on notions of proximity. By ignoring individual-level factors, it follows that geographical analysis has the potential to provide skewed representations of accessibility, which may propagate into downstream investigations of transport equity.

The time geography approach was introduced by Torsten Hägerstrand as a general geographical perspective where the concept of space is broadened by societal and environmental aspects related to time (Hägerstrand, 1970). This allows researchers to reveal relationships that are unidentifiable when studied in isolation from its given environment and context, for example, in the domain of transportation (Lenntorp, 1999). In addition, individual behavior and experience related to contextual influences create spatial and temporal uncertainty. Kwan (2012) refers to this issue as the

Measuring Transport Equity. https://doi.org/10.1016/B978-0-12-814818-1.00004-4

uncertain geographic context problem, recognizing that no researcher has full knowledge of the true causally relevant context. The shortcomings attributed to the use of purely place-based methods have thoroughly been addressed in the domain of transportation. Incorporating temporal and individual restrictions allows researchers to approach transport-related issues in a more detailed way, therefore, addressing the actual distribution of benefits–and related transport disadvantages and aspects of social equity–more accurately through an accessibility framework. The focus on person-based accessibility enables to evolve to more person-based transportation models that aim to align demand and provision as correctly as possible.

1.2   Toward a person-based equity framework

Accessibility to vital activities such as employment, education, or health care has an important impact on an individual's level of embeddedness in the society and, therefore, his/her quality of life. The degree of equity in access to these opportunities is a complex matter, and primarily focuses on a fair distribution of the costs and benefits generated by the transport system. The person-based approach described in this chapter can be applied within a broad range of overarching definitions of equity that can be used by policy makers. The structural graph in Fig. 1 indicates the necessity of extending place-based accessibility methods by incorporating temporal and individual restrictions when considering equity appraisal. Many factors influencing accessibility go beyond the merely spatial dimension and these restrictions at different levels are strongly interrelated. Distance or travel time, for example, from a place-based point of

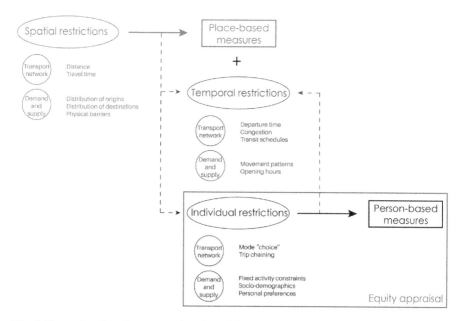

Fig. 1 From place-based to person-based models: the importance of all three dimensions.

view is a very static interpretation of an individual's travel cost along the transport network. Temporal restrictions such as public transport operating times influencing availability or higher travel times due to congestion can have a strong impact on the actual travel cost experienced by the individual. Nonetheless, incorporating spatial and temporal restrictions in space-time accessibility (STA) measures primarily allows us to examine accessibility on an aggregated level. Due to their overall aggregate level of analysis, impersonal STA hinder us to make important claims on equity issues at the individual level. Various person-based factors additionally impact an individual's level of accessibility. Car ownership, for example, delineates the ability or necessity to use a certain transport mode, which in turn impacts the departure time, movement pattern, or affordability and, resultantly, the general travel cost for that specific person. Another example is the age of the individual, which determines a person's dependence on other family members to reach places. As such, these individual characteristics are necessary for person-based STA because they pinpoint differences in accessibility levels and prove to be vital in assessing the equitability of the distributional benefits that can only be examined on the individual level.

Examples of more complex, person-based STA, however, also show one of the downsides of striving for a more accurate representation of reality: elaborate datasets are required to account for the temporal and personal restrictions, and, therefore, the level of detail is strongly dependent on the data availability. In addition, each case study is context specific, which also defines the extent to which spatial, temporal, or individual constraints can be considered. As a result, accessibility measures vary according to the research question, the policies being addressed and the available data, and are, therefore, not fixed on one specific dimension. The following section will assess the way accessibility analysis changes according to the data availability and the specific research question by comparing a place-based accessibility measure to a person-based STA. Using an elaborate dataset for 11,599 individuals in the Wasatch Front region, Utah (United States), the benefits and limitations for both accessibility measures are examined, using the average accessibility across socioeconomic groups as a benchmark. Salt Lake City– and its surroundings–is an interesting case for demonstrating the benefits of a time-geographical, person-based, equity assessment due to its unique demographic makeup. The state of Utah has the largest average household size in the United States (3.19 people per household), and is the youngest state in the nation (median age 30.7). This largely has implications for measuring accessibility for parents in large households, where time spent performing household responsibilities may severely limit the opportunities available to an individual given a purely spatial measure. The case study example shows that STA is a desirable method to use in equity appraisal as it encompasses aspects of equity that are inherently related to the individual for whom accessibility is measured.

2 Methodology

In the following case study, we address the various dimensions of accessibility and determine the benefits and limitations related to the implementation of place- and person-based measures for assessing accessibility to discretionary activities (e.g., health care, shopping, leisure, recreation, etc.) for inhabitants of the Wasatch Front region. In this case study, it is assumed that work, school, and sleeping activities are fixed in space and time, and all other activities are considered discretionary, not because they are not needed, but instead because they are associated with a higher degree of spatial and temporal flexibility. The Wasatch Front is the most densely populated area of the state of Utah. The region poses an interesting case study for detailed accessibility research, as the Wasatch Front Regional Council conducted the elaborate 2012 Utah Statewide Travel Study for 9155 households (consisting of 21,046 individuals making 101,405 trips), which enables us to conduct a detailed STA analysis. In this chapter, a commonly applied place-based measure is constructed and, subsequently, compared with an elementary person-based STA. Herein, both the data requirements and the level of detail—and, therefore, the suitability for equity appraisal using equality in access as a justice standard—are altered to indicate each measure's applicability. For a more thorough comparison between commonly applied place- and person-based accessibility measures, the authors refer to the work by Miller (2007).

2.1 Place-based measure

For the place-based measure, we start from the premise that only data on the spatial, aggregated level is available, as data availability is in practice often the main determinant for the choice of accessibility measure. For the proposed case study, this means that the necessary information is limited to the number of activities for each census tract in the study area of the Wasatch Front region–data that is almost always at hand without any additional data collection. Considering the zonal distribution of activities, a place-based measure can be applied to examine accessibility by summarizing the number of potential activities within a threshold travel time from each origin zone (weighted based on a distance decay, with higher weights for opportunities closer by). As such, the place-based accessibility for each origin zone is determined by summarizing the number of locations for each destination zone accessible within a predetermined maximum cut-off travel time. Often termed an isochronic or cumulative opportunities measure, the number of reachable opportunities given a particular cut-off travel time—and its many adaptations—is one of the most commonly applied place-based accessibility measures.

Place-based accessibility measures in general do not require detailed data, are easy to implement and provide results that are easy to interpret and map, especially for larger-scale policy interventions. However, they fail to address accessibility on a detailed, individual level, as a person's accessibility is generally assumed to coincide with the accessibility level for the zone he or she resides in and, therefore, will be similar to another inhabitant with potentially vastly different preferences, time-geographic constraints or socio-demographic characteristics living in the same zone. The general aggregated nature of place-based accessibility measures provides a static representation of a dynamic situation and hinders researchers to highlight specific individual differences in accessibility levels, thereby failing to address key issues relevant for equity appraisal.

2.2   Person-based measure

For person-based accessibility measures, detailed information on the individual level is necessary if we want to address the more complex relationship between individuals, space, and activities. As such, data collection for more complex accessibility measures is even more demanding in comparison with place-based measures, which can be applied with a minimum of data. Activity diaries are a commonly applied dataset for person-based accessibility analysis, as they contain information on each person's activity schedule throughout the day. To calculate the person-based accessibility levels, two major inputs are needed. First, an origin-destination matrix for the travel times from all individuals' fixed activity locations to all activity opportunity locations and vice versa is calculated. Due to the level of detail (individual data are often made available on the address level), this step requires a large amount of computational power and calculation time. Second, a detailed travel diary is used to determine each individual's space-time prisms (STPs), or the physical representations of every point in space he or she could reach at a certain time given the start and end locations for the fixed activities and the available time budget one has in between two fixed activities. The proposed STA is one of the most simplistic representations of a person-based accessibility measure and determines the accessibility score as the number of minutes a person can spend at accessible locations given his or her spatiotemporal constraints throughout the day. As such, the person-based accessibility for an individual is determined by the sum of the available free time in between different fixed activities one can spend at each reachable activity location, while accounting for the travel time to reach that location.

A well-known visualization method for person-based accessibility is the use of STPs and their respective potential path area (PPA). The PPA depicts the spatial extent a person can reach given his or her individual, space-time constraints, and provides a useful tool for analyzing complex paths. Fig. 2, for example, shows the PPAs for a person with multiple fixed activities such as sleeping, work and picking up or dropping off kids at school, and his or her access to potential discretionary activities. The figure shows that one of two possible discretionary activity opportunities is within reach considering this person's daily time budget and spatial constraints related to the fixed activities. The vertical red line shows the amount of time one can spend at the accessible discretionary activity, or in this case the person-based accessibility. On the one hand, this visualization technique could be beneficial for highly detailed research focusing on a specific person, or comparison between multiple individuals. On the other hand, it does not enable policy makers to easily make general assumptions on accessibility and the equitability of its distribution for the study area and (groups of) people residing here.

As activities take place at different locations at various times of the day, defining the fixity of various types of activities can be tedious. Therefore, it is a common practice to derive simple assumptions based on the activity type, for example, in this case study, by considering all sleep, work, and education-related activities as fixed. Activity opportunities within the spatial projection of the STP are considered as accessible given the person's spatiotemporal constraints, and the time a person can spend at this

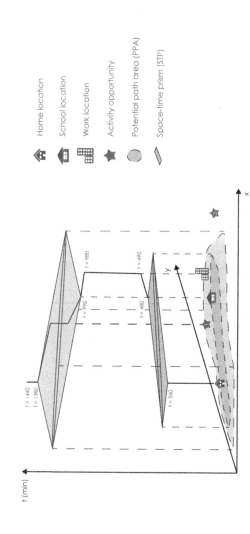

Fig. 2 Space-time prisms and corresponding potential path areas for an individual given his or her daily space-time constraints (Fransen et al., 2018b).

location represents his or her accessibility. As such, the proposed STA is a type of person-based accessibility measure, as the individual's fixed activity constraints determines the anchors of the STPs. The resulting measurement unit for the STA immediately indicates the difference in applicability in comparison to the place-based accessibility measure: the STA provides an indicator of opportunity as the available portion of the time budget one can spend at a specific location given his or her spatiotemporal constraints, whereas the place-based accessibility measure delineates the number of activities a person residing in a specific zone can reach given the spatial constraints inherent to that zone. The latter does not provide individual information, and, therefore, fails to address the aspects of equity appraisal and thus cannot deliver targeted policy recommendations or interventions on an individual level. Nonetheless, the person-based accessibility measure requires representative information on both activity locations and individual mobility, in turn leading to more complex calculations. In addition, the results are difficult to map in a straight-forward manner, especially on the zonal level often strived for in transport policies.

3 Application

In all areas of spatial analysis, the ability to present the results of the analysis in a clear and concise manner to a broad range of practitioners, researchers, and policy makers is of vital importance. The way the information is presented strongly determines the applicability at different scales and for various policies. The more detailed the analysis, however, the more difficult to provide clear and concise maps, graphs, or tables to answer the research question. This section explores this "visualization conundrum" of how more detailed and thus complex results for a person-based STA can be visualized for a broader public in a straight-forward manner. In addition, it shows the possible policy applications while considering both methods' strengths and weaknesses. In terms of equity appraisal, the main goal is to determine intergroup differences in accessibility levels related not only to the place where people live, but also to their socio-demographic status, preferences, and time constraints. This allows us to highlight inequitable distributions of benefits rooted into our society or granted by existing policies, caused by the layout of the transport system, the land-use pattern, and the built environment.

3.1 Place-based measure

Maps are an adequate way of representing the results for a place-based accessibility measure because of its spatial outcome and often aggregated nature. A map succeeds in delineating the actual location where a phenomenon—in this case, high or low accessibility—takes place. Fig. 3, for example, shows the accessibility levels for the census tracts in the Wasatch Front region according to the place-based accessibility measure. Generally, the outcome is relatively predictable, with higher accessibility levels in the denser, more urbanized areas—here, Salt Lake City. Overall, the result is easy to read and understand, making this type of analysis suitable for general policies

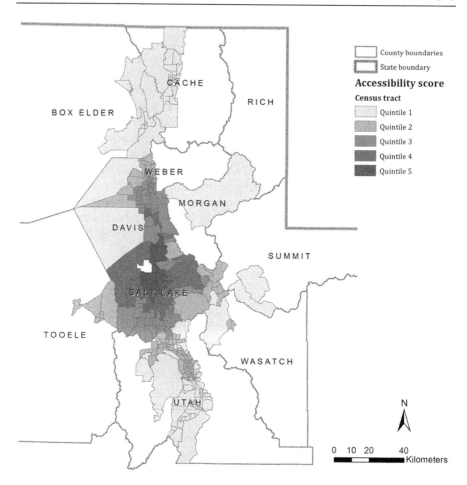

Fig. 3 Place-based accessibility levels for the census tracts (minimum density of 20 inhabitants per square mile), organized from low accessibility (quintile 1) to high accessibility (quintile 5) in the Wasatch Front region, Utah.

aimed at providing an overview of overall accessibility levels in a certain study area. As mentioned earlier, it is, however, necessary to acknowledge the limitations related to the place-based measures in terms of the level of detail and, consequently, not advisable to use such maps for detailed equity appraisal.

Due to the absence of information on the individual level, place-based accessibility measures fail to address the question of who actually benefits. In general, place-based measures only address the locational characteristics of where one lives. From Table 1, similar conclusions as for the map are drawn. The highest quintile in accessibility levels consists of areas with high population densities and a large number of opportunities. This goes to show that if no additional information on the personal level is provided, tables will not provide a better insight in the mechanisms at work in addition

Table 1 Characteristics of the quintiles for the place-based accessibility levels

Accessibility quintile	Population (inh)	Population density (inh/sqmi)		Number of opportunities[a]
	1	4302.58	2937.89	71.06
	2	4559.37	3469.21	91.24
	3	5290.24	3081.78	95.91
	4	5015.73	4734.09	110.44
	5	4414.46	5965.17	120.04
Total		4717.93	4035.95	97.75

inh, inhabitants; *sqmi*, square miles.
[a]With decimals due to the gravity-based weighting function.

to maps. Additional zonal data, however, allow for the examination of correlations between access scores and, for example, age groups or income. Statistical analysis (Pearson correlation between the census tract's accessibility and various socio-demographic variables.) shows that the strongest association is found for income, indicating that a higher income is significantly related to higher levels of accessibility. Nonetheless, these findings are still subject to the same risk of fallacy due to the aggregated nature of the analysis (Fotheringham and Wong 1991; Openshaw 1979).

3.2   Person-based measure

Because of the complex outcomes and individual level of detail for person-based measures, maps are less adequate in portraying individual accessibility levels. A map similar to Fig. 4 for the place-based accessibility measure can be constructed when the accessibility at the residence of the individual is depicted. These maps, however, are often illegible due to symbol overlap and lack of clear patterns, especially for larger datasets in larger study areas. Fig. 4, for example, shows the difficulty in presenting large datasets on an individual level, as the map is difficult to understand and no specific configurations in accessibility can be discerned. A possible solution is to smooth or aggregate the accessibility score. Nonetheless, this would render useless the high level of detail of analysis and the integration of temporal and individual constraints into the analysis.

A more accurate way of focusing on specific population groups without losing the detailed level of analysis is by applying statistical analysis on the person-based outcomes. Regression analysis is used to assess differences in accessibility for various socio-demographic subgroups, and, for example, in this case study, highlights the relationship between accessibility and multiple socio-demographic characteristics. The statistical analysis highlights certain inequitable distributions in accessibility (Table 2). Lower income, for example, is negatively associated with accessibility, indicating that individuals in the lowest income group have a significantly lower accessibility to discretionary activities in comparison with the reference group of

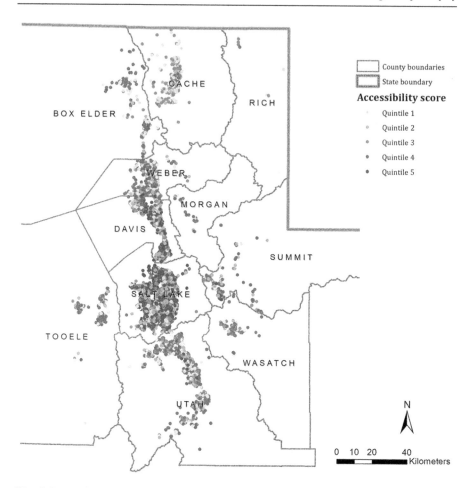

Fig. 4 Person-based accessibility levels for all individuals residing in the Wasatch Front region, Utah.

average incomes. In addition, individuals under 18 and over 65 have a significantly higher accessibility level than the reference group of middle-aged individuals. Young adults, on the contrary, have a significantly lower accessibility level. In combination with the significantly negative access of larger households, this shows that, as mentioned in the Introduction section, this group of young, large households is strongly limited in their access to opportunities due to temporal restrictions not apparent in the place-based analysis. The results for the person-based analysis show various new associations on a more refined level of detail in comparison to the results of the place-based accessibility analysis illustrated above. As such, statistical analysis of the outcomes shows the benefits of the high level of detail in addressing equity issues and, therefore, proves to be an adequate tool for policy support.

Table 2 Ordinary least squares regression model for the person-based accessibility levels (full regression results have been removed for the sake of brevity)

Variable	Subcategory	Effects on accessibility		
		Positive	Negative	No significant effect
Age (reference "35–64")				
	Under 18	X		
	18–34		X	
	65 or older	X		
Income (reference "$35,000–$74,999")				
	Under $35,000		X	
	$75,000–$149,999			X
	$150,000 or more			X
Employment status (reference "Full-time")				
	Not currently employed	X		
	Student, unemployed	X		
	Student, employed	X		
	Homemaker	X		
	Part-time	X		
	Self-employed	X		
	Retired	X		
Household size (reference "3–4")				
	1			X
	2			X
	5 or more		X	

4 Policy relevance

The results in Section 3 show the importance of adapting accessibility measures to incorporate temporal and personal constraints when considering equity appraisal in policy and targeted interventions. Although place-based measures succeed in providing an overall indicator of the distributional benefits of transportation in a specific study area, they do not reach an adequate level of detail that allows policy makers to address interpersonal differences in accessibility. They are also open to criticism due to the ecological fallacy, because characteristics of the individual are often mistakenly deduced from the characteristics for the population group to which they belong. As a result, the excessive use of place-based measures for policy support has led to an overall underestimation of the issues of social exclusion and transport poverty in policy making. A well-known example is the extensive application of cost-benefit analysis (CBA) in a wide range of policy domains. Especially for assessing transport projects and investments, CBA has proven to primarily favor the higher income groups because it lacks transparency on which population groups benefit from policies or investments. The application of person-based accessibility measures provides researchers and policy makers with an opportunity to assess these issues in an explicit manner.

In addition, the results indicate that the often aggregated nature of place-based accessibility measures—such as the one provided in this paper—hinders the production of an adequate representation of equity issues that affect individuals on a personal level. Suppose, for example, that a researcher or policy maker is interested in gender-based differences in accessibility. A typical aggregate appraisal would include computing accessibility scores for each zone in a region, and then proceeding with one or more of the following analysis options:

- computing and comparing weighted average access scores by gender;
- plotting a scatter of accessibility vs percentage of females or males to identify systematic trends in the provision of access for both groups; and
- identifying hot spots in the region with low levels of access and high levels (raw or percent) of women or men for targeted intervention.

One problem with this aggregate approach is that it (a) assumes that all women or men face the same levels of time-geographic constraints and (b) assumes that women and men are subjected to equal constraints. Of course, neither of these assumptions are valid. The person-based approach attempts to incorporate interpersonal differences in time-geographical opportunities and constraints, therefore, obtaining a more valid measure of accessibility for each individual in the sample survey. Differences in access by gender within the survey data can then be inferred for the population, subject to classical sampling theory and hypothesis testing best practices. These specific foci can support policy makers in making targeted decisions that benefit those specific population groups with the highest needs.

Due to an increased complexity, the first necessary step in the transition from place- to person-based accessibility measures consists of a collection of elaborate and ready-to-use information for the demand and supply of activity opportunities as well as the transport network. As mentioned earlier, travel diaries provide a valuable source of information, as not only data on travel behavior are collected, but also—dependent on the extent of the questionnaire—data on travel preferences, motives, or socio-demographics. Unfortunately, assembling these datasets is time consuming and costly. In addition, there is an increased demand for more detailed information on the transport networks, for different transport modes. This allows researchers to accurately assess potential accessibility for a broad range of users. It is possible that adequate datasets already exist, but are not made publicly available due to their high economic value. For example, historical or current locational data for shops and services are quite costly. Because equity appraisal does not serve an economic goal, purchasing the data is often not an option. Second, researchers, practitioners, and policy makers should aim to better understand the use of person-based accessibility measures and comprehend that the benefits outweigh the costs. Although they require more data and computational complexity, they allow to examine the transport-related aspects that simply cannot be studied when applying place-based accessibility measures. This is vital in counteracting the phenomenon of transport poverty and social exclusion. As such, more applied case studies in which equity appraisal is done by person-based accessibility measures are needed. They will serve as a guideline for other similar case studies. Herein, it is crucial that policy makers understand that providing one ideal map that clarifies every aspect of accessibility—or transport in general—is no longer sufficient.

Besides data considerations, one drawback of the person-based approach is the difficulty in disentangling the place- and person-based contributions to the overall accessibility score. This is incredibly important from a policy perspective, as place-based interventions (including the provision of more supply of destinations or of better transport) are generally quite different to interventions that might serve to loosen personal constraints in accessing destinations, such as relieving time-use burdens and increasing disposable income. Despite this drawback, if the intention of the research is to properly understand the current state of inequality in access, the person-based approach provides the most valid measure of accessibility. Moreover, if the research objective is to determine whether inaccessibility leads to differences in higher-order outcomes, such as economic and health status, well-being, quality of life, etc., then starting with a valid measure of accessibility that is tailored to the individual is of paramount importance. A large number of existing case studies are available with ready-to-use examples of the application of an STA to determine accessibility levels for various study areas with different contexts. Especially, person-based STA has proven to be valuable in assessing the equitability of the distributional benefits of a transport system among individuals. This has a strong effect on policies related to transportation, but also on a wide range of related policy domains such as spatial planning, housing, sustainability, etc. STA measures—and person-based measures in particular—can encompass multiple policy domains, as they additionally focus on the relationship between the individual and the built environment he or she interacts with.

5   Further reading

The final section provides some interesting studies that can offer the reader more background in why one should apply person-based accessibility measures, how to construct them, and what limitations they might bring.

It is important to understand that the place-based measure proposed in this chapter is a simplistic spatial accessibility measure. There is, however, a large number of place-based measures available, ranging from basic population-to-provider ratios to highly complex methods that incorporate aspects of attractiveness or competition (e.g., the floating catchment area methods). Given a certain context, some of the existing methods might be adequate in assessing certain aspects of equity (Delmelle and Casas, 2012; Grengs, 2015; Talen and Anselin, 1998). Talen and Anselin (1998), for example, applied various spatial analytical methods to assess the relationship between accessibility to public playgrounds and socioeconomic characteristics, and, as such, the equitability of urban public services. Nevertheless, various authors argue that spatial analysis for equity appraisal often leads to noncoherent results that are strongly dependent on the applied accessibility measure. Neutens et al. (2010) evaluated four place-based and six person-based accessibility measures' applicability in determining the equity of the urban public service distribution. They concluded that utility-based STA measures provide a more solid foundation for equity appraisal, and that substantial differences within the group of person-based accessibility measures exist. This claim is supported by Fransen et al. (2018b), who assessed the relationship between participation in discretionary activities and person-based or place-based accessibility. They inferred that the latter can provide counterintuitive results in terms of equity appraisal because it fails to grasp important aspects related to individual space-time constraints.

In the past decade, there has been a growing interest in the application of STA for equity appraisal. Herein, a large number of spatiotemporal accessibility studies use general transit feed specification (GTFS) files to assess the temporal variability in access through the transit network (Farber et al., 2014; Fransen et al., 2015; Ma and Jan-Knaap, 2014). Farber et al. (2014), for example, demonstrated the ability to use GTFS to factor schedule-dependent transportation into accessibility analysis to assess food deserts—or areas where people lack access to healthy food. In their study on transport gaps in Flanders, Belgium, Fransen et al. (2015) examined the accessibility to key destinations at various times of the day, and compared the accessibility to the need for public transportation. However, examples listed above are aggregated zone-based measures, indicating that incorporating temporal constraints does not necessarily mean that the proposed measures will automatically introduce individual constraints. More complex person-based accessibility measures illustrate how activity diaries specifying individual activity participation and travel behavior allow for more detailed accessibility analysis, for example, in the mobility of caring (Fransen et al., 2018a; Neutens et al., 2012; Patterson and Farber, 2015; Schwanen and de Jong, 2008). Schwanen and de Jong (2008), for example, used a narrative STA analysis to illustrate a highly educated mother's ability—based on both spatial as well as temporal constraints—to reconcile employment and caregiving responsibilities. Patterson and Farber (2015) provided a systematic review of the literature applying STA's key concepts of STPs, PPAs, and activity spaces, and highlighted that methods based on these concepts are primarily used in accessibility analysis. Fransen et al. (2018a) constructed a prediction model for job seekers' risk for long-term unemployment based on the spatiotemporal accessibility to job openings and concluded that STA enables detailed equity analysis on an individual level.

Along with the high data requirements, various limitations inherently related to the existing person-based accessibility measures exist. Contrary to temporal constraints related to the transport network or the individual, temporal variability related to the activity locations is often overlooked. Delafontaine et al. (2011), for example, examined the extent to which the opening hours of public libraries in Ghent (Belgium) affects the equity of accessibility levels across the individuals. In addition, a uniform definition of which activities should be considered as discretionary or fixed is still lacking to this day. Most studies make simple, static assumptions based on the type of activity reported in the travel survey (e.g., work, school, or sleep are often considered as fixed). Another common critique is that the majority of person-based studies examine accessibility over a short time span. This is mostly due to the high requirements for both data collection and computational complexity, which greatly increase when accessibility is examined over a longer time span. In addition to daily variations, travel behavior, however, is influenced by temporal fluctuations over longer time periods (e.g., weekly appointments, season-based activities, etc.). Spissu et al. (2009), for example, used a multiweek analysis to understand the determinants of and variability in weekly activity engagements in activity-travel modeling. These limitations should be further elaborated on to make the application of person-based accessibility measures both more accessible and more accurate.

References

Delafontaine, M., Neutens, T., Schwanen, T., de Weghe, N.V., 2011. The impact of opening hours on the equity of individual space–time accessibility. Comput. Environ. Urban. Syst. 35 (4), 276–288. https://doi.org/10.1016/j.compenvurbsys.2011.02.005.

Delmelle, E.C., Casas, I., 2012. Evaluating the spatial equity of bus rapid transit-based accessibility patterns in a developing country: the case of Cali, Colombia. Transp. Policy 20, 36–46. https://doi.org/10.1016/j.tranpol.2011.12.001.

Farber, S., Morang, M.Z., Widener, M.J., 2014. Temporal variability in transit-based accessibility to supermarkets. Appl. Geogr. 53, 149–159. https://doi.org/10.1016/j.apgeog.2014.06.012.

Fotheringham, A.S., Wong, D.W.S., 1991. The modifiable areal unit problem in multivariate statistical analysis. Environ. Plan. A 23 (7), 1025–1044. https://doi.org/10.1068/a231025.

Fransen, K., Boussauw, K., Deruyter, G., De Maeyer, P., 2018a. The relationship between transport disadvantage and employability: predicting long-term unemployment based on job seekers' access to suitable job openings in Flanders, Belgium. Transp. Res. Part A Policy Pract. https://www.sciencedirect.com/science/article/pii/S0965856417307140.

Fransen, K., Farber, S., Deruyter, G., De Maeyer, P., 2018b. A spatio-temporal accessibility measure for modelling activity participation in discretionary activities. J. Travel Behav. Soc. 10, 10–20.

Fransen, K., Neutens, T., Farber, S., De Maeyer, P., Deruyter, G., Witlox, F., 2015. Identifying public transport gaps using time-dependent accessibility levels. J. Transp. Geogr. 48, 176–187.

Grengs, J., 2015. Nonwork accessibility as a social equity indicator. Int. J. Sustain. Transp. 9 (1), 1–14. https://doi.org/10.1080/15568318.2012.719582.

Hägerstrand, T., 1970. What about people in regional science? Pap. Reg. Sci. Assoc. 24, 6–21.

Kwan, M.-P., 2012. The uncertain geographic context problem. Ann. Assoc. Am. Geogr. 102 (5), 958–968. https://doi.org/10.1080/00045608.2012.687349.

Lenntorp, B., 1999. Time-geography—at the end of its beginning. GeoJournal 48 (3), 155–158. https://doi.org/10.1023/A:1007067322523.

Ma, T., Jan-Knaap, G., 2014. Analyzing Employment Accessibility in a Multimodal Network Using GTFS: A Demonstration of the Purple Line, Maryland.Paper presented at the Association of Collegiate Schools of Planning (ACSP) Annual Conference, Philadelphia, PA.

Miller, H., 2007. Place-based versus people-based geographic information science. Geogr. Compass 1, 503–535. https://doi.org/10.1111/j.1749-8198.2007.00025.x.

Neutens, T., Delafontaine, M., Scott, D.M., De Maeyer, P., 2012. An analysis of day-to-day variations in individual space-time accessibility. J. Transp. Geogr. 23, 81–91. https://doi.org/10.1016/j.jtrangeo.2012.04.001.

Neutens, T., Schwanen, T., Witlox, F., De Maeyer, P., 2010. Equity of urban service delivery: a comparison of different accessibility measures. Environ. Plan. A 42 (7), 1613–1635. https://doi.org/10.1068/a4230.

Openshaw, S., Taylor, P.J., 1979. A million or so correlation coefficients: three experiments on the modifiable areal unit problem. In: Wrigley, N. (Ed.), Statistical Applications in the Spatial Sciences. Pion, London, pp. 127–144.

Patterson, Z., Farber, S., 2015. Potential path areas and activity spaces in application: a review. Transp. Rev. 35 (6), 679–700. https://doi.org/10.1080/01441647.2015.1042944.

Schwanen, T., de Jong, T., 2008. Exploring the juggling of responsibilities with space-time accessibility analysis. Urban Geogr. 29 (6), 556–580. https://doi.org/10.2747/0272-3638.29.6.556.

Spissu, E., Pinjari, A.R., Bhat, C.R., Pendyala, R.M., Axhausen, K.W., 2009. An analysis of weekly out-of-home discretionary activity participation and time-use behavior. Transportation 36 (5), 483–510. https://doi.org/10.1007/s11116-009-9200-5.

Talen, E., Anselin, L., 1998. Assessing spatial equity: an evaluation of measures of accessibility to public playgrounds. Environ. Plan. A 30 (4), 595–613. https://doi.org/10.1068/a300595.

Equity analysis of dynamic bike-and-ride accessibility in the Netherlands

5

John P. Pritchard, Marcin Stępniak, Karst T. Geurs

1 Introduction

In this chapter, the authors rely on an egalitarian perspective of distributive justice, particularly Rawls' (1999) egalitarianism and its strong focus on equality of opportunities, to apply the concept of accessibility as a measure of transportation equity. This theory, and particularly the *maxi-min* principle (which calls for the greatest benefits to be distributed to the least advantaged) is the driving force behind the goal of analyzing the impact of the *bike-and-ride* policies as a way of increasing accessibility to basic opportunities for all, while simultaneously reducing accessibility disparities between different modes.

Particularly since the turn of the century, academics have increasingly called for policy makers to make equity considerations more central in transport appraisal and planning. Accessibility is a better measure for egalitarian transport equity analysis than travel time savings and other mobility-oriented measures. A focus on travel time savings tends to result in policies that increase inequalities due to concentrating the benefits amongst those who tend to be better off to begin with (e.g., by focusing on road investments). Furthermore, mobility-focused studies are unable to distinguish between actual and desired mobility (i.e., whether the system provides opportunities to travel elsewhere or differently). Accessibility provides a potential measure that is not influenced by the restrictions and constraints currently imposed on personal mobility, and importantly, is not impacted by unfulfilled mobility due to personal preferences. It is a measure of the opportunities that individuals can access.

From an equity perspective, being able to access an opportunity is more important than whether an individual chooses to use the access that is provided. As a result, an equitable society should strive to provide access to a wide range of opportunities. The analysis in this chapter focuses on one particular type of opportunity: employment. However, the underlying accessibility concept and methodology can and should be applied to other types of opportunities (e.g., health care).

The approach presented highlights the benefits of cycling as an additional transport alternative that can be used independently or as part of a multimodal trip to access the Dutch transit network. While the health benefits associated with cycling are well known, here the focus is on exploring the impact of cycling as a way of reducing the disparities in the potential accessibility provided by different modes.

Measuring Transport Equity. https://doi.org/10.1016/B978-0-12-814818-1.00005-6

The integration of cycling and public transport is important because cycling can significantly increase the spatial reach of the transit system, particularly as an access mode during the *"first mile."* It can effectively increase the catchment area of transit stations beyond the walking radius and reduce the burden during this segment of the trip. This is particularly relevant within the scope of restricted choice sets that condition personal mobility and the fact that the dominant transport mode (in this case the car) shapes the land use and distribution of opportunities. Effective policy should seek to minimize the disparities in accessibility between the dominant mode (the car) and the remaining available modes. Thus, the aim is to investigate the extent to which integrating cycling and public transport improves the fairness of the distribution of accessibility to jobs in the Netherlands, while reducing the intermodal gap.

2 Methodology

This section first describes the methodology used to estimate potential job accessibility, and second, the methodology to estimate the associated equity.

2.1 Accessibility methodology

The backbone of the methodology is the detailed potential job accessibility estimated for different modes following the general gravitational form. It includes the number of opportunities (jobs) at any location (postcode area), the travel time between the origin/ residential location and any area that could be a destination/employment location, and an associated distance decay function (in this case of the log-logistic form). In simple terms, this function weighs the employment opportunities as a function of how long it takes the potential worker to reach them because the propensity to travel decreases as travel times increase. Thus, by applying greater weight to opportunities that are closer, potential accessibility models the likelihood of traveling a certain amount of time or distance to work. This provides more realistic results than isochrones which assume that all trips within certain time or distance bands are equally accessible.

From a methodological perspective, intermodal comparisons of accessibility require ensuring the comparability of the measured travel times by mode. Thus, a *door-to-door* approach as described by Salonen and Toivonen (2013) is recommended. In the current analysis, the accessibility by car is estimated considering network geometry, speed limits, free flow speeds during uncongested times, and speed profiles of real traffic speeds for road segments provided by TomTom. Job accessibility by public transport is estimated using general transit feed specification (GTFS)-based transit models. The models include access time (walking or biking to a station/stop), waiting time at the stop, in-vehicle travel time, any transfer time (relying on GTFS schedule data for these last three), and finally the egress time to reach the final destination. The public transport and car models are calculated in 15-minute intervals for 24 hours.

Two separate *door-to-door* GTFS-based transit models are estimated. The first GTFS model is a typical transit model with pedestrian access and egress, referred to here as a *walk-and-ride* model. The second is the *bike-and-ride* model which incorporates cycling as a potential access mode and as an alternative for certain trips. The cycling speeds are calculated based on network geometry and variable average speeds for each segment of the Dutch cycling network. The *bike-and-ride* model presents the best-case scenario of cycling and transit integration by maximizing the estimated accessibility of the areas following a set of conditions summarized in Fig. 1.

Option A is the *walk-and-ride* model and is the default selection. Option B models cycling access to the transit system and option C models unimodal cycling trips to destinations. Option B is chosen if it is faster than option A and the cycling segment has an associated travel time of 30 minutes or less while being longer than 200 m. Option C is chosen if it is faster than options A and B and meets the same cycling conditions as option B.

The goal is to provide realistic alternatives and results. If it is faster to walk to the stations, then the default should be to walk. Likewise, if it is faster to cycle to the destination instead of cycling to a station to then use public transport the former should be the alternative chosen. In addition, to ensure the applicability of this model, only cycling to the largest train stations in the country is modeled in option B. Cycling is not modeled as a potential egress mode because it was found that while a large percentage of national railways passengers cycle to stations, the impact for the egress segment is significantly reduced and multimodal trips including only buses and bikes are rare.

The analysis is conducted at a high spatial resolution (five-digit postcode areas—PC5). These areas are smaller than a neighborhood and allow for a disaggregate exploration of variations in accessibility, for example, the province of Zuid Holland is made up of 6164 units. Using the larger, four-digit postcode areas (PC4) was considered. However, preliminary analysis showed that when aggregating PC5 results (using a weighted average) to a PC4 level and comparing it to the estimated PC4 results there was a high correlation (0.95) in the estimated accessibility but with a relatively high mean absolute percentage error (MAPE) of 31.8%. That is, that while the spatial pattern is quite similar, using PC4 units makes detection of low-accessibility areas very complicated.

The georeferenced employment information (opportunities) used in the analysis relies on the Landelijk Informatiesysteem van Arbeidsplaatsen (LISA) database.

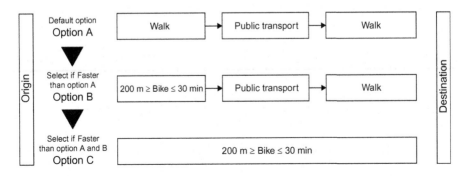

Fig. 1 *Bike-and-ride* model methodology.

It includes a census of all registered enterprises in the Netherlands including their location and number of employees. The same values are used for all of the calculated models.

2.2   Equity methodology

With the accessibility to jobs calculated, the analysis now seeks to answer the main question: does cycling and the *bike-and-ride* reduce the gap between the accessibility provided by the public transport system and the private car? In addition, the analysis focuses on the fairness of the distribution of the estimated accessibility and in particular to the benefits that can be associated with the *bike-and-ride* model.

Given the stated goal of minimizing accessibility disparities while increasing total accessibility to opportunities, in this case to jobs, this analysis goes beyond absolute values of accessibility. The Gini coefficient is used to determine which mode results in a better distribution of accessibility amongst the population. This egalitarian measure of statistical dispersion is commonly used to measure income distributions but can be equally applied to other distributions including accessibility. It measures the degree to which the accessibility to employment is distributed amongst the population, with zero being perfectly equal and one being completely unequal. It is calculated using graphical Lorenz curve approximations, relating the ranked empirical distribution with the line of perfect equality (45 degrees).

The car (the benchmark dominant mode), the *walk-and-ride* and *bike-and-ride* results are compared to determine whether public transport and cycling can be integrated to provide not only higher accessibility (reducing the intermodal gap), but also importantly, do so with a more egalitarian distribution of accessibility than under the *walk-and-ride* model.

3   Application

This section describes the results of the application at the national and city scales.

3.1   Analyzing job accessibility at the national scale

The results (Fig. 2) show that the level of accessibility provided by the car is vastly superior to the job accessibility provided by public transport and cycling throughout the day. The lower accessibility of the *walk-and-ride* and *bike-and-ride* models is caused by the lower speeds and the distribution of jobs.

The temporal disaggregate analysis, in 15-minute intervals, shows that congestion negatively impacts accessibility by the car, particularly during the morning and afternoon peaks. During these peak periods national average accessibility decreases by more than 20% from nighttime, when a car driver can travel at free-flow or near free-flow speeds. This is in stark contrast to transit, which provides the highest accessibility during the day (particularly during the morning and afternoon peaks). Nighttime accessibility by public transport plummets due to reduced service, providing

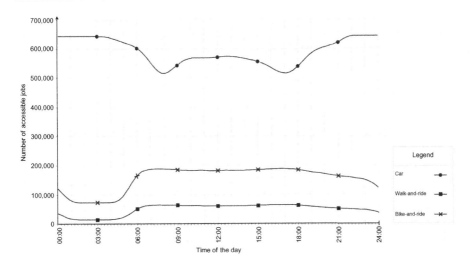

Fig. 2 Temporal variation of potential job accessibility.

much lower access to opportunities in both the *walk-and-ride* and *bike-and-ride* models. While not surprising, this large drop-off can have a large and negative impact on the individuals who work during these hours. Furthermore, the *walk-and-ride* accessibility is surprisingly low. Accessibility levels by bicycle alone are comparable to those of the *walk-and-ride* model during the day and higher than the accessibility provided at night.

The difference between the car and the *walk-and-ride* is lowest during the morning peak, but the car still provides accessibility values up to seven times higher. The *bike-and-ride* model provides better accessibility than the *walk-and-ride* model, but follows a similar pattern. Even with the added benefit of the cycling integration, it still falls well below the accessibility levels provided by the car. Nevertheless, this integration enhances the accessibility by public transport significantly, doubling during the day and having an even greater impact during the night. While falling short of providing similar levels to the car, it can be concluded that integration significantly increases access to job opportunities for those who cannot or do not want to commute by car.

This first snapshot of the Dutch reality provides the reader with two important insights. The first is that the level of accessibility provided by the competing modes is extremely unequal. The dominance of the car is not threatened by network congestion factors nor transit and cycling integration. Public transport accessibility levels are relatively low compared to the car due to the nonfavorable spatial distribution of jobs (most jobs are not located in close proximity to public transport stops) and longer *door-to-door* travel times. However, in relative terms, the value of integration is still significant and results in much higher levels of accessibility.

From a justice perspective, it is important to understand if the increase in average accessibility results in a more egalitarian distribution of this transport good. Thus, the second stage of analysis calculates the level of inequality in the accessibility provided by each mode, relying on the Gini coefficient. This is of particular interest in the comparison of the *bike-and-ride* and *walk-and-ride* to ensure that the previously presented improvements do not result in more unequal outcomes, and that these accessibility benefits are not disproportionally distributed.

The most equal distribution of job accessibility is provided by the car, with a low Gini coefficient ($G=0.11$) that is almost a quarter of the resulting coefficient for the walk-and-ride model (see Fig. 3). Of course, these levels of accessibility by car can only be achieved by those that have access to a car. The level of accessibility provided by public transport is not as equally distributed amongst the Dutch population even after incorporating cycling as an access mode, although the *bike-and-ride* model shows a more egalitarian distribution ($G=0.33$) than the *walk-and-ride* model ($G=0.42$).

3.2 Analyzing job accessibility at the city scale

In absolute terms, the largest Dutch cities (Amsterdam, Rotterdam, The Hague, and Utrecht) have the highest levels of the *walk-and-ride* (Fig. 4) and *bike-and-ride* (Fig. 5) accessibility, followed by secondary cities (e.g., Groningen and Amersfoort) and lastly by peripheral cities such as Enschede.

The added benefit of the cycling integration is not equally shared, even among these larger cities. Some cities benefit more than others in total terms and during key times of the day. As an example, The Hague and Utrecht, both show very similar results during the morning, afternoon, and evening periods under the typical *walk-and-ride* model (Fig. 4). However, the impact of the bicycle in Utrecht is much higher during the day, where it outperforms The Hague under the *bike-and-ride* model (Fig. 5). In the nighttime, however, the added value of the bike integration cannot

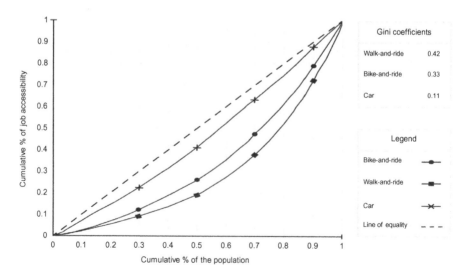

Fig. 3 Accessibility Lorenz curves for the Netherlands (by mode).

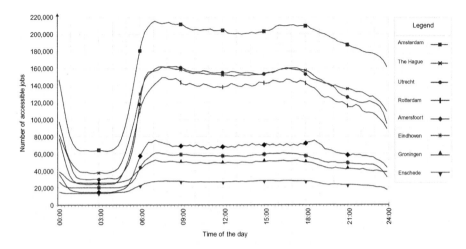

Fig. 4 *Walk-and-ride* accessibility in Dutch cities.

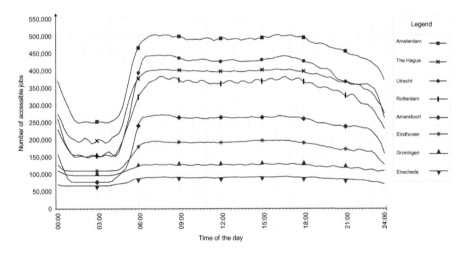

Fig. 5 *Bike-and-ride* accessibility in Dutch cities.

compensate for other factors such the lower level of service being provided by the transit network and The Hague provides better accessibility levels to its residents during these hours.

The gap between the car and public transport is significantly reduced in the larger cities. For example, under the *bike-and-ride* model even the postcode area with the lowest job accessibility in The Hague has a much higher accessibility than the average *walk-and-ride* accessibility for the municipality. In Rotterdam, the postcode with the lowest *bike-and-ride* accessibility is comparable to the average *walk-and-ride* accessibility in that city. However, the modal comparison shows that even in the most urbanized areas of the country the car still provides higher accessibility. That is, that despite the higher levels of both road congestion and public transport service, the *bike-and-ride* enhanced accessibility does not result in public transport overtaking the car as the dominant accessibility-providing mode.

The best-served areas in terms accessibility by public transport (i.e., the postcode areas within the cities with the highest levels of *bike-and-ride* accessibility) exceed the national average of accessibility by car. Unfortunately, despite these comparatively high levels, the local levels of accessibility remain lower for transit than car. Moreover, the relatively high *bike-and-ride* accessibility (above the mean national accessibility by car), occurs only temporally. In Rotterdam during mornings and afternoons (starting and ending at the peak hours), and in The Hague only during the morning and afternoon peak hours. This confirms that some cities gain more from cycling integration than others. Most importantly, it also shows that those who work nonstandard hours, such as night shifts, have significantly lower potential job accessibility if they depend on public transport, even while living in centrally located and well-served metropolitan areas. As a result, it is important to underline that bike integration only provides a partial remedy for the reduction of the car-transit imbalance in job accessibility. It works well during peak hours but has a limited applicability for the off-peak times, particularly during the night.

4 Policy relevance

The analysis shows that the accessibility by car remains several orders of magnitude higher than the best-case scenario for public transport (the *bike-and-ride* model), both nationally and within individual cities. This is also the case during peak hours in the center of metropolitan areas, despite the negative impact of congestion on the accessibility by car being coupled with the highest frequencies and levels of service of public transport. The degree to which the car outperforms the public transport system and the bicycle in the Netherlands, which has a strong history of investment in both cycling and transit, should give policy makers some pause. Clearly, more needs to be done to minimize this disparity between those with and those without access to a car.

When assessing the accessibility provided by transit, it is seen that the *bike-and-ride* is effective in providing better absolute accessibility, and on a national scale also achieves a better distribution of this transport good. It reduces the gap in accessibility between the dominant (car) and nondominant modes. The distribution of accessibility provided by the *bike-and-ride* model is more equal than the *walk-and-ride* model at the national level with a lower Gini coefficient (0.33). The *bike-and-ride* is successful in providing more equal access to jobs across a larger spatial area, with peripheral areas outside the largest cities enjoying accessibility levels by transit that could only be found in central cities if the access and egress modes were limited to walking. However, this is not enough to overcome the full extent of the inequality, in part because more urbanized areas still have more advantages than more suburban and rural areas in terms of the distribution of jobs and the transport system itself.

Nevertheless, the remarkably marked increase in accessibility achieved by effectively integrating the bicycle in the *bike-and-ride* model seems to benefit all areas of the country, and in doing so it also reduces the inequality in accessibility to jobs. The fact that it results in a system that is more equitable is highly relevant to policy makers and planners, given the associated costs of expansions to transit networks. The integration with the cycling infrastructure provides practitioners with an additional tool to consider. This integration is particularly important for large transport hubs and heavy rail infrastructure, as the effective expansion of the catchment area of each of the stations helps those that are further removed to more easily access the system. In addition, it is also beneficial for the service providers. This can have important positive equitable impacts across the world because this increase is achieved without any additional heavy infrastructure investment (e.g., public transport network expansion).

Having said this, it should be noted that integrating the bicycle as a viable access mode to transit is not as easy as simply asking individuals to cycle to the stations. Effective integration still requires investments. It needs to be encouraged through infrastructure integration (including cycle lanes and paths) to serve as feeders to and from the stations. In addition, sufficient and secure cycling parking alternatives at the stations are also needed. The Dutch government and the Netherlands Railways have continuously invested in bicycle parking facilities at train stations since the 1990s, including free bicycle parking facilities at main railway stations, digital signs indicating available parking spots, and high-quality uniform design.

In addition, it should be clear that even perfectly integrated bike and public transport is not an option for everyone. While the bicycle can be seen as an egalitarian mode of transport in terms of monetary costs, it requires, amongst other things, a level of ability and physical stamina that are not universal. The bicycle cannot be used by everyone and personal modal preferences should also be considered. There are significant spatial and social variations in bicycle use in the Netherlands. In particular, nonwestern immigrants in the Netherlands cycle significantly less (with a 18% share of cycling in the total amount of trips) than native Dutch (with a 28% share of cycling trips) (Harms et al., 2014).

Finally, the average accessibility by bicycle shows that it can be treated as competing mode to public transport under certain conditions. This highlights a potential policy pitfall that could be tempting to policy makers, but could have negative equity implications. While the bicycle does compete with public transport, especially for shorter trips, care should be taken when making decisions regarding the elimination or alteration of public transport routes, or levels of service. As previously mentioned, the bicycle is not a viable alternative for everyone. Moreover, our analysis shows that the close integration of cycling and public transport offers far more benefits than either of them separately. From an egalitarian perspective of justice, the focus should be oriented toward improvements to public transport as well as the *bike-and-ride* integration to equalize the accessibility provided by different modes.

5   Further reading

This work takes advantages of some of the new data that has allowed researchers and practitioners to provide greater nuance to the temporal dimension of accessibility. The importance of the temporal dimension is implicitly understood by many; for example, few would argue against the frequency and hours of service of the public transport system, in addition to the proximity of the stations and stops, all being components of the level of accessibility being provided. Furthermore, regardless of the presence (or not) of public transport, different temporal constraints may limit the accessibility of certain groups or areas to particular activities/opportunities. It is precisely for this reason that from a justice or equity perspective it is very important to consider the temporal variability across the day. Quite simply, by aggregating accessibility levels to provide a simple daily average and ignoring the daily variability, we lose a lot of information and potentially hide systemic issues that negatively impact access.

Among the transportation methods that have been used to better incorporate the temporal variability of accessibility, we can highlight the use of GTFS data for public transport schedules (e.g., Owen and Levinson, 2015; Widener et al., 2015), and detailed speed estimates through either the use of speed profiles (e.g., Moya-Gómez and García-Palomares, 2017) or travel times based on the Google Maps API (e.g., Delamater et al., 2012). Temporal constraints unrelated to the transport system itself have also been incorporated in several studies. Amongst these, we can highlight including opening hours (e.g., Neutens et al., 2012), the start times of jobs when calculating job accessibility (e.g., Boisjoly and El-Geneidy, 2016) as well as temporal constraints at the individual level (e.g., Neutens et al., 2010). Finally, Salonen and Toivonen's (2013) description of their *door-to-door* approach constitutes a good point of the departure for all studies which deal with intermodal accessibility comparisons, while the review by Järv et al. (2018) sheds light on how to better consider the temporal dimension of accessibility.

Acknowledgments

This work has been funded by the Netherlands Organisation for Scientific Research (NWO Project number: 485-14-038) within the framework of the joint FAPESP-ESRC-NWO Joint Call for Transnational Collaborative Research Projects Sustainable Urban Development.

M. Stępniak gratefully acknowledges the support of the Polish National Science Centre allocated on the basis of the decision no. DEC-2013/09/D/HS4/02679.

References

Boisjoly, G., El-Geneidy, A., 2016. Daily fluctuations in transit and job availability: a comparative assessment of time-sensitive accessibility measures. J. Transp. Geogr. 52, 73–81. https://doi.org/10.1016/j.jtrangeo.2016.03.004.

Delamater, P.L., Messina, J.P., Shortridge, A.M., Grady, S.C., 2012. Measuring geographic access to health care: raster and network-based methods. Int. J. Health Geogr. 11 (1), 15. https://doi.org/10.1186/1476-072X-11-15.

Harms, L., Bertolini, L., te Brömmelstroet, M., 2014. Spatial and social variations in cycling patterns in a mature cycling country exploring differences and trends. J. Transp. Health 1 (4), 232–242. https://doi.org/10.1016/j.jth.2014.09.012.

Järv, O., Tenkanen, H., Salonen, M., Ahas, R., Toivonen, T., 2018. Dynamic cities: location-based accessibility modelling as a function of time. Appl. Geogr. 95 (April), 101–110. https://doi.org/10.1016/j.apgeog.2018.04.009.

Moya-Gómez, B., García-Palomares, J.C., 2017. The impacts of congestion on automobile accessibility. What happens in large European cities? J. Transp. Geogr. 62 (June), 148–159. https://doi.org/10.1016/j.jtrangeo.2017.05.014.

Neutens, T., Delafontaine, M., Schwanen, T., Weghe, N.V.d., 2012. The relationship between opening hours and accessibility of public service delivery. J. Transp. Geogr. 25, 128–140. https://doi.org/10.1016/j.jtrangeo.2011.03.004.

Neutens, T., Schwanen, T., Witlox, F., De Maeyer, P., 2010. Evaluating the temporal organization of public service provision using space-time accessibility analysis. Urban Geogr. 31 (8), 1039–1064. https://doi.org/10.2747/0272-3638.31.8.1039.

Owen, A., Levinson, D.M., 2015. Modeling the commute mode share of transit using continuous accessibility to jobs. Transp. Res. A Policy Pract. 74, 110–122. https://doi.org/10.1016/j.tra.2015.02.002.

Rawls, J., 1999. A Theory of Justice. revised ed The Kelknap Press of Harvard University Press, Cambridge, MA.

Salonen, M., Toivonen, T., 2013. Modelling travel time in urban networks: comparable measures for private car and public transport. J. Transp. Geogr. 31, 143–153. https://doi.org/10.1016/j.jtrangeo.2013.06.011.

Widener, M.J., Farber, S., Neutens, T., Horner, M., 2015. Spatiotemporal accessibility to supermarkets using public transit: an interaction potential approach in Cincinnati, Ohio. J. Transp. Geogr. 42, 72–83. https://doi.org/10.1016/j.jtrangeo.2014.11.004.

Can the urban poor reach their jobs? Evaluating equity effects of relocation and public transport projects in Ahmedabad, India

Mark Brussel, Mark Zuidgeest, Frans van den Bosch, Talat Munshi, Martin van Maarseveen

1 Introduction

A city's transportation system plays an integral role in enabling the mobility that is essential to socioeconomic participation. Indeed, insufficient access to opportunities (employment or otherwise) can cause social exclusion (Lucas et al., 2016). This concept of transport-related social exclusion is of particular relevance to emerging economies, where a lack of accessibility is hampering the urban poor from participating in economic, social, and political activities.

As cities continue to grow and (in many places) their economies continue to develop, levels of congestion and land prices are likely to rise, potentially exacerbating social exclusion of the urban poor. High land prices force the urban poor to either squat in the inner parts of the city or live in areas with low land and property prices, mostly located in the peripheral areas. Low-income dwellers in cities in India typically experience high levels of social exclusion. They are forced into long daily commutes to and from low-paying jobs on overcrowded public transport systems for which fares continue to rise and are thus left with insufficient mobility choices, as walking and cycling are generally not an option for those trips (Joshi, 2014).

Thus, the debate on where the urban poor live and how they can access their workplaces using public transport modes is central to a more sustainable future of cities in the developing world. Despite the importance of these issues, most urban transport planning has avoided measuring the direct impacts of residential and job location and has limited its focus to understanding the efficiency of the transport network itself. Better integration between urban development and transport may provide the way forward to prevent the low income and excluded groups from being locked out of activities that are essential to support a good quality of life (Lucas, 2004). Accessibility analysis can help to quantify this integration by analyzing the land use and transport system simultaneously, and by developing metrics that measure, for example, the number of destinations (generally jobs, but also other urban services) that can be accessed by a particular group in society in a given time using a given mode (or combination of modes) of transport.

Measuring Transport Equity. https://doi.org/10.1016/B978-0-12-814818-1.00006-8

Likewise, the impact of new developments—such as new mass transit systems or new affordable housing can thus be compared regarding their contribution to a more equitable distribution of accessibility, using a standard set of metrics. Agreeing that transport equity can be viewed as the distribution of a minimum required level of accessibility based on principles of social justice and fairness (Martens, 2017), this study focuses on measuring the transport equity impacts of two related projects, both targeting low-income residents, in the city of Ahmedabad, India.

Ahmedabad, like many other cities in India, has embarked on an urban renewal program under the Jawaharlal Nehru National Urban Renewal Mission (JnNURM) with the explicit intention of providing more sustainable and equitable transport (MOUD, 2017) and pro-poor housing solutions (MOHUA, 2017). Initiatives sponsored under this urban renewal program across India include the development of rapid transit systems [bus rapid transit system (BRTS) and metro rapid transit system (MRTS)], investment in nonmotorized transport (NMT) infrastructure, and the provision of affordable housing. Whereas these initiatives are directed at the urban poor, the effect on these groups is not systematically analyzed.

Our focus, therefore, lies with the urban poor; we define three different urban poor groups with distinct characteristics regarding income, housing and housing location, and jobs and job location. The equity standard we employ is based on a before and after scenario of two projects: a housing relocation project and a BRT project. We consider these projects to be fair (i.e., to promote equity) if they increase accessibility to jobs (even if limited) for all urban poor groups, which is an application of the well-known Pareto criterion. We consider the outcome of the project more equitable if the poorest group profits more than the middle poor and the least poor group. We do not apply a minimum accessibility norm; our approach is to evaluate whether the implemented projects have contributed to more equitable accessibility for the poorest groups by comparing the situation before and after the project.

The metrics used in this study help to assess the effectiveness of the different programs currently being developed in Ahmedabad and elsewhere to reduce social exclusion. The presented metrics and the developed geographic information system (GIS) tool can thus help to highlight critical investment or policy reform needs in cities in India and beyond.

2 Ahmedabad

Ahmedabad is the largest city and former capital of the Indian state of Gujarat located on the bank of Sabarmati River in the western part of India. The river divides the city into two halves, mostly referred to as East Ahmedabad and West Ahmedabad. Ahmedabad, with currently more than 5.5 million inhabitants (Fig. 1) is the fifth largest city and the seventh largest metropolitan area in India, and is one of the vital trade and commerce centers. Its flourishing textile industry collapsed in the late 1980s, but the present city still accounts for 19% of the total urban workers in the state, while the city houses only 9% of the state inhabitants, and still hosts several large industries, such as for textile, chemical engineering, and pharmaceuticals.

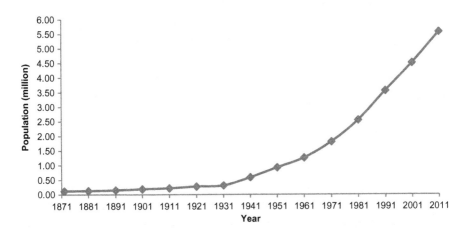

Fig. 1 Ahmedabad population growth since 1871.
Data from 2011 Census of India (Government of India, 2011).

Lopsided and heterogeneous development marks the built form pattern of the city. The population density ranges from 2293 persons per hectare in the (old) walled city area to densities of 150–370 persons per hectare in the western part of the city. Ahmedabad still has a substantial urban poor population; about 25% of the total population (AMC et al., 2006) live in slums, and an additional 14% live in tenement houses, also called *chawls* (Mahadevia, 2001; MOHUPA and Government of India, 2010), which are spread over the city.

In terms of transport, the present mean trip length of 5.5 km in Ahmedabad is lower than same tier cities such as Bengaluru, Hyderabad, and Pune (Pai, 2008), but the fast sprawling city and rapid rise in motorized vehicle ownership and use are matters of concern. Two mass transit modes are currently in operation in the city. The main system is the Ahmedabad Municipal Transport Service (AMTS), with around 540 buses, and routes oriented mostly to connect to the central portions of the city. A newly constructed system is the BRTS, which now runs successfully on the main radials (see Fig. 2). Also, Ahmedabad has advanced plans for the construction of a MRTS.

The BRTS project is implemented under the JnNURM mission. This urban renewal mission also supports several slum improvement programs, such as the Basic Services for the Urban Poor (BSUP) program, which includes the Socially and Economically Weaker Section Housing (SEWSH) project, which is considered in this study. In this project, in total 976 buildings are built to relocate 78,080 poor residents from slum locations, mostly at locations which are redeveloped through the Sabarmati Riverfront Development project.

The main questions addressed by this study are (i) what is the change in accessibility to jobs of those urban poor that have been relocated to new housing sites? and (ii) what are the anticipated impacts of the proposed investments in the BRTS and future MRTS on the level of accessibility to job opportunities of the urban poor vis-à-vis the defined equity standard?

Fig. 2 Existing and proposed public transport systems in Ahmedabad.

To answer these questions, we have developed a GIS-based three-dimensional (3D) multimodal network model, which we elaborate further below. The model combines all public transport modes and walking and cycling access/egress modes into an integrated and connected network, suited to analyze travel time with unlimited modal change within a single trip. Such a model is very suited to evaluate the effect of various policy scenarios on accessibility and social exclusion as discussed below.

We apply two accessibility measures. The first, a gravity-based measure, evaluates the city-wide impact of the proposed BRTS and MRTS on potential accessibility for the urban poor in the city as a whole, whereas the second, a contour-based measure, evaluates the accessibility impact of the housing relocation project involving 21 social housing complexes for different combinations of modes (AMTS, BRTS, MRTS, walking, and cycling). Both measures are analyzed and discussed in view of transport equity. The measures used are further explained below.

We conclude on the contributions of the different public transport systems on accessibility for the urban poor and the effects of the social housing program on transport equity in Ahmedabad.

3 Methodology

The following section explains our methodological approach, which involves a number of steps. First, we determine the locations of the urban poor, by the identification of slum locations and the categorization in three levels of housing quality, associated with three levels of poverty. These groups are then linked to their associated classes of employment, providing us with a spatial distribution of the poor and their jobs. Subsequently, we model all transport systems, each with their particular characteristics, in a multi-modal network model. In the next step, we calculate two accessibility measures, one associated with the housing relocation project and the other associated with the city as a whole. For the first, we implement a travel time contour measure which identifies all jobs within distinct travel time bandwidths. We then calculate the difference in the number of jobs accessible before and after the housing relocation project, for the three poverty groups and for different travel time bandwidths. If overall (for most groups and locations) accessibility is improving, we consider the project to be promoting equity. For the city-wide analysis, we use a so-called gravity-based measure, which calculates the job accessibility from each location in the city to any other location in the city. We do this for all transport systems and compare changes in accessibility before and after the implementation of the BRTS and MRTS and look at effects on spatial and social equity.

3.1 Accessibility metrics

The interaction between land use and transport is complex. Everything that happens to land use has transport implications and vice versa. Urban development generates the need for travel, which often is translated into the enhancement of transport infrastructure and services, which attracts further development. Because of this, levels of accessibility are continuously changing. These interconnections are particularly vivid in a city like Ahmedabad where rapid urbanization and urban restructuring are transforming the urban area, and the location of the urban poor population is continuously changing (formally through social housing programs or development induced evictions, informally through squatting). At the same time, urban infrastructure is being reshaped and redeveloped in response to this rapid urbanization and the city's fast-growing economy.

Accessibility metrics are particularly suited to evaluate the interaction between transport and land use, as they value both the infrastructure and the activity system. These metrics also allow distinguishing between socioeconomic groups, hence making them ideally suited for the study of transport equity. The development of accessibility metrics is aided by recent advances in GIS that make the use of detailed spatial operations and high-quality visualizations possible in a way that can be more readily used and understood by planners, policymakers, and the general public. The rapid development of these tools is a benefit for all those interested in understanding the complex interactions that take place in cities.

Accessibility metrics can be used to analyze the spatial and social equity impact of interventions by quantifying the extent to which accessibility levels change for one location and group of people compared with another location and group of people.

Table 1 Analysis and data sources

Analysis activity	Key data sources	Data source to test model assumptions	Data source for model validation
Determining locations of the urban poor	Locations of slums and chawls	Expert interviews	
Determining locations of employment	Ahmedabad property tax data	Expert interviews	
GIS-based network modeling	Various networks, AMTS and BRTS with their characteristics Mode use of urban poor	n.a.	n.a.
Contour-based accessibility modeling	BSUP housing locations		Focus group discussions
Gravity-based accessibility modeling	Ahmedabad household survey Distance decay curves		Focus group discussions

When compared to a normative value of accessibility, the same analysis can be used to gauge transport justice levels.

In this study, we apply location-based accessibility metrics, linking locations of opportunity (i.e., job locations) to locations of residence (i.e., locations of the urban poor). We consider the resistance of space (i.e., traveling through a multimodal transport network) to study the transport equity impact of public transport projects in combination with a social housing project in the context of a city in the developing world.

Below, the main methodological approaches that were followed are explained. Prior to this, an overview of data sources is provided for the key elements in the research.

To support key assumptions on the locations of the urban poor, the locations of their employment and their sensitivity toward travel time, two activities were carried out to gather qualitative data: (i) a number of focus group discussions and personal interviews were conducted on eight locations with (groups of) poor dwellers and (ii) a number of interviews were held with experts from the CEPT University in Ahmedabad in the field of transport and development. In the following sections, the various analytical steps are discussed, and their assumptions and data validation explained. Table 1 provides an overview of the main types of analysis performed, their associated data sources, and assumptions.

3.2 Locations of the urban poor

In Ahmedabad, about 40% of the population resides in informal settlements. A substantial number of the urban poor reside in these locations. The two dominant types of informal settlements are slums that have developed out of the illegal occupation of the marginal areas of the city by migrants and squatters, and chawls, which are residential units originally built for workers in the mills and factories. Most slum dwellers tend to settle along the waterways in the city, like Sabarmati River, on vacant land or in low-lying areas (Bhatt, 2003).

In the absence of reliable and disaggregated census data on poverty in Ahmedabad, we have used the locations of informal development and the quality of buildings in informal areas to identify the locations of the urban poor. We assume that the urban poor mostly live in these slum and chawl areas in the city. This assumption was tested and confirmed by expert interviews. Given the absence of poverty data, housing data are typically used as a proxy for identifying the residential location of the urban poor.

The data on slum locations were collected by the CEPT University in Ahmedabad as part of the Slum Free City Ahmedabad project. The survey data for these areas contain the number of huts in total, the number of huts that are poorly built (*kutchha*), the number of huts that are of good construction (*pucca*), and one class in between (*semipucca*). The three types of housing conditions are used as proxies to classify the urban poor into the least poor (occupying pucca housing), middle poor (occupying semipucca housing), and poorest (occupying kutchha housing). This classification is used to estimate the number of (potential) workers assuming two potential workers per hut irrespective of housing type, following Bhatt (2003). Fig. 3 shows concentrations of (potential) workers (all urban poor classes combined) in the city based on the slum and chawl locations.

3.3   Locations of employment opportunities

We derived data on job locations, job types, and their densities, using 2011 property tax data of Ahmedabad (Munshi, 2013), to identify employment opportunities and map their locations at an appropriate spatial scale. These data were spatially disaggregated to obtain job density grids (using 100×100 m grid cells) and clusters by employment sector, that is, distinguishing industrial, retail, government, education, transport and logistics, and office and commercial jobs. The employment data per grid were then grouped into three categories: salaried (24% of the potential jobs, typically in education, banking, government, hotels, and commercial sectors), self-employed (33% of the potential jobs, one for each retail job), and casual labor jobs (43% of the potential jobs, typically construction, storage warehouses, and industrial jobs). This urban employment subdivision can be typically (but not exclusively) linked to the identified worker categories, that is, the least poor (11% of the urban poor in Ahmedabad), middle poor (67%), and very poor (22%), respectively, following Ray (2010). The three worker categories represent different levels of wages associated with different levels of poverty and uncertainty of income. The percentages of these job categories and worker classes in Ahmedabad are depicted in the chart in Fig. 4, where matching colors indicate matching job categories and urban poor classes. There is a surplus of about 100% in potential jobs; these jobs may also be occupied by nonpoor workers. Competition for jobs as such is not considered in this study.

For the accessibility analysis, both the locations of the urban poor and employment locations have been aggregated to a 400×400 m grid for computational reasons.

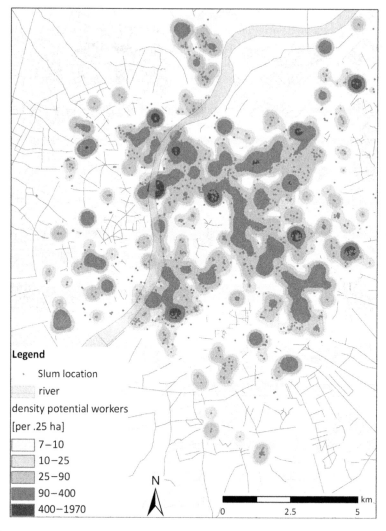

Fig. 3 Concentration of all potential urban poor workers per quarter of a hectare (based on so-called "kernel density'").

3.4   Modeling public transport systems

We model each specific mode as a subsystem of the whole transport system with its own network and routes and with contact points or exchange points at the stops or terminals where it is possible for people to change from one mode to another. Recent advances in 3D GIS provide us with opportunities to represent multiple routes that run on the same street segment in three dimensions. This approach allows for the possibility to precisely define and store the networks of the individual modes, their network connectivity, and the attributes of routes, stops, and connections. Moreover, the

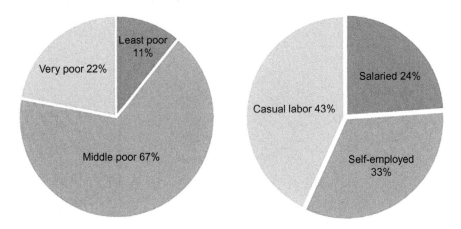

Fig. 4 Distribution of urban poor classes and employment categories.

disconnected nature of routes into multiple overlaying layers in 3D allows for shortest path algorithms. To adequately model the transport system in the city of Ahmedabad, we considered the following modes:

- NMT modes (walking and cycling), operating mostly on sidewalks for walking and the general road network for cycling except some bicycle paths along the BRTS. For these modes, separate walking and cycling networks have been generated based on the general road network.
- The AMTS, operating fixed routes on the general road network. For this mode, we have generated separate route networks connected to each other at the locations of bus stops.
- The Ahmedabad BRTS, operating fixed routes on dedicated BRTS infrastructure, phases 1 and 2 of which are in operation and implemented in the model (Fig. 2). For this mode, we generated a separate network.
- The Ahmedabad MRTS, which will be operated on dedicated rail infrastructure in the future. Also here, a separate network has been generated.

There are no private motorized modes used in the model. We assume that the urban poor hardly own and use these, an assumption that was confirmed by the focus group discussions and interviews. The influence of these motorized modes on the average operating speeds of the other modes such as cycling and the AMTS is considered though. A GIS network dataset that contains all four modal networks has been developed, that is, a geo-database including the general road network layer (used for modeling access and egress trips by walking or cycling), the AMTS network, the BRTS network, and a part of the proposed MRTS network. All networks include stops or stations where trip makers can enter, exit, or transfer within or between the modal networks. As such, the fully connected and functional 3D multimodel network model has been developed and implemented in the software ArcGIS (Fig. 5).

Fig. 5 shows a visualization of how the lines are modeled in 3D. Each AMTS route is modeled in 3D, in a horizontal plane. This approach allows for the possibility to model more than one bus route on a single street segment. Likewise, the BRTS and walking and cycling networks have been modeled. In the model, travel time

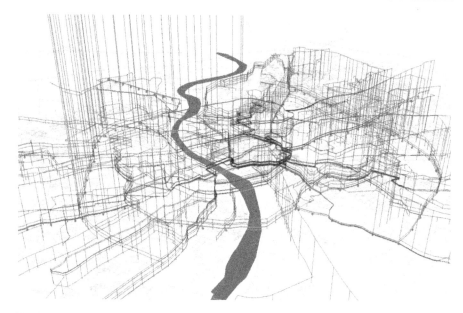

Fig. 5 The 3D representation of the public transport model for Ahmedabad.

and distance are considered as the main impedances, although the database in principle allows for adding other attributes such as distance-based fares, etc. The time cost is the sum of all time spent using a mode or transferring between modes. Fig. 6 shows how the various transport system attributes are combined into one multimodal network model. The multimodal network model is complemented with walking or bicycle access and egress times. In this way, the GIS database can be used to link the urban poor locations and their respective job locations.

3.5 Modeling accessibility

Two major policy initiatives that have an impact on accessibility for the poor have been implemented during the same period; the BSUP housing relocation schemes and the BRTS. We first analyze the city-wide effects of the BRTS on the accessibility of all urban poor. Then, we zoom in on the effect of housing relocation based on the relocation itself under the condition of current urban poor mode use (walking and AMTS), followed by the inclusion of the BRTS as a mode. To carry out these two analyses, two types of accessibility metrics have been implemented. A gravity-based measure is used that is suited to evaluate accessibility for several scenarios of transport system improvement and different types of users (varying between mode combinations, poverty classes, and locations of interest). A contour-based measure that is suited to evaluate the quality of the relocated sites in terms of their accessibility. The contour-based measure is chosen for the analysis of accessibility for the housing relocation sites. It can be more easily explained and communicated to policymakers

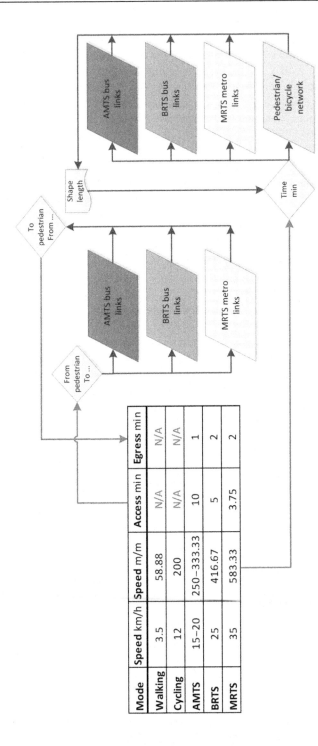

Fig. 6 Modeling of network impedances. N/A means not applicable, as walking and cycling trips do not have access and egress trips.

and is based on the total number of jobs, which is easily understood than the more abstract discounted number. Moreover, it *is not based* on assumptions associated with distribution curves. It allows us to evaluate changes in equity based on travel bands, which is not possible with a gravity-based measure that works by a distance decay function and is therefore continuous. For the area-wide analysis, we do find the gravity-based measure more suited, as its application in the GIS is cell-based and provides a summative count for all job locations in the city, using a continuous measure.

Contour-based accessibility maps show the area that can be reached in different time bands of travel (up to 10, 20, 30, 45, and 60 min) around each of the locations where new housing projects are being developed. Travel times are calculated in the multimodal network model, based on the estimated travel speeds and attributes of the modes used and average waiting times at stops. The number of jobs (by employment category) within each contour can be calculated in a GIS overlay operation.

The gravity-based accessibility metric is an extension of the contour measure and discounts jobs that are further away from a location using a negative exponential decay function that is based on the travel behavior of the poor in Ahmedabad. The decay functions have been estimated following methods proposed by Skov-Petersen (2001) and Salze et al. (2011) in such a way as to not provide a generic travel time decay function for all trips, but to generate mode-specific decay functions (walking vs general public transport). The curves are based on a large household survey of Ahmedabad consisting of 4950 valid household samples containing almost 30,000 trips of over 16,000 individuals. Out of this data, the trips of the urban poor (19,000, or 63% of all trips) were extracted and again classified by their housing type. In this way, curves were estimated for the poor only, for employment purpose trips for public transport users and walkers.

The curves of both public transport and walking (Fig. 7) show that the travel time decay is quite strong in both modes. The walking decay, however, is particularly

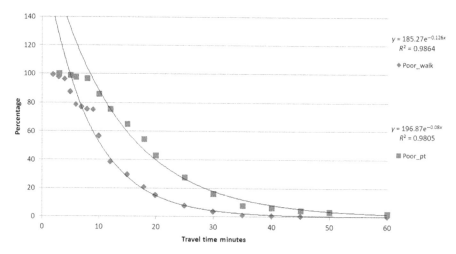

Fig. 7 Travel time decay curves for the urban poor for walking and public transport trips, based on 19,000 urban poor trips, classified with a class width of 5 min increments.

strong, indicating that less than 20% of the poor are traveling on foot longer than 20 min to reach their job location, as opposed to 40% in the case of public transport.

4   Results

4.1   City-wide accessibility analysis

The potential accessibility measure explicitly combines job opportunities for the poor and the difficulty of travel. Job opportunities are discounted with increasing travel time using the above given negative exponential decay functions; a distant job is valued less than one close by. The differences in this potential accessibility value can be substantial across modes.

Fig. 8 shows the gain in potential accessibility levels for all urban poor classes combined. We compare the situation with the walking and AMTS only combination to the

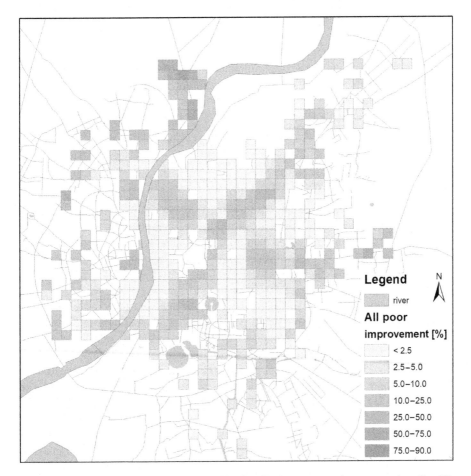

Fig. 8 Ratio of job-based potential accessibility for all urban poor workers comparing all public transport options with the walking and AMTS only.

situation where the BRTS and MRTS have been implemented fully. The BRTS and MRTS corridors are clearly visible in the resultant map and have a direct impact on local accessibility, indicating that the effect of the BRTS and MRTS on potential job accessibility is substantial in these areas.

The contribution of the AMTS and BRTS to potential job accessibility is highest in the areas surrounding the center locations with high job density. More jobs can be reached in shorter travel time, and these are valued higher because of the decreased travel time to reach them. The average overall contribution of the BRTS and MRTS to the level of potential job accessibility (for the whole city) compared to the walking and AMTS combination only is calculated at 11%. The contribution of the AMTS and BRTS phase 1 to potential job accessibility for the urban poor class compared to walking alone is calculated at 138% (not shown in Fig. 8).

Finally, the three urban poor classes, who live in different locations and who are employed in different job categories are looked at specifically. Analyzing the expected gain in their potential accessibility levels from the current AMTS and BRTS phase 1 systems to one with the BRTS phase 2 and MRTS phases 1 and 2 fully implemented, reveals a potential increase of 5.1% for the least-poor workers, 5.7% for the middle-poor workers, and 3.9% for the very poor workers. The very poor workers (accessing casual labor jobs) will benefit less than the other two groups from the planned extensions, as they are mostly located further from the BRTS and MRTS corridors, while the middle-poor workers (accessing self-employment jobs) benefit the most. The new systems, therefore, do not contribute to reducing the gaps between the poorest group and the other poor groups.

4.2   Accessibility of relocated communities

In this section, we zoom in on the housing relocation sites in particular and validate results using focus group data obtained during site visits (Fig. 9). We discuss how the forced move of people has impacted their accessibility and how this has led to further inequity. A comparison of levels of accessibility to jobs by multimodal combination, including a defined access and egress mode (walking or cycling) is shown. We apply a contour-based measure for the 21 BSUP housing locations.

Using the contour-based accessibility measure, the number of job opportunities of the working population (all three urban poor classes together) living in 21 selected BSUP locations is derived. Various travel time bandwidths are distinguished. Fig. 10 shows a contour map for one central BSUP location only (Ahmedabad cotton mill—BSUP No. 5) demonstrating the impact of the current and planned investments in the BRTS and MRTS on job accessibility as compared to the situation with the walking and AMTS only. The spatial extent of the job opportunities reachable within 1 h travel time clearly increases as, particularly near the current and planned corridors, travel times reduce. A similar analysis was done for each of the 21 BSUP locations. To see the effect on job accessibility regarding the number of opportunities, we spatially overlay the contour maps with the employment map (all three urban poor classes

Fig. 9 Interview at one of the new housing locations.

combined) to get the chart in Fig. 11. The chart shows the total number of job opportunities reachable for each of the 21 BSUP locations in stacked bars indicating the different travel time bandwidths. For all 21 locations together, the BRTS and MRTS investments increase the level of job accessibility for the urban poor within 30 min travel time by 16.5% as compared to the AMTS situation only, while this figure is almost 50% for trips up to 60 min.

Fig. 11 provides a fascinating picture of spatial inequity. It shows enormous spatial variations in job accessibility of the poor, depending on the location they have migrated to. Six of the locations (BSUP locations nos. 5–10) show very high levels of accessibility, with, in the BRTS scenario, up to 350,000 jobs that are accessible within half an hour. This half an hour is essential, as it is the travel time band in which 96% of the walking trips and 82% of the public transport trips of the poor take place (see Fig. 7). Locations 5–10 are in the old city area, where most of the jobs for the urban poor are located. On the other hand, five other locations (BSUP locations nos. 1, 13–16) show deficient overall levels of job accessibility.

This result is a clear indication of a very inequitable situation. Also, from locations 1, 14, and 15, few jobs are accessible within 45 min of travel. People who are relocated to these areas are, therefore, further marginalized and disadvantaged. Some of the locations they were forced to migrate to do not provide enough accessibility to livelihood sustaining activities. The inequity in accessibility is thus contributing to further inequity in income.

The maps in Fig. 12 demonstrate clearly how spatial inequity works, by highlighting the spatial configuration of the various transport systems as well as the cells with

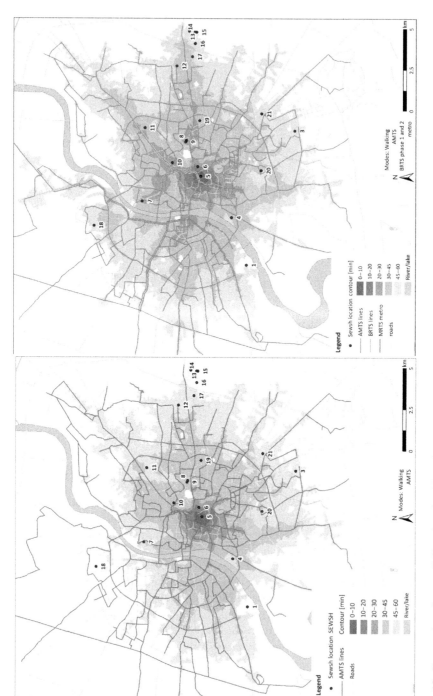

Fig. 10 Contour-based accessibility plots for Ahmedabad cotton mill (no. 5) for the walking and AMTS only (*left*) and all current and planned public transport modes + walking (*right*) for different contour bandwidths (all urban poor workers combined). Names of the BSUP locations are given in Table 2.

Table 2 Names of the BSUP locations

Shahwadi	Odhav-1, 187
Vatava	Odhav-3, 23
Vatva site A and site B	Odhav-3, 37
Calico Mill	Odhav-3, 38
Ahmedabad Cotton Mill, Sarangpur	Odhav-3, 51
Kesar Hind Mill Ni Chali	Odhav-3, 86
Rustam Mill	Vadaj BSUP
Vivekanand Mill	Ajit Mill, Rakhiyal
Raipur Mill	Ishanpur
Saraspur Mill	Bag-e-Firdosh
Vijay Mill	

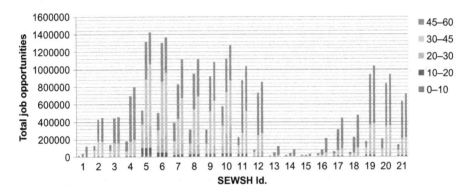

Fig. 11 Contour-based accessibility levels per BSUP location for different contour lengths (in minutes) in stacked bars. Each housing location shows three bars: walking *(left)*, walking + AMTS *(middle)*, and all modes *(right)* (all urban poor workers). Names of the BSUP locations are given in Table 2.

job locations and their density. Where both transport options and employment options are absent, people are at a clear disadvantage. Detailed analysis of locations 13–16 reveals that these are located relatively far away from current or planned public transport stops, and also in areas with no jobs or relatively lower job densities. Access to the BRT from these locations is time consuming, with around 20–30 min of access trip by walking to the nearest BRT station, in the absence of the AMTS service. In the lower two maps of Fig. 12, locations 1 and 4 are shown, and, as can be seen in Fig. 11, these score very differently. Location 4 is closer to the city center and both the AMTS and BRT systems, whereas location 1, although not so far from the main job concentrations in Euclidean distance, scores very low because it is on the other side of the river and less favorably located in terms of access to public transport.

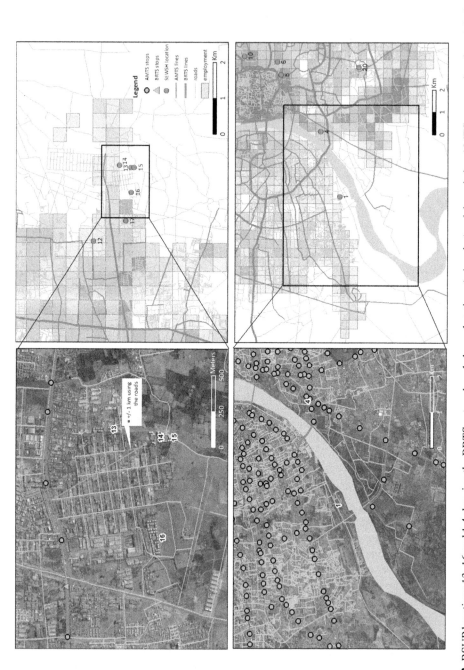

Fig. 12 BSUP locations 13–16 and 1,4 showing the BRTS network and planned stations (*triangles*) and the existing AMTS route and stations (*circles*); job densities indicated in *gray* scale intensities (all urban poor workers). Names of the BSUP locations are given in Table 2.

Overall, the ratio of accessibility values of the highest (5) and the lowest (15) location for all modal combinations is around 40. Although there is no information on the exact origin of people who were relocated to a particular housing project, we do know that all slums from which people originated are located along the riverfront where the Sabarmati Riverfront Development Project is being implemented (Patel et al., 2015). After determining the average accessibility of three representative central riverfront locations in aggregated travel times from 0–30 to 30–60 min, we see the following results (Table 3).

It is clear that, although for some people the relocation has worked out well, for most people this is not the case. Comparing the average accessibility of the low scoring locations in Fig. 11 with the values before relocation reveals large reductions in the number of jobs accessible, both for trips below 30 min and trips between 30 and 60 min, for all modal combinations. The effects are stronger, however, for trips below 30 min, which are the trips most of the poor make.

From an equity perspective, one could, therefore, conclude that for the majority of people who were relocated to locations further away, the relocation has had a detrimental effect on their accessibility to jobs, in all travel time bandwidths. The new BRTS and MRTS can only partially alleviate this situation.

To analyze the impact of cycling as a feeder/last mile mode to and from the BRTS and MRTS stations, we looked at the change in accessibility levels for the 21 BSUP locations in the situation that all proposed public transport interventions have been

Table 3 Average accessibility values before relocation by mode, compared to average accessibility values after relocation, with locations that win or lose, for two aggregated travel time bandwidths

0–30 min	Walking	Walking +AMTS	All modes
Before relocation	78,000 jobs	148,000 jobs	215,000 jobs
After relocation	40,000 jobs	61,000 jobs	80,000 jobs
Winners	Four locations (5, 6, 10, 11)	Three locations (5, 6, 10)	Three locations (5, 6, 10)
Losers	17 Locations (1–4, 7–9, 12–21)	18 Locations (1–4, 7–9, 11–21)	18 Locations (1–4, 7–9, 11–21)

30–60 min	Walking	Walking+AMTS	All modes
Before relocation	353,000 jobs	798,000 jobs	910,000 jobs
After relocation	155,000 jobs	545,000 jobs	637,000 jobs
Winners	Six locations (5–10)	Seven locations (5–11)	Nine locations (5–11, 19, 20)
Losers	15 Locations (1–4, 11–21)	14 Locations (1–4, 12–21)	12 Locations (1–4, 12–18)

implemented (Fig. 13). We use the gravity-based measure (without travel time band-widths) to illustrate the effect of the access and egress function. Our findings show a huge increase in accessibility levels in all locations, even the ones that are relatively close to the center. The strongest effects are seen in the five locations with the lowest (contour-based) accessibility levels as described above and depicted before in Fig. 11) (nos. 1, 13–16). These locations are relatively far from public transport stops. The use of bicycles in access and egress makes that more jobs are reachable in the first section of the distribution curve, which results in less discounting of jobs.

5 Policy relevance

The objective of this work was twofold: to measure the effect of public transport improvements on the overall level of job accessibility of the urban poor in Ahmedabad, as well as to evaluate the accessibility of the urban poor after relocation through a housing relocation program.

Our findings show that there is variation between accessibility to jobs for the different urban poor groups. Compared to walking, public transport does improve job accessibility, particularly through the extensive AMTS network, that can be accessed relatively easily from all locations in the city. The current and planned BRTS and MRTS projects improve this accessibility to jobs considerably further, but mostly in the close vicinity of these systems. The contribution of these projects quickly drops as the distance to the BRTS and MRTS stations increases.

These findings suggest that the planning of new mass transit lines should always encompass improvements in access and egress options. In addition, accessibility would improve if the BRTS frequency and speed would increase if fares of the AMTS, BRTS, and MRTS would be integrated and physical connections improved.

Our analysis shows that if the urban poor could use the bicycle as an access mode accessibility levels improved further as cycling provides an excellent first-mile access and last-mile egress to and from the BRTS and MRTS stations, combining the strengths of both systems. While bicycle mode share is currently 19%, few people make use of the cycling option to access stations because of a lack of facilities for safe parking at the BRTS and MRTS stations. Cycling should, therefore, be considered more seriously and specific policy needs to be developed to make the BRTS more accessible to cyclists. Such policy could involve the safeguarding of current cycling infrastructure facilities and the provision of new facilities, safe crossings, new guarded bicycle parking facilities, and the like. Also, the implementation of public bike schemes that are designed to be used by the poorest could be considered at strategic locations, particularly for egress trips in central locations.

The analysis of accessibility of the BSUP housing locations clearly demonstrates that most locations are wrongly chosen, given their position relative to employment and transport systems. Families that were moved to these locations have very limited access to jobs within a reasonable travel time (30 min), which significantly impedes their ability to take part in economic life. On the basis of our first defined equity

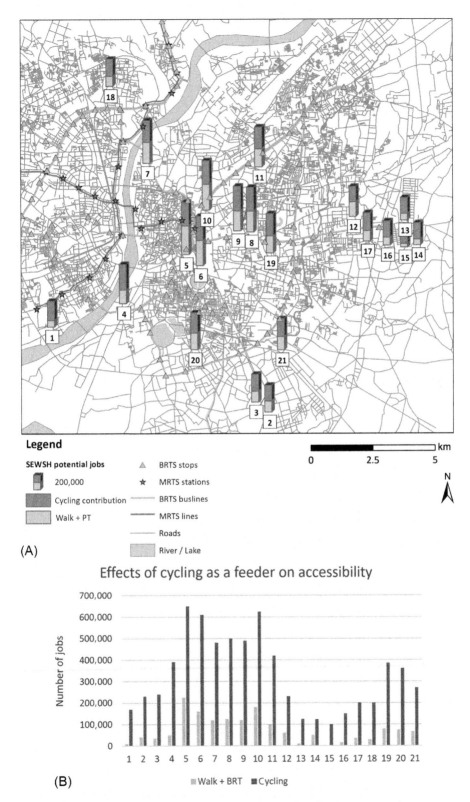

Fig. 13 (A) Potential accessibility in the BSUP locations for all urban poor workers. (B) Comparing walking and cycling feeders to all public transport options.

standard—remember we consider the project to be fair if it increases accessibility to jobs for all urban poor groups—we conclude that the housing relocation is not equitable, as accessibility levels have dropped for a large section of the urban poor population.

Although the relocated groups do benefit to a degree from the planned public transport interventions, these benefits are too marginal to compensate the negative effect of the relocation. To limit the negative effects on spatial and social equity, more attention should be paid to both the locational characteristics of the new sites and a more equitable transport system. Only if both elements are jointly considered, can these negative effects be controlled.

To improve the benefit of systems like the BRTS, particularly for the urban poor, its spatial coverage should expand, and more attention needs to be paid to the routing of the various systems given the locations of the urban poor and their jobs. New low-cost housing projects such as BSUP, should, therefore, be planned on or close to mass transit corridors.

To push the agenda of social inclusion of the urban poor forward, local planning efforts should concentrate on public transport improvement and the NMT feeder function, and particularly the development of more integrated urban land use and transport-development strategies.

6   Further reading

Various studies have discussed the application of location-based measures. For instance, in Tel Aviv and Ha Noi, these have been used to assess the difference between potential accessibility by car and public transport (Benenson et al., 2010; Hong Ha et al., 2011); in Boston, Los Angeles, and Tokyo between potential accessibility to jobs versus different urban form (Kawabata and Shen, 2006); in Finland to study the relation between potential accessibility by road and railway to population change (Kotavaara et al., 2011); and in China to develop an Urban Accessibility Planning Support System (Shi et al., 2012). More complex location-based measures explicitly incorporate capacity restrictions of supplied activity characteristics to include competition effects (Geurs and Ritsema van Eck, 2003; Cheng and Bertolini, 2013). However, these indicators also require more analytical skills from users (Handy and Clifton, 2001) and place a high demand on data availability.

Other studies have looked at the effect of transport projects on social inclusion of the poor. Teunissen et al. (2015), for example, show this is the case for the low-income population in Bogotá, Colombia, while Lucas (2011) shows this for the Tshwane Region in South Africa.

An interesting study that looked into the equity effects of a BRT system was carried out in Cali, Colombia by Delmelle and Casas (2012). They applied a gravity-based accessibility measure to three classes of activities (education, recreation, and hospitals) on a single mode BRT system, using z-scores to indicate deviations from the city average of accessibility.

Various authors have looked at measuring equity in relation to accessibility, including Martens (2017), van Dijk et al. (2016), again Delmelle and Casas (2012), Teunissen et al. (2015), Neutens et al. (2010), Preston and Rajé (2007), and many others. Whereas many useful approaches have been developed, questions remain on which metrics are suited for which context, scale level, and level of aggregation at which they are used, whether or not simple measures are sufficient, etc. More work is needed on effective measures that are both robust in terms of equity appraisal of transport projects, are easily understood and communicable, but also work in relatively data poor environments.

The principle of 3D network modeling was described by Thill et al. (2011) in an interesting paper in which this approach was primarily tested on indoor environments. The paper discusses a prototype approach in a controlled campus area in which the accessibility calculations are somewhat limited. However, it provides an interesting overview of the methodological issues and possibilities of the 3D modeling approach.

The case of displacement in relation to the riverfront development projects in Ahmedabad has been researched and discussed in depth in Patel et al. (2015). In this paper, the policies and governance processes surrounding the relocations are discussed. Its findings indicate that the poor, who have not been included in the infrastructure planning and resettlement process, have been further marginalized and impoverished as a result of these projects.

Acknowledgments

This work is based on a research project commissioned by the World Bank India. The project team wishes to acknowledge Mr. Anand Patel of the Ahmedabad Municipal Corporation (AMC) for his inputs and permission to use data, Mr. Nguyen Ngoc Quang for his assistance in the geodatabase and model development, as well as students in ITC's UPM course for their contribution in further developing and testing part of the concepts and model.

References

AMC, AUDA and CEPT, 2006. City Development Plan Ahmedabad 2006-2012. Ahmedabad Municipal Corporation and Ahmedabad Urban Development Authority, Ahmedabad.

Benenson, I., Martens, K., Rofé, Y., Kwartler, A., 2010. Public transport versus private car GIS-based estimation of accessibility applied to the Tel Aviv metropolitan area. Ann. Reg. Sci. https://doi.org/10.1007/s00168-010-0392-6.

Bhatt, M., 2003. Understanding Slums: Case Studies for the Global Report on Human Settlements 2003, A Case of Ahmedabad City. Report. UN-Habitat, London.

Cheng, J., Bertolini, L., 2013. Measuring urban job accessibility with distance decay, competition and diversity. J. Transp. Geogr. 30, 100–109. https://doi.org/10.1016/j.jtrangeo.2013.03.005.

Delmelle, E.C., Casas, I., 2012. Evaluating the spatial equity of bus rapid transit-based accessibility patterns in a developing country: the case of Cali, Colombia. Transp. Policy 20, 36–46.

Geurs, K.T., Ritsema van Eck, J.R., 2003. Accessibility evaluation of land-use scenarios: the impact of job competition, land-use and infrastructure developments for the Netherlands. Environ. Plann. B 30 (1), 69–87.

Government of India, 2011. 2011 Census Data. Office of the Registrar General & Census Commissioner, India. Available at: http:/censusindia.gov.in/2011-Common/CensusData2011.html (Accessed 11 May 2018).

Handy, S.L., Clifton, K.L., 2001. Evaluating neighbourhood accessibility: possibilities and practicalities. J. Transp. Stat. 4 (2/3), 67–78.

Hong Ha, P.T., Van den Bosch, F., Quang, N.N., Zuidgeest, M.H.P., 2011. Urban form and accessibility to jobs: a comparison of Hanoi and Randstad Metropolitan areas. Environ. Urban. ASIA 2, 265–285.

Joshi, R., 2014. Mobility Practices of the Urban Poor in Ahmedabad (India). (PhD dissertation). University of the West of England.

Kawabata, M., Shen, Q., 2006. Job accessibility as an indicator of auto-oriented urban structure: a comparison of Boston and Los Angeles with Tokyo. Environ. Plann. B 33, 115–130.

Kotavaara, O., Antikainen, H., Rusanen, J., 2011. Population change and accessibility by road and rail networks: GIS and statistical approach to Finland 1970–2007. J. Transp. Geogr. 19 (4), 926–935.

Lucas, K. (Ed.), 2004. Running on Empty; Transport, Social Exclusion and Environmental Justice. The Policy Press, University of Bristol, Bristol.

Lucas, K., 2011. Making the connections between transport disadvantage and the social exclusion of low income populations in the Tshwane region of South Africa. J. Transp. Geogr. 19, 1320–1334. https://doi.org/10.1016/j.jtrangeo.2011.02.007.

Lucas, K., Wee, B., Maat, K., 2016. A method to evaluate equitable accessibility: combining ethical theories and accessibility-based approaches. Transportation 473–490. https://doi.org/10.1007/s11116-015-9585-2.

Mahadevia, D., 2001. Informalisation of employment and poverty in Ahmedabad. In: Informal Sector in India: Perspectives and Policies. Institute for Human Development, New Delhi, pp. 142–159.

Martens, K., 2017. Transport Justice: Designing Fair Transportation Systems. Routledge, New York.

MOHUA, 2017. Ministry of Housing and Urban Affairs (MOHUA). [Online]. Available from: http:/mohua.gov.in/. (Accessed 12 December 2017).

MOHUPA and Government of India, (Ed.), 2010. Rajiv Awas Yogna, towards a slum free India: guidelines.Ministry of Housing and Urban Poverty Alleviation, Government of India.

MOUD, 2017. Jawaharlal Nehru National Urban Renewal Mission (JNNURM) Ministry of Urban Development, Government of India. [Online]. Available from: http:/jnnurmmis.nic.in/. (Accessed 12 December 2017).

Munshi, T., 2013. Built form, travel behaviour and low carbon development in Ahmedabad, India. PhD thesis. University of Twente.

Neutens, T., Schwanen, T., Witlox, F., de Maeyer, P., 2010. Equity of Urban service delivery: A comparison of different accessibility measures. Environ. Plan. A 42 (7), 1613–1635.

Pai, M., 2008. India: Sustainable Transport Indicators. Center for Sustainable Transport. Embarq.

Patel, S., Sliuzas, R., Mathur, N., 2015. The risk of impoverishment in urban development-induced displacement and resettlement in Ahmedabad. Environ. Urban. 27, 231–256. https://doi.org/10.1177/0956247815569128.

Preston, J., Rajé, F., 2007. Accessibility, mobility and transport-related social exclusion. J. Transp. Geogr. 15 (3), 151–160.

Ray, C., 2010. Livelihoods for the Urban Poor: A Case Study of UMEED Programme in Ahmedabad. Report. CEPT University, Ahmedabad.

Salze, P., Banos, A., Oppert, N., Charreire, H., Casey, R., Simon, C., Badariotti, D., Weber, C., 2011. Estimating spatial accessibility to facilities on the regional scale: an extended commuting-based interaction potential model. Int. J. Health Geogr. https://doi.org/10.1186/1476-072X-10-2.

Shi, Y., Zuidgeest, M.H.P., Salzberg, A., Sliuzas, R.V., Huang, Z., Zhang, Q., Quang, N.N., Hurkens, J., Peng, M., Chen, G., van Maarseveen, M.F.A.M., van Delden, H., 2012. Simulating urban development scenarios for Wuhan. In: Proceedings of 6th International Association for China Planning Conference (IACP), 17–19 June 2012, Wuhan, China. IEEE, Washington, ISBN: 978-1-4673-4907-9.

Skov-Petersen, H., 2001. Estimation of distance-decay parameters: GIS-based indicators of recreational accessibility. In: Proceedings of the ScanGIS 2001, Aas, Norway, 24–27 June 2001pp. 237–258.

Teunissen, T., Sarmiento, O., Zuidgeest, M.H.P., Brussel, M.J.G., 2015. Mapping equality in access: the case of Bogota's sustainable transport initiatives. Int. J. Sustain. Transp. 9 (7), 457–467.

Thill, J.-C., Diep Dao, T.H., Zhou, Y., 2011. Travelling in the three-dimensional city: Applications in route planning, accessibility assessment, location analysis and beyond. J. Transp. Geogr. 19, 405–421.

van Dijk, J., Krygsman, S., de Jong, T., 2016. Toward spatial justice: the spatial equity effects of a toll road in Cape Town, South Africa. J. Transp. Land Use 8 (3), 95–114. https://doi.org/10.5198/jtlu.2015.555.

Transport equity in low-income societies: Affordability impact on destination accessibility measures

Imuentinyan Aivinhenyo, Mark Zuidgeest

1 Introduction

1.1 Accessibility as a measure of transport equity

The overall goal of any functional transport system in any society is to provide accessibility to key opportunities and services for its population. In a "perfect" city system, from an equity perspective, every member of the society would enjoy equal levels of accessibility to such opportunities. However, due to the multidimensional complexities of cities, it is rarely the case to have such perfection. The implication of this is that, in the real sense, it would be practically impossible for every member of society to enjoy equal levels of accessibility. Transport provision can, therefore, be evaluated from an accessibility perspective to reflect the levels of transport opportunities available to various persons or groups and also the level at which certain groups of persons are excluded or transport disadvantaged. The issue of transport disadvantage has numerous dimensions. It can be as a result of total lack of transport infrastructure and services, unaffordability of available services, physical inability to access the system, lack of safety, etc.

In the South African context, the issue of social exclusion has been recognized in numerous studies, which have identified transport-related exclusion as a part of the fallout of the apartheid planning regime, which created a high level of segregation among the population. As a result of this, the majority of low-income residential neighborhoods are still located along the urban outskirts, popularly known as "townships," far away from major economic centers, when compared with affluent neighborhoods. These areas are also known to lack transport infrastructure including for bus rapid transit (BRT) and nonmotorized transport (NMT). The overall implication is that low-income earners are bound to bear high transport costs due to their relatively longer travel distances to central business districts (CBD) and other economic hubs, which is affecting their access to goods, services, and activities. This chapter intends to look at the measurement of accessibility from a transport affordability perspective for the low-income population in Cape Town. In comparison to the other chapters in this volume, its main methodological contribution is to implement an accessibility measure that incorporates income effects and transport affordability as a measurement of transport equity.

Measuring Transport Equity. https://doi.org/10.1016/B978-0-12-814818-1.00007-X

1.2   Affordability as a transport equity issue

Tariffs or fares are fundamental to the operation of a public transport system as they form a major source of revenue for operators. From the literature on transport economics and policy, the price of transport is one of the key factors determining the quantity of travel people consume (Paulley et al., 2009; Litman, 2013). Based on the premise that an elastic relationship exists between the cost of a service and trip demand, an increase in user fares would result in a decrease in consumption. While this might hold true based on the economic theory, users' responses to fare changes are also usually dependent on the value they place on the trip, in addition to their individual level of affordability.

Although transport affordability can be seen as one of the key factors that impacts on accessibility, especially for low-income households, most accessibility measures from literature have ignored this component, with the emphasis instead placed on the transport network and service supply characteristics in relation to the land use and spatial distribution of opportunities. The underlying implication of such a framework is that potential for interaction or ability to reach opportunities is assumed to be wholly dependent on spatial access of transport facilities, as well as the travel impedance from the origin of interest to the destination of opportunity. In the context of the developing cities, however, where a good number of the population falls in the low-income category, trip making is expected to be more sensitive to available personal or household income and subsequent transport and/or housing budget, especially for those who are reliant on public transport for daily commutes. Therefore, the consideration of affordability is important when evaluating accessibility in these contexts.

Transport affordability can be described as the financial burden individuals and households bear in purchasing transportation services. From an accessibility perspective, a user's ability to pay for transport service plays an important role in determining whether potential opportunity destinations can be accessed, and in the number of trips that can be made, based on the proportion of income that can be spend on transport services. Therefore, if affordability is regarded as a constraint to trip making, a measure that quantifies such affordability should be included within the generic accessibility model. In this chapter, the consideration of affordability is seen to be relevant in the analysis of accessibility in low-income cities. A high affordability level should have an increasing effect on potential accessibility while low affordability should have a decreasing effect. In the case of a highly fragmented city like Cape Town where certain parts of the city are predominantly low-income areas, while others are predominantly high-income, an analysis of accessibility based on the transport supply characteristics and the variation in income has great relevance to planning policies aimed at reducing transport-related social exclusion and promoting equity.

2   Methodology

2.1   Measures of transport affordability

Several approaches have been developed by the experts to evaluate or measure transport affordability. A framework as proposed by Fan and Huang (2011) considers three key attributes as affecting transport affordability, which are; (1) household sociodemographic characteristics, (2) the built environment, and (3) the policy environment. The effect of household sociodemographics is seen in terms of how a household income level determines the financial resources available for goods and services (including transportation). Traditional measures of transport affordability have mostly been represented in terms of the proportion of household income spend on transportation for every household.

In this chapter, affordability of public transport is considered in terms of the proportion of household monthly income spent on commutes to work for the lowest income population. Accessibility is then computed for each income group within the zone for travel costs within a preestablished affordability benchmark. In this case, the accessibility of a zone is not only measured in terms of travel time, but also considers the income of the subjects (person and household) that make up the zone.

Considering that the accessibility measure is zone based, it is necessary to aggregate the characteristics of the population by income level, as it becomes impractical to measure zonal accessibility taking account of the exact income of every household within a zone. The approach utilized in this chapter is to assume an aggregated best-case income situation for the low-income household, where a household earns the maximum amount of the low-income wage range. In other words, if the low-income wage ranges from say, 0 to a maximum value x, x is applied in estimating the affordable travel monetary budget for every low-income household. Since this income assumption is made for the purpose of our zone-based analysis, it must be noted that household earnings less than the maximum value, would invariably translate to less travel resources.

2.2 Analysis of public transport expenditure and travel time by income group

The accessibility measure proposed in this chapter incorporates an element of user-group income and affordability. To justify the consideration of affordability in accessibility measurement, it is essential to carry out a transport expenditure/income ratio analyses for the various person groups in order to give a better picture of the level of disparity in the proportion of income spend on transport among the various income groups. Information regarding travel expenditure is usually gathered through a household travel survey.

For the case of Cape Town, a citywide household travel survey was conducted by the City of Cape Town in 2013 to investigate the transport situation and travel behavior and choices of residents. The survey comprised of both revealed preference and stated preference components (City of Cape Town, 2013). The purpose of the survey was to determine where people live, where they work, when they travel, the frequency of their travels, as well as their travel expenditure and the various modes of transport used. Trip makers' personal information, such as age, gender, mobility impairments, as well as details on travel costs, travel time, and location of service hubs and transfers were gathered as well. The survey involved face-to-face interviews of approximately 25,000 households (a 2% representative sample) in selected locations across the entire city (City of Cape Town, 2013). Personal travel information from a maximum of six persons per household was recorded in the survey, yielding a total of about 63,000 persons entries in the entire survey.

The mode of travel to work by income level of respondents' household, as cross-tabulated from the survey data, is shown in Table 1. Household income is defined as the total take home pay for a household, and is stratified into four groups; low, middle-low, middle-high, and high-income.

From Table 1, it can be seen that walking and the minibus taxi are the major modes of travel to work for the low-income population as it is used by about 31% and 21%, respectively, among the respondents from that income group. Only about 13% of the respondents in the low-income group travel by car as driver. This suggests that quite a good number of the low-income population only afford jobs that are within walking distance. In contrast, about 80% of those in the high-income group drives to work, while 5% walk. The proportion of the high-income population that uses any form of public transport to work amounts to less than 5%. Similar characteristics are also exhibited by the middle-high-income population.

The monetary cost of travel by public transport to work for residents according to their regular payment method (single, return, daily, weekly, or monthly ticket), their income level, and the number of work trips they make per week were also recorded. For every payment method used for public transport trips, the monthly equivalent expenditure is calculated based on the number of work days per week. Using this information, an average monthly expenditure/income ratio is computed for persons of the various income groups.

The average percentage of income spent on public transport to work among the various population groups is shown in Fig. 1. The data only relate to the house-holds/persons that actually use public transport to travel to work.

Considering that only the income range (and not the exact income) of households were captured in the City of Cape Town survey, the medians of the different income ranges were applied in estimating the proportion of income used for travel to work. The analysis does not include expenditure for other trip purposes as work trips are the main focus in this chapter.

From Fig. 1, it can be seen that, on average, a low-income household spends about 27% of their income on travel to work by public transport only. There is a disparity when compared to the 6% for the low-middle income group and 0.9% for the upper middle-income group. Considering that these proportions are averages from households that only use public transport, the disparity can only be attributed to the wide variance in monthly take home pay. By relating the ratios in Fig. 1 to the proportion of population that rely on public transport (Table 1), we further see a picture of the likely extent of transport burden borne by the poorer population. Based on the values in Fig. 1, we argue that accessibility measures that attempt to quantify accessibility for all the income groups without taking into consideration such expenditure/income ratio disparity would result in an incomplete and unfair evaluation of accessibility. The reason is not that com-plicated; someone with a travel expenditure of 27% of income will most likely be deterred from engaging or taking up opportunities that would consume such proportion of income in travels, compared to someone with transport expenditure of 6% or 0.9% of income, for the low-middle and the upper middle/high-income class, respectively.

Table 1 Main mode of travel to work by income group

Income group/ income range of respondent's household		Respondents' main mode of travel to work													
		Walk	Car driver	Car passenger	Train	Bus	Minibus taxi	Bicycle	Motorcycle driver	Motorcycle passenger	MyCiti BRT	Employer transport	Scholar transport	Other	Total
Low income (ZAR0-3200)	Count (N)	1296	538	215	464	438	865	15	13	4	2	268	9	2	4129
	% Within income group	31.02	13.02	5.24	11.23	10.65	20.95	0.44	0.32	0.09	0.04	6.7	0.25	0.05	100
Middle-low (ZAR3,201-25,600)	Count (N)	3085	4324	1084	808	1192	2059	62	72	31	31	747	18	31	13,544
	% Within income group	22.80	31.93	8.00	5.97	8.80	15.20	0.46	0.53	0.23	0.23	5.52	0.13	0.23	100
Middle-high (ZAR25601-51200)	Count (N)	160	1526	183	41	48	53	5	22	3	17	37	2	3	2100
	% Within income group	7.62	72.67	8.71	1.95	2.29	2.52	0.24	1.05	0.14	0.81	1.76	0.10	0.14	100
High (ZAR51201 or more)	Count (N)	49	760	62	10	12	19	6	8	0	5	15	0	2	948
	% Within income group	5.17	80.17	6.54	1.05	1.27	2.00	0.63	0.84	0.00	0.53	1.58	0.00	0.21	100
Total	Count (N)	4595	7150	1544	1323	1690	2996	88	115	38	55	1067	29	38	20,728
	% Within income group	22.17	34.49	7.45	6.38	8.15	14.45	0.42	0.55	0.18	0.27	5.15	0.14	0.18	100

Data courtesy of the City of Cape Town.

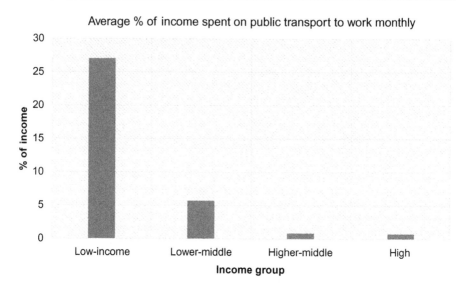

Fig. 1 Percentage of income spent on public transport to work.
Data courtesy of the City of Cape Town.

The key question, however, is, where do we draw the boundary of affordability considering the heterogeneous travel behavior, varying sensitivity and different willingness to pay among individuals of different or similar income groups? Again, there is no straightforward answer to this, considering that a host of other factors contribute to individuals' choices. The approach adopted in this chapter is basically to carry out an accessibility analysis based on various assumed thresholds of affordability, in other to get a picture of what effective accessibility might be, if we are to take such thresholds into account. Three thresholds of travel budget restrictions as percentages of income were applied: 10%, 15%, and 20%. These thresholds were selected in line with the public transport affordability benchmark in South Africa, which has stipulated, in accordance with World Bank's recommendation, a travel expenditure of not more than 10% of income. The selected thresholds will, therefore, give an indication of accessibility levels within and beyond the affordability benchmark. The emphasis in the analysis is not necessarily on the absolute numbers of accessibility, but on the sensitivity of accessibility under travel budget restrictions, which could have a great policy relevance to integrated land use and transport planning as well as policies aiming to redress transport equity issues.

3 Application

3.1 Indicator of accessibility for Cape Town

In this chapter, we define public transport accessibility of a zone as the aggregated ease of reaching opportunities at all possible destination zones using any mode or combination of modes from the available multimodal public transport system. For this study, a total of 1787 traffic analysis zones (TAZs) covering the entire city of Cape Town are considered, and accessibility is computed for each of the zones. The adoption of the TAZ system for this analysis is in line with the current transport planning model system in Cape Town, which uses the same TAZ system. The accessibility measure is, therefore, a location-based potential accessibility measure with consideration of person and household characteristics. While the location-based class of measures usually analyzes accessibility of locations at a macro level, mostly of a TAZ, suburb or neighborhood (Van Wee et al., 2013), the consideration of person or household income attributes further enables computation of accessibility, specifically for persons or household groups that make up the zone. Since only public transport is considered in this study, the accessibility measure is derived as a component of the 2013 public transport network and service characteristics, as well as the income characteristics of the users as reflected in the 2013 household travel survey. The public transport system consists of Cape Town's scheduled modes (regular scheduled bus services, BRT, and urban train) and the unscheduled minibus (paratransit) mode.

The accessibility measure is adapted from the widely applied gravity-based potential accessibility measure proposed by Hansen (1959). This measure captures the number of jobs that can be reached from a certain point in space, with the value of each job weighted by the distance, travel time, or other measure of impedance to the job. The measure can be used to determine the accessibility to all jobs, or to a specific subset of jobs, for instance by required educational level. In our case, we will use travel time as the impedance function. In addition, we have included affordability into the impedance measure. Our cost-related impedance measure consists of three components. It considers (1) the income of a household; (2) a preestablished travel affordability index benchmark given as a percentage of income (for instance, 20% of income), and (3) the average monetary costs of traveling between an origin and a particular destination (for instance, added-up across a workweek or month). Note that the time- and cost-related impedance functions we employ are not identical in character. The time-related impedance allocates weights to the jobs at the destination based on the travel time from the zone of origin. The implication is that the accessibility increases with decreasing time cost and vice versa. The cost-related impedance function has a binary character: a job can either be reached within a predefined "reasonable" monetary cost of travel or it cannot be reached within reasonable cost. The former set of jobs are all taken into account to the same extent in the measurement of accessibility levels (i.e., each job within the predefined monetary cost threshold counts as 1), while the latter are not taken into account at all (i.e., each job beyond the predefined monetary cost threshold counts as 0, even if that job can be reached within reasonable travel time).

3.2 Multimodal public transport network modeling

A key part of the public transport accessibility modeling process involves the development of a multimodal public transport network data model to simulate travel between origin and destination zones. The multimodal network considered consists of the road and rail network with the current public transport routes. The four modes of public transport represented in the network data model are: (1) the regular bus service, (2) BRT, (3) the train, and (4) the minibus taxi, which is a paratransit mode in South Africa. Among the four modes, the regular bus service has the widest network coverage and has been in operation for over a century, serving the majority of the low-income population. In addition to the various public transport modes, walking is also considered as a part of the system as an access and egress mode. Due to the lack of data on the pedestrian network, the existing street network is utilized for modeling pedestrian movements. The zone-based potential accessibility measure in this chapter assumes all trips from a zone to start from its centroid toward the transport network. As such, the location of different households relative to the transport network is aggregated into a single point, and is not accounted for individually. Differences in access time to the network from the various zones are, however, accounted for using the impedance weighting.

A network model was built using the ArcGIS Network Analyst and various geoprocessing tools. Building of the network data model involves a combination of various processes such as: editing network elements, creating stop-link connectors, defining connectivity typologies, setting connectivity groups for each of the route type, and specifying key network attributes, such as travel speed and travel cost measure (e.g., distance, time, and monetary cost). The network model for the accessibility modeling also involves the development and incorporation of procedures to handle aspects such as intermodal transfer within the public transport network.

The origin-destination (OD) matrix calculation tool was run on the built multimodal network dataset to generate matrix of travel cost (both time and distance) between the 1787 TAZs. Travel time on each public transport mode was calculated using the predefined average travel speed on the routes and the distance of travel. Using a linear cost—distance function, the monetary out-of-pocket cost per OD pair was estimated. While travel time was used to establish the impedance weight for the opportunities of interest, the distance traveled determines the out-of-pocket cost, which is critical to the consideration of affordability impact on accessibility. The impedance function applied is a simple negative exponential decay function as shown in Fig. 2.

The figure gives a rough representation of the distance decay behavior, with the value of a job on the y-axis (ranging from 0 to 1), and travel time on the x-axis. The function was based on the data about the actual travel times for home-to-work trips of the low-income group using public transport. From the curve, the value of a job decreases rapidly with increasing travel time. Jobs located further away than 2h have virtually no value (see Fig. 2).

3.3 Measuring monetary cost of public transport

The accessibility framework utilized for the evaluation of equity in this study requires the computation of potential journey costs for trip makers, based on the public transport pricing system as applied in the city of Cape Town. The relationship of fare vs distance is established for the bus and minibus modes using a simple linear regression of a combination of empirical survey data of actual fares paid by the users of the

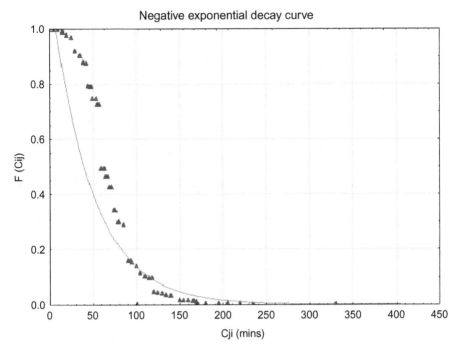

Fig. 2 Decay curve estimated for public transport.
Data courtesy of the City of Cape Town.

various modes for OD pairs of preestablished distance. The regression plot of the 2003 data of fares vs distance for the regular bus and minibus (Taxi) modes are shown in Fig. 3. The linear fare-distance relationship for the other modes (BRT and train) was derived from the preestablished price per distance band for these modes.

The plot shows that a linear relationship exists between fares and distance for the two modes considered in the survey, with the bus mode having a better coefficient of determination of $R^2 = 0.91$ as compared to the minibus (paratransit) with an $R^2 = 0.75$.

Due to a lack of reliable data on fares for the year 2013 (on which this study is based), a linear adjustment was applied on the regression function estimated for year 2003. The adjustment to the year 2013 was carried out by applying a 10-year average inflation rate of 5.5% for the period 2003–13. The linear relationship of fare vs distance traveled for the various modes is given in Fig. 4, with the y-axis representing the user fare in South African Rands (US$ 1 = ZAR 13.5 as at December 2017) (ZAR), and x-axis is travel distance in kilometers.

From the graph (Fig. 4), it can be seen that for travel between 0 and 12 km, the BRT (which is the newest among the modes) is the most expensive option while the minibus taxi (or paratransit mode) becomes the most expensive option of all the modes for distances beyond 12 km. The proportion of households by income group using the various modes is shown in Section 2.2 (see Table 1).

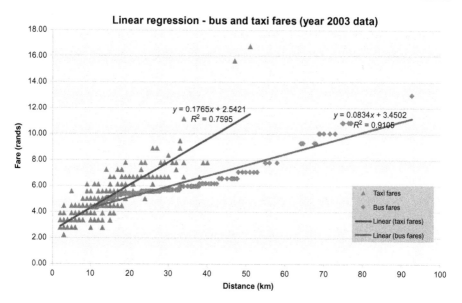

Fig. 3 Bus and paratransit fares for 2003.
Data courtesy of the City of Cape Town.

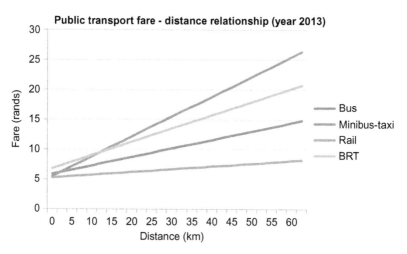

Fig. 4 Public transport fare-distance relationship 2013 (inflation-adjusted from 2003 data).
Data courtesy of the City of Cape Town.

3.4 Low-income job accessibility under no budget restriction

The potential accessibility measure without the affordability component was first
applied in measuring accessibility to jobs for the low-income population in the entire

city of Cape Town. Levels of accessibility are analyzed for travel thresholds of 30, 45, 60, and 120 min. Although the impedance function of the gravity measure allocates appropriate weights to the jobs depending on the travel time, it is essential to set these travel time thresholds, for ease of travel time computation within the geographic information system (GIS) software. The thresholds were selected based on the actual experiences of public transport users as revealed from travel survey data. The survey showed that average travel times from origin to destination including access and egress times vary from 50 to 90 min depending on the mode. Based on these values, we have considered a 30-min travel time as a best-case travel scenario and 120-min travel time threshold as a worst-case travel scenario or scenario of maximum potential accessibility. The 120-min accessibility threshold, therefore, serves as a reference point for analyzing accessibility under budget restrictions or affordability considerations. The map of accessibility under these two conditions drawn using same interval values is shown below.

In Fig. 5A and B, accessibility is represented as the total number of jobs potentially reachable from any given location. The jobs in this case are specifically low-income jobs. A comparison of both maps reveals a wide gap in accessibility levels for travel time thresholds of 120 and 30 min. For travel within 120 min, zones with the highest accessibility level can potentially reach up to 335,000 jobs, while for a 30-min travel time, only about 40,000 jobs are potentially reachable for the zones with the highest accessibility level.

3.5   Low-income job accessibility under restricted travel budget

Fig. 5 shows the job potential accessibility levels for travel within time threshold of 30 and 120 min. In other words, what was displayed is the sum total of weighted jobs that can be potentially accessed from every TAZ, assuming people are going to spend whatever monetary cost it takes. The impact of income and budget restriction is now analyzed by applying 20%, 15%, and 10% of income travel budget to represent different levels of affordability, while setting the travel time threshold at 120 min. By applying these budget thresholds, we compute the number of low-income jobs that can be potentially accessed by a low-income person (living in that zone) within a travel time of 120 min assuming the person is restricted to 20% or 10% of their income for travel expenditure. From the previously calculated 120-min accessibility (as seen in Fig. 5B), only OD pairs that have associated monetary travel cost within the specified percentage of income (20% and 10%) are now selected. OD pairs having monetary travel cost beyond these thresholds are thus discarded. The difference between the numbers of jobs reachable within 120 min without budget restrictions and the jobs reachable given restrictions of budget is, therefore, considered as a measure of equity in accessibility.

3.6   Accessibility loss index as a measure of equity

The measure of equity in accessibility in this chapter is regarded as the accessibility loss index. This index is a measure of the difference in accessibility level when there is

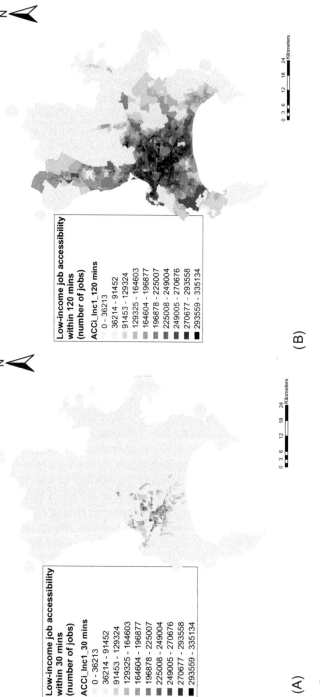

Fig. 5 Low-income job accessibility within (A) 30 min and (B) 120 min.

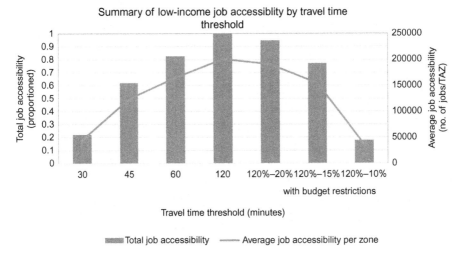

Fig. 6 Summary of low-income job accessibility.

no restriction in travel budget and the accessibility level under budget restrictions. To show the effect of budget restriction on accessibility, we have drawn a comparison of accessibility under various budget thresholds, with accessibility under a maximum travel time of 120 min. In other words, we have assumed that the maximum available accessibility is achieved within a travel threshold of 120 min. Fig. 6 presents a summary of the variation in accessibility levels with and without budget restrictions.

In Fig. 6, the total accessibility available within a travel time of 120 min is normalized to a value of 1, since the absolute value (sum of potential accessibility of all zones) becomes a very large number, which does not have much meaning in terms of interpretability. The first four bars in the chart show the level of accessibility computed without a budget restriction for various thresholds of travel time, while the last three bars show accessibility levels when budget restrictions are factored at various percentages of income under travel time threshold of 120 min. The values in the vertical axes are sums and averages across all zones.

Accessibility loss, which is regarded as the measure of equity, is calculated for every zone by subtracting the accessibility values under budget restrictions from accessibility values with no restrictions of budget under a 120-min travel time. Figs. 7 and 8 show the accessibility loss across zones for a 10% and 20% of income travel budget.

Due to the wide gap in values, both maps have been drawn using different interval scale. The darker areas in both maps indicate locations with higher accessibility loss. From the maps, it is seen that the loss in accessibility is much higher across zones for a travel budget of 10% income (Fig. 7) as compared to that of the 20% income group (Fig. 8). The accessibility loss at 20% of income is generally lower across most parts of the city, except in areas on the outer edge of the city, which are relatively far from the CBD (area shown with rectangular outline).

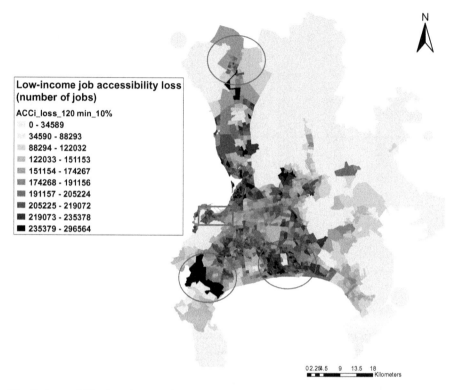

Fig. 7 Accessibility loss for travel budget of 10% income.

To further evaluate whether the low-income group are really affected by accessibility loss, we relate the maps of accessibility loss to the population dot density distribution of the low-income population (see Fig. 9).

In Fig. 9, the areas with high concentration of low-income dwellers are shown under the oval outlines. From a visual assessment of Figs. 7–9, it is seen that, with 10% of income travel budget, accessibility loss is quite high in these areas with high concentration of low-income dwellers. The loss is, however, significantly reduced with a travel budget of 20% income, except in areas at the outer edge of the city which are relatively far away from the city's CBD. In terms of equity, it can be concluded that the low-income dwellers are surely suffering potential accessibility loss.

3.7   Setting an equity standard for accessibility

Setting an equity standard for accessibility will require establishing (1) the level of accessibility that can be considered "sufficient" and (2) the minimum resources in terms of proportion of income required to achieve such sufficiency in accessibility. Sufficiency in accessibility can be established in terms of a benchmark travel time. That is, setting a standard on what travel time can be considered "reasonable" or "excessive." In Section 3.6, a travel time threshold of 120 min was applied in establishing accessibility

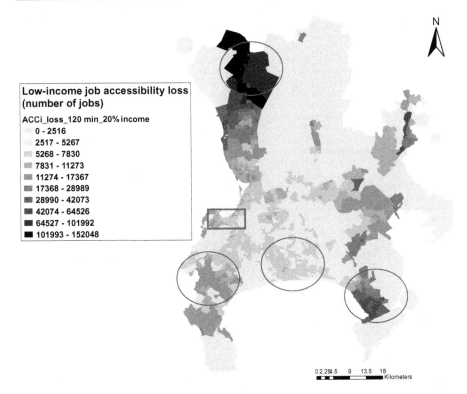

Fig. 8 Accessibility loss for travel budget of 20% income.

loss. In terms of setting equity standard, a much lesser travel time of say 60 or 45 min can be adopted, depending on the existing characteristics of the area. This should, however, be at the discretion of the land use or transport planning professional and should be judged from observed average travel time in travel surveys.

The second aspect of setting an equity standard will involve determining the average monetary cost of travel within the stipulated travel time threshold across various public transport modes or combination of modes. The average cost of travel should be within pre-established benchmark of affordability (maximum share of income) for the low-income group and thus, should guide the pricing system of public transport. In essence, a fair pricing system to achieve equity standard of accessibility would be such that public transport within the benchmark travel time, cost no more than the benchmark threshold of affordability (maximum share of household income) for the low-income group. In other words, fair pricing would not lead to a loss of accessibility, as it would be possible to reach all destinations that can be reached within reasonable travel time with a reasonable monetary budget.

4   Policy relevance

In this chapter, we presented a pragmatic approach for measuring accessibility under an affordability constraint, demonstrating how limitations of travel budget could

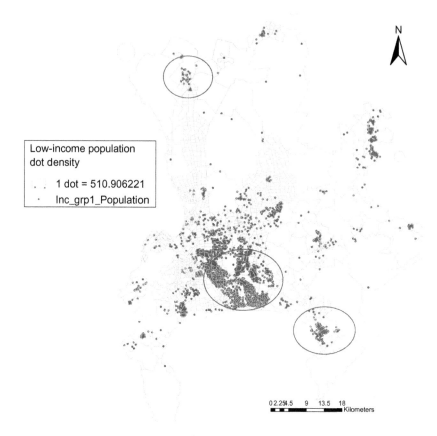

Fig. 9 Low-income population distribution.

potentially reduce the ability to overcome spatial separation and thus reduce the level of accessibility to opportunities for the low-income earners. We emphasize that analyses of accessibility for any locality must acknowledge income gaps across the population and the implication of income and travel cost on accessibility for the poorest group. If equity issues around transport for the poor population are to be addressed, then "affordable accessibility" should be the major goal of planners and policymakers.

Equitable access would be considered here as affordable access. The underlying policy questions would then be: *How do we define the parameters of affordable access? What proportion of income should be used to define an affordable system considering that people usually exhibit varying degrees of willingness to pay? How do we facilitate equitable and affordable access for the poor? What are the key policy measures to be taken?* Again, these are quite complex questions with no direct answers, and they are very context sensitive. While the objective of this study is not to propose a definitive and specific policy response measure, it, however, poses these questions as challenges that need to be dealt with, in defining or implementing strategies for promoting equitable access.

One of the key policy aspects that this study has challenged is the fare policy of public transport in Cape Town, which utilizes a distance-based pricing model for all modes. Although distance-based pricing has been regarded as economically efficient and is utilized by numerous agencies around the world, it could be argued that such approach to pricing in the context of Cape Town has some social and equity implications for the majority of the poor population, especially those who happen to find themselves residing on the outskirts of the city, not as a matter of their own choice but because of the legacy of the apartheid planning system (City of Cape Town, 2013).

The question would then be: what can justify the distance-based pricing to the welfare of the poor who have been confined to a situation where they have to travel longer distances to access opportunities? Is it justifiable from an equity perspective for a system that has (over the years) created the spatial dislocation in the first place implement a pricing system that would further disadvantage the already disadvantaged in terms of accessibility? These are a few of the questions that need to be interrogated at a much deeper level, which goes beyond the scope of this chapter. However, what has come out of the analyses in this chapter is that the current distance-based fare structure of public transport could reduce the amount of potentially accessible opportunities for the low-income households if we assume some common percentage of income as benchmark for transport affordability. Suggested policy interventions would be implementing a trip-based pricing structure sensitive enough for the welfare of the low-income population.

With such pricing mechanism, there is potential to access opportunities (such as jobs), even if they are located far from the low-income residential zones. Other possible pricing mechanism would be a zone-based structure that would allow trips originating from, or terminating at the predominantly low-income residential zones, to pay lower fares. Subsidy schemes could also be streamlined and directed toward the benefit of those who are likely to suffer from the consequences of the current distance-based pricing system. In other words, rather than having a holistic public transport subsidy which benefit every user of public transport, including those who have the capacity to afford the system, subsidy could be directed only toward the poor. Again, implementing these kinds of systems would require further investigation and measures to ensure it only benefit the right people, which is the low-income group.

5 Further reading

In this chapter, we have presented an approach to accessibility analysis that takes into account, income and affordability dimension of transport. This section provides some interesting studies that can offer the reader additional insight on measuring accessibility, transport affordability and equity in transport.

Accessibility is a multidimensional concept with no generally-accepted "best" approach to its measurement. This chapter has specifically focused on location-based gravity measure, as it was considered adequate based on the context and available data. There are however, certain limitations with this kind of measure. For example, it does not account for individuals' personal choices of transport or preferred destinations. Some studies (Dong et al., 2006; Cascetta et al., 2016) have employed other kind of measures such as the utility-based measures to account for individuals' choices.

Further, the accessibility measure discussed in this chapter accounts for monetary cost of reaching destinations as well as travel time between origin and destination. The consideration of both monetary cost and travel time within accessibility measurement have also been discussed in studies such as El-Geneidy et al. (2016), who, for example, found that measures based only on travel time do lead to overestimation of "reachable" opportunities especially for the poor, when compared to measures that consider both user fare and travel time.

Finally, the evaluation of transport equity in this chapter is based on accessibility within reasonable time and affordable cost (given as percentage of income). It must be noted however, that no generally-accepted standard exists for affordability, which will vary across different cities or regions. Other useful studies (Talen, 1998; El-Geneidy et al., 2016; Manaugh and El-Geneidy, 2012) have also developed various approaches to evaluating and mapping equity in transport.

References

Cascetta, E., Cartenì, A., Montanino, M., 2016. A behavioral model of accessibility based on the number of available opportunities. J. Transp. Geogr. 51, 45–58. https://doi.org/10.1016/j.jtrangeo.2015.11.002.

City of Cape Town, 2013. Development of a City Wide Integrated Public Transport Network (IPTN) and the Concept Design and Operational Plan for the IRT Component of the LANSDOWNE WETTON Corridor. Household Survey Report First Draft, Cape Town.

Dong, X., Ben-Akiva, M.E., Bowman, J.L., Walker, J.L., 2006. Moving from trip-based to activity-based measures of accessibility. Transp. Res. A Policy Pract. 40 (2), 163–180. https://doi.org/10.1016/j.tra.2005.05.002.

El-Geneidy, A., Levinson, D., Diab, E., Boisjoly, G., Verbich, D., Loong, C., 2016. The cost of equity: assessing transit accessibility and social disparity using total travel cost. Transp. Res. A Policy Pract. 91, 302–316. https://doi.org/10.1016/j.tra.2016.07.003.

Fan, Y., Huang, A., 2011. How Affordable Is Transportation? A Context-Sensitive Framework. Retrieved from: http://www.cts.umn.edu/.

Hansen, W.G., 1959. How accessibility shapes land use. J. Am. Inst. Plann. 25 (2), 73–76. https://doi.org/10.1080/01944365908978307.

Litman, T., 2013. Transport Elasticities: Impacts on Travel Behaviour—Understanding Transport Demand to Support Sustainable Travel Behaviour. Federal Ministry for Economic Cooperation and Development. GIZ.

Manaugh, K., El-Geneidy, A.M., 2012. Who benefits from new transportation infrastructure? Using accessibility measures to evaluate social equity in transit provision. In: Accessibility and Transport Planning: Challenges for Europe and North America. Edward Elgar, London, pp. 211–227. https://doi.org/10.4337/9781781000106.00021, January 2011.

Paulley, N., Balcombe, R., Mackett, R., Titheridge, H., Preston, J.M., Wardman, M.R., Shires, J.D., White, P., 2009. The demand for public transport: the effects of fares, quality of service, income and car ownership. Transp. Policy 13 (4), 295–306. https://doi.org/10.1016/j.tranpol.2005.12.004.

Talen, E., 1998. Visualizing fairness: equity maps for planners. J. Am. Plan. Assoc. 64 (1), 22–38. https://doi.org/10.1080/01944369808975954.

Van Wee, B., Annema, J.A., Banister, D., 2013. The Transport System and Transport Policy: An Introduction. Edward Elgar Publishing Inc. ISBN 978 1 78195 204 7.

Part Three

Burdens of transport: Health, environment and other externalities

The health impacts of urban transport: Linkages, tools and research needs

8

Haneen Khreis, Mark J. Nieuwenhuijsen

1 Introduction

In this chapter, we analyze how health impact assessment (HIA) can be used to identify the range of (negative and potentially positive) health impacts related to transport and how these impacts may differ across population groups.

HIA is often used to study and pinpoint the health impacts of transport on populations or subpopulations. HIA can be defined as a combination of procedures, methods, and tools by which a policy, program, or project may be judged as to its potential impacts on the health of a population and, importantly, the distribution of those impacts within the population (World Health Organization, 1999). The distributional effects require specific consideration in the HIA as they demonstrate whether the policy will affect different groups of society differently by for example, age, gender, race, socioeconomic status, and geographical positioning. HIA is generally patterned after environmental impact assessment (EIA), containing a number of procedural steps, which are accompanied with opportunities for stakeholders' involvement (Bhatia and Wernham, 2008).

The most common form of HIA, especially in practice, is qualitative. The aim of qualitative HIA is to only identify the range of the health impacts associated with a policy and the direction of its impacts (risks or benefits). Qualitative HIA can be performed using freely available guidance and screening tools that are specific to each country or region but that are similar enough. These guidance and screening tools broadly resemble the tools provided in the UK Department of Health guidance and series of publications to support HIA (Herriott et al., 2010; Herriott and Williams, 2010), as an example.

HIA can also include a quantitative assessment, following a comparative risk assessment approach. This includes, first, estimating the burden of disease attributable to specific transport-related exposures [(e.g., cases of disease attributable to traffic-related air pollution (TRAP), or injuries and deaths attributable to motor vehicle crashes (MVCs)], and then comparing this burden of disease with the impacts of a change associated with a proposed intervention or policy. The aim of quantitative HIA is to provide a numeric estimate of the expected health impacts attributable to an environmental exposure and/or intervention or policy and its distribution across the exposed population. In quantitative HIA, a range of potential scenarios could

Measuring Transport Equity. https://doi.org/10.1016/B978-0-12-814818-1.00008-1

be evaluated, ideally, with the participation of different stakeholders to ensure the plausibility and relevance of the investigated scenarios. As such, quantitative HIA can provide numeric indices of health risk factors, inform the health benefit-risk trade-off of public policies, and provide basis for transport investment appraisals such as cost-benefit analyses.

In the following sections, we present a conceptual model linking urban and transport planning, environment, and health. We then synthesize the key traffic-related exposures and their health effects, to frame the issues related to HIA. We review equity issues related to these exposures, with a focus on the example of TRAP. We emphasize traffic-related exposures as opposed to transport-related exposures as motor vehicle traffic is dominant in urban spaces and acts in close proximity to an increasing number of people. Furthermore, we describe a case study of TRAP and childhood asthma in Bradford (UK) and give some estimates (numeric indices) of the magnitude of the health impacts of traffic-related exposures and alternative scenarios and policy implications. Children are a particularly vulnerable group and tend to suffer disproportionately from the impacts of their exposures. We finally give recommendations on how future quantitative HIA can explore equity issues more explicitly and systematically and expand the focus on TRAP to the other framed issues and traffic-related exposures.

2 Framing a Health Impact Assessment

An important aspect of any HIA is how to frame the assessment, that is, what will be included and excluded in the assessment? Therefore, a review of the current knowledge and a conceptual framework are required.

2.1 Underlying methodological framework

Urban and transport planning, environmental exposures, physical activity, and health are linked (Fig. 1). These linkages have been discussed in detail in the literature (see Section 4). In general, large investment in infrastructure for cars has led many present cities to become car dominated. These investments have often happened at the expense of investments in public and active transport. The catering for motor vehicle traffic has led to land uptake and more traffic-related infrastructure such as roads and parking spaces which in turn led to greater use of motor vehicles and changing land-use patterns (e.g., decreased density, accessibility, connectivity, and land-use diversity). These changing land-use patterns go hand in hand with increasing traffic and reduced walking, cycling, public transport use, and investment. In many cities and regions, the results were higher levels of air pollution, noise, temperature through the heat island effects and less active travel and physical activity. Further, stress during commuting and reduced social contacts has been reported too. These changes have in turn led to increased premature mortality and morbidity, across a wide variety of health outcomes including cardiovascular and respiratory disease, cancers, reduced cognitive function, and mental health problems, among other acute and chronic outcomes.

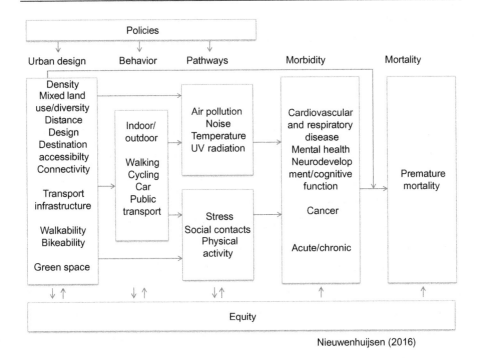

Fig. 1 Interlinkages between urban and transport planning, environment, physical activity, and health.

Furthermore, infrastructure for cars takes up a large amount of public space in cities that can be used for other purposes like green space or public space for people to meet, relax, and exercise. On the other hand, a move away from car infrastructure to infrastructure for public and/or active transport can lead to an increase in use of public and/or active transport and reduce air pollution, noise, heat island effects, and stress while increasing physical activity and social contacts, ultimately reducing morbidity and premature mortality (Nieuwenhuijsen et al., 2017). The linkages described earlier are depicted in Fig. 1.

Equity is a relevant issue at the different stages of this framework. Where people live, what their environment looks like, what transport mode they can or choose to use, what environmental exposures they experience, and subsequently what disease they acquire are not equally or randomly distributed among different population groups. The unequal distribution of health impacts is often determined by socioeconomic status and race, implying that lower income and ethnic minority populations are disproportionately negatively affected, as are described later in this chapter.

2.2 Health effects and impacts associated with urban transport

Before health impacts can be addressed in transport planning and policy, they need to be clearly scoped. We focus on urban areas and document that the health impacts associated with the abovementioned traffic-related exposures and practices occur through nine key pathways:

1. motor vehicle crashes
2. traffic-related air pollution)
3. noise
4. increased local heat exposures
5. reduced green space exposures and biodiversity loss
6. reduced physical activity
7. climate change
8. social exclusion
9. community severance

These pathways and the health impacts associated with them are broader and bigger than previous documentations (Khreis et al., 2016). Specifically, the health effects of community severance, noise, local heat exposures, and green space exposures (beyond mental health and stress), are matters of emerging research and have not been common inquiries in contemporary health and transport research.

However, this evidence base has strengthened, and further research and synthesis are underway, supporting the inclusion and consideration of these pathways and their health outcomes in practice. For example, emerging evidence suggests that the impact of noise on premature mortality is comparable to, and independent of, the impacts of air pollution on premature mortality. Furthermore, when morbidity is considered, the health burden of noise is even higher than that of air pollution or physical inactivity. In comparison, very little quantitative evidence is currently available for the health impacts of traffic-related heat, green space, and community severance.

2.3 Equity considerations

The abovementioned traffic-related exposures, and their associated health impacts, are not equally distributed among population groups. Perhaps the most prominent factors that determine the distribution of these exposures/lifestyles and their associated health impacts are age, income, and race. These exposure-related health inequities further contribute to well-established and large health inequities that reflect social inequalities (Centers of Disease Control and Prevention, 2011). They further impact the most deprived groups disproportionality, not only because these groups are often more exposed, but also because these groups exhibit a variety of other factors which make them more vulnerable to their adverse environmental exposures (e.g., poor diet, suboptimal health care, stress, violence, different height and metabolism, and different genetics).

The unequal distribution of health impacts, as determined by age, race or economic status, is seen at different geographical levels ranging from national to neighborhood-level. Some key examples to consider are given further.

Low-income and middle-income countries, where motorization started later and where investments in road safety campaigns, safe infrastructure, and road safety technologies are generally less, account for over 90% of the world's roads fatalities, despite only having 48% of the world's registered vehicles. The number of road deaths per 100,000 population in low-income countries is now at a level of 24, comparable to the level in developed countries such as The Netherlands in the 1970s. Although there is a high variability between different regions, MVC rates remain highest for motorbike commuters and active travel commuters (pedestrians and cyclists), followed by public transport commuters and finally car commuters. For example, half of the world's road traffic deaths occur among motorcyclists, pedestrians and cyclists, with 31% of deaths among car occupants (remaining percentage is unspecified).

As with MVC, physical inactivity and subsequently its associated health impacts may be disproportionately distributed according to socioeconomic factors. The scientific evidence demonstrates that available resources for physical activity participation, including parks, walking, and biking trails, vary by neighborhood socioeconomic status with the pattern of fewer options for the more deprived. Similarly, high socioeconomic groups appear to engage in more leisure-time physical activity.

In addition, TRAP is often disproportionately distributed among socioeconomic and vulnerable groups including children, low-income groups, and minorities, as their schools and residences are often located in high traffic exposure areas, although a recent study in Europe showed a more mixed picture (Temam et al., 2017).

Race has also been shown as an important factor linked to exposure and health disparities, especially in the United States. A recent study estimating annual average NO_2 concentrations demonstrated that disparities in air pollution exposure were larger by race-ethnicity than by income. On average, estimated NO_2 concentrations remained 37% higher for nonwhites than whites in 2010, which showed no progress compared to 2000 (Clark et al., 2017). Another pioneer United States national-level study paired information about the geographic locations and demographics of 84,969 public schools with air neurotoxicant exposure estimates pertaining to 24 known neurotoxicants. The study found that students attending "high risk" public schools nationwide (in the top 10% most burdened by air neurotoxicant exposures) were significantly more likely to be eligible for free/reduced price meals, and to be Hispanic, black, or Asian/Pacific Islander than white or another race. The study also showed that schools serving the youngest students (e.g., prekindergarten) have greater presence of air neurotoxicants than schools serving older students (Grineski and Collins, 2018).

Similarly, studies indicated that low-income individuals and visible minorities also tend to be located in areas most polluted by road traffic noise. Other exposures follow the same trend. The distribution of (access to) public green spaces can be differential by socioeconomic status in favor with those with resources to move to greener areas. Often, low-income groups and ethnic minorities are least able to relocate to protect themselves and little is done to mitigate the adverse impacts and protect vulnerable groups.

In the following assessment, we focus on one aspect that drives the unequal distribution of adverse health impacts, namely age. Childhood is a particularly vulnerable life period and children are a population who are unable to drive changes in their (school or residential) locations or exposures to protect themselves. Exposure to TRAP is of particular importance to infants and children, who are more susceptible to the hazardous effects of air pollution due to various reasons including their imma- ture detoxification, immune and respiratory systems, their higher respiratory rates, and their higher activity levels and time spent outdoors where exposure to TRAP is generally elevated. As such, both infancy and childhood, from birth to 18 years old, represent exposure windows that are crucial for some medical outcomes, includ- ing respiratory diseases. Exposure during these critical windows of time (or life periods) can result in permanent changes to the body's structure and function and, therefore, we have life-long effects.

While we focus the assessment below on age, other issues related to differential exposures by race and socioeconomic status can and should be included in future assessments. Our assessment is in fact set in Bradford, which is one of the 10% most deprived local authorities in the United Kingdom, and an ethnically diverse city, where over 20% of the population are of South Asian origin and 45% of the kids born in Bradford are of Pakistani origin. Following the assessment, we give specific rec- ommendations on how a broader HIA can be conducted in the future, also expanding the focus on TRAP to the other framed issues and exposures.

3   The Health Impact Assessment

As the key pathways and health impacts associated with urban transport have been determined (see earlier), the question remains as how to better incorporate this knowl- edge in transport planning and policy and how to judge whether certain transport plans and policies contribute to more or less health and equity in health. In this context, HIA offer a valuable tool to systematically assess the health risks and benefits of transport projects and their distribution.

In the remainder of this chapter we focus on a full-chain HIA in a case study to show the impact of TRAP on childhood asthma.

3.1   A full-chain HIA of TRAP

One form of quantitative HIA can be conducted using a full-chain approach. In a full- chain HIA model, the modeling considers the full-chain from exposure source, through pathways to health outcomes and as such traces the health impacts under investigation back to their particular sources. This form of HIA has been predomi- nantly used to assess the health impacts of TRAP. In the case of TRAP, the exposure is assessed starting from the source (e.g., traffic flows and speeds); to source emissions (e.g., traffic exhaust emissions); to resulting air quality and exposures (e.g., emissions dispersion and TRAP exposures); and finally, to the associated health effects or impacts (e.g., new asthma cases) (Fig. 2).

In practice, this can be done by integrating existing models of traffic activity, traffic emissions, and air dispersion to predict air quality and people's exposure and subse- quently estimate the associated health impacts (Fig. 2). Data on traffic counts, origin and destination zones, and fleet composition can be used to construct traffic models for cities. Often, such traffic models are readily available for other applications in

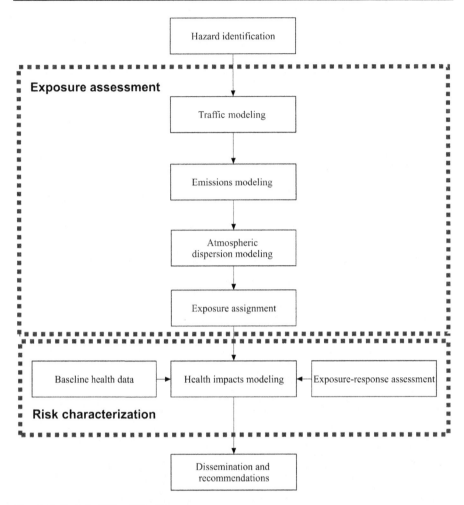

Fig. 2 Full-chain HIA of TRAP.

cities such as strategic transport planning. The outputs from traffic models, most importantly the traffic flows and average traffic speeds, are then linked to vehicle emissions models such as the European leading emission model known as COPERT (COmputer Programme to calculate Emissions from Road Transport). From this data, vehicle emission inventories are calculated and are then entered into air dispersion models such as the widely used European model ADMS-Urban (Atmospheric Dispersion Modelling System-Urban). In dispersion models, traffic/emissions data alongside terrain, meteorological, and boundary layer data are used to estimate seasonal and/or annual air pollution concentrations in cities. Exposure can then be assigned at the residential or census tract level, or even at the exposure microenvironments or routes (although this is less common in the literature and practice), and the health impacts associated with the exposure then estimated.

Next, we demonstrate the use of the full-chain quantitative HIA model to estimate the health impacts of TRAP, focusing on childhood asthma as an example. The full-chain model, however, can be used to quantify the impacts of TRAP on other health outcomes such as premature mortality, cancers, birth outcomes, hospital admissions, and others. Further, the full-chain approach can be used to quantify the health impacts of other traffic-related exposures such as noise.

3.2 Case study

Using the framework presented earlier, we present here a full-chain HIA of TRAP and childhood asthma for the multi-ethnic city of Bradford, United Kingdom. The aim of the analysis was to estimate how many new cases of asthma, a year, may be attributable to children's exposure to TRAP, at the smallest census tract level. The age group considered was from birth to 18 years old, in line with the World Health Organization definition of childhood and other biological evidence about that age group's susceptibility to air pollution. All analyses were undertaken at the smallest census tract at which census population data were available.

Exposure-response functions that quantify the strength of association between the exposure and the health outcome of interested were needed. Exposure-response functions for the association between exposure to TRAP and the subsequent development of childhood asthma from birth to 18 years old were extracted from metaanalyses we undertook earlier. The exposure-response functions expressed the percentage change in the risk of developing childhood asthma in association with the selected unit of exposure for two different pollutants: nitrogen dioxide (NO_2) and nitrogen oxides (NO_x). The NO_2 exposure-response function was based on the synthesis of 20 studies and equaled 1.05 (1.02, 1.07), per the exposure to $4\,\mu g/m^3$ NO_2. The NO_x exposure-response function was based on the synthesis of seven studies and equaled 1.48 (0.89, 2.45), per the exposure to $30\,\mu g/m^3$ NO_x.

Using the exposure-response functions earlier, the risk estimates for asthma development were scaled to the difference in exposure level between the counterfactual (no exposure) and reference (current exposure as estimated from the atmospheric dispersion model) scenarios to be able to estimate the risk that is due to that difference in exposure. To scale a risk estimate to the exposure difference between the counterfactual and reference scenarios, standard methods were used. The result was a new risk estimate at each census tract which corresponded to the difference in exposure level between the counterfactual (no exposure) and reference (current exposure) scenarios.

The population attributable fraction (PAF) was then calculated. PAF is a standard metric used in quantitative HIA. PAF defines the proportional reduction in morbidity that would occur if the air pollution exposure was reduced to the counterfactual scenario (no exposure scenario in this case). PAF is calculated using standard methods which use the proportion of the exposed population (100% in this case as all kids are exposed to some level of air pollution) and the previously scaled risk estimate at each census tract which corresponded to the difference in exposure level between the counterfactual (no exposure) and reference (current exposure) scenarios.

Finally, the number of childhood asthma cases attributable to the excess exposure compared to the counterfactual (no exposure) scenario was calculated by multiplying the PAF by the overall number of new asthma cases in Bradford that year (i.e., number of new asthma cases due to all causes). The overall number of new asthma cases in Bradford that year is equal to the childhood population multiplied by the childhood asthma incidence rate observed in Bradford that year.

The results of this exercise indicated that up to 638 (or 35% of all) annual childhood asthma cases in Bradford may be associated with air pollution, specifically NO_x exposures (Table 1). Up to 219 cases (12%) are specifically associated with the traffic component of NO_x pollution, i.e., TRAP (Table 1). As shown in Table 1, the choice of the pollutant to be studied (NO_2 versus NO_x) also makes a measurable impact on the final estimates, with NO_x having larger impacts but a wider/less precise confidence interval.

3.3 Consideration of equity in future HIA

The population of Bradford is multi-ethnic, and income deprived, but we did not directly consider these aspects in the HIA reported earlier. We, however, note here the great importance of including equity analyses in future full-chain HIA. This can be done by assigning deprivation levels and/or ethnicity categorizations to each of the census tracts included in the HIA, and then stratifying the HIA results by categories of deprivation and/or ethnicity. In the case study of Bradford, this can be done specifically by:

- Undertaking the analysis at the lower layer super output area (LSOA) and extracting the English residential area index of multiple deprivation (IMD) for all the analyzed LSOAs. Each LSOA can then be assigned an IMD rank, which usually ranges from the most deprived to the least deprived. The exposures estimates can then be assigned at the LSOA area level and the HIA repeated. The exposure and HIA estimates can then be stratified by the IMD ranks established. Such analyses will shed light on differential exposure levels and associated health burden across the different IMD ranks.
- Undertaking the analysis at the LSOA and extracting the proportion of white versus nonwhite residents for all the analyzed LSOAs. Each LSOA can then be assigned in a category depending percentage of nonwhite residents. The exposures estimates can then be assigned at the LSOA area level and the HIA repeated. The exposure and HIA estimates can then be

Table 1 Estimated annual attributable asthma cases in Bradford using the full-chain model (baseline asthma incidence = 137 per 10,000 person-year)

Model	Pollutant	Attributable cases	Attributable cases lower confidence interval	Attributable cases upper confidence interval	Percentage of all cases	Attributable cases to traffic
Full-chain AD	NO_2	394	173	520	22%	128 (7%)
Full-chain AD	NO_x	638	−256	1125	35%	219 (12%)

stratified by the ethnicity categories established. Such analyses will shed light on differential exposure levels and associated health burden across the different ethnicity categories.

4 Policy relevance

There is an urgent need for policy makers to act and reduce the health burden of TRAP in cities, while paying particular attention to the burden in different places and the vulnerability of different population groups. The approach we described provides quantitative data on the impact of TRAP and could be extended to other exposures such as noise or lack of green space or physical activity. The quantitative estimates are essential as there is a need to better include the health burden and related costs in cost-benefit appraisal of new transport schemes. Further improvements to our proposed methodology are yet needed to estimate the burden in different population groups (e.g., by ethnicity, or socioeconomic status), as the burden is likely to be unequally distributed among different population groups, with a higher burden in the more deprived and ethnic minority populations, as has been established by the literature. The full-chain HIA tool we show cased in this chapter can be used for such applications and could be further extended to describe the distribution of the exposures and the associated health impacts by socioeconomic status or ethnic group. We provided specific guidance on how this could be done in the future focusing on our case study in Bradford.

As yet equity considerations in this and similar tools, especially when quantitative, are not a focal point for analysis. And overall HIA is still not mainstreamed or a requirement of policy. Further work is needed to consider equity more systematically in HIA and to develop more sophisticated models such as full-chain models, which identify the health impacts from specific sources through different pathways. These models can be helpful for policy makers to identify the right sources to target and the policy interventions that are likely to be most effective. Health and environmental regulatory agencies should also advocate for formal guidance on incorporating HIA in policy to maximize the potential for protecting and/or improving public health through public policy.

5 Further reading

In this final section, we point the reader to relevant studies exploring equity issues of transport policies and related exposures alongside seminal and formal guidance documents on how to conduct qualitative and quantitative HIA of transport policies and related exposures.

A seminal paper in this field is the Gothenburg Consensus Paper: Health Impact Assessment: Main Concepts and Suggested Approach, published by the World Health Organization in 1999. The intention of this paper was to create a common understanding of the rapidly developing concept of HIA and introduce feasible approaches to carry out this assessment on international, national, and local levels. The paper discusses the need to develop HIA, the elements of HIA, the timing, stages, and types of HIA and importantly, outlines the key values governing HIA: equity, democracy, sustainable development, and ethical use of evidence. The paper also contains one of the most frequently cited definitions of HIA that is still used in present day.

A more recent paper published by Bhatia and Wernham in 2009 focuses on the overlap between EIA and HIA while also overviewing existing regulatory requirements for health effects analysis, and the barriers to and opportunities for integrating human health concerns within the EIA. This paper sheds new light on potential mechanisms for incorporating health impacts in the well-established, and often regulated, EIA procedure. However, as the authors note, the practice of integrating HIA in EIA is still in its infancy. The paper also emphasizes the value of collaboration and communication between community stakeholder groups, public health professionals, and regulatory agencies to make real-world impact. This latter massage is further reiterated in the work by Nieuwenhuijsen and colleagues in 2017 where the authors demonstrate the lack of participatory integrated and full-chain HIA models, methods, and tools. In this paper, the authors review and document a variety of studies that undertook quantitative HIA of transport policies or related exposure at the local level. These studies provide the reader with examples of methods and tools that have been used to date. The paper contains specific recommended actions to better assess and formally consider the health impacts of transport at the local level, targeted at politicians/authorities, urban and transport experts, public health practitioners, and researchers. In terms of framing the impacts of transport on health, we refer the reader to the paper by Khreis et al. (2016) which documents a wide list of transport-related exposures and their associated health impacts as established by the literature. Framing the impacts of transport on health is essential in HIA as the process often depend on the subjective knowledge of the assessor, in the lack of formal documentation of which exposures and impacts should be considered and why.

Over the years, there have been many formal guidance documents on how to conduct qualitative and quantitative HIA of public policies. These guidance documents are often tailored to the specific context of the locations they originate from but are broadly consistent and follow suit of the guidance given in the Gothenburg Consensus Paper. A document by the UK Department of Health offers a high level and comprehensive overview of this guidance including the specific steps for carrying out a HIA and supplementary tools/tables which can be used in the process (Herriott and Williams, 2010). Another practical document from the same source overviews sources of data that is needed to undertake HIA, published reports, case studies, and gray literature alongside examples of guidance and previous HIAs from across the world (Herriott et al., 2010).

Finally, a select list of papers and reports which explore equity issues as it relates to transport-related air pollution exposures can be found in Centers of Disease Control and Prevention (2011), Clark et al. (2017), Grineski and Collins (2018), and Temam et al. (2017). These papers focus on the US and the European context and provide a starting point for a search of quantitative information on the differential health burden associated with air pollution by socioeconomic status and ethnicity. A wider overview of the differential health burden associated with other transport-related exposures such as noise, green space, and MVCs can be found in Khreis et al. (2016).

References

Bhatia, R., Wernham, A., 2008. Integrating human health into environmental impact assessment: an unrealized opportunity for environmental health and justice. Ciên. Saúde Colet. 14 (4), 1159–1175.

Centers of Disease Control and Prevention (2011). CDC Health Disparities and Inequalities Report—United States, 2011. Morb. Mortal. Wkly Rep. Supplement/Vol. 60.

Clark, L.P., Millet, D.B., Marshall, J.D., 2017. Changes in transportation-related air pollution exposures by race-ethnicity and socioeconomic status: outdoor nitrogen dioxide in the United States in 2000 and 2010. Environ. Health Perspect. 125 (9), 097012.

Grineski, S.E., Collins, T.W., 2018. Geographic and social disparities in exposure to air neurotoxicants at US public schools. Environ. Res. 161, 580–587. Available at: https:/ www.sciencedirect.com/science/article/pii/S0013935117317188.

Herriott, N., Williams, C., 2010. Health Impact Assessment of Government Policy A guide to carrying out a Health Impact Assessment of new policy as part of the Impact Assessment process. UK Department of Health. Available at: https:/www.gov.uk/government/uploads/ system/uploads/attachment_data/file/216009/dh_120110.pdf.

Herriott, N., Williams, C., Ison, E., 2010. Health Impact Assessment: Evidence on Health. A Guide to Sources of Evidence for Policymakers Carrying out Health Impact Assessment as Part of Impact Assessment of Government Policy. UK Department of Health. Available at: https:/www.gov.uk/government/uploads/system/uploads/attachment_data/file/216006/dh_120109.pdf.

Khreis, H., Warsow, K.M., Verlinghieri, E., Guzman, A., Pellecuer, L., Ferreira, A., Jones, I., Heinen, E., Rojas-Rueda, D., Mueller, N., Schepers, P., et al., 2016. The health impacts of traffic-related exposures in urban areas: understanding real effects, underlying driving forces and co-producing future directions. J. Transp. Health 3 (3), 249–267.

Nieuwenhuijsen, M.J., Khreis, H., Verlinghieri, E., Mueller, N., Rojas-Rueda, D., 2017. Participatory quantitative health impact assessment of urban and transport planning in cities: a review and research needs. Environ. Int. 103, 61–72.

Temam, S., Burte, E., Adam, M., Antó, J.M., Basagaña, X., Bousquet, J., … Le Moual, N., 2017. Socioeconomic position and outdoor nitrogen dioxide (NO_2) exposure in Western Europe: a multi-city analysis. Environ. Int. 101, 117–124.

World Health Organization, 1999. Health Impact Assessment. Main Concepts and Suggested Approach. Gothenburg Consensus Paper WHO European Centre for Health Policy, WHO Regional Office for Europe, Copenhagen.

Assessing health inequalities related to urban and transport determinants of mental health

9

Giulia Melis, Matteo Tabasso, Morena Stroscia, Giuseppe Costa

1 Introduction

According to the World Health Organization, health inequities are defined as inequalities that are systematic, socially produced (and therefore modifiable) and unfair. Health inequalities (HIs) are the result of the circumstances in which people grow, live, work and age, and the health systems that they can access, which in turn are shaped by broader political, social, and economic forces. In other words, health is widely influenced by socioeconomic factors, known as social determinants of health, which include educational attainment, employment, income, ethnicity, and living conditions.

The living conditions, through the unequal distribution of resources inside a city, influence differences in health between neighborhoods since built environment and social context have a direct impact on the level of health that each individual can reach.

As a matter of fact, harsh inequalities emerge in the health profile of the population in big urban agglomerations: people living in less affluent neighborhoods show a lower health status and shorter life expectancy when compared to people living in more advantaged urban areas.

Mechanism underlying differences in health observed within a city are essentially linked to two causes. The first is the selection process due to residential mobility: wealthier (and healthier) people can afford housing in better served, more comfortable, and more desirable urban neighborhoods, while less advantaged population (which also shows a worse health status) do not have many choice opportunities, thus moving to cheaper housing in lower quality neighborhoods. As a consequence, differences in life expectancy between an affluent and a deprived neighborhood may simply reflect the different social composition of their inhabitants. The second cause of inequalities in health is directly linked to the contextual health effects of neighborhoods, independent of the individual characteristics of their inhabitants. The living (natural, built, social) environment characteristics are recognized to have an influence, either in positive or risk terms, on human health: for example, noise, pollution, fear for own safety, or social isolation have been identified as risk factors. Many studies have demonstrated the impacts of physical environment (noise, pollution, built context, green areas, accessibility to services, public transport) and socioeconomic factors (fear of violence and aggressions, socioeconomic deprivation, segregation) on physical and mental health, and well-being of city dwellers.

Measuring Transport Equity. https://doi.org/10.1016/B978-0-12-814818-1.00009-3

When looking at health impacts, the influence of transport services on mental health is one of the pathways cited by WHO and recognized by experts worldwide: having a poor accessibility can cause stress and mental health problems. As urban and transport planners, we were interested in understanding which urban features most significantly affect our daily life, in order to identify the most urgent and promising policy intervention opportunities to increase well-being in the city.

In the next paragraphs, we present a methodology, which can be applied to different health equity analysis and different contexts, and then we present the application of these methods to a case study in Turin.

2 Methodology

We present here the methodology used for assessing the impacts of different urban built environment features on the health inequalities in Turin. The results in our case helped decision makers in understanding health disparities patterns in the city and in orienting their investments in case they want to reduce mental health inequalities, from a broad perspective (e.g., better to invest on public transport than on public security).

The possible approaches to identify the target of the interventions can be three: (i) to target the most disadvantaged groups/social classes; (ii) to reduce the health gap between the most wealthy and most disadvantaged groups, thus addressing the extremes of the social scale; (iii) to reduce health inequalities along the whole urban population, trying to reduce the association between social disadvantage and health at every level.

This last approach was pointed out by experts as the most efficient and beneficial in terms of health gain, especially if considered in its proportionality, that is, the action is universal but it affects different social groups in proportion to their needs.

Our primary aim was, therefore, to assess which are the most influential factors in shaping health disparities (in our case mental health) among a selected group of factors (illustrated in Fig. 1), identified thanks to a literature review on the topic. Once we identified the most important factors, through statistical analysis we were able to assign a specific incidence rate ratio (IRR) in relation to each one of them. For example, an individual has $x\%$ more risk to take antidepressants when living in a low urban density neighborhood than the same individual (by gender, age, education, employment, etc.) living in a high-density neighborhood.

Our equity approach, therefore, assigns a risk ratio to each one of the individual characteristics (certainly the most influential in shaping health) as well as to contextual factors.

2.1 Individual characteristics and health inequalities

When analyzing the distribution of health in urban contexts in order to better understand (and consequently address) the inequalities within a city, the health status of different population groups must be described separately, for example:

- males and females
- young and elderly
- minorities

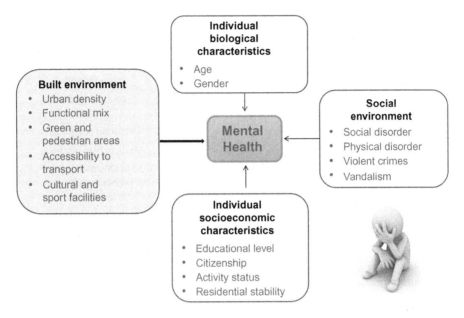

Fig. 1 The scheme illustrates the variables considered in the study, plausibly connected to mental health in urban areas.

- vulnerable groups (disable, homeless, unemployed)
- different socioeconomic groups (by educational level, income, or occupational status)
- different family composition types
- residential history

Health effects vary considerably according to each one of these characteristics: therefore, a first step toward understanding inequalities is the ability to isolate them through a searchable database.

The methodology adopted in this case study counts on a very precious and complete source of data: the Turin Longitudinal Study started in 1971. It collects and links together different archives (Fig. 2), which are useful to describe the health status of a community (e.g., causes of death, drug prescriptions and hospital admissions data, data on individual socioeconomic status–income, educational level, employment, housing conditions, civil status).

By collecting these different sources of data at several points in time during a period (e.g., since 1981–2011 every 10 years), researchers are allowed to describe the health status considering also changes in socioeconomic status or contextual characteristics.

2.2   Contextual characteristics: Social and built environment

While many researchers have already presented evidence on the importance of urban trees and parks, which can have a profoundly beneficial impact on psychological well-being and general mental health, not many studies have analyzed the urban built

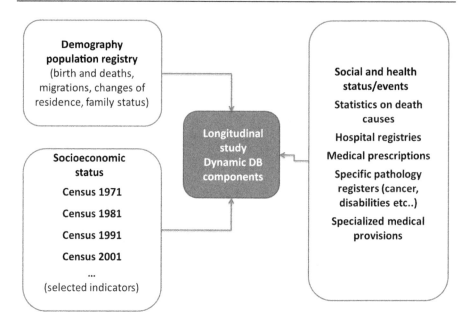

Fig. 2 Basic database structure in the Turin Longitudinal Study.

environment in its complex functioning. We therefore gathered data both on the structure of the city (how dense it is, where are the parks for recreational activities, which is the mix of functions in one area) and its services (Is the nearest library placed within an accessible distance? Is the area well-served by public transport? Are there public sport facilities? Are there Cinemas, theaters? etc.) in order to isolate and quantify their specific influence on health. When considering the urban system, which one of this features is able to increase health risks for individuals? Is the risk significant and can we assume policy indications?

Data on the **built environment variables** of neighborhoods were collected through the municipality administrative datasets. They were classified in two macro-categories representing, respectively, the structure of a neighborhood (density, functional mix, and green/pedestrian areas), shown in Fig. 3, and the presence of services (described by cultural and leisure facilities and accessibility by public transport), shown in Fig. 4.

The first set of indicators, concerning the urban structure, includes:

-   Green and pedestrian areas: the surface area occupied by green areas (tree-lined shore, forest, garden, park, tree-lined square, river banks, school grounds, …) and pedestrian areas was mapped; a density index was calculated for each statistical area, and values were then normalized in a 0–100 scale.
-   Urban density: the built volume, calculated by the multiplication of the sum of all buildings footprint area by the eaves height over the surface of the statistical area.
-   Functional mix: land use mix calculated by using the Shannon index (1948), then normalized in a 0–100 scale.

Fig. 3 Distribution of built environment structural variables.

Fig. 4 Distribution of built environment availability of services.

The second set of indicators, representing urban services, includes:

- Average accessibility by public transport, calculated as minutes in origin to reach all the other zones from a given one, by using public transport. It represents the ability to reach desired goods, services, activities from the residence by using only the public transport service. The central area, served by many public transport lines with a high frequency is the most connected, while peripheral areas are the most disadvantaged due to poorer service and geographical reasons.
- Cultural, leisure, and sport facilities: this indicator represents the availability of free time services within an area. It is a composed index, which takes into account the number of public libraries, day-care centers, cinemas, theaters and bowls club per statistical area, and the ratio between the surface area occupied by sports facilities (indoor activities, outdoor activities, football, canoeing, golf, multipurpose plate, indoor swimming pool, outdoor swimming pool, tennis), and the statistical area surface. It has been normalized in a 0–100 scale.

Neighborhood **social environment variables** refer to the occurrence among the resident population of events related to urban safety and neighborhood coexistence, as measured through local police registries (Fig. 5).

The social environment is represented by the following indicators:

- Social disorder: complaints to municipal police for noises and neighborhood's conflicts and annoyance.
- Physical disorder: complaints to municipal police and to the trash pick-up company for dirtiness, urban decay and acts of vandalism on garbage bins.
- Violent crimes: all the crimes in which the perpetrator uses physical violence against the victim. It includes homicides (all the typologies), fights, insults, assaults, and battery, kidnapping, sexual violence (and related offenses). It is worth considering that most of them are reported to the police because they happened in public (this indicator do not include violence inside the family).
- Vandalism: rate of malicious mischief in the city of Turin. It includes criminal offenses popularly defined as acts of vandalism. It is worth considering that in the legal systems of different European countries, these offenses are not exactly the same.

2.3   Statistical analysis

We used Poisson multilevel regression models stratified by gender and age groups (internally age-standardized), with individuals nested within neighborhoods. Models were fitted using the backward-stepwise selection method with a significance level of 5% for removal of variables from the model. Statistical analyses were performed using the STATA System. In the stepwise procedure we kept in the models the individual socio-demographic variables (model 1) and added one by one the built environment (as variables of interest) and the social environment (as control variables) predictors (models 2 and 3). We kept only the models with significant IRR presented in Section 3.2.2.

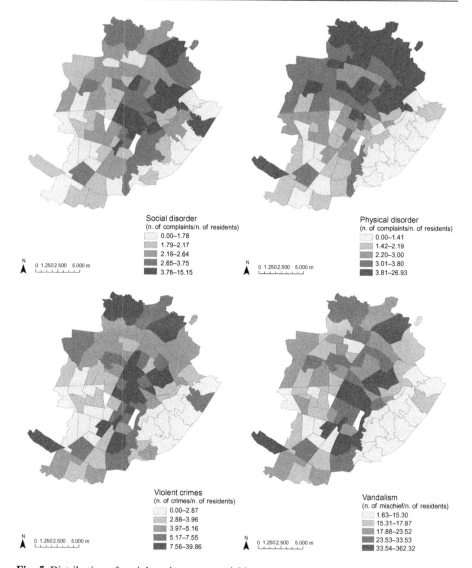

Fig. 5 Distribution of social environment variables.

3   Case study application

3.1   The context: Turin city

Over the last 20 years, the city of Turin had to face several urban transformations due to the need to reconvert large industrial areas located just outside the border of the historical city center.

With the industrial crisis of early 1990s, Turin had to face a huge change: with the decline of car industry, the city shifted paradigm from an urban mobility based on cars to a more sustainable one. In particular, the approval of the Urban Masterplan in 1995 defined huge urban transformations and some interventions to facilitate pedestrian mobility in the city center, playing a key role in this transition.

Looking at the social geography, in the central part of the city, along with the eastern and western suburbs, wealthier people live with the least economic and social problems, while in the northern and southern parts are located the most disadvantaged neighborhoods. For this reason, during the last 20 years, most of the investments in regeneration programs were directed toward to these latter areas. Thanks to this kind of investments and other policies aimed at increasing the quality of such areas, some positive effects on the quality of life took place and life expectancy in these areas increased more than in other areas.

For what concerns the transport system, the city also underwent huge infrastructural changes, such as the so called "*Spina Centrale*" (Central Backbone). This massive urban project consisted in burying the railway tracks (railway junction) "cutting" the city. The railway tracks were covered at the ground level by an urban boulevard and contextual urban renewal, enhancing above ground connectivity.

The cross-city railway link, with its five stations, is integrated with the only Metro line crossing the city from west to south, lying on the edge of the historical city center and reaching two neighboring municipalities (Fig. 6).

Such recent infrastructures are linked to a bus/tram-based public transport network, which serves (more) homogeneously the remaining portions of the city.

In addition to public transport, a bike sharing service has been successfully developed in recent years only in the most central areas of the city; there is a project to extend it toward the periphery, which has not been developed yet.

3.2 The case study

There is scanty evidence of the impact on—and inequalities in—mental health due to the different dimensions of the built environment in urban areas. This limits the ability of urban and transport planners to take into account the health and health equity impacts of their decisions. The aim of this study is to identify the effect on mental health of the various components of the built environment, irrespective of the roles played by individual socioeconomic characteristics. The method adopted looks at variations in antidepressant prescriptions depending on specific dimensions of the built environment and urban services, namely urban density, land use mix, green areas, public services, and accessibility through public transport. Transport was, therefore, one of the features we considered, as a fundamental asset in the complex urban functioning, but not the only focus of our analysis. Its contribution to health inequalities was estimated in a comparative system together with the other features.

Prescriptions of antidepressants appear to be a useful proxy indicator for all types of depressive and anxiety disorders, which is also one of the health impacts that have the shortest incubation period.

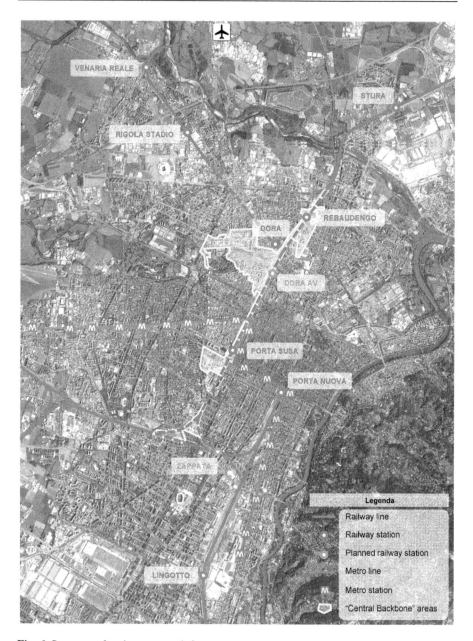

Fig. 6 Structure of main transport infrastructures.

3.2.1   Data collection and analysis

Data were drawn from the Turin Longitudinal Study, which is based on the city's historical population records from 1971 to the present. Demographic information from the registry is individually linked to census variables and routinely registered health events.

The availability of data allowed us to base the study on a significant statistical sample, with more than 500,000 individuals selected: these people appeared in the database every year. Adult residents in Turin were monitored for the consumption of antidepressant medications over a 3-year period (2004–06), with attributes on their individual and contextual socio-demographic circumstances and their residential stability.

- Men and women aged between 20 and 64 years were included in the study, and the champion was stratified by age ranges (20–34, 35–49, and 50–64), in order to consider differences in exposure to neighborhood characteristics by age and gender.
- Individual socio-demographic conditions were classified according to educational level, activity status, citizenship (native vs migrant), and residential stability (3 or more years at the same address versus less than 3 years).
- Built environment and social environment characteristics were then measured at the neighborhood level (79 statistical areas with an average of 10,000 inhabitants each).

The outcome (antidepressant prescription) was tested as a function of individual socio-economic variables (educational level, citizenship, activity status, residential stability), contextual built environment variables (density, functional mix, green and pedestrian areas, cultural and leisure facilities, accessibility by public transport), and contextual social environment variables (social disorder, physical disorder, violent crimes, vandalism), in order to identify the dimensions mostly affecting mental health, irrespective of individual and contextual socioeconomic disadvantage. The main hypothesis formulated was that living in "liveable" contexts (generally the richest areas of the city) with high functional mix and high opportunity to move, by public transportation or through green and pedestrian areas (more opportunities for an active life), positively affects mental health and can reduce the risk at psychiatric illness.

3.2.2   Results

The first model (Fig. 7) accounts for the main individual predictors of antidepressants prescription. Among all variables, activity status shows the strongest association with antidepressants: men are especially sensitive to this risk factor even if it has a

Age	20–34		35–50		51–64	
School attainment (low vs high)	1.16*	1.20*	0.98	1.11*	0.85*	0.94*
Citizenship (foreign vs italian)	0.29*	0.40*	0.25*	0.49*	0.31*	0.42*
Residential mobility (stable vs moving)	1.01	0.97	0.9*	0.90*	0.69*	0.77*
Activity status (other vs employed)	1.49*	1.14*	1.92*	1.15*	1.34*	1.19*

Fig. 7 Model 1: individual variables.

significant effect at all ages in both genders. Women significantly differ about it: this is probably due to the definition of "inactive" that produces different social and psychological features in men and women: in fact, also homemakers and mothers who stay at home are considered "inactive." The importance of the economic and social traditional role of men can explain their frailty in case of unemployment, while women tend to compensate the lack of paid jobs playing their socially recognized role of mothers and homemakers.

Among our subgroups, women and elders tend to stay longer at home. Some authors considered the effect of the neighborhood as dose-related in previous studies. In Turin, these two groups and those which have been residentially stable confirm it.

In the second step of the analysis, we kept in the models the individual socio-demographic variables (presented in model 1) and added one by one the built environment (as variables of interest) and the social environment (as control variables) predictors.

Density showed up to be a protective factor for elderly population. This is coherent with the consolidated literature describing health effects of sprawl: for aged people higher density means bigger availability of daily services and more frequent social relationships. This is evident in both genders. Accessibility is particularly important for women all ages, and in fact we know they use public transport more, for a variety of different reasons.

These two variables were mutually excluding each other when tested in the model: even if they represent two different phenomena, as we can see from the map, their distribution is similar: in fact denser areas normally report increased the presence of services as well as better public transport connection.

When we try to run the model with all the three groups of variables, it comes that accessibility remains the only protective factor above women over 35 (Model 3, presented in Fig. 8). The protective effect of accessibility is evenly distributed across the population by educational level and by employment status, and it does not interact with the risk due to individual social disadvantage.

Women (of all ages) and older people (age 50–64) were found to be prescribed fewer antidepressant drugs when they lived in places better connected to public transport, and in places with higher urban density, compared with counterparts in more remote or sparse areas. That connection held up even when social factors were taken into account. This means that if everybody had the same level of education, same citizenship, and were all employed, all living in a neighborhood that had equivalent levels of crimes and social and physical disorder, there would still be differences in antidepressant consumption according to the level of connectivity of an urban area (i.e., the efficiency level of public transport, density, and liveliness of the neighborhood).

This study, therefore, shows that good accessibility to public transport, as well as a dense urban structure (versus sprawl), could contribute to a reduced risk of depression, especially for women and elderly, by increasing opportunities to move around and enjoy an active social life.

This type of large-scale data analysis cannot pinpoint causal mechanisms. Nevertheless, it is easy to speculate on the reasons why transit and density might reduce stress: the former relieves the need to drive everywhere (and to own a car); the latter enhances the potential for social connectivity. For older populations, in particular,

Age	20–34		35–49		50–64	
School attainment (low vs high)	1.17*	1.20*	0.98	1.12*	0.85*	0.94*
Citizenship (foreign vs italian)	0.29*	0.40*	0.25*	0.49*	0.31*	0.42*
Residential mobility (stable vs moving)	1.01	0.97	0.9*	0.90*	0.69*	0.77*
Activity status (other vs employed)	1.49*	1.14*	1.92*	1.15*	1.34*	1.19*
ACCESSIBILITY	0.93	0.94	0.99	0.96*	0.91	0.95*
VIOLENT CRIMES	0.88	1.05	0.97	1.11*	1.00	1.04

Fig. 8 Model 3: Built environment and social environment variables (simplified). *Statistical significance of the result (<0.05 confidence).

both aspects help guard against feelings of isolation or loneliness. They also stand in contrast to remote suburban living that is likely to have a serious impact on mental health, particularly when it results in unmet trips.

4 Policy relevance

There is still a lot to understand about the key stressors of city life, but some advices to urban planners could already be outlined: in order to address health inequalities, urban policies should invest in the delivery of services that enhance resilience factors, above all a good public transport network, carefully and equally designed throughout the city.

Therefore, after collecting evidence from data in our study, we decided to involve decision makers in a Health Equity Audit process, and try to stimulate them taking action against inequalities in the city.

If health inequalities widely derive by social determinants of health, it is recognized that the most effective way to tackle them is through policies involving all sectors of society and not merely the health-care sector, according to the "Health in All Policies" (HiAP) approach.

Actions which can effectively reduce HI require partnerships between government (at different levels: regional, national, and international) and society, consolidated through the development of cooperation initiatives that include actors coming from different settings such as civil societies, industrial sector, and health and public health services.

A promising way to advocate for health equity is the implementation of the "health equity audit (HEA)" process, as it provides a framework to act against HI in an informed and systematic way. Health equity audit consists of "forming partnerships among actors that systematically review inequities in the causes of ill health and in the access to services among population groups and define priorities to implement informed actions to reduce HI into local plans, services, practices and community strategies" (Hamer et al., 2003).

In other words it consists of a systematic screening of inequalities and the analysis of mechanisms which could explain them in order to find effective solutions, conducted in a jointly manner.

This process is then useful to detect priorities of intervention in order to better allocate resources and services according to the real needs of the population, where the gain of health could be higher.

In order to contrast urban inequalities with effective actions, some factors should be carefully considered. Firstly, a solid monitoring and assessment have been done by using disaggregated data, and by using the results as an **evidence base for taking informed decisions**. Actions should be feasible, sustainable, and based on scientific evidences. When a solid evidence base cannot be carried out on the local context, we suggest to use the "best available evidence." Even when the study design is not as rigorous as we would expect, a good explanatory framework behind it—able to explain and consider all potential mechanisms, determinants, and effects—could be a reasonable and solid base for taking action.

Secondly, try to address the '**Health in all policies' approach**: supported by WHO in the last two decades, it promotes health and health equity as driving principles of public policies. This goal can be reached if the health-care system is able to activate advocacy and information processes, and stakeholder (politics and administrative) engagement on the health impacts of cross-sectoral actions; in particular, impacts on vulnerable and psychosocial disabled population should be carefully analyzed. This process of stakeholder engagement is based on the knowledge and evidence transfer from the health sector toward all the others that may be involved in a decision process.

5   Further reading

The World Health Organisation (2014) provides a general framing of the health equity approach and of the relationships between contextual factors and people's health, which is relevant for countries in both the Global North and Global South. Gilormino et al. (2014) provide a literature review of the connections between inequalities and urban environment, with references to a number of key scientific studies that have measured health equity impacts on specific links between the built environment and health. Weich et al. (2002) and Bocquier (2013) provide an explanation and justification for the use of data on antidepressant treatment as a proxy for measuring mental health, in particular when considering the influence of neighborhood context. The effect of the neighborhood as a dose-related phenomenon has been considered and explored by Galster (2008) and Vallée et al. (2013). Hamer et al. (2003) and Rijk et al. (2007) are good introductions into Health Equity Audit and an integrated policy approach to tackling health inequalities, with the first presenting practical guidelines on how to set up and conduct a HEA, and the second team of authors testing a method to foster cooperation in public health settings. Finally, for readers interested in the particular case of Turin, we refer to two studies extensively dealing with health inequalities in this Italian city. Stringhini et al. (2015) present the Turin Longitudinal Study in its components, and use its data to trace a history in the last 40 years. Melis et al. (2015) present the results of the case study narrated in this chapter more in depth, with a rich scientific bibliography useful for readers who want to explore the themes briefly presented in this chapter.

References

Bocquier, A., Cortaredona, S., Verdoux, H., Sciortino, V., Nauleau, S., Verger, P., 2013. Social inequalities in new antidepressant treatment: A study at the individual and neighborhood levels. Ann. Epidemiol. 23, 99–105.

Galster, G., 2008. Quantifying the effect of neighbourhood on individuals: Challenges, alternative approaches, and promising directions. Schmollers Jahrb. 128, 7–48.

Gelormino, E., Melis, G., Marietta, C., Costa, G., 2014. Causal pathways of built environment on health inequalities: a synoptic framework based on evidence. Preventive Medicine Reports 2, 737–745.

Hamer, L., Jacobson, B., Flowers, J., Johnston, F., 2003. Health equity audit made simple: a briefing for primary care trusts and local strategic partnerships. Retrieved March 27, 2017 from: http://www.thehealthwell.info/node/26838?source=relatedblock.

Melis, G., Gelormino, E., Marra, G., Ferracin, E., Costa, G., 2015. The effects of the urban built environment on mental health: A cohort study in a large northern Italian city. International journal of environmental research and public health 12 (11), 14898–14915.

Rijk, A.D., Raak, A.V., Made, J.V., 2007. A New Theoretical Model for Cooperation in Public Health Settings: The RDIC Model. Qualitative Health Research *17* (8), 1103–1116. Retrieved April 30, 2017 from: https://www.ncbi.nlm.nih.gov/pubmed/17928482.

Stringhini, S., Spadea, T., Stroscia M, et al. 2015. *Decreasing educational differences in mortality over 40 years: evidence from the Turin Longitudinal Study (Italy)* J Epidemiol Community Health Published Online First: 16 July 2015. https://doi.org/10.1136/jech-2015-205673.

Vallée, J., Cadot, E., Roustit, C., Parizot, I., Chauvin, P., 2011. The role of daily mobility in mental health inequalities: The interactive influence of activity space and neighbourhood of residence on depression. *Soc. Sci. Med.* 73, 1133–1144.

Weich, S., Blanchard, M., Prince, M., Burton, E., Erens, B., Sproston, K., 2002. Mental health and the built environment: Cross-sectional survey of individual and contextual risk factors for depression. Br. J. Psychiatry 180, 428–433.

World Health Organisation, 2014. Governance for health equity. Taking forward the equity values and goals of Health 2020 in the WHO European Region. Retrieved March 8, 2017 from: http://www.euro.who.int/__data/assets/pdf_file/0020/235712/e96954.pdf.

A public health approach to assessing road safety equity—The RoSE cycle

10

Adrian Davis, Paul Pilkington

1 Introduction

This chapter focuses on equity goals relating primarily to the reduction of adverse effects of the transport system, particularly road traffic collisions (RTCs), with a strong emphasis on the protection of vulnerable population groups. It describes the current equity issues relating to deaths and injuries on the road, from the global to national and then local. However, the chapter challenges a reductive approach to the assessment of equity in relation to transport interventions designed, at least in part, to reduce collisions. The authors argue that an approach that seeks to address not only injury outcomes, but also other equity issues, is a fairer method of evaluating the true impact of transport interventions on road danger-related equity outcomes. A road safety equity (RoSE) cycle approach is proposed.

The case for this approach is made through the examination of a case study in the UK city of Bristol, where a "road danger reduction" approach has been pursued since the year 2012. This approach has involved the creation of 20 mph speed limits across the city. Importantly, the aim of this transport intervention, and of the overall approach, was to not only reduce deaths and injuries on the road, but also to encourage greater levels of active travel (such as walking and cycling), play, and improved general feelings of health and well-being among the resident population. This intervention itself is located within a broader ambition of a Safe Systems Road Safety Plan reflecting still broader public policy ambitions. Safe Systems is a practical tool for introducing an ethical dimension—that life and limb should no longer be sacrificed for mobility—and that the aim must be for zero fatalities and life-changing injuries. The approach recognizes that road risk is a combination of road infrastructure, vehicle, and individual behavior, and that casualties are a result of a systems failure.

RTCs are a public health problem of significant importance. The number of road traffic deaths continues to climb, reaching 1.35 million in 2016 and there are few signs of any significant change in this burden. Road safety is an international priority, with the UN Decade of Action on Road Safety (2010 – 20) aiming to cut deaths on the road by ensuring that evidence-based interventions are in place across the world. Road safety is a key component in the UN Sustainable Development Goals (SGGs), with a target to halve the number of global deaths and injuries from RTCs by 2020. Urgent action is needed to achieve the 2030 Agenda for Sustainable Development. Yet, road

Measuring Transport Equity. https://doi.org/10.1016/B978-0-12-814818-1.00010-X

safety when discussed in the literature usually has referred to the unsafety of the transport system and this is only slowly changing. We define road safety as the freedom from fear of exposure to harm or injury on the road network.

In terms of discussing equity, we commence with a definition of health equity. We follow that used by the World Health Organization, which states that equity is:

The absence of avoidable or remediable differences among groups of people, whether those groups are defined socially, economically, demographically, or geographically.

Equity in transport has been defined variously and the definition we apply here is how appropriately and equally the impacts of transportation are distributed among different types of users and members of a given population. There are many aspects of equity to consider when examining the issue of RTCs. At a global level, there are clear equity issues in relation to the burden of deaths and injuries faced by low- and middle-income countries as compared with high-income countries. While high-income countries have road traffic death rates of 9.2 per 100,000 population, this figure is 18.4 among middle-income countries and 24.1 in low-income countries. The factors accounting for this are many, but include issues relating to vehicle safety (low-income countries are more likely to have older vehicle fleets with lower safety standards even for newer vehicles), driver behavior (low-income countries are less likely to have laws and enforcement on speed, use of mobile phones, seatbelt and helmet use, driving standards, etc.), and the environment (low-income countries are likely to have more dangerous road networks). This inequity in provision of road safety promoting interventions and features in low- and middle-income countries is assessed in the annual Global Status Report on Road Safety. Equity is also apparent in the disproportionate burden of deaths and injuries experienced among so-called vulnerable road users–in particular, pedestrians, cyclists, and motorcyclists. Nearly, half of all deaths globally are among this group.

Although the clearest equity issues in RTCs are evident at the global level, there remain important issues of equity even in high-income countries. Most notably, socioeconomic differences in risk of death and injury on the roads are evident, especially for vulnerable groups such as pedestrians. One interpretation is concerned with the distribution of impacts between the individuals and groups that differ in income and social class or in mobility need and ability. At the core of equity is providing at least equal access to meet basic needs. By way of example, low-income mothers walk mostly not out of choice but due to necessity and often in traffic environments with high motor traffic volumes and hence higher risk of injury per unit of exposure (Bostock, 2001). In contrast, as income rises car ownership rises so that higher social classes tend to use modes of travel which externalize the danger of that mode through the exporting of kinetic energy into the transport network.

Studies on hospital admissions in the United Kingdom suggest that there is both an increased number of injured people and severity of the injury from RTCs with increasing deprivation and that the increase is more pronounced for pedestrian injuries. An area's socioeconomic characteristics are strongly associated with pedestrian casualties, once other aspects of the neighborhood/environment have been considered. This includes where population (density and proximity), employment (number, density, and proximity), type, and length of road and weather, are controlled for. This association holds for both adults and children, although is more pronounced for young people. Children from disadvantaged backgrounds are five times more likely to be killed on the roads as pedestrians than children from more affluent backgrounds.

It is well documented that the reasons for such differences are complex (Hippisley-Cox et al., 2002). Reasons for this effect include higher exposure rates for deprived children (as fewer parents own cars), less adult supervision in the traffic environment, and educational disadvantage in understanding issues of road safety. There is also evidence that risk varies with area-based characteristics (e.g., living near main roads) and that deprived children exhibit different behavioral patterns that increase their susceptibility to road traffic injuries. Where children play is also crucial, the absence of safe play spaces is known to be associated with the higher incidence of child pedestrian casualties. A UK study has reported that as the area of domestic gardens as a proportion of total area decreases, the number of casualties increase (Green et al., 2011). Separately, the significance of crime and child pedestrian casualties is supported by the presence of index of multiple deprivation crime indicators. The causal mechanism in the relationship between high crime areas and child pedestrian casualties is unclear, but areas of high crime influence activity patterns, behavior, and child traffic exposure.

Historically, 20 mph zones (traffic-calmed areas) have been introduced with the aim of being self-enforcing to reduce RTCs and associated nonintentional injuries. These zones use engineering measures, such as speed humps to reduce vehicle speed across a length of road and are self-enforcing because in theory it is hard to exceed 20 mph when driving through them. In all, 20 mph zones have been evaluated with before-after studies, with and without controls, and these evaluations have concluded that 20 mph zones reduced collisions, deaths, and injuries. For example, a 1996 review of the impact of the introduction of 200, 20 mph zones found reductions in child pedestrian accidents of 70%, child cyclist accidents by 48%, and overall accidents by around 60%. Significantly, there was a 6.2% reduction in collisions for each 1 mph reduction in vehicle speed. A more recent controlled interrupted time series analysis of 20 mph zones in London found a 42% reduction in road traffic casualties. The authors were also able to report that 20 mph zones are effective interventions for reducing road injury with no apparent evidence of casualty migration to nearby roads outside the intervention zones. A caveat was that this study was not able to account for potential confounders, such as other road safety initiatives (including road safety cameras).

Default 30 kph (18.6 mph) speed limits in residential areas is a key aspect of the Safe System approach to road safety promoted by the WHO, in which the road system allows for human error while reducing the risk of death or serious injury. By contrast to traffic calmed 20 mph zones, signs-only 20 mph speed limits are increasingly being promoted and implemented by local authorities in England as a cheaper way to reduce road traffic casualties and improve residential quality of life. Signs-only 20 mph speed limits have signs placed on poles and painted on the road surface indicating the speed limit. They do not usually feature traffic calming and do not, therefore, enforce drivers to reduce their speed to 20 mph or below. An obvious advantage of signs-only 20 mph speed limits is that a far larger number of streets can be covered than with more expensive 20 mph zones. Some cities and towns in Britain have implemented signs-only 20 mph on residential streets citywide. In Portsmouth, introduction of residential streets 20 mph signs-only limits is reported to have led to a 22% reduction in casualties with an average speed reduction of 1.4 mph. Such programs are supported by evidence such as a reduction of just 1 mph in average speed on urban roads with low average traffic speeds can reduce the frequency of collisions by around 6%. A 2015 review of 20 mph zones and limits concluded that they are an effective means of improving public health via reduced collisions and injuries (Cairns et al., 2015). Nonetheless, the Portsmouth evaluation, as with most of the evidence from studies on 20 mph limits to date, is cross sectional, often lacking control groups, and potentially confounded by a range of factors. In addition, other potential wider benefits of 20 mph limits, including improved levels of well-being and community cohesion among residents, have not been researched.

The current move toward lower speed limits is only in part powered by the injury prevention agenda. Certainly, in the United Kingdom, previous national targets to reduce deaths and injuries on the road have been a motivating factor. However, also significant is the desire to tackle obesity through the promotion of physical activity in the form of walking, cycling, and active play. There is recognition that in many societies, an "obesogenic" environment, of which motorized road traffic is a contributory factor, dissuades the population from engaging in healthy behaviors. In the United Kingdom, policy reports on obesity have called for reductions in speed limits. The perceived wider equity outcomes from lower speed limits means that the policy also intersects with the sustainability agenda, which seeks to promote sustainable forms of travel.

2 Methodology

We postulate that the multifaceted aims of reducing speed limits to 20 mph in urban areas challenges the reductionist approach to assessment of transport interventions involving casualty reduction that often occurs. It is certainly the case that the evaluations of the impact of 20 mph speed limits, particularly those undertaken "in-house" by municipal authorities responsible for their introduction, have focused on changes in vehicle speeds, collisions, and associated deaths and injuries. Such studies use routine data on RTCs and associated deaths and injuries in the United Kingdom based on Police STATS19 data, which is gathered from the roadside of a crash by the attending police officer. It includes data on date, location, and casualties.

This narrow focus may be because of resource limitations, or from a lack of data with which to assess wider effects, or it may reflect a lack of understanding of the wider benefits of 20 mph and/or a siloed approach. Assessments of the equity impact of such interventions must focus not only on the reduction of vehicle speeds, collisions, and associated deaths and injuries, but also on the changes in levels of walking and cycling, feelings of health and well-being among residents, social cohesion impacts, and other issues such as air quality. Consequently, the focus on the potential for addressing broader equity goals as road danger reduction interventions necessitates the collection and measurement of a broader range of data from which to make an assessment. In addition to routine data, it may be necessary to collect information from surveys of local residents (for instance, representative sampling of households through surveys were used in Bristol pre- and postimplementation of all phases of 20 mph speed limit roll out) in order to understand changes in perceptions regarding the quality and safety of local environments, to assess self-perceived feelings of health and well-being. Taking a holistic, public health approach to evaluating the equity impact of 20 mph limits enables wider public policy benefits of this transport intervention to be assessed.

Consequently, we contend that assessment of equity entails an analysis utilizing socioeconomic data, for example, from routine sources such as the census, geocoded (using geographical information system software) alongside data on RTCs and associated deaths and injuries to determine impacts of the 20 mph limit across different socioeconomic areas. This is an approach taken by a number of studies examining the impact on inequalities in RTCs following the introduction of measures to reduce traffic speeds to 20 mph (both 20 mph zones and 20 mph limits). Such an approach should be extended beyond collisions, deaths, and injuries. More broadly, as the UK House of Commons Select Committee has also identified, there is a need for a change in approach to road safety strategies. They called for:

> a strategy that explains how casualty reduction, danger reduction and the various other important policy objectives such as sustainable transport systems, economic efficiency, climate change, social inclusion, and physical health are integrated.

House of Commons Transport Select Committee (2008)

We then suggest that the concept of proportionate universalism can be used as an approach to achieve more just and healthier societies through road safety decision making. Universal proportionalism, developed by Marmot in the seminal 2010 report Fair Society, Healthy Lives, argued that "Focusing solely on the most disadvantaged will not reduce health inequalities sufficiently. To reduce the steepness of the social gradient in health, actions must be universal, but with a scale and intensity that is proportionate to the level of disadvantage" (Marmot, 2010). Marmot looked beyond economic costs and benefits toward a goal of environmental sustainability. The review contends that creating a sustainable future is entirely compatible with action to reduce health inequalities although promoting sustainable local communities, active transport, sustainable food production, and zero carbon houses, all of which have health benefits. In road safety terms, this would require tackling danger at source to make a significant positive contribution to RoSE. This could change the focus of the debate around road safety at local, national, and global levels. It supports both 20 mph speed limits and Safe Systems approaches to road safety in that they are arguably both universal and proportionate in the effects to the level of disadvantage imposed through the current distribution of road traffic injuries.

Lastly in this section, drawing on a Safe System approach, we propose a RoSE cycle (Fig. 1). This takes a holistic public health approach for assessing equity in road

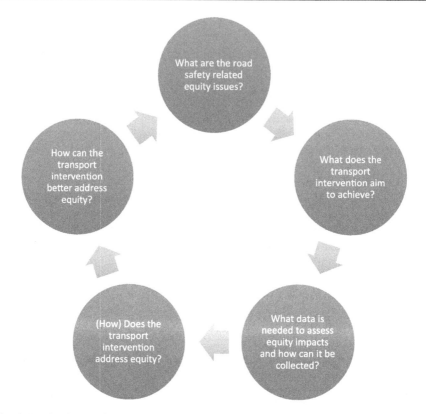

Fig. 1 Road safety equity (RoSE) cycle.

safety and feeding back findings into the design and implementation of interventions in order to maximize equity benefits.

Stage 1: What are the road safety-related equity issues?
A strategic, holistic Safe Systems assessment of the current RoSE issues affecting a given population is conducted on an annual basis, using a range of data sources including routine data from transport, road safety, and health, and well-being sectors. Sociodemographic data will enable analysis of equity by socioeconomic deprivation. The focus should not just be on collisions and casualties, but also on wider aspects of health and well-being, equity between different modes of road users, and community social cohesion.

Stage 2: What equity benefits might the transport intervention achieve?
This stage involves clarifying the potential equity benefits of the proposed transport intervention, in terms of what aspects of RoSE (as identified in Stage 1) the intervention might have an impact on.

Stage 3: What data are needed to assess equity impacts and how can it be collected?
Stage 3 involves identifying the data that is required in order to assess the potential equity impacts of the transport intervention, including whether this data are available from routine

sources or whether it needs to be collected ad hoc for the purposes of the evaluation. Data will include that beyond traditional transport-related data sets, including socioeconomic and health data. Data should be available before (baseline), during, and after the implementation of the intervention to assess potential equity impacts.

Stage 4: (How) Does the transport intervention address equity?
Evaluation of the impact of the transport intervention, with a particular focus on equity, using the data identified in Stage 3.

Stage 5: How can the transport intervention better address equity?
Reflection on how the transport intervention can better address equity across the population. Identify and address any unintended consequences of the intervention. Feed in learning from the evaluation to the ongoing implementation. Reassess equity impacts at specified time points, repeating the equity cycle.

The following section will demonstrate how the RoSE cycle process has been applied in Bristol, with regards to the introduction of 20 mph speed limits across the city.

3 Application: Bristol 2006–2016

This case study illustrates how transport interventions can address equity through a proportionate universalism approach, taking population-wide action that aims to have a more beneficial effect on those at greatest risk, whether that can be defined by geography, socioeconomic status, or travel mode. Assessment of the impacts on equity of such an approach necessitates the monitoring and analysis of a wide range of data.

Bristol is the eighth largest city in England and economic capital of the south west. The City Council administers an area of 18 mile^2 and serves a resident population of over 440,000. The city is also a home to over 17,000 businesses and is the national headquarters for more than 160 companies. Bristol's gross domestic product per head is higher than that of any city in England except London. Bristol is then both prosperous although there are major challenges with stark differences in income and life expectancy between the wealthiest and the poorest communities including life expectancy differences of 10 years between the two (Bristol City Council, 2017).

The municipal and public health authorities in Bristol recognized that health and health inequalities are influenced more by the circumstances in which people live and by way they live than they are by the provision of health services, although the latter are also important for health and well-being. This is reflected in the definition of health contained in the Constitution of the World Health Organization, where health is defined as "a state of complete physical, mental, and social well-being and not merely the absence of disease or infirmity." In pursuit of this goal, public health is concerned with the determinants of health, the patterns of distribution of those determinants in a population and also about how those determinants and their distribution might be modified "through the organized efforts of society" (Faculty of Public Health, 2017). From a public health perspective, how people live in a city and how healthy and happy they are depends to a considerable extent on their urban environment, their access to employment, to services, to travel and transport, to green space, and on the community around them. Bristol's public health leadership was determined to improve the urban environment, including that relating to transport, in pursuit of broader public health and well-being goals.

Stage 1: What are the road safety-related equity issues?
Inequity, as reflected in road casualty data, reveals significant differences in Bristol, as with most if not all the UK cities and as noted globally. That is, that those road users who pose least threat to other road users, are those most significantly represented in reported casualty data. Local health data highlighted the major differences in casualties between the least and most deprived areas, demonstrating inequities by socioeconomic status. As an example of gross inequity, for the period 2011–13 the most deprived areas of the city sustained 18% of child casualties while the least deprived sustained 3%. In Bristol for a typical year, 2013, the killed and seriously injured comprised 40 pedestrians, 19 cycle users, 31 motorcyclists, and 16 vehicle occupants.

Stage 2: What equity benefits might the transport intervention achieve?
A new Director of Public Health (DPH) for Bristol from 2006 took up the challenge to address the wider determinants of health and especially that of the built environment as a part of a strategy to increase population levels of physical activity. Recognizing that the role of the DPH alone is insufficient to address the range of wider health determinants the DPH brought together a spectrum of inputs through built environment "experts" who also had influencing skills at different levels of the system of local government so that change can be effected. Yet, influencing officers alone is insufficient and so the "experts" need also to be skilled at developing political support. One of these postholders working inside the Bristol City Council is the first author, a transport and health specialist.

As noted above, work on transport and health in Bristol was driven by a concern to address low levels of physical activity. Low levels of physical activity have become a major public health problem in most western societies. The evidence shows that the health impact of inactivity in terms of coronary heart disease, for example, is comparable to that of smoking, and almost as great as high cholesterol levels. In addition, there is a social class gradient so that lower economic groups are most at risk of disease and ill-health through low levels of physical activity. By 2008, together with the DPH, the transport and health specialist had identified the importance of 20 mph speed limits across most of the road network of the city as an intervention which would impact on all citizens but disproportionately benefit the poorest communities given both the lower levels of physical activity among poorer communities as well as the steep social class gradients in road traffic deaths and injuries. In deciding the approach, as public health practitioners, we drew on a public health strategy contribution to public policy. This was the concept of population-level strategies. This means rather than the targeting of small numbers within the population who may be at high risk, for example, through lifestyle behaviors, to instead address whole populations. The rationale is that in the case of road traffic injuries (as with other health threats) the majority of cases do not occur in the individuals at high risk. Thus, "a large number of people exposed to a small risk may generate many more cases than a small number exposed to a high risk" (Rose, 1992). Through this approach, we sought to reduce health inequities through transport.

In making the case for this work, a successful Knowledge Transfer Partnership (KTP) bid between NHS Bristol, Bristol City Council, and the University of the West of England (UWE) in 2009 involved researching best practice in road safety globally. These both had the ambition of further informing an ongoing pilot of 20 mph speed limits, and how this might contribute to a broader vision for road safety across the city. The output of the KTP project was a report drawing on the international literature and focused on reducing road danger across the city's road network, principally, but not wholly, through more effective speed management. It was partially stimulated by broader developments in road safety internationally, most notably the Vision Zero road safety policy of Sweden commenced from 1997. Underpinning Vision Zero is the judgment that the transport system will always create a substantial number of crashes, but it is possible to limit the effect on the human body by reducing speeds to a level which will almost eliminate fatalities and prevent most serious injuries. This report then underpinned work to support the citywide roll out of 20 mph speed limits across Bristol which was approved by City Council's Full Council meeting in June 2012 after evaluation of the pilot 20 mph areas being assessed as positive. Assessment was in terms of three key elements: road traffic casualties; social cohesion; and total physical activity time. Given the challenge with capturing meaningful data on the first two of these within 12 months, objective monitoring of pedestrian and cycle user movements did report a small but notable increase in travel by these modes and together with no significant change in casualties in that first year this data were used to make an assessment as to the effectiveness of the 20 mph speed limits pilot.

Stage 3: What data are needed to assess equity impacts and how can it be collected?
The Bristol City Council, understanding the importance of taking a more holistic, safe-systems approach to the evaluation of the 20 mph speed limit roll out, sought to identify the most appropriate data sources from which to assess the effectiveness of the transport policy, particularly its impact on equity. This included more traditional data sources, such as vehicle speed and RTC data, as has been used in evaluations of 20 mph in other UK cities. But it also included a number of other data sources. To evaluate impact on modal shift, particularly changes in the number of people walking and cycling, before-after data from manual counts using roadside cameras was collected in the intervention areas. To assess impacts on perceptions among the local community, household interview surveys were undertaken pre- and postimplementation. This data were assessed alongside the results from the Bristol Quality and Life Survey, and supplemented with data on attitudes toward 20 mph speed limits gained from a national tracker survey with a boosted sample size for Bristol. The latter was commissioned by the UWE (Bristol) from a nationally respected polling agency, YouGov. Air quality data were also available. Socioeconomic data, particularly relating to measures of geographical deprivation, enabled an assessment of how the 20 mph intervention was impacting on socioeconomic equity.

Stage 4: (How) Does the transport intervention address equity?
The Bristol City Council undertook a detailed analysis of the 20 mph speed limit pilot initiative, and found that the introduction of 20 mph limits had been accompanied by a small but important reduction in average daytime vehicle speeds, an increase in walking and cycling counts especially at weekends, a strengthening of public support for 20 mph, maintenance of bus journey times and reliability, and no measurable impact on air quality or noise. It was too soon at that stage to draw statistically valid conclusions on the impact on road traffic casualties. Although this interim evaluation did not specifically address equity issues in the analysis, the pilot areas deliberately included parts of the more socioeconomically deprived neighborhoods of the city. Therefore, positive findings in these areas indicate a positive impact on equity. More importantly, the data collected for the pilot intervention, and the interim evaluation, tested the feasibility of assessing the impacts on equity of the 20 mph limit intervention using a holistic, systems-wide approach. This approach was applied to the evaluation of the impact of the wider rollout of the intervention across the city. The citywide evaluation of the 20 mph intervention

has found reductions in speeds and casualties across the city, including those in the more socio-economically deprived areas. There have also been increases in self-reported walking and cycling, and improved self-reported quality of life.

Stage 5: How can the transport intervention better address equity?
The evaluation of the 20mph intervention is currently feeding directly into a wider review of the intervention that will influence high-level decision making within the Bristol City Council, particularly relating to addressing issues of equity across the city. Discussions will focus on how the citywide 20mph limits can better address equity considerations. This may involve engaging with local communities in specific areas of the city where speeds and collisions have not reduced as much as hoped for, targeting problematic roads with engineering and other environmental measures, and considering increasing enforcement.

4 Policy relevance

In urban areas, there are a number of ways to reduce risk of injuries—strongly discourage pedestrian and cycle use—which has been successfully achieved in some US car-dependent cities and increasingly also in some Asian cities—with consequent increasing levels of kinetic energy in the transport network. Car-dependent cities tend to the highest traffic fatality rates. The United States has the worst traffic safety performance of all developed countries. North Dakota registers more than twice the national average and five times the rate of Massachusetts (Ahangari et al., 2017). In their modeling work, the authors of a US study found that the biggest two contributions to the traffic fatality rate across the United States were vehicles per population, and vehicle miles traveled. Here, risks to those who do walk or cycle are much higher than in more mixed modes cities given the levels of car dependency.

Recent policy in Bristol, United Kingdom, has been to promote road safety through tackling danger at source by reducing motor vehicle speeds. This conforms with the now dominant orthodoxy across the developed world for a Safe Systems approach, one endorsed by the WHO, the World Bank, and the OECD. Given the gross inequity in road casualties in Bristol, reflecting the wider global disparity between those unprotected by a vehicle cage and in-vehicle occupants in road safety terms alone, a Safe Systems approach would reduce the burden on both those from lower income and social class groups. More broadly, this approach meets with wider public policy goals including the pressing need also to promote active travel forms for both health, economic, and sustainability reasons, as Marmot noted. This should, we contend, be a course to be followed by many other countries and cities.

However, we also contend that political elites across the globe are complicit in failing to utilize known effective road safety and transport interventions which could massively reduce the prevalence not only deaths and life changing injuries but also importantly in making significant advances in the goal of freedom from fear of harm of injury through the transport system. For example, there is overwhelming evidence that lower speeds result in fewer collisions and in reduced severity of collisions including injuries (MASTER Project; Allsop, 1998). Road traffic injury is the result of energy transfer and there is a straightforward relationship between speed and crash involvement such that as the speed goes up so also does the crash involvement. Kinetic energy management in traffic systems needs to focus more on speed as an important measure in injury prevention. Fear of injury itself also acts in a range of ways to curtail the lives and damage the livelihoods of millions of the world's poorest people through reduced physical activity, increased pollution exposure, and degraded environments. If national programs were more aligned to Safe Systems and applied proportionate universalism greater progress could be made to reduce the gross inequity in road traffic deaths and injuries across the globe.

In Bristol, the choice has been to choose the latter and positively encourage and support walking and cycle use. The KTP report led to the drafting of a Safe Systems Road Safety Plan for Bristol in 2015 with the long-term ambition of eliminating fatal and life changing injuries and thus removing the inequity through road traffic injuries that currently exists.

As a coda, beyond reported casualties, there is also the suppressed and latent demand for walking and cycle use typified by the desire of children to walk and cycle the school journey but often vetoed by parents and carers on the grounds of lack of road safety. If transport equity is a serious ambition of decision makers, we contend that they will need to tackle the causes of suppressed and latent demand for the two most equitable modes of travel, modes which both provide health benefits to the individual as well as to populations at large through reduced traffic danger, reduce air and noise pollution, and more equitable use of urban space for movement.

The RoSE cycle approach, as used in Bristol in the 20 mph speed limit intervention, offers guidance for other areas to take an equity focus to transport interventions that meet broader, public health goals. It is a means by which a Safe Systems approach, focusing not just on casualty reduction, but more on reducing danger on the roads that genuinely transforms the road environment and tackles important equity issues.

Many countries have ambitions to encourage mode shift from motorized individual transport to walking and cycling to address societal goals such as reducing air pollution and climate change as well as road safety goals (Christie, 2018). We would note that even with the political commitment, even for high-income countries, there is a threat from funding cuts which negatively impact on road safety and which are further likely to hit poorer communities hardest.

5   Further reading

The steep social class gradient in child pedestrian casualties has now been well reported in the United Kingdom for decades. As a background to equity and road safety, we would also encourage readers to delve into the broader and supporting literature around road safety. The Black Report was first published in the United Kingdom in the early 1980s. It reported that among children "the risk of death from being hit by a motor vehicle is multiplied by five to seven time in passing from class I to class IV" (Inequalities in Health, The Black Report, 1982). Reports and studies since have confirmed this structured social inequality which is reported in many countries.

Pursuing the concept of proportionate universalism, as discussed in our chapter, we highlight the value of intervention measures targeted not solely at high-risk groups but rather than whole populations, as proposed elsewhere by Geoffrey Rose (1992). Such whole populations thinking are not far removed from Safe Systems Road Safety. Wegman provides a helpful global overview for the future of road safety differentiated by the challenges for high-, medium-, and low-income countries. Importantly, he recommends that sustained political commitment is required, along with the active commitment of the public sector.

References

Ahangari, H., Atkinson-Palombo, C., Garrick, N., 2017. Automibile-dependency as a barrier to vision zero, evidence from the states in the USA. Accid. Anal. Prev. 107, 77–85.

Allsop, R.E., 1998. MASTER Project (Managing the Speeds of Traffic on European Roads). Report for the EC (DGVII) R1.3.1. Centre for Transport Studies, University College London, London, pp. 1–37.

Bostock, L., 2001. Pathways of disadvantage? Walking as a mode of transport among low-income mothers. Health Soc. Care 9 (1), 11–18.

Bristol City Council, 2017. Joint Strategic Needs Assessment 2016–17. Bristol. https://www.bristol.gov.uk/documents/20182/34740/JSNA+2016+to+2017+final+version/1ffc45f9-0a75-4e04-8b0d-a1ee86f23bf2, (Accessed 21 August 2017).

Cairns, J., et al., 2015. Go slow: an umbrella review of the effects of 20mph zones and limits on health and health inequalities. J. Public Health 37 (3), 515–520.

Christie, N., 2018. Is Vision Zero important for promoting health? J. Transp. Health 9, 5–6.

Faculty of Public Health, 2017. What is public health? http://www.fph.org.uk/what_is_public_health, Accessed 31 August 2017.

Green, J., Muir, H., Maher, M., 2011. Child pedestrian casualties and deprivation. Accid. Anal. Prev. 43 (3), 714–723.

Hippisley-Cox, J., et al., 2002. Cross sectional survey of socioeconomic variations in severity and mechanism of childhood injuries in Trent 1992-97. Br. Med. J. 324, 1132–1138.

House of Common Transport Committee, 2008. Ending the Scandal of Complacency: Road Safety Beyond 2010, 11th Report of Session 2008. The Stationery Office, London. https://publications.parliament.uk/pa/cm200708/cmselect/cmtran/460/460.pdf, Accessed 23 August 2017.

Marmot, M., 2010. Fair Society, Healthy Lives: The Marmot Review: Strategic Review of Health Inequalities in England Post-2010. http://www.instituteofhealthequity.org/resources-reports/fair-society-healthy-lives-the-marmot-review/fair-society-healthy-lives-full-report-pdf.pdf, Accessed 21 August 2017.

Rose, G., 1992. The Strategy of Preventive Medicine. Oxford University Press, Oxford.

Distribution of transportation "goods" and "bads" in a Canadian metropolis: A diagnosis of the situation and potential interventions to tackle environmental disparities

11

Mathieu Carrier, Philippe Apparicio

1 Introduction

The first studies in the field of environmental justice looks at the interrelations between the characteristics of the urban environment and those of the people living in a certain area. Researchers in this stream try to determine whether environmental nuisances or urban resources are equitably distributed between all population groups in a specific place. As an example, in the past few years, the studies performed in the field of transportation have tried to look at both the benefits and the burdens to a specific group in a particular place. Since the early 1990s, a number of environmental justice studies performed in the United States, Europe, and Oceania have looked at the distribution of the negative effects linked to the functioning of road transportation, whether in connection with the socioeconomic position of households, their ethnic origin, or the age of the individuals in question.

In many cases, it has been reported that low-income persons and, to a lesser extent, individuals belonging to certain ethnic groups were seen to be more likely to live along highways and other major traffic arteries, in areas where the air is found to be more polluted from road transportation and where noise levels are higher, and in environments where they are more at risk of suffering an accident. As well as living in areas where negative elements related to road transportation are concentrated, low-income populations are said to be more likely to have less access to positive urban resources in the urban living environment such as parks, municipal facilities, and supermarkets. This situation was measured in several US cities. It has also been shown that children from lower-income families and those belonging to ethnic minorities are more likely to attend a school located near a major traffic artery and, consequently, where the concentration of certain air pollutants is significantly higher.

In recent years, increased traffic flows on the road networks of many cities around the world have sparked interest in the literature on environmental equity in regard to

Measuring Transport Equity. https://doi.org/10.1016/B978-0-12-814818-1.00011-1

the issue of the distribution of pollutant emissions (air pollutants and road traffic noise) from transportation. The area of transportation has thus been approached from a distributional justice perspective, that is: "Who gets what, when, and, to some degree how (Schweitzer and Valenzuela, 2004: 384)." The existence of an equitable distribution is then said to derive from an imbalance between the benefits and costs stemming from, among other things, the functioning of road transportation infrastructures for certain population groups, namely, mostly low-income individuals and people belonging to visible minorities in a specific area. The main objective of these studies is to understand the social patterning of costs and benefits related to road transportation in terms of distributional justice in a particular place.

2 Objectives

Some authors have defined a framework to characterize the concept of environmental justice. Environmental justice involves more than an equal sharing of harmful environmental burdens for a specific group of the population. It must, for instance, provide a sufficient protection for various population groups exposed to such hazards. Other authors have also noted that "an unequal distribution of environmental "bads" by itself may not necessarily be unjust it is rather the "fairness" of the processes through which the distribution has occurred and the possibilities which individuals and communities have to avoid or ameliorate risk, which are important (Walker and Bulkeley, 2006: 655)." This chapter specifically focuses on the distribution of burdens of road transportation (road traffic noise, air pollution, and accidents), which, because of the unequal spatial distribution of different social groups, leads to an increased exposure to risks for certain populations. These have been developed in accordance with certain basic principles in an attempt to evaluate the impacts associated with the functioning of road transportation systems. Among these, one stream is attempting to analyze whether certain population groups are more at risk of being exposed to the negative impacts of transportation compared with the potential benefits related to their immediate environment. Whit this in mind, we have based our chapter on the equity principle that everyone should share the same level of burdens of a road network, regardless their socioeconomic status or their ethnic origin.

More specifically, in regard to the negative elements of the environment under study, we look at the distributional analysis of road transportation-generated air pollution, road traffic noise, and accidents. The main objective is to determine the spatial patterning of some of these costs related to the road transport network in our study area. The likelihood of visible minorities and low-income individuals living in the areas most polluted by road transportation, require that attention be accorded to these population groups. Once the three burdens related to transportation combined by means of a transportation index, the second objective of this chapter is to determine whether visible minorities and low-income individuals are overrepresented in areas where there are both high concentrations of NO_2, road traffic noise levels, and risk of accidents, compared with the rest of the population and compared with their presence in the rest of the study area.

Then, the positive elements being considered are related to the accessibility that the road network provides to urban resources in the immediate residential environment, namely, parks, supermarkets, and municipal amenities (arenas, pools, sports grounds, libraries, municipal cultural centers, and other infrastructures managed by municipal public authorities) by using the network distance. The creation of this global index of the quality of the urban environment could then allow authorities and municipal organizations working in local-level urban planning to quickly and easily target the portions of their territories affected by an imbalance between the negative elements of the urban environment directly related to road transportation and the perceived benefits in this environment in order to prioritize the corrective actions needed to reduce the environmental disparities measured for low-income individuals or visible minorities.

3 Methodology

3.1 The approach

Specifically, the main objective of this chapter is to determine the spatial patterning of road transportation burdens (air pollution, road traffic noise, and accidents) for low-income individuals and visible minorities based on where they live. Then, the next step is to measure the potential disproportionately effect of transportation burdens for low-income individuals and visible minorities by using indicators of distributional justice such a multidimensional index of transportation burdens and an index of the global environment. Finally, the balance between transportation burdens and amenities is calculated toward low-income individuals and visible minorities in order to obtain a wider perspective in terms of distributional justice. The following sections specify how we operationalize the measure of the balance between the burdens of road transportation and the accessibility to amenities directly related to the presence of a road network for low-income individuals and visible minorities.

3.2 The methods

Analyzing variations in the urban environmental indicators requires that analyses be performed at a fine geographic scale, as air pollution and road traffic noise levels, for example, can vary greatly on the scales of a neighborhood, a census tract, or a dissemination area. In examining the important criteria for a rigorous evaluation of distributional justice, some authors have pointed directly to the question of the choice of the scale of analysis. Concretely speaking, this spatial division must be as precise as possible. This means that analyses must be performed at a fine geographic scale as the levels of air pollutants and road traffic noise, for example, can vary considerably. The analysis was consequently performed at the geographic scale of the 10,290 inhabited city blocks on the study area, each of which contains an average of 100–300 people. Once the spatial scale had been selected, we proceeded to measure the characteristics of the urban environment for each of the 10,290 city blocks in the study area. In terms of measuring, we aggregated all the values of each environmental indicator at the city block level. In this way, it would then be possible to add up all the positive elements and subtract the nuisances considered at a common geographic scale.

3.2.1   Transportation burdens (transportation index)

The first step of the methodology is to construct an index of transportation burdens. To do this, we have considered three of the principal burdens that are generated by the road transportation network in an urban area. We first used a set of data developed by Dan Crouse of the McGill University and his team regarding road transportation-related air pollutants. These researchers measured, during three nonconsecutive months in 2006, at 133 locations on the Island of Montreal determined according to a spatial allocation model based on proximity to major traffic arteries and urban density, the concentration of nitrogen dioxide (NO_2), which is one of the main road transportation-related air pollutants. With the help of a regression equation that included, notably, urban density, and the proximity to major traffic arteries, they then estimated NO_2 concentrations on the entire Island of Montreal. It was thus possible to estimate the mean concentration in each city block in the study area.

The average level of noise over an entire day, in decibels (dBA)—a unit used to express the noise level measured using a device that accentuates components of average frequency, thus imitating the response of the human ear—was modeled by using the variables of traffic flow, number of heavy vehicles, road geometry, building heights, land elevation, and atmospheric conditions with the help of software designed for this purpose (Predictor-LiMA Type 7810). To do this, the area under study was divided into more than 200 zones, and calculations were done at distances of 20 m each. Ultimately, the average noise level was calculated for each city block.

Finally, for accident rates, we calculated the average accident rate for all intersections located less than 500 m from the geographic center of the residential function of the city blocks in the study area for the period from 2008 to 2013. In order to do this, a weighting established by the Société d'Assurances Automobile du Québec (SAAQ) (Quebec Automobile Insurance Board) was first assigned to each of the accidents based on their seriousness. Weightings of 10, 5, and 1 were, respectively, associated with fatal, serious, and minor accidents. Once the weightings had been assigned, an accident rate was calculated for each intersection based on the annual average daily traffic flow (AADTF). Ultimately, the average accident rate was ultimately calculated based on the number of intersections located less than 500 m walking distance from the place of residence in each city block.

Once all the data had been collected on the scale of the city block, a Z-score was calculated for each of the indicators in order to determine a global value for the transportation burdens. The Z-score considers both the average and standard deviation of each of the distributions of the transportation indicators. So, in the end, the lower the value is, the more the block is characterized by a relatively unfavorable environment in relation to transportation burdens and vice versa.

3.2.2   Distribution of the two groups in the most disadvantaged areas by road transportation burdens

The second step is to measure the presence of the two groups under study in sectors associated with the lowest value of the transportation index. The lowest values of the transportation burdens index indicate that a city block is potentially characterized by higher concentration of air pollution, higher level of road traffic noise, and higher accident rates in comparison with the mean value of the study area. To do so, we have considered the city blocks located in the first quintile related to the transportation index as the potentially most disadvantaged areas. Then, two indicators have been considered.

The first indicator allows us to assess whether one of the two groups (low-income individuals and visible minorities) is overrepresented in disadvantaged areas compared with the rest of the population. This involves comparing the proportion of the groups present in disadvantaged areas with that of the rest of the population in the same area. If one group is overrepresented in the disadvantaged areas compared with the rest of the population, an indicator value of greater than 1 is obtained. The second indicator allows us to determine whether one of the groups is overrepresented in disadvantaged areas compared with its presence in the rest of the study area.

3.2.3 Positive elements associated with the urban living environment (global index)

In terms of positive elements associated with road transportation, we have considered a few aspects of the urban living environment that are directly accessible from the road network. Starting from the geographic center of the residential function of each city block, we considered the surface area, in hectares, of accessible parks less than 500 m away, as well as the number of supermarkets and municipal amenities located less than 1 km away, using accessibility indicators directly related to the network distance.

Once all the data had been collected on the scale of the city block, a Z-score was calculated for each of the six indicators in order to determine a global value for the urban environment, as had already been done in the literature. The Z-score considers both the average and standard deviation of each of the distributions of the urban environmental indicators. We, therefore, added up the positive elements (parks, municipal amenities, and the food supply) together. Then, we subtracted the transportation burdens considered (NO_2, noise level, and accident rate) on the scale of the 10,290 city blocks in the study area, using the adjusted values obtained. A similar weight has been given to each component of the urban environment for the purposes of this chapter. Ultimately, the global environmental quality index is calculated on the scale of the city block based on the Z-score values for each variable by adding the positive aspects (equipment, parks, and supermarkets) and by subtracting the burdens from road transportation (NO_2, noise, and accidents).

3.3 The case study

This study was conducted on the territory of the Island of Montreal (Canada). Despite the geographical proximity to the United States, it is noteworthy that the history of urbanization in Canada is quite different from the situation in the United States. Canadian urbanization processes have not been accompanied by a racial dimension, which has meant in particular that there is less ethnic segregation than in the United States.

More specifically, the study area is the Island of Montreal, in the center of the Montreal metropolitan region (the second most populous area in Canada after the Toronto metropolitan area), and which, in 2006, had 1.9 million inhabitants spread over a territory of 499 km^2 (Fig. 1). Occupation of the territory of the Island of Montreal is characterized by variable urban densities: lower at the eastern and western ends of the Island, which are suburban and essentially residential areas, and with higher densities found in neighborhoods in the center of the Island. Moreover, the central portions of the study area are characterized by a significant concentration of the main traffic arteries that link the major centers of attraction on the Island of Montreal and provide access to the bridges and the principal suburban cities of the metropolitan region.

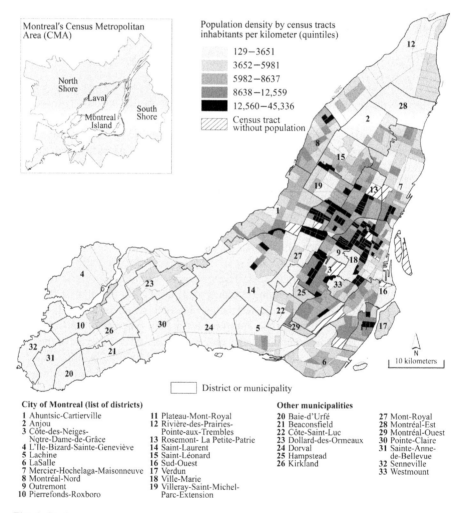

Fig. 1 Study area.

Two population groups were selected for the purposes of this chapter: namely, low-income individuals and people having stated that they belong to a visible minority. The reality in Canada making this group (visible minority) a more relevant category than African Americans or Hispanic Americans. The variable of visible minorities refers to all nonwhite individuals, except Aboriginal people: that is, the census categories of Chinese, South Asian, Filipino, Latin American, Black, Arab, Korean, Japanese, South East Asian, West Asian, and South Sea Islander. We are, therefore, looking at two groups that are often studied in the environmental equity field, that is, low-income individuals and members of visible minorities. The numbers of these groups and of the total population were taken from the 2006 Statistics Canada census on the level of the geographic scale of the dissemination area, that is, the most precise spatial unit of analysis, in which some 400–700 people live. It should, however, be noted that Statistics Canada only provides data on the total population on the level of the city block. A city block generally corresponds to a block of homes. To deal with this limitation, we estimated the numbers of the groups of low-income individuals and visible minorities on the level of the city block. Descriptive statistics on low-income individuals and visible minorities are shown in Table 1.

4 Variations in the transportation and the global indexes in the study area

A first index was applied on the level of the city blocks in the study area, in only considering environmental burdens relating to transportation (air pollution, road traffic noise, and accident rate). Fig. 2 shows the distribution of the index in the study area.

Residential areas with the lowest index values are those presenting higher levels of air pollutants, road traffic noise, and risk of accidents compared with the average for the study area. In an even more marked way than in Fig. 3, we can see that the blocks in the urban area that concentrate the weakest index values, identified by the darkest shade, are almost all located in the central boroughs and thus prove to be, due to this very fact, the most densely populated, as well as being the areas where the main traffic arteries are concentrated. The residential areas with the lowest index values, identified by the darkest shade, are mostly located along highways, near the CBD, and in the central boroughs (in the district Côte-des-Neiges, Plateau-Mont-Royal, Sud-Ouest, Ville-Marie, and Villeray-Saint-Michel-Park-Extension). These areas are,

Table 1 Univariate statistics for the two groups studied at the city block level

Group	N	Mean	S.D.	Median	Max
Visible minorities (%)	10,290	21.20	16.51	17.44	96.60
Low-income population (%)	10,290	23.88	16.18	21.27	94.42

N, number of dissemination area in the study area; *Mean*, mean values of visible minorities and low-income individuals per dissemination area; *S.D.*, standard deviation; *Median*, median value of visible minorities and low-income individuals per dissemination area; *Max*, maximum value of visible minorities and low-income individuals per dissemination area.

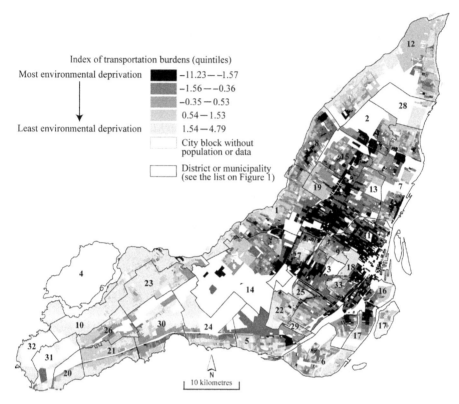

Fig. 2 Application of the transportation burdens index on the scale of the city blocks.

respectively, labeled with the numbers 3, 11, 16, 18, and 19 in Fig. 1. Then, a global index was calculated for each of the 10,290 inhabited city blocks on the Island of Montreal. The global index values range from −10.90 (the least advantageous situation) to 10.32 (the most advantageous situation). Fig. 3 shows that the most disadvantageous and advantageous areas are more evenly geographically distributed on the Island of Montreal in comparison with the transportation index.

4.1 Diagnosis of distributional justice for the two groups targeted

4.1.1 Distribution of the groups studied in quintiles of the transportation and global indexes

Once all the indicators had been generated on the scale of the city blocks, we used a few statistical tests to check for the existence of environmental disparities for low-income individuals and visible minorities. The distribution of the groups studied was then calculated for each quintile related to the transportation index and the global index (Table 2). First, low-income individuals and visible minorities are more strongly concentrated in the lowest quintile of transportation index than is the population as a

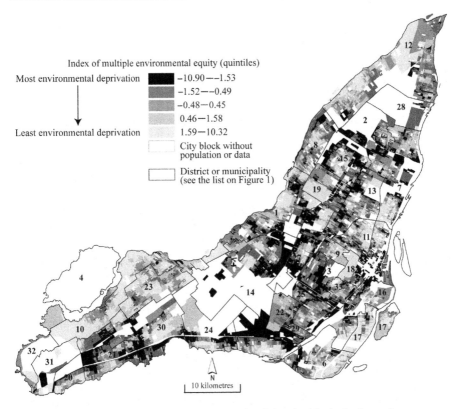

Fig. 3 Application of the global index on the scale of the city blocks in the study area.

Table 2 Distribution (%) of population groups in block quintiles of the two indicators

	Total population (%)	Low-income individuals (%)	Visible minorities (%)
Quintiles of the transportation index			
1	23.75	31.67	29.16
2	23.09	26.16	24.01
3	21.07	20.78	20.84
4	17.57	13.39	14.64
5	14.52	8.00	11.35
Quintiles of the global index			
1	21.03	23.78	25.04
2	20.23	21.37	21.97
3	19.88	19.61	20.30
4	19.18	17.71	16.84
5	19.68	17.53	15.86

whole (31.67% and 29.16%, respectively, compared with 23.75%). The situation signifies that low-income individuals, and, to a lesser extent visible minorities, tend to be more located in areas where the concentrations of traffic-related pollutants and accidents are higher. Second, these two groups are also slightly more concentrated in the lowest quintile of the global index in comparison with the total population.

4.1.2 Using the indicators to identify environmental disparities for the two groups

In this section, we present the results of the calculations of the two types of distributional justice indicators for the population groups under consideration. These results will enable us to determine whether any of the two groups are overrepresented in the areas with the highest concentration of transportation burdens (transportation index) and those where the costs of transportation are higher than the benefits (global index). For any of the two indicators, a value over 1 will signify that a group is overrepresented in the most problematic areas compared with the rest of the population (indicator 1) and overrepresented in disadvantaged areas compared with its presence in the rest of the study area (indicator 2). The results shown in Table 3 indicate that low-income individuals, and to a lesser extent, visible minorities, are overrepresented in the areas characterized by the highest costs of road transportation (indicator $1 = 1.54$ and 1.33 and indicator $2 = 1.49$ and 1.32). It appears that low-income individuals are more susceptible than the rest of the population to live in the areas where the transportation burdens are more important. However, the values obtained for the two indicators in relation with the global index are lower for low-income individuals. It seems to indicate that low-income individuals potentially benefit from a better accessibility to urban amenities than visible minorities.

4.1.3 Correlation between the values of the indicators and the proportions of the groups considered

Spearman correlation coefficients were calculated to check for the existence of significant linear relationships between the proportions of the two groups in each zone considered and the urban environmental indicators (Table 4). On one hand, it is of note

Table 3 Indicators of representation of the groups under study in the lowest quintiles of the transportation and global indexes

	Low-income individuals	Visible minorities
	Indicator 1	Indicator 1
Transportation index (Q1)	1.54	1.33
Global index (Q1)	1.19	1.27
	Indicator 2	Indicator 2
Transportation index (Q1)	1.49	1.32
Global index (Q1)	1.17	1.25

Table 4 Spearman coefficients between the indicators and the presence of the different groups

Indicators	Low-income individuals (%)	Visible minorities (%)
NO_2	0.425***	0.123***
Noise—dB(A)	0.302***	0.146***
Average accident rate	0.375***	0.102***
Parks	−0.02*	−0.065***
Supermarkets	0.399***	0.126***
Equipments	0.383***	0.005
Transportation index	−0.489***	−0.200***
Global index	−0.116***	−0.148***

*0.05, **0.01, ***0.001.

that some of the correlations are positive and significant: between the proportion of low-income individuals and the levels of road transportation-related air pollutants [namely, NO_2 (0.425)] and average accident rate (0.375). It is also noteworthy that the index associated only with road transportation burdens (−0.489) are the strongest with the proportion of low-income individuals per city block. Similar results, from every point of view, were obtained for visible minorities, but in a much less marked fashion. This, therefore, means that, for the entire Island of Montreal, and moderately so, the more the proportion of low-income individuals increases in a given city block, the lower the air quality is, the more the level of road traffic noise increases, the greater the risk of accidents is. This ultimately results in a lower index of transportation burdens. On the other hand, this is compensated by a stronger presence of supermarkets (0.399) and municipal amenities (0.383) by using the network distance, which is explained by the fact that low-income individuals in the study area are more concentrated in dense environments near the downtown core of the study area. In the end, the costs of transportation burdens for low-income individuals, and, to a lesser extent for visible minorities, are reduced by benefits from accessibility.

5 Policy relevance

Within the framework of their urban planning, all the boroughs in the study area are required to make an assessment of the quality of their environment in their urbanization plan in order to plan their development orientations and measures to improve quality of life for their residents. The objective is to seek out quality of life, and to harmonize activities in considering the needs of the population as a whole and the characteristics of the urban environment. This is generally done every 5 years. At the moment, the boroughs are not using this type of composite index to evaluate the quality of their environments in order to target areas where priority interventions need to be made in terms of transportation. The boroughs' assessment is generally made by identifying specific factors where concrete actions need to be taken.

Currently, for most boroughs in the study area, the quality of life dimensions that are chiefly targeted are to reduce heat islands, reduce air pollution and road traffic noise, to increase urban vegetation, and to lower accident rates, with the latter two based on the municipal tree policy and the local transportation plan. In terms of air pollution and road traffic noise, municipal authorities in the study area have not yet developed a monitoring plan or adequate data to properly measure these nuisances related to road transportation, which makes it harder to prioritize the interventions to be made due to the low level of reliable data sampling. In the following sections, we discuss the interventions that could be done in order to reduce transportation costs through the planning policies at the level of the most populous borough of the study area.

5.1 Potential interventions to improve the urban living environment

On the level of the entire study area, the transportation index and the global index can vary considerably from one place to another, especially due to the location of the main transportation infrastructures and of urban density. However, this scale of analysis is not the scale prioritized by actors and decision makers involved in urban planning and improvement of the urban living environment since the corrective actions taken must be done locally under the planning framework in effect in the Montreal study context. In this sense, in the Montreal context, the planning and operationalization of interventions in terms of improving the living environment are done by organizations working on the level of the boroughs or the autonomous municipalities, identified by the numbers in Fig. 1.

We, therefore, applied the transportation index on the level of the city blocks of one of the boroughs on the Island of Montreal. The borough of Côte-des-Neiges-Notre-Dame-de-Grâce was thus targeted because of a few specific factors. First, it is the most populous borough in the study area, with more than 165,000 inhabitants, that is, 8% of the total population of the Island of Montreal, over a territory of $21.4\,km^2$. In some sectors, the density there is greater than 15,000 inhabitants/km^2. Second, authorities in this borough have already raised the idea of reducing disparities in regard to the transportation burdens by using existing urban planning and development tools. Third, the borough exhibits similar variations on the level of each of the components compared with the study area, which allows actions to be targeted that could apply to other sectors on the Island of Montreal. Finally, this borough presents a socioeconomic profile which is similar to that of the entire study area.

The borough of Côte-des-Neiges-Notre-Dame-de-Grâce presents substantial disparities in regard to the quality of the urban environment, as well as being characterized by considerable disparities in terms of the proportion of low-income individuals on the level of the 571 city blocks that make up its territory. The concentrations of transportation-related air pollutants, the level of road traffic noise, and the risk of accidents also tend to be significantly higher in blocks with high concentrations of low-income individuals. The transportation index in this borough thus ranges from -6.41

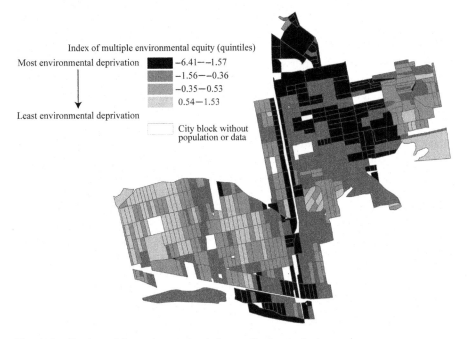

Index of multiple environmental equity (quintiles)

Most environmental deprivation
- ■ −6.41−−1.57
- ■ −1.56−−0.36
- ▧ −0.35−0.53
- ▨ 0.54−1.53

Least environmental deprivation

☐ City block without population or data

Fig. 4 Application of the transportation index on the level of a borough.

in the city block with highest concentration of transportation burdens to 1.53 in the area with the lowest presence of traffic-related pollutants and accidents (Fig. 4).

Various public policies including a transportation plan have recently been developed on the level of the Island of Montreal boroughs so as to better plan and develop living environments, encourage active transportation, and provide better quality of life and better health for the people living there. In its urbanization plan, the borough of Côte-des-Neiges-Notre-Dame-de-Grâce also intends to improve the quality of the environments there in order to mitigate the nuisances generated by urban activities and transportation and ensure safer living environments. To do this, the borough wants to implement measures to increase the quality of the planning of the public domain in order to make it more pleasant, safer, and more attractive.

The diagnosis made of the quality of the environment through the transportation index, illustrated in Fig. 4, shows sizeable differences on the level of the borough. In this regard, one can distinguish one sector of more than 50 blocks in Fig. 4 that concentrate several transportation burdens compared with the average for the borough of Côte-des-Neiges-Notre-Dame-de-Grâce. In that case, all the city blocks which in total make up a little less than 15% of the entire area under study, and more than 40% of the population of which is considered to be of low income, are characterized by significantly higher levels of accident rates, NO_2 and road traffic noise, compared with the average for the borough of Côte-des-Neiges-Notre-Dame-de-Grâce. This situation is due to the higher road density, and the greater concentration and lengths of collector roads and arteries in these city blocks. The geography of road transportation in the center of the Island of Montreal explains, in part at least, the higher concentration of traffic-related pollutants for these city blocks.

Using this assessment, the borough could intervene on several levels in its territorial local planning in order to implement corrective measures to reduce the burdens from road transportation in these areas. First, through its local urban planning regulations, the borough could require a sufficient quantity of trees on all residential and commercial lots in its territory so as to reduce air pollution. Through this measure, the proportion of vegetation covering the city block would increase, thereby reducing summertime temperatures and heat islands, while fostering a decrease in the concentrations of air pollutants. The borough also has the power to rationalize parking spaces through its urban planning regulations by allocating a certain number of spaces based on the types of land use. The space thus freed up from parking areas could then be reallocated for greening and tree planting. Second, in the Montreal context, the boroughs have full jurisdiction over the local road network in partnership with the central city, in order to make the interventions that it deems necessary there. The boroughs in the study area recently developed local transportation plans that identify in particular the main problems associated with road transportation as well as potential solutions to remedy these problems. For example, the boroughs are targeting sections of road and intersections with the highest accident rates in order to make local interventions, especially in terms of traffic calming measures, curb extensions, coordination of traffic lights, and reduced speed limits on problematic sections of road. By directly intervening in its road network, the borough is helping to reduce the number of accidents and to lower traffic speeds, which has the potential to also minimize the concentrations of air pollutants and levels of road traffic noise.

5.2 Policy relevance

It is known that the combined effect of a number of environmental nuisances and the lack of certain urban resources can have negative impacts on residents' health and quality of life. A distributional justice analysis including different road transportation-related burdens was first applied at a fine spatial scale on the territory of the Island of Montreal. We have shown that low-income individuals and, to a lesser extent, visible minorities tend to live in the city blocks that combine the highest concentrations of environmental burdens related to road transportation. We have also added three urban amenities related to the environment in line to calculate the balance between the "goods" and the "bads" associated with road transportation in a broader view. The results obtained with the urban amenities have reduced the burdens previously measured toward low-income individuals and visible minorities.

The transportation index that we present in the context of this chapter can be used to quickly pinpoint specific sectors of the urban environment where quality of life is lower compared with an area under examination due to the presence of the road network. More particularly, this type of index can be useful for municipal actors working in urban planning, where one of the objectives of this discipline is to attain equity and to control certain environmental nuisances (e.g., pollutant emissions). Then, the consideration of one or another of the six components that make up the global index makes it easier to identify parameters on the level of which public authorities can improve residents' quality of life, while also having spatial references that help them to know where to prioritize certain specific interventions.

Through their urbanization plan and municipal regulations (zoning and subdivision by-laws), municipal authorities can, for example, set quantified thresholds to be respected, for a given area, in terms of the allocation of municipal services and the space allocated to vegetation, as well as to urban parks, with the aim of reducing the impacts associated with heat islands. If municipal authorities decide to develop specific thresholds in public policies for particular elements of the urban environment, as well as systematic monitoring measures to estimate the concentrations of environmental nuisances that cover the entire territory in question, the environmental quality index would be an appropriate tool to support them in these approaches.

Municipal authorities could thus develop an operational framework characterized by minimum thresholds (for urban resources) or maximum thresholds (for environmental nuisances) for all the elements of the urban environment, supported by specific interventions should these thresholds not be respected. With this goal in mind, distributional imbalance related to road transportation could potentially be reduced and it would thus be possible to strive toward a more equitable city for everyone in the North American context. These indexes and indicators represent a tool to potentially help municipalities and boroughs in the search to reduce disparities, as stipulated in local urban planning and development policies and urban planning documents in effect in many contexts of study, particularly in Canada.

6 Further reading

We suggest further readings in line with the concept of environmental equity and the methods to measure equity. Walker and Bulkeley (2006) and Walker (2009, 2011) provide rich discussions of the concept and phenomenon of environmental equity. For a classic reading on environmental equity and planning, we refer to Talen (1998). Key readings in environmental equity and transportation include Feitelson (2002) and Schweitzer and Valenzuela (2004). Finally, Chakraborty (2006), Carrier et al. (2016), and Manaugh et al. (2015) present and discuss different advanced methods for measuring environmental equity in transportation.

Acknowledgments

We thank Mark Goldberg (Department of Medicine, McGill University) and Dan Crouse (University of New Brunswick) for the provision of the NO_2 data pollution. We would also thank the *Director of Direction régionale de santé publique*. Finally, we warmly welcome Anne-Marie Seguin (National Institute of Scientific Research) for her valuable guidance during the project.

References

Apparicio, P., Séguin, A.M., Dubé, J., 2016. Spatial distribution of vegetation in and around city blocks on the Island of Montreal: A double environmental inequity? Applied Geography 76, 128–136.

Carrier, M., Apparicio, P., Séguin, A.M., Crouse, D., 2016. The cumulative effect of nuisances from road transportation in residential sectors on the Island of Montreal–Identification of the most exposed groups and areas. Transportation Research Part D: Transport and Environment 46, 11–25.

Carrier, M., Apparicio, P., Kestens, Y., Séguin, A.M., Pham, H., Crouse, D., Siemiatycki, J., 2016. Application of a Global Environmental Equity Index in Montreal: diagnostic and further implications. Annals of the American Association of Geographers 106 (6), 1268–1285.

Chakraborty, J., 2006. Evaluating the environmental justice impacts of transportation improvement projects in the US. Transportation Research Part D: Transport and Environment 11 (5), 315–323.

Feitelson, E., 2002. Introducing environmental equity dimensions into the sustainable transport discourse: Issues and pitfalls. Transportation Research Part D: Transport and Environment 7 (2), 99–118.

Goldberg, M., Mercer, J., 2011. The myth of the North American city: Continentalism challenged. UBC Press.

Manaugh, K., Badami, M.G., et al., 2015. Integrating social equity into urban transportation planning: A critical evaluation of equity objectives and measures in transportation plans in North America. Transport Policy 37, 167–176.

Schweitzer, L., Valenzuela, A., 2004. Environmental injustice and transportation: the claims and the evidence. Journal of Planning Literature 18 (4), 383–398.

Talen, E., 1998. Visualizing fairness: Equity maps for planners. Journal of the American Planning Association 64 (1), 22–38.

Walker, G., 2011. Environmental justice: concepts, evidence and politics. New York.

Walker, G., 2009. Beyond distribution and proximity: exploring the multiple spatialities of environmental justice. Antipode 41 (4), 614–636.

Safety and daily mobilities of urban women—Methodolgies to confront the policy of "invisibility" 12

Tanu Priya Uteng, Yamini Jain Singh, Tiffany Lam

1 Introduction

This chapter drew its initial momentum from the Indian case, where the previously unspoken issue of "female molestation and rape in public spaces" was being publicly discussed for, what many of us would like to posit, the very first time in the history of the subcontinent. While both mainstream and social media might have given a voice to this previously unacknowledged and highly unsafe status quo of women in public spaces, and might have paved the way for minor wins, "safety of women" has been neither streamlined nor prioritized.

Not surprisingly, the issue of daily mobilities, the ways in which the corporeal dimension of women intersects with their movement, creates varied patterns of unsafe-safe domains.

Gendered norms and values are a socially constructed and propagated phenomenon. Although the cultural elements are difficult to tackle from the perspectives of urban and transport planning, the materiality and physicality of urban structures play a dominant role in sanctioning or challenging the meanings constructed around "gender." From a young age, girls are taught to avoid walking on certain streets after certain hours, being alone in certain neighborhoods, wearing certain types of clothing, etc. These instructions are repeatedly reinforced in the media and from the family and friends, ultimately becoming embedded into societal norms and beliefs.

The resounding message is that cities are unsafe for women and girls. Women often feel the need to alter their routes, clutch their keys or mobile phones, alter their clothing, or modify their behavior when out and alone at night in order to avoid perceived threats. Violence against women, ranging from seemingly benign sexual harassment on city streets to physical acts of violence constricts female access to public space. In particular, perceived and actual threats of violence constrain female mobility in public space. While some efforts are being made to address patriarchy, sexism, and systems of oppression that give rise to everyday inequalities in public space, society still often puts the onus on women worldwide to learn "safety work," as if they can somehow "avoid" sexual harassment and violence.

Given the patriarchal relegation of women to the private sphere, a "public woman" is a seen as woman out of place. The increasing privatization of public space in cities worldwide reduces the availability of space accessible for all, thereby

Measuring Transport Equity. https://doi.org/10.1016/B978-0-12-814818-1.00012-3

disproportionately jeopardizing women's right to the city and abilities to claim public space due to the existing uneven, gendered access to urban public space. *The right to the city*, therefore, is not an abstraction but a concrete demand for safety so that women can freely inhabit public space and participate in public life, without physical or verbal threat.

Ensuring women's safety in public space, therefore, is an equity issue. Without freedom from gender-based harassment and violence, women are less free to be mobile—both physically, in and around the city, and figuratively, in social, political, and economic endeavors—and consequently less able to exercise their right to the city. We, therefore, need to integrate a better understanding of gendered perceptions of safety in urban and transport planning, where it has been and remains markedly absent. The failure of urban designers, planners, and engineers to consider differential gendered experiences of the city compounds structural sexism and other inequalities. Without an understanding of gendered urban mobility, cities cannot be truly inclusive and accountable to diverse and pluralistic populations.

2 Background

The realm of "transportation" often tends to focus on roads, highways, and (public) transport systems while ignoring other dimensions of mobility and the built environment. Consequently, "safety" in the domain of transport is often understood as road/vehicular safety. The issue of people's safety, especially women's, goes beyond that and is affected by the design of our transport systems, access points, and routes to transport stations. In this chapter, we highlight issues around gendered perceptions of safety, gendered transport systems, and gendered mobility, describe indicators to understand and measure safety, and lastly, show the way forward.

Mobility studies worldwide have shown that women and men have different travel patterns: women tend to make more trips, often during off-peak hours, of shorter distances, for multiple purposes; they also depend mostly on public transport, cycling, or walking. This pattern exists in the developing and developed nations alike. Women have complex travel needs as managers of households, working and engaging with communities, taking care of children and the elderly, and often also working to earn. This is not the case of "different but equal," but "unequal burden" of activities or roles placed on women in patriarchal societies, in which men are entitled to the most appropriate, fastest, or most expensive mode of travel. Thus, women also have limited access to private modes of transport, such as cars, that can provide them the personal space and safety that they desire. Women's reliance on public transport, especially buses, and walking is higher in the developing countries, where most women belong to lower- and middle-income groups and cannot afford private modes of transport.

Women's safety on streets and public transport is an important global issue, especially as public transport is paramount for them to pursue educational and work opportunities, often to support their families. Based on past studies, women's safety concerns can be divided into two broad categories: (1) concerns over sexual harassment on public transport or in public spaces in general and (2) concerns regarding poor physical infrastructure provision (the absence of footpaths, street lightings, etc.).

Globally, studies show that compared with men, women's perceptions of safety more significantly govern their use of public spaces. Women typically have lower perceptions of safety in public spaces, due to realities and threats of gender-based violence. Fear and safety concerns have repercussions that extend beyond acts of violence. They influence women's decisions on where they go or which jobs they accept, therefore, affecting the socioeconomic well-being of a considerable demographic in society. Public space and public transport are where many women experience sexual harassment or violence. Sexual harassment and violence in public space and public transport not only limits women's and girls' physical mobility, but also it also decreases their perceptions of safety and community cohesion.

Infrastructure provision, particularly street lighting and public toilets, are tangible examples that underscore the need for a more holistic and nuanced perspective of gendered dimensions of safety. These infrastructural fixtures may seem to be less relevant to transportation, but they support and enable urban mobility and moderate people's comfort and duration in public space. Street lighting mediates women's movement on city streets and public toilets impact women's abilities to linger in public space for extended periods. The treatment of basic infrastructure provisioning, like street lighting and toilets, as gender-neutral issues ignores women's legitimate safety concerns, trivializes violence against women, and normalizes the patriarchal exclusion of women from the public realm.

While most perpetrators of sexual violence against women tend to be people they already know—friends, family, colleagues, acquaintances, etc.—instead of strangers, "stranger danger," the idea of the unknown male sexual predator lurking in the bushes or in an alleyway remains prevalent. The fact that most violence against women will occur in a private setting by an acquaintance does not negate the importance of enhancing women's perceptions of safety in public. Ensuring sufficient street lighting and toilets is the bare minimum that urban planners and engineers can do to facilitate women's safety and mobility; yet, this need remains largely unmet.

Like street lighting, toilet provisioning also tends to be framed as an engineering project. The myopic focus on pipes, plumbing, and "hard" infrastructure results in poorly designed toilets that fail women and girls by causing safety, hygiene, and public health issues. Disabling women's access to safe facilities reinforces patriarchy by endangering women's safety, health, well-being, and lives.

Vegetation also impacts gendered perceptions of safety as it can provide cover for illegal activities by enabling people to hide. For women walking on city streets, geometric landscapes invoke a greater sense of safety than naturalistic vegetation: the former implies a stronger sense of stewardship, greater visual accessibility, and less opportunity for ambush. As such, the urban built environment plays a pivotal role in shaping gendered perceptions of safety. Unlike societal attitudes, behavioral norms, and cultural factors—which also influence gendered perceptions of safety but are intangible and cannot be transformed overnight—the built environment can be used as a medium for more tangible and immediate change, even if small in scale and scope. To optimize the potential of built environment designs and interventions in enhancing women's safety, we first need to understand and evaluate women's safety in cities to then plan accordingly. Some of the methods adopted internationally are elaborated in the following section.

3 Methods to measure and plan for women's safety in urban public spaces

In order to improve women's safety in public urban spaces, we must first identify unsafe areas and understand what makes them unsafe. In that way, we can generate evidence to inform policy, which is also the first commitment of UN champion cities. In this section, we outline three case studies to discuss methodologies to study women's safety in public space. We describe the methods adopted by METRAC's safety audit tool, the Mexico City government's approach, and the Safetipin (2017) smartphone app in India. Through these case studies, we gain insight into different methods across scales, purposes, and contexts that can be applied to other cases.

3.1 METRAC's community safety audit tool

The METRAC pioneered the first Women's Safety Audit in 1989 in Canada. It partnered with the Council of Ontario Universities and Colleges to launch a Campus Safety Audit Process in 1992 and 2 years later, in 1994, it partnered with the Toronto Transit Commission (TTC) to audit public transit. METRAC's Safety Audit tool (see for details of the tool and questionnaire: https://www.metrac.org/resource-category/safety-2/) has been used widely in Canada and other countries like Russia, Poland, Tanzania, and India, among others. People who use certain public spaces or streets conduct its safety audit by walking around the target neighborhood, streets, or areas at night and recording on a questionnaire their feelings of insecurity in relation to the urban design and built environment structures. In advance of the audit, auditors are trained to understand and respond to the questionnaire. After the audit, auditors discuss their results with each other, collectively identify unsafe "hotspots," and come up with creative solutions to safety problems. The results and the recommendations are put together in a Safety Report Card and taken to the responsible authorities for action. People reported the process as empowering since they were consulted as experts and were, therefore, more committed to supporting or implementing solutions.

Under the UN-Habitat's Safer Cities Program, the local UN-Habitat Office in Warsaw, Poland conducted a Women's Safety Audit pilot project in 2007 in the Srodmiescie district in Warsaw's city center (Buckingham, 2009). The project also referred to and adapted METRAC's Safety Audit Tool for their audit. Eight female participants comprising of women from the Warsaw municipality, police headquarters, UN-Habitat office, Chamber of Town Planners, a local nongovernmental organization (NGO), and the media were involved. They walked around the target neighborhood at night with a questionnaire and recorded their observations. An evaluation session was then held to gather the group's findings and joint recommendations for policy makers and urban planners were made. Participants identified concerns

related to lighting, signage, receiving emergency assistance, infrastructural maintenance, and urban amenities. They also suggested improvements to enhance the safety
and design of the neighborhood and creating mixed-use spaces in the neighborhood to
attract more human presence.

3.2   Mexico city safe city and safe public spaces for women and girls program: Scoping and evidence-based interventions

Women in Mexico City rely on public transport more than men: 75% of women who
travel daily use public transport (UN Women, 2017: 7), yet, 90% of women have experienced harassment or violence on public transport (UN Women, 2016). Mexico
City's public transport system is notoriously dangerous for women, as per five indicators: (1) how safe women feel traveling alone at night, (2) risk of being verbally or
physically harassed, (3) likelihood that other passengers would come to their assistance, (4) trust in authorities to investigate reports of harassment or violence, and
(5) availability of safe public transport (Thomson Reuters, 2014). A total of 70%
of women felt their mobility was disrupted or limited so that they could "avoid" sexual
harassment in public: They avoided going out alone or at night, modified their daily
routes, pretended to have a male partner, wore inconspicuous clothing, and avoided
even slight physical contact (Campos et al., 2017: 104). To reduce sexual harassment
and violence on public transport, Mexico City, a UN Women champion city, launched
the "Mexico City Safe City and Safe Public Spaces for Women and Girls program" in
2015, implemented in two steps.

Step 1: Scoping: The National Institute for Statistics and Geography and the Cole-
gio de Mexico conducted a scoping study to gather data on women's experiences of
sexual harassment and violence on public transport to inform women's safety interventions. The scoping study had five objectives: (1) understand women's and girls'
experiences of gender-based violence in public spaces, especially on public transport,
(2) aggregate and analyze data about women's experiences of public harassment and
violence, (3) identify knowledge and data gaps that need to be filled, (4) evaluate existing and forthcoming policies, programs, and resources to improve women's safety in
public spaces, and (5) identify best practices to prevent sexual harassment and violence at the local, national, and international level (Garcia et al., 2017). The
researchers developed a methodological framework to analyze gender-based violence
in Mexico City across three dimensions: (1) public space (i.e., spatial-temporal
aspects of public space usage, gender norms, and feelings of vulnerability), (2) secu-
rity/insecurity (i.e., facts about gender-based violence and perceptions of fear), and (3)
right to free and safe mobility in public space (conditions necessary to enable
women's safe mobility).

The scoping study employed mixed quantitative and qualitative methods, and contained the following five components: (1) an analysis of existing frameworks to com-
bat gender-based violence in institutional and legal documents, (2) aggregating data
about the prevalence of gender-based violence from various national surveys (i.e., the
National Survey on the Dynamics of Household Relations and the National

Victimization Survey and Perception on Public Safety), as well as academic and NGO publications, (3) a review and analysis of legal actions taken to address sexual violence, (4) obtaining data from the Mexico City Survey of Origin and Destination of Trips of Residents, disaggregating it by gender, and contrasting routes and modes of transport, and (5) organizing several focus groups with a diverse sample size (across age, socioeconomic class, and geographic locations) for more qualitative data collection.

Step 2: Evidence-Based Interventions: Mexico City's attempts to reduce sexual harassment on public transport predate its UN Women involvement. In 2008, the government created the Viajemos Seguras program, which entailed the installation of support centers for women to seek assistance and report cases of sexual abuse aboard/around public transport, the launch of the Athena program to provide bus transport exclusively for women, and women-only areas in metrobus and light rail systems (Granada et al., 2016: 18). In response to scoping efforts in 2015 and onwards, the government added two new Athena bus routes and three new support centers in the metro and metrobus systems for women to report and seek help for sexual harassment and violence. In addition, people can file administrative complaints for catcalling, and reported perpetrators must either pay a fine or spend a night in jail (Deb and Franco, 2017). Local authorities have also increased lighting and surveillance at bus stops and other public spaces to enhance women's and girls' safety in the city through gender-aware urban planning.

3.3   Mapping-based exercises to measure and plan for women's safety in urban public spaces (Safetipin)

The first commitment of the UN champion cities is to identify unsafe areas and understand what makes them unsafe. Systematic data collection provides the evidence base to inform the policy. We, therefore, now expand on the concept of hazard mapping and a smartphone app-based tool, SafetiPin, to discuss the mapping methodology being adopted by this tool to generate information as a basis for creating safer public spaces for women. Through this case study, we gain insight into the uptake of this method across scales, purposes, and contexts that can be applied to other cases.

In 2014, an app for women's safety, called "Safetipin" was launched in India to help women navigate the city with less fear by identifying its safe zones (Viswanath, 2016a, b). It is a location-based mobile app that collects safety-related information and conduct safety audits of different places by calculating a safety score. Users of the app can identify how safe certain areas are and can plan their travel routes and timings accordingly.

The safety audit is based on nine parameters:

1. Lighting: refers to the amount of illumination after sunset.
2. Openness: evaluates the availability of clear lines of sight in all directions.
3. Visibility: assesses how visible is one to others on the street.
4. Security: refers to the presence of visible security officers–either police officers or private security guards.

5. Crowd: indicates the number of people in that space–higher is better.
6. Public transport (connectivity): based on the distance to the nearest public transit stop or station.
7. Gender usage: evaluates the proportion of women and children in the crowd and surrounding area.
8. Feelings (of safety): refers to how safe one feels in the area.
9. Presence of footpaths or walkways: indicates whether footpaths and walkways are easily accessible.

Each of these parameters, except for the eighth one, Feelings (of safety), is measured by volunteers using a rubric and scored on a scale of 1–4 (from "poor" to "good" conditions). Below is an example of the rubric used to evaluate the second and third parameters, open and visible (Table 1).

The data on these parameters are collected through trained volunteers of partner organizations, such as NGOs and city governments, and through crowdsourcing from the general public. Interestingly, the data are collected only after 6 pm, when it is (or begins to get) dark to address women's increased vulnerability at dusk. The Safetipin Nite app is another source of data collection. Mobile phones with this app are mounted on the windshields of moving cars to take photographs of the roads, streets, and footpaths at regular intervals. All photographs are geo-tagged and carry time stamps, which are later coded on the abovementioned parameters. A safety score is calculated for each pinned location by aggregating the parameters' scores using the weighted mean function. Adopting this approach, safety audit can be done at different scales, such as street scale, the ward scale, or even for a specific location, like a bus stop. App users can also contribute safety input by posting their own safety-related experiences or observations. The app founders believe that involving people to crowd source data will initiate a broader conversation around safety, thereby inducing positive behavior change. The app also contains a "Track" feature that helps friends and family track the

Table 1 Safetipin—scoring methodology

| Parameter | Scores | | | |
	1	2	3	4
Open	**Not Open** Many blind corners and no clear sightline	**Partly Open** Able to see a little ahead and around	**Mostly Open** Able to see in most directions	**Completely Open** Can see clearly in all directions
Visible	**Not visible** No windows or entrances (to residences/ shops), or street vendors	**Less visible** Less than 5 windows or entrances or street vendors	**Fairly visible** Less than 10 windows or entrances or street vendors	**Highly visible** More than 10 windows or entrances or street vendors

user's movements, be adequately informed about her whereabouts, and even help her raise an alarm if needed.

The safety scores help women make more informed decisions about which places are best to avoid and concerned authorities, like police and urban planners, know about and correct the situation. The safety data are available in multiple forms, including maps, reports, and csv files, which can support urban stakeholders in making judicious urban planning and monitoring decisions, such as identifying areas that need more lighting, security, CCTVs, and/or public transport at night. In 2016, Safetipin also assessed the bus stops and 10 most popular tourist places in Delhi using the same parameters and audit process. Safety audits of metro stations, railway stations, and bus terminals have also been conducted, although the experiences of passengers on transit journeys once aboard metros, trains, and buses have not been assessed. Safetipin has now extended to more than 20 cities, including some outside India, such as Bogota, Manila-Quezon, Jakarta, and Nairobi.

In the following sections, we will elaborate more on the use of Safetipin in the three cities of Delhi, Bogotá, and Nairobi.

3.3.1 Safetipin in Delhi

Delhi, or the National Capital Territory (NCT) of Delhi, is a city and Union Territory of India. It is also one of the five megacities of India with a population that exceeds 16 million. For the city's safety audit, a total of 44,396 safety audits were collected from all over the city, 5296 of which app users conducted and 39,100 of which the Safetipin Nite app generated, covering 3910 km of road length (Bhatla et al., 2012). The audit results showed that half the audited area had a safety score of 4.0 or above on a scale of 1–5. The city's overall safety score was 3.5 and about one-third of the area scored less than 3. Of the nine parameters, security and gender usage received poor ratings while visibility and crowd parameters received below average ratings. Access to public transport facilities was rated as average. Lighting, openness, and the presence of walkways and footpaths were all rated above average. Meanwhile, people's feelings of safety in the city overall were rated as average. The current methodology to calculate a safety score places the most weight on lighting, which, therefore, has the most significant impact on the safety score. Gender usage and visibility come next. Thus, the implications are to improve street and public space lighting, ensure that activities which attract women and children find place in the design scheme, foster walkability, bikeability, active space making, and the notion of "eyes on the street" to improve women's safety in the city (Fig. 1).

3.3.2 Safetipin in Bogotá

Bogotá is the capital and largest city of Colombia with a population of around 8 million. It has 19 localities, or districts, forming an extensive network of neighborhoods. For a total of 19,351 locations, safety audit was conducted by volunteers; the audits

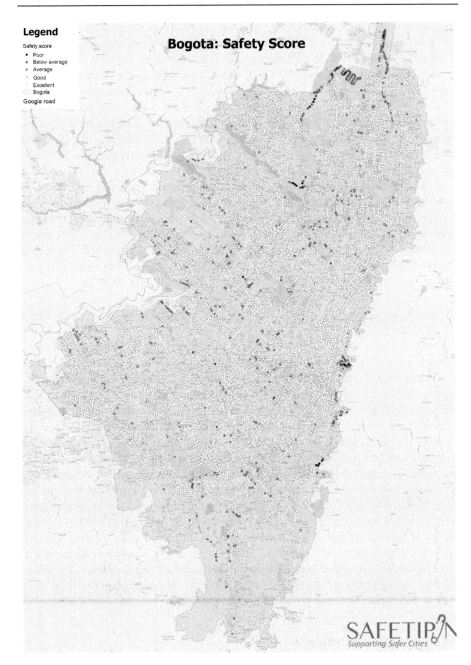

Fig. 1 Safety score for Delhi.

generated through the Safetipin Nite app covered 1927 km of road length. In addition to cars, bicycles were also used to collect data using the Safetipin Nite app. The results of the audits indicate that 81% of the area audited has a safety score of 4.0 or above, which exceeds the safety score of Delhi. Compared to Delhi, in which about a third of audited area scored less than 3, only 4% of Bogota's audited areas scores less than 3 out of 5.

What Bogotá does well that lends itself to a higher safety score includes having properly paved footpaths, separate cycle lanes, and a well-planned bus-rapid transit (BRT) system. This explains why the safety scores are particularly high for the public transport, openness, and visibility parameters. However, the city's streets become inactive post sunset, due to the lack of activity and people out and about, which lowers the scores for the security and gender usage parameters. Meanwhile, people's feelings of safety were rated as average citywide, with a safety score of 4 out of 5. Safety audits should also be conducted aboard public transport to ensure that both the public transport network and the experience of traveling on public transport allow for women's safety. Moreover, creating more vibrant public spaces and street life at night is paramount to increasing women's safety when traveling after dusk (Fig. 2).

3.3.3 Safetipin in Nairobi

Nairobi is Kenya's capital and largest city, with a population of nearly four million. The city is a rapidly growing commercial and economic center of the country. For 11,807 locations and road links, safety audits were conducted in the city: 4956 audits were conducted by app users and 6851 were generated with the Safetipin Nite app, which covered 685 km of road length. About 40% of the area audited scored less than 3 out of 5 and hence, the average safety score for the entire city is only 3.1.

Of the nine parameters, security, gender usage, crowd, and visibility were given a below average rating. This may be due to heavily congested roads and streets, crime, and poverty. As such, it is essential to first focus on providing physical infrastructure in the built environment that is currently missing or inadequate. For example, lighting, footpaths and walkways, access to public transport, and visibility are parameters that relate to infrastructure and could be improved, potentially reducing crowding and thus the risk of harassment and crime. Another important first step is to improve security and enforcement to tackle crime and ensure a safer city. Both considerations—infrastructure improvements and increased security—could help to attract more users to public spaces at night, thereby activating public spaces and public life (Fig. 3).

Figs. 1–3 show the safety scores of the audited locations in the three cities.

3.3.4 From audits to action

The safety scores that Safetipin has generated in these three cities have driven city leaders to take action to improve women's safety. In Delhi, the government commenced a citywide project to improve lighting in the dark spots that Safetipin

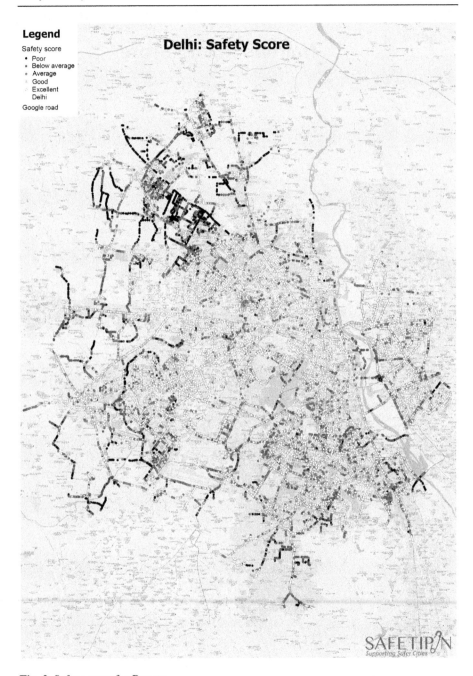

Fig. 2 Safety score for Bogota.

Fig. 3 Safety score for Nairobi.

identified. Between January and March 2017, the Safetipin team accompanied electrical engineers around the city to do site visits, and in April 2017, the government produced a list of roads where lighting improvements had been made, such as the installation of new street lights and the regular pruning of trees that previously blocked lighting. Safetipin subsequently conducted a second round of safety audits in May 2017 in several locations in East and South Delhi to evaluate the lighting improvements using Safetipin Nite, which confirmed that the lighting in both parts of the city had, indeed, significantly improved.

Similarly, in Nairobi, the city council used Safetipin data to identify two neighborhoods for targeted infrastructure improvements, like improved lighting, road infrastructure, solid waste management, public transport, and traffic circulations. A second round of safety audits of lighting and pathways were conducted in March 2017 in one of the intervention areas with the Safetipin Nite app, which also confirmed that infrastructure improvements had increased safety.

In Bogotá, Safetipin has tremendously useful for policy makers in helping to create a data-driven approach to women's safety in public space. City officials have been able to combine data based on the safety audits with other data sources in order to better understand urban problems. For instance, the city was able to overlay maps indicating Safetipin's security parameter rating with maps of police station locations and incidences of crime. Based on Safetipin data, the city identified five priority locations for interventions to generate a broader dialog about women's safety at night that included local operative councils for women and gender, local women's organizations, and citizens. These public engagement activities are key to educating people and changing people's perceptions and attitudes about women, gender, and gender-based violence.

4   Policy relevance

As city leaders increasingly realize that public spaces cannot be truly public and inclusive if half the population feels endangered and unwelcome, there must be more research, monitoring, and impact assessments of interventions to make cities safer for women and girls. Women's safety in public space is a complex issue for which there is no one-size-fits-all solution. Rather, it requires multipronged, mutually reinforcing efforts, including new laws and policies, physical changes in the built environment, "smart" digital innovations, behavioral change campaigns, and education of young generation (in particular men).

Policy making needs to prioritize women's safety in public spaces, particularly city streets and public transportation. This demands an intersectional approach to urban planning making the following fields intersect–urban planning and mobility, public health, education, economic participation, welfare, and social justice. Methods adopted in different contexts to measure women's safety in public space, such as the METRAC Community Safety Audit Tool pioneered in Canada, women's safety audits in Durban, Mexico City's Safe City and Safe Public Spaces for Women and Girls program in collaboration with UN Women, and the Safetipin app to measure women's safety in Delhi, Bogotá, and Nairobi, can act as catalysts in operationalizing future policies.

The overwhelming share of policy attention and program formulation given to physical and digital infrastructure needs to be revisited. Education and creativity is needed to transform social norms and end harassment and violence against women.

An example of an effective campaign to raise awareness and provoke debate around gender-based violence in public space is the #NoEsDeHombres (It's not manly) campaign that UN Women and the Mexico City government launched in March 2017. #NoEsDeHombres targeted men between 20 and 50 years old who commute daily on public transportation and puts the onus on men and men's behavior, which counters typical victim-blaming messages directed at women. The campaign contained filmed social experiments, such as "Experimento Asiento" (experiment with a seat), which went viral online. This video showed people's reactions to subway seats that were changed to look like naked male bodies, including penises, with signs beneath the seats reading, "It is annoying to travel this way, but not compared to the sexual violence women suffer in their daily commutes" (Deb and Franco, 2017).

Digitalization comes with its own set of restrictions and cannot offer a single-handed solution to the entire gamut of challenges to improving women's safety in public spaces. Digital platforms must be supplemented with formal follow-up procedures. Smart innovations in digital space hold much potential to make cities safer and more equitable, but they must include corresponding legal and policy changes, tangible changes in the urban built environment, and behavioral change interventions.

If cities are to be truly liveable, sustainable, and smart for all, we must acknowledge and incorporate women's experiences into the way we design, plan, and govern cities. This requires having difficult and uncomfortable conversations and challenging our own implicit biases. Throughout 2017 allegations of sexual harassment and assault against powerful, wealthy men broke around the world and across industries— politics, academia, entertainment, and technology. Multiple perpetrators have faced consequences, such as resignation, which is unprecedented in a culture that silences, shames, and doesn't believe women. We have arrived at a critical juncture of public reckoning with how and why we live in a society that normalizes and sanctions violence against women. Collectively, we must challenge our culture of silence and complicity and take action to make cities equitable and inclusive for all.

5 Further reading

The final section takes a step back and revisits a few studies and projects which can inform and inspire future research work.

We are increasingly in the world of Big Data and need to be creative in how to harness the potential of big data to inform evidence-based policy making. Data-driven approaches to women's safety are increasingly gaining traction. The three case studies described in this chapter are certainly not the only examples. For instance, Melbourne has launched a campaign [similar to Safetypin app (Viswanath, 2016a, b)] and web-based interactive map "Free to Be" (Kalms et al., 2017), enabling women to report on how safe and welcome they felt in spaces all over the city by dropping "pins" on the interactive, geo-locative map of Melbourne and suburbs. This is just one more example. These micro-initiatives are on the rise across both the developed and developing parts of the world, but a review study of these initiatives is still missing. One way to go forward could be through studying these different tools to reflect on how these different initiatives could inform building a universally applicable robust tool.

Readers interested to gain a deeper understanding of the highly gendered character of infrastructure design, provision, and impacts at all the levels–macro, *meso*, and micro–are kindly referred to Benjamin (1994), Lynch and Atkins (1988), Sham et al. (2013), Sideris and Fink (2008), or Yavuz and Welch (2010). Even when the gendered character of infrastructure provision is more and more acknowledged, the interlinkages with women's opportunities remain often poorly understood. In the background paper prepared for World Bank's 2012 development report on "Gender and Development," Priya Uteng (2011) has attempted to highlight some of these interlinkages, providing fertile grounds for further research focusing on safety. Granada et al. (2016) also provide insight on how the element of "safety" interlocks with access to markets and fair competition, and thus shed light on how lack of safety shapes women's opportunities.

Acknowledgments

We would like to acknowledge Dr. Kalpana Viswanath (cofounder, Safetipin) and Ms. Sonali Vyas (Program Manager, Safetipin) for their cooperation and helpfulness in sharing valuable information about Safetipin that significantly contributed to this chapter.

References

Benjamin, J.M., 1994. Perception and incidence of crime on public transit in small system in the southeast. Transp. J. Adv. Transp. 195–200.

Bhatla, N., Achyut, P., Ghosh, S., Gautam, A., Verma, R., 2012. Safe Cities Free from Violence against Women and Girls - Baseline Findings from The 'Safe City Delhi Programme'. International Center for Research on Women.

Buckingham, S., 2009. Addressing Women's Urban Safety through the Right to the City: UN-Habitat's Women Safety Audit Pilot Project in Warsaw. Poland. Available at http://base.d-p-h.info/es/fiches/dph/fiche-dph-8058.html.

Campos, P.A., Falb, K.L., Hernandez, S., Diaz-Olavarrieta, C., Gupta, J., 2017. Experiences of street harassment and associations with perceptions of social cohesion among women in Mexico City. Salud Publica Mex. 59 (1), 102–105. https://doi.org/10.21149/7961.

Deb, S., Franco, M., 2017. 'Penis seat' causes double takes on Mexico City Subway. New York Times. (March 31). https://www.nytimes.com/2017/03/31/world/americas/penis-seat-mexico-city-harassment.html.

Garcia, A.G., Capobianco, L., Osman, Y., Espinosa, M.A.M., Castro, P.M., Romero, T.I., Saucedo, S.E.G., Mendoza, A.A., 2017. Diagnostico Sobre La Violencia Contra Las Mujeres Y Las Ninas en el Transporte Publico de la Ciudad de Mexico (Diagnostics about

Violence against Women and Girls on Public Transport in Mexico City), UN Women Global Programme for Safe Cities and Safe Spaces for Women and Girls.

Granada, I., Urban, A., Monje, A., Ortiz, P., Perez, D., Montes, L., Caldo, A., 2016. Inter-American Development Bank—The Relationship between Gender and Transport.

Kalms, N., Matthewson, G., Salen, P., 2017. Safe in the city? Girls tell it like it is. 2017, From https://theconversation.com/global.

Lynch, G., Atkins, S., 1988. The influence of personal security fears on women's travel patterns. Transportation 15, 257–277.

Priya Uteng, T., 2011. Gender and Mobility in Developing World, Background Paper for the World Development Report 2012—Gender Equality and Development. World Bank.

Safetipin, 2017. Using Data to Build Safer Cities: Delhi, Bogota, Nairobi. Available at: http://safetipin.com/resources/files/Report%20Cities%20Alliance.pdf.

Sham, R., Hussein, M.Z.S.M., Ismail, H.N., 2013. A dilemma of crime and safety issues among vulnerable Travellers in Malaysian Urban environment. Procedia Soc. Behav. Sci. 105, 498–505.

Sideris, A.L., Fink, C., 2008. Addressing Women's fear of victimization in transportation settings. Urban Aff. Rev. 44, 554–587.

Thomson Reuters, 2014. Ranking the most Dangerous Transport Systems for Women in Major Cities. Available at https://www.thomsonreuters.com/en/articles/2014/most-dangerous-transport-systems-for-women.html.

UN Women, 2016. Improving women's safety in Mexico City, November 28, 2016. http://www.unwomen.org/en/news/stories/2016/11/improving-womens-safety-in-mexico-city.

UN Women, 2017. Safe Cities and Safe Public Spaces: Global Results Report.

Viswanath, K., 2016a. Using data to improve women's safety in cities. Transport. Retrieved from https://blogs.adb.org/blog/using-data-improve-womens-safety-cities-transport.

Viswanath, K., 2016b. Using Data to Improve women's Safety in Cities. (transport. Asian Development Blog).

Yavuz, N., Welch, E.W., 2010. Addressing fear of crime in public space: Gender differences in reaction to safety measures in train transit. Urban Stud. 47, 2491–2515.

Part Four

Social outcomes from transport interventions

Applying a subjective well-being lens to transport equity

Louise Reardon, Lucy Mahoney, Wenbo Guo

1 Introduction

This chapter focuses on equity from a subjective well-being perspective. It argues that it is in interrogating the inequalities in levels of subjective well-being and how these link to objective factors that subjective well-being can shed new light on the nature of transport equity and potential ways in which transport inequity can be mitigated. Subjective well-being is understood here as an individual's own assessment of how they feel their life is going determined by their positive and negative emotional responses and evaluations of their personal experiences. In turn it assumes that it is the individual that is best placed to make a judgment on their own well-being (OECD, 2013). Subjective well-being is often understood in common parlance as a happiness measure, however it is more nuanced than that. Subjective well-being measures enable the understanding of three different key aspects of well-being: the experiential, the eudemonic, and the evaluative (Phillips, 2016).

The experiential aspect of subjective well-being refers to an individual's emotional reaction to an experience, for which happiness could be one such response. The experiential element of subjective well-being derives from a utilitarian understanding of well-being; the experience of pleasure and the absence of pain. In order to measure this aspect of well-being, an individual could be asked to rank how happy/sad/anxious they felt on a scale of 1–10. The eudemonic aspect of subjective well-being refers to the extent to which an individual feels that they are able to fulfill their own potential, and relates to the Aristotelian notion of the process of human flourishing as the embodiment of well-being. This aspect of well-being can be measured by asking individuals to rate on a scale of 1–10 how worthwhile they feel their life is. The evaluative aspect of well-being relates to an individual's contentment with their life overall. This aspect of well-being can be measured by asking individuals to rate on a scale of 1–10 "how satisfied are you with your life overall,".

Advocates for the use of subjective well-being in policy argue that the practice of asking people directly about their well-being, rather than relying on objective proxies, democratizes the basis upon which policy is made. It is the standards and values that the individual has chosen for themselves that becomes the basis on which a society is evaluated, and not the standards of a powerful elite. However, there are two key concerns with the use of subjective well-being measures that need to be considered here. The first is methodological and the second normative.

Measuring Transport Equity. https://doi.org/10.1016/B978-0-12-814818-1.00013-5

Methodologically there have been concerns raised about the validity and reliability of self-report subjective well-being measures. Different individuals may interpret the same subjective well-being question differently for example, or have different thresholds for the number at which they rank "satisfaction" or "worthwhileness" on a scale. Even where a shared understanding could be assumed, there are also concerns that individuals may lie about their level of well-being. There are also concerns that responses are too vulnerable to the respondent's current mood and therefore may not be a reliable reflection of their underlying well-being. However, a growing body of research has alleviated these concerns.

Subjective well-being scores have been found to correspond well with objective indicators of well-being, including the assessments of friends and family, and for instance indicators of health and sleep quality. Furthermore, the use of multiple subjective well-being questions has been found to counteract the risk of random variance. Where only single measures of well-being are used, such as in large-scale surveys (typically due to cost constraints), large sample sizes compensate for potentially low reliability, meaning that national or local indicators can still provide valid information on the well-being of subgroups (e.g., men and women) even if they may be too unreliable to measure the well-being of a single individual.

The second, more normative challenge relates to the notion of the "contented slave." When asked, slaves may consider themselves happy and satisfied with their life. However, in looking at their circumstances objectively, including their absence of freedom and autonomy among other things, an outsider would not consider the individual to be experiencing high levels of well-being. This paradox derives from the potential for an individual's level of aspiration to affect what they consider to be their full potential and what they consider they should rightfully expect from life, which in turn affects the parameters through which they judge their own well-being. The slave, who has come to terms with their captivity, has lower aspirations than the slave who has not adapted to their captivity, and indeed has lower aspirations than an individual who is not enslaved.

There is therefore the risk that rather than measuring the quality of someone's life, subjective well-being measures are actually measuring how well individuals are able to adapt to their present circumstances. However, while there is a considerable body of evidence to show that an individual's level of subjective well-being does not fully adapt to changes in circumstance (e.g., to divorce, bereavement, or unemployment), the risk of the contented slave means that the use of subjective well-being data at the exclusion of objective indicators is an unsatisfactory basis for policy making. Thinking conversely for example, policymaking may risk supporting the discontented rich; those with the highest well-being in objective terms may be the least satisfied by subjective measures and in turn redirect resources from the people who need them most in objective terms.

In using subjective well-being measures as a basis for interrogating transport equity, it is therefore essential that levels of subjective well-being are considered in the context of life circumstances, typically understood through objective indicators. This is best practice as identified by the OECD (2013) and others who not only analyze levels of subjective well-being in relation to demographics such as gender and geographical location, but also in relation to domains deemed necessary for well-being from a needs-based perspective—as necessary preconditions for well-being—such as income, employment, health, relationships, civic engagement, and quality of governance; all of which have relevance to the transport domain.

Utilizing subjective well-being indicators alongside objective indicators therefore enables researchers and policymakers to interrogate the relationship between the social environment (uncovered through objective indicators) and emotion (uncovered through subjective indicators). It may, for example, aid in understanding whether those who are more socially disadvantaged, and therefore have lower levels of well-being in objective terms, also experience the biggest impacts on their subjective well-being from transport interventions. Utilizing subjective well-being alongside objective measures therefore provides a more holistic picture of the well-being impacts on different groups and the well-being trade-offs, and therefore sheds greater light on the nature of transport inequities but also on the potential ways in which the inequities can be reduced and mitigated for.

In this chapter we posit the day reconstruction method (DRM) as one means through which the effect of transport on subjective well-being can be identified. Here we examine the levels of subjective well-being experienced by commuters using different transport modes and show how these levels of subjective well-being can be analyzed in relation to different demographics in order to understand the equity implications. Demographics have been found to play an important role in shaping individual's travel behavior and travel-related subjective experience, for example, those with disabilities, the elderly, children, those on low-incomes and women. Travel is therefore important to analyze from a subjective well-being equity perspective. People with disabilities for example have potentially lower resilience in their schedules and therefore less choice of travel behavior as compared to a nondisabled person and therefore their subjective well-being may be disproportionately affected due to these travel constraints. Low-income groups that may need to rely more heavily on public transport may also be disproportionately affected in terms of the impacts on their subjective well-being.

2 Methodology

The DRM is used to assess how individual's spend their time and how they experience the various activities and contexts of their lives; combining features of time-budget measurement and experience sampling (Kahneman et al., 2004). The DRM requires participants to systematically reconstruct their activities and experiences from the previous day and in doing so builds on the "gold standard" of experience sampling. Experience sampling asks participants to record where they are, what they are doing, and how they are feeling several times throughout a day. Experience sampling therefore reduces the distortion that may occur when respondents are asked to recall information after a time delay and the result is a thick description of a sample of moments experienced by the respondent. However, this is burdensome on the respondent and is often expensive to administer. The DRM reduces this burden and expense through a hybrid approach which combines a time use study with a diary-based technique that can be used to recover subjective experiences.

The time-use dimension of the DRM provides insights into the subjective experiences felt in a specific situation and moment; something that cannot be gleaned from typical subjective well-being surveys which tend to ask questions in generality; for example "Overall, how happy did you feel yesterday?.". In assessing feelings in relation to their context, the DRM therefore goes beyond asking "are you happy?" to asking "when are you happy?" The responses can then be used alongside data on the social circumstances of the individual to better understand the equity impacts of subjective well-being across different demographic groups in relation to these experiences.

The first stage of the DRM requires respondents to recall their previous day through the creation of a diary in which they break down the day in to a series of "episodes," for example "lunch in the park" or "commute home," and recall the approximate times at which each episode began and ended. Episodes might be discerned when the respondent goes to a different location, ends one activity and starts another, or the respondent starts interacting with different people.

The second stage of the DRM is a survey in which the respondents have to answer a series of questions about each episode. These questions include what they were doing during the episode (ticking one or more from a list of provided options) such as "eating," "sleeping," and "housework"; where they were during the episode, for example at home or work; and how they felt during the episode. Respondents are required to report the intensity of their feelings relating to each activity (or episode) from their diary on a scale from 0 ("not at all") to 6 ("very much"), through 12 affective dimensions including happy, sad, anxious, focused, for example. For methodological reasons it is important that respondents complete the DRM diary before they are aware of the survey questions that relate to the diary. This is because early knowledge of the survey questions may affect day reconstruction and introduce selection bias.

The third stage of the DRM is to ask a number of contextual and demographic questions of the respondent relating, for example, to the nature of their job and household.

Once this data have been collected, the DRM allows for the examination of the "spill-over effects" of an episode on a person's moment-to-moment mood. Spill-over effects occur when a problem arising from the preceding time period or its effects persist, because an individual has been unable to cope with an issue, or because it takes some time to cope with the issue successfully. Examining these spill-over effects enables a deeper understanding of the psychological processes and emotions before, during and after undertaking activities and coupled with analysis of life circumstances allows discerning equity impacts of SWB over time for one individual, and across demographic groups.

We propose that as a fourth stage and as a compliment to the standard DRM, the addition of a semistructured interview with each respondent. These interviews are an important compliment to the DRM because they provide a better understanding of the respondent's life circumstances and the rationale for decisions on activities to be better understood. Interview data also aid the triangulation of the findings from the DRM survey. Therefore, these methods in combination allow researchers to measure equity between respondents. Socio-demographic data of each participant is recorded, subjective well-being data in relation to activities is collected through the survey, and more detail on the activities and potential reasons for well-being levels are discussed with participants through interview.

3 Application

Here we apply the DRM approach to gain a fuller picture of equity in subjective well-being of transport users in and around the Pont-y-Werin walking and cycling bridge in Cardiff, Wales (more details on the study are provided in Section 5). The study collected, analyzed, and evaluated empirical data gathered in 2011 with a follow-up DRM survey and interview in 2012. Participants were recruited through the edited electoral register. The 402 households contacted for this study consisted of adults aged 18 years and over who live in private residential accommodation within a defined buffer zone around the Pont-y-Werin Bridge. Approximately 50% of participants lived in buffer zone A (i.e., within 0.5 km of the bridge; 200 households); 34% of participants in buffer zone B (between 0.5 and 1 km of the bridge; 136 households) and 16% of participants lived in buffer zone C (between 1 and 1.5 km of the bridge; 66 households). Households who lived outside buffer zone C were excluded. Households varied socio-demographically with respondents' ages ranging from 23 to 77 and from single occupancy homes to families of five. In terms of socioeconomic classification, approximately one-third of respondents are classed as A/B (employers/managers/high professionals), one-third classed as C/D/E (lower professional/nonmanual) and one-third F/G/other (semiskilled/unskilled/other, i.e., retired).

Each household received a recruitment pack and a 35% response rate was achieved with 141 respondents. To reach the final sample ($N = 60$), further criteria were applied to exclude respondents with a low-to-moderate intention to increase their active travel levels ($N = 81$). The final sample focused on respondents who "had intentions to do more active travel over the coming months" and who had stated a moderate-to-high intention to increase their active travel levels (with or without a long-term illness). These respondents were targeted to ensure that people who travel actively, or who intend to travel actively were represented and that the sample was not disproportionately dominated by car or public transport users. This way the effects of transport on well-being could be captured for all modes. Across April to June 2011, 60 households took part in DRM surveys and household interviews, the follow-up data collection (i.e., DRM surveys and household interviews) in June 2012 received a 30% attrition rate with 42 households taking part.

In accordance with the DRM, respondents were first asked to create a short diary which consisted of a sequence of episodes to help revive memories and re-instantiate the previous day. Respondents then used their completed diaries to answer a series of structured questions about each episode. The survey first asked respondents to state the duration of the episode, with start and end times, and whom they were interacting with (e.g., alone, spouse, children, boss, and pets). The survey asked respondents to tick any of 20 activities that may have applied to the episode, including "shopping," "voluntary work," and "exercise."

Table 1 Key dimensions of subjective wellbeing included in the survey

	Affective dimension
Experiences	Happy, relaxed, frustrated, sad, anxious, impatient, engaged, focused, competent
Eudemonia	Worthwhile and meaningful, benefitted someone else, helped achieve goals
Evaluation	Day satisfaction, life satisfaction

There was also an "other" option where respondents could provide their own answer if they felt none of the suggested activities were appropriate.

As there was a specific interest in transport and travel in this application of the DRM several modes of transport were given as activities (e.g., cycling, walking, taking the bus, using the car) in order to provide more detail to an activity that may otherwise have only been understood as "going to and from work," for example. Respondents were then asked to report the intensity of their feelings for each of the episodes on a scale from 0 ("not at all") to 6 ("very much") in order to identify the activities and other factors that affect subjective well-being. The factors cover the three key dimensions of subjective well-being discussed in the introduction: experiential, eudemonic, and evaluative Table 1).

A semistructured interview was then conducted with each respondent. The focus of each interview was on transport and travel, in particular the journey to work/school and how they moved around their local area. Questions included by what mode these journeys were typically made; how much time each of these journeys typically takes; whether the respondent considered it possible to do these journeys by foot or on bicycle (if not the stated mode) and the reason for this; and whether they had considered using a different mode of transport for each of the discussed journeys. Such questions can help assess fairness by unlocking discussions on whether modes are "chosen" or are in fact the only viable option for individuals. This enables policymakers to delve into social disparities in income, age, gender, location, and the social consequences of such differences and how this then links to subjective well-being.

Of those respondents who commuted to work every day by car (or if retired, before retirement), 31% were socioeconomically classified as A/B, 53% were classified C–G (16% were retired). Of those who commuted everyday by sustainable modes 62% were A/B and 38% C–G. Of those who alternated their commute through a combination of car and sustainable modes, 45% were classified A/B, and 55% C–G. The findings of the DRM analysis in this study found that all groups experienced less pleasant emotions during travel compared to all other everyday activities, in line with other research findings. When assessing overall changes in happiness before and after use of transport, the study found that drivers were more relaxed than public transport users. Public transport users were 16% less relaxed when compared to drivers, and were 30% less focused. Drivers were also 37% more engaged than public transport users in the activities immediately after the transport episode.

Examining this through an equity lens and linking mode to socioeconomic status, the results demonstrate that more individuals with a "lower" socioeconomic status are commuting by car and therefore not experiencing the worst subjective well-being outcomes; they are more relaxed and engaged in activities post travel than those who are traveling by public transport. However, transport poverty research has found that lower income groups often have little choice but to own a car in order to get to work or support family and this therefore has a disproportionate effect on their income and increasing financial stress, with negative consequences for subjective well-being.

The findings also show inequity across time of travel. For example, when comparing weekday and weekend travel, the weekday drivers spend 9% more time experiencing more unpleasant emotions. Again, understanding who is driving at the weekend as opposed to the weekday is vital for identifying fairness in transport outcomes. This suggests that the well-being of those drivers who are working during the week is more negatively affected than those who travel to work at the weekends. Furthermore, when comparing rush hour driving to rush hour active travel, for 11% of the time, active travelers are experiencing more pleasant emotions than drivers. Finally, comparing nonrush hour driving against nonrush hour walking and cycling, 13% of experiences for nonrush hour active travel users are more pleasurable. In our sample, it is those in higher income groups that more readily travel by these active travel modes and therefore disproportionately benefit from the subjective well-being benefits of these travel modes.

The main findings from the spill-over analysis are that car drivers have 32% higher levels of happiness than public transport users after transport activities. Furthermore, levels of relaxation reported before and after a transport episode by public transport users were significantly lower than those reported by walkers, cyclists, and drivers. Additionally, public transport users perceive activities undertaken after a transport activity to be 22% less worthwhile and meaningful when compared to drivers. The longitudinal data were pooled to identify whether a larger sample would replicate these findings. Overall, while data pooling did reduce the magnitude of the effects of public transport episodes observed, mean levels of happiness, relaxation, engagement, focus, competence, worth and meaningfulness generally remained lower for public transport users in the episodes after their transport activity, than for drivers.

The pooled data and findings suggest that people using public transport suffer a disproportionate impact on their subjective well-being than those who drive, walk, or cycle; they are generally less happy and less relaxed for example. Importantly for policy however, after the study's longitudinal data were pooled, the mean levels of subjective well-being (i.e., happiness, relaxation, engagement, focus, competence, worth and meaningfulness indicators) of activities for public transport users generally remained lower during posttransport activity than for car drivers, showing a sustained impact on subjective well-being for the public transport group. While public transport may be one in a range of mode choices for many travelers, those who have no choice but to use public transport, because they are not old enough, able, or cannot afford to drive, and for which walking and cycling are not considered an option (e.g., because of commute distance, health reasons, or other perceived barriers such as safety risks), are compelled to use a mode that has a potentially detrimental or suboptimal effect on their subjective well-being.

Further to this, the study examined the impact of transport interventions at the household level. The findings highlighted, in particular, the impacts on children and young adults. Parents looked to establish active travel habits for their children by suggesting that they should be encouraged to engage critically with active travel to establish social norms. Parents, however, perceived a trade-off between fostering independent mobility and ensuring their child's safety with 34% of respondents agreeing that the roads in Penarth and Cardiff were still too dangerous for walking and cycling, and 11% expressing fears for their children's safety due to their vulnerability, experience, and confidence levels.

Conversely, for young adults active travel fostered wider access to opportunities and improved mobility as well as a perceived increase in independence for themselves and their parents. This freedom can have a substantial impact on the well-being of young adults, and therefore their families. It can therefore be suggested that travel behavior and well-being are linked through improved opportunities for increased life satisfaction, improved experiences and activities, and greater opportunities for personal flourishing. All of which are important for later social outcomes.

The use of the DRM crucially permits the measurement and comparison of an array of subjective variables across a diverse sample of respondents. Moreover, in providing a framework through which such variables could be measured periodically throughout a single day, this method facilitated the identification of broad patterns and trends in the time-based relationships between individuals' travel behavior choices, other everyday activities, and their subjective well-being. However, taken alone, the quantitative data supplied by the DRM provide limited insight into the meanings, beliefs, and deeper experiences of respondents. Understanding these intangible meanings, beliefs and values is vital in order to enable the researcher to generate more nuanced interpretations of the underlying causes of the broad patterns and trends in well-being identified through the DRM.

The DRM analysis demonstrated effects of travel on subjective well-being by revealing differences in reported well-being during transport episodes and also average overall reported well-being across the day. The qualitative interviews however reveal nuances behind DRM survey responses suggesting that the relationships between transport behaviors and subjective well-being are not intrinsic to individual transport modes but rather are context-dependent (e.g., public transport is perceived by some as unreliable and not clean, while many cyclists are happier not just because they enjoy the experience of cycling as a form of mobility, but also because they want to be healthier, contribute to a wider environmental cause, and save money).

Therefore, the relationships between transport behavior and subjectively measured elements of well-being should be understood as governed not only by affective experiences of mobility, but also by the wider structures of meaning within which respondents interpret the nature and characteristics of the transport mode itself. Given spatial and demographic constraints, the successful redistribution of the subjective well-being benefits of travel by various modes therefore entails more than just the nudging of people to use one mode instead of another, but rather requires that all transport options are accessible and considered viable options regardless of motivations.

4 Policy relevance

The application of the DRM outlined here goes only a small way into analyzing the potential equity implications of transport on subjective well-being, by reflecting on the nature of the demographics that use the transport modes, and how these modes link to levels of subjective well-being. However, there are many other ways in which transport equity in relation to subjective well-being can be analyzed—for example, spatially in relation to commutes within and between different areas, gender, and age. Each of which may have relevance for different areas of policy.

In relation to the application of the DRM outlined here, the lower levels of well-being experienced by public transport users supports the notion that improving not only the availability and reliability of public transport, but also the quality of the experience of the mode itself, may help to bolster levels of subjective well-being. The higher levels of well-being experienced by those using active travel also highlights the value of facilitating access to walking and cycling through infrastructure investment and transport and land-use planning.

Perceptions of independence and freedom, as well as actual and perceived safer routes, between Penarth and Cardiff also positively affected children and young adults' mobility and well-being in the study households, suggesting a role for education and training as part of the transport policy mix. Moreover, it must also be recognized that subjective well-being changes experienced by individuals can impact on the well-being of others. Therefore, policy evaluations should not only examine the immediate well-being consequences of infrastructure interventions, but also their wider ramifications beyond the individuals who use them.

More broadly, the collection of subjective well-being data in and of itself adds a new dimension to understanding equity impacts and casts a new light on, and can challenge, the traditional assumptions of policymaking. In relation to its application to understanding the emotional effects of travel, for example, the widely held assumption is that individuals will trade-off the negative effects of a journey in order to maintain their well-being. An individual might accept a longer commute in order to have a larger house in the suburbs, and might live closer to work if they do not want to suffer the effects of a longer commute. However, most disadvantaged groups may not have the luxury of this trade-off and may have a long commute coupled with poor living conditions. Even assuming such a choice, the application of the DRM shows that this trade-off is not straightforward. There is still a well-being affect related to the journey, not only in relation to the time the journey takes, but also the mode. This in turn has an effect on well-being posttravel such as work and time with family, and therefore transport and travel should be considered in relation to employment and social policy, rather than as a "transport" issue in isolation. It also begs for a wider range of transport interventions to be taken seriously, for example not only speeding up journeys (seen as integral to productivity), but also enhancing the quality of the experience while on a journey (regardless of time).

The availability of subjective well-being data also means that the actual and potential impact of policy interventions on well-being can be known and considered explicitly within the policy process, including in cost–benefit analysis and project evaluation. Subjective well-being indicators can therefore help resolve the "apples versus oranges problem" of deciding which policy option should take priority by providing a standard unit of comparison.

However, as discussed above, due to concerns over the "contented slave" it is important that these subjective elements are considered alongside objective factors that are also integral to well-being, such as health, income, and effect on the environment.

The power of quantifying the subjective element of well-being, however, is that it brings well-being into the policy equation, where it is commonly overlooked at present due to the power of appraisal mechanisms and current cost–benefit analysis techniques that bias toward economic impacts, rather than more socially orientated ones.

However, a subjective well-being orientated understanding of equity requires a policy approach that is not just data driven (be this data "subjective" or objective). A well-being approach recognizes that the factors that contribute to well-being are people and community orientated rather than driven by systems and processes and in turn requires policy actors to address inequalities in well-being by working across boundaries rather than in policy silos. Subjective well-being research recognizes the importance of personal resources such as trust and autonomy as an integral to subjective well-being. To build these personal resources requires a policy process that builds personal capabilities rather than relying on the implementation of top-down choices. Therefore, inequities in subjective well-being will not be rectified through new infrastructures or behavioral incentives alone, but through enabling the participation of those experiencing lower levels of well-being, in the policy process. Enabling conversations about what is important for them in relation to transport and travel, and the subsequent identification of policy priorities within a deliberative forum.

5 Further reading

Explicit and systematic attention on well-being within policy has been on the rise over the past two decades, as discussed by Booth (2012) and Bache and Reardon (2016), among others. Well-being is increasingly being used by governments around the world as a performance indicator (O'Donnell et al., 2014) and organizations like the OECD (2013) have developed guidelines regarding the measurement of well-being and its use in policy.

The attention on well-being in relation to transport is more recent. Nordbakke and Schwanen (2014) have developed a theoretical framework for linking well-being and mobility, while Reardon and Abdallah (2013) provide an overview of the literature and present a research agenda. The complex trade-off between the commute length, housing and job location, and well-being and satisfaction with travel is discussed by Stutzer and Frey (2008).

The DRM employed in this chapter has been developed by a range of authors, notably by Kahneman et al. (2004). Diener and Tay (2013) provide an accessible overview of the method and its advantages and disadvantages.

This chapter is based on the PhD Thesis by Mahoney (2015), who has carried out detailed analyses of the interactions between travel behavior and well-being.

References

Bache, I., Reardon, L., 2016. The Politics and Policy of Wellbeing: Understanding the Rise and Significance of a New Agenda. Edward Elgar, London.
Booth, P. (Ed.), 2012. … and the Pursuit of happiness: Wellbeing and the role of government. Institute of Economic Affairs, London.

Diener, E., Tay, L., 2013. Review of the day reconstruction method (DRM). Soc. Indic. Res. 116 (1), 255–267.

Kahneman, D., Krueger, A.B., Schkade, D.A., Schwarz, N., Stone, A., 2004. A survey method for characterizing daily life experience: The day reconstruction method. Science 306, 1776–1780.

Mahoney, L. (2015) Investigating the Interactions of Travel Behaviour and Wellbeing: A Mixed-methods Case Study of Penarth and Cardiff, Wales, Unpublished PhD thesis, presented to University of Oxford, Oxford.

Nordbakke, S., Schwanen, T., 2014. Wellbeing and mobility: a theoretical framework and literature review focusing on older people. Mobilities 9 (1), 104–129.

O'Donnell, G., Deaton, A., Durand, M., Halpern, D., Layard, R., 2014. Wellbeing and Policy. Legatum Institute, London.

OECD, 2013. OECD Guidelines on Measuring Subjective Well-being. OECD Publishing, Paris. Available from: https://doi.org/10.1787/9789264191655-en. (Accessed 13 June 2018).

Phillips, D., 2016. Quality of Life: Concept, Policy and Practice. Routledge, London.

Reardon, L., Abdallah, S., 2013. Well-being and transport: taking stock and looking forward. Transp. Rev. 33 (6), 634–657.

Stutzer, A., Frey, B., 2008. Stress that doesn't pay: the commuting paradox. Scand. J. Econ. 110, 339–366.

Social impact assessment: The case of bus rapid transit in the City of Quito, Ecuador

14

Alvaro Guzman Jaramillo, Ian Philips, Karen Lucas

1 Introduction

This chapter presents an approach to assess the equity of public transport provision in a metropolitan context in the Global South. In Quito, the principal public transport improvement in recent years has been bus rapid transport (BRT). This intervention is relevant for measuring equity as the social benefits of the introduction of BRT projects in developing cities are increasingly being questioned, and in particular their ability to satisfy the unmet transport needs of the poor. The scope of this chapter is to present a high-level strategic analysis for use by policymakers at the initial stages of their investigations into the equity implications of (proposed) BRT interventions.

In practice, a delicate balance between the positive and negative economic, environmental, and societal impacts of transport projects often needs to be achieved within the decision-making process. This sometimes requires difficult trade-offs between one area of impact and another. In order to make such trade-offs, decision-makers, both in the public and private spheres of influence, need to be able to employ robust assessment tools, so that they can formulate and support their decision processes based on evidence. Making the (possibly less obvious) social benefits and disbenefits more visible to transport decision-makers is part of the process to ensure that the most appropriate interventions to achieve the desired policy outcome are taken forward–in this case transport equity.

We analyze the disparity between public transport need and public transport supply to measure equity. Equity issues arise when the disparity is too large. We will specify how we define "too large" in what follows.

Our intention is that the measurement of transport equity is kept simple as it is to be conducted in the early stages of the planning process. Furthermore, we have developed a tool that utilizes open source government datasets, as these are increasingly being made readily available online, also in the Global South. The method we present does not assess individual need, but is rather an *area-based measure*, which also takes account of the social characteristics of the population within areas, specifically focusing on multiple dimensions of deprivation. The actual travel needs of individuals living within these areas should subsequently be investigated in more depth using follow-up techniques which are briefly described at the end of this chapter.

Measuring Transport Equity. https://doi.org/10.1016/B978-0-12-814818-1.00014-7

The main aim of this chapter is to present a basic method, which can be easily replicated by policymakers in their assessment of the social equity of major new transport infrastructure projects, and to demonstrate its application in a "real-world" case study of Quito, Ecuador's capital city. The applied case study seeks to better understand the specific accessibility effects of the implementation of the BRT focused transport system in the Quito case study area, using an index of public transport disparity.

2 Approach

This section explains, in general terms, the proposed method for analyzing equity in the provision of public transport. The key steps of the proposed method are as follows: (1) assessment of public transport needs by calculating a need index, based on need of index deprivation data; (2) assessment of public transport supply by calculating a supply index, which is designed to quantify the level of public transport service; and (3) calculation of disparity between need and supply by calculating a disparity index. All calculations are carried out using GIS-based analysis and publically available datasets.

2.1 The need index

In many cities, particularly in Latin America and other regions of the Global South, the population in highly deprived areas is reliant upon public transport to meet their mobility needs. This is caused by low car ownership rates and the spatial separation of peripheral poorer residential areas and the concentration of economic activity in city centers, among others. Given the strong correlation between socioeconomic status, residential location, and the need for efficient (public) transport service, indicators of deprivation represent an appropriate proxy for public transport need.

The need index uses a statistic called the index of unsatisfied basic need which is commonly abbreviated as "IBD." It is a composite measure, which captures the level of deprivation in residential neighborhoods. It was developed by the Economic Commission of Latin America and the Caribbean (ECLAC) during the 1980s. The need index is an indicator which is calculated for all the countries that are members of ECLAC (i.e., all South American Countries and the Caribbean) (IBD data, n.d.). The dimensions of the need index are housing quality, access to drinking water, sewage disposal, access to education, economic status, and overcrowding. It is used here because this data is available for many (Latin American) countries, not just in the case study described further, and our method can thus be easily employed in other cities. The need index, like many similar measures of deprivation, is calculated using census data. Census-based deprivation measures provide a way to create a single measure of deprivation in every neighborhood within a region.

When calculating the need index for each zone in a study area, the number of households in the area whose basic needs are not met are recorded. This value is then divided by the total number of households in the area. The result is then multiplied by 100 to gain a percentage, providing a value between 0% and 100%. A value of 0 indicates that there are no households whose basic needs are unmet. A value of 100 indicates that none of the households in the zone has their basic needs met. Note that the set of variables used to determine whether basic needs are met can be adjusted to local circumstances, depending on the situation in a region or country, for instance regarding the availability of particular services.

2.2 The supply index

There are many ways in which public transport supply can be measured, and the actual use of a particular measure will depend upon data availability, among others. In our method, a minimum requirement is that the supply index captures the number of stops in an area and the frequency of services at each stop.

2.3 The disparity index

Finally, the index of public transit deprivation (disparity index) measures the gap between the two components: the need index and the supply index. Before measuring the disparity gap, it is useful to think about the range of values in the needs and supply indices. For example, if the need index has values ranging from 1 to 100 and the supply index has values ranging from zero to one, the need index will have a bigger influence on the disparity index. If both the needs and supply indices have a range of values from zero to one, they will have equal importance. In our approach we assume need and supply have the same importance. We thus converted the need index and supply index so that they both have a minimum value of 0 and a maximum value of 1. It is similar to converting money from two different currencies into one, so that it is easier to compare them. This process is called "normalization" and most spreadsheets, statistics software and GIS software can perform this conversion. (See Jaramillo et al., 2012 in further reading for a detailed explanation of this method.)

The disparity index measures the gap between deprivation (the need index) and public transit provision (the supply index) in each census area. For each census area, the disparity index is equal to the need index minus the supply index. If both the needs and supply indices have a range of values from zero to one, a value of −1 indicates that a census area has no deprived inhabitants and the highest level of public transport provision in the city. A value of +1 indicates that all inhabitants in an area live in deprivation and that the area also has the poorest level of public transport provision in the city. Note that this index describes differences between whole areas, not the situation of individuals living within these areas, which can vary to some lesser or greater extent depending on the homogeneity of the population in each area. This is an issue to be analyzed at a later stage, once the key areas of inequity have been identified.

The data should be mapped to illustrate the spatial variation of the index of public transport deprivation (disparity index). Any GIS and data manipulation software could be used (R and QGIS software were used in the following application). We map the data by grouping the values into quintiles (five groups each containing one-fifth of the census areas, with quintiles distinguished based on disparity index scores). We have used quintiles as they are often used by practitioners to set thresholds for different sectors of the population, for example, income quintiles. Quintile maps are useful when comparing several mapped inputs and where we want to find a set of areas which are likely to be experiencing disparity.

3   Application of the method

3.1   Case study description

The case study city, Quito, the capital of Ecuador, is located at an altitude of 2800 m, in a narrow and long valley which has forced the urban growth northwards and southwards. As of 2017, the city was approximately 44 km long and 3–8 km wide. In recent decades, the city has grown considerably. The population grew from 1.4 million people in 1991 to 2.2 million inhabitants in 2015 and is expected to grow to 2.7 million by 2020. The urbanized area grew by approximately 500%, while the population density decreased from 213 to 68 inhabitants per hectare. During this period, new residential areas for the lower income segments of the population appeared in the urban peripheries. This has produced urban sprawl, as is particularly evident in the 2015 map in Fig. 1.

The central area, which includes the historic town and its immediate surroundings, is also known as the extended center (Fig. 2 Centro extendido). Despite urban sprawl, the majority of jobs, services and other opportunities are still concentrated in the extended center.

The extended city center has an increasing number of services such as health, leisure activities, and education; it is also the area with better-paid jobs and better quality of life. On the other hand, the peripheries, diverse in character, have a concentration of the population with the lowest level of quality of life, education, and jobs, their settlements and areas of leisure are characterized by overcrowding, while services are often absent or in decline. As a result, residents of poorer peripheral areas, where

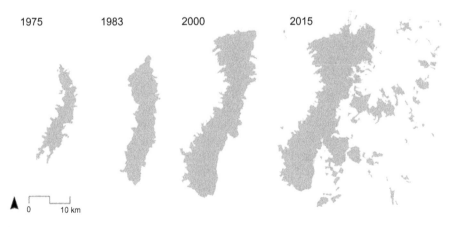

Fig. 1 Quito-Urban Growth.

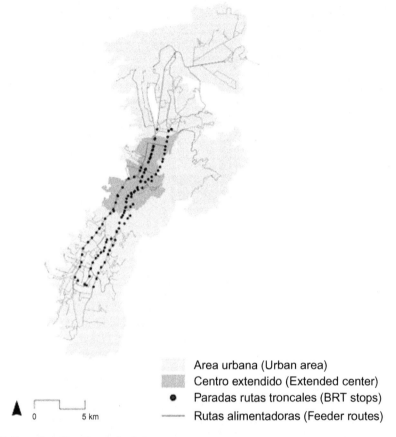

Area urbana (Urban area)
Centro extendido (Extended center)
● Paradas rutas troncales (BRT stops)
—— Rutas alimentadoras (Feeder routes)

0   5 km

Fig. 2 Extended City Center in dark gray.

car ownership is very low, rely heavily on public transport to access the opportunities concentrated in the city center.

The car ownership rate in Quito is still quite low, estimated at 120 per 1000 people, which is approximately double that for Ecuador as a whole (by comparison the European average is approximately 500 per 1000 people). In recent years, new gated communities have been developed in the suburban areas for higher-income car owners, with new highway infrastructures to support their use. This model of development has encouraged further capital investment in the renovation of the existing city center and intensification of high revenue land uses. Further out in the periphery, in contrast, there is a constant growth of the population through inward migration from the surrounding region and beyond, but with a very low provision of physical infrastructures or economic opportunities. The consequence of this in terms of transport is the need for high mobility to access opportunities in the center of the city. Households without access to a car and poorly served by public transport have constant difficulties accessing the better opportunities of the labor market, education, cultural, and leisure activities.

Fig. 3 Ecovia System Quito.
Source: ITDP.

Prior to the early 1990s, public transport routes were determined by the existing transport provider cooperatives, with the system operating in a largely deregulated way except for fares being set by the national government. There was no local government or service user input. Historically, the bus system has suffered several conflicts around fares and contracts, with no investment in service improvement and ad-hoc staffing arrangements. The practical problems included that full-size buses were effectively being operated in the same manner as paratransit. This basic phenomenon was repeated in many different parts of Latin America and elsewhere in the Global South. In addition to these governance issues, the fleet, made up of regular buses and smaller buses (called "colectivos" and "busetas"), was old and poorly maintained, creating emissions and noise problems exacerbated by the altitude (2800m). The spatial coverage of services was also poor.

In 1998, the transit system was brought under a new authority. The transport strategy included adding a BRT backbone (see Fig. 3) along the valley to the existing bus system, improving the bus fleet and eliminating redundant services. The first section of BRT infrastructure opened in 1999. Currently there are five BRT corridors concentrated along the valley through the extended center, with a total length of 69 km, 101 stations, and 11 transfer stations. There are also key feeder bus routes extending the reach of the BRT system but not covering all peripheral areas (see Fig. 2).

3.2 Application of the disparity index methodology to Quito

The analysis was conducted at the level of census areas within the Quito metropolitan district. The Quito metropolitan district is divided into 5993 census areas. Each census area in the urban area is composed of one or two residential blocks. The number of inhabitants recorded as living in each census area on the day of the census has a

Table 1 Index of unsatisfied basic needs (need index)–dimensions and variables used in Quito, Ecuador

Basic needs	Dimensions	Census variable
Access to dwelling	Quality of the dwelling	Construction materials of the floor, walls and roof
Access to Sanitary Services	Access to drinking water	Source of supply of water
	Excreta Elimination	Access to sewage
Access to Education	Children between 6 and 12 years who do not go to school	Age of dwellers
	Scholarity level of the Head of Household is less than 2 years	Assistance to education
Economic Capacity	There are more than 3 persons per working person in the Dwelling	Age of dwellers
		Highest level of education Number of dwellers Economic activity
Overcrowding	Number of persons per bedroom is more than three	Number of People
		Number of Rooms

Source: National Statistics Office of Ecuador: http://app.sni.gob.ec/sni-link/sni/Portal%20SNI%202014/ ESTADISTICA/Reportes/indicadores_pnbv/fichas/26.pdf.

maximum of 2033 inhabitants, a minimum of 0 with an average of 371 persons. Non-urban Census Areas (with less than five persons per hectare) were excluded from the analysis. The indicators are calculated for each of the remaining census areas (a total of 5606 areas).

As previously stated, the equity assumption is that the more deprived a population group, the more it depends on public transport. This is because in the more affluent parts of cities people are more likely to be able to solve their travel needs by using cars or getting a lift or paying for private taxis.

In Table 1, the component parts of the need index in Quito are listed (National Statistics Office of Ecuador, n.d.). In Fig. 4A, a map of the need index is shown in the left-hand panel, based on a differentiation of the population into five deprivation quintiles (five groups each containing one-fifth of the census areas). The lightest areas are the least deprived and the darkest areas are most deprived. In the most deprived quintile over 44% of the population of each census area are living with unsatisfied basic needs, i.e., in deprivation. The population of the most deprived quintile totals 373,376 people, which is 17% of the population. The spatial pattern of deprivation shows generally less deprivation close to the city center because this area is the center of economic opportunity. Deprivation is more pronounced in the peripheral areas where low-income residential areas have been built during the period of urban sprawl and inward migration, as described above.

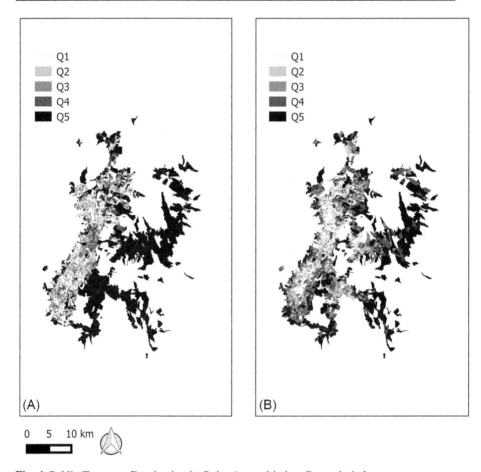

Fig. 4 Public Transport Deprivation in Quito A: need index, B supply index.

The supply index which is an indicator of public transport provision was produced with data provided by the Municipality of Quito (METRO-DE-QUITO, 2011). It is calculated as follows for each census area. The supply index is equal to the number of stops in that census area multiplied by the average capacity of busses stopping there multiplied by the average bus frequency. This number is subsequently divided by the population of the census area. The calculation of the supply index for each census area identifies the areas with low public transport provision and areas with high public transport provision, relative to the population. The provision of public transport was calculated for a weekday, but similar analysis for weekends can also be relevant in determining levels of access to leisure pursuits and for certain groups of workers (e.g., health care workers).

Fig. 4B areas present an overview of the level of public transport provision relative to the population for each census area (dark-shaded areas are poorly served; light-shaded areas enjoy the highest service provision). Quintile 5 of the supply index is the fifth of census areas with the lowest supply index values. They have no public transport provision at all. The combined population of the census areas in quintile five

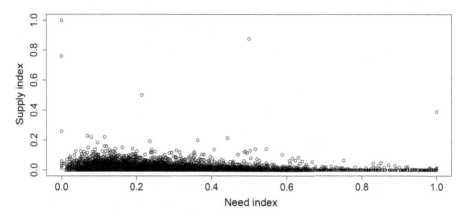

Fig. 5 The relationship between the need index and the supply index.

of the supply index is 520,000 people, which is 24% of the population. The location of this group can be seen in Fig. 4B by those areas shaded darkest (quintile 5). Note that the darkest areas in Fig. 4B are generally in the same areas as those shaded darkest (and most deprived) on the need index map Fig. 4A. Quintile 1 of the supply index is well served by BRT stops and feeder services (442,000 people or 21% of the population). Note that in Quito the supply index is highly skewed, with relatively few census areas enjoying high public transport supply while most have very low levels. The reasons for this spatial pattern are, first, that the BRT routes are concentrated in the city center, which is partly caused by the narrow shape of the valley in which the city is located. Second, feeder routes to the BRT system do not cover all peripheral areas.

The deprivation and public transport supply data allow us to ask the question: Are the deprived population groups served well by public transport in comparison to the affluent groups? Fig. 5 shows the relationship between transport need and transport supply. In general, as public transport supply decreases, transport need increases, a pattern clearly suggesting a substantial level of transport inequity.

The mean supply index value for the most deprived fifth of census areas (need index Quintile 5) is 0.009, while the mean supply index value for the least deprived fifth of census areas (need index Quintile 1) is 0.028. This demonstrates that on average the most deprived areas have a worse transport supply. This illustrates an inequitable situation. The deprived census areas are located mostly in the periphery, where residents need to travel to the city center to access opportunities. These peripheral areas have poor public transport provision, even though the population relies heavily on public transport because of very low levels of car ownership. As a result of this mismatch, residents of these areas may experience a restricted access to opportunities.

Fig. 6 shows the spatial pattern of the disparity index. Those areas where deprivation is high and transport provision is poor are shaded darkest (Quintile 1). Areas where affluence is high and public transport supply is relatively good have light shading (Quintile 5). It is quite easy to determine from the map that the areas of greatest disparity are in the newer peripheral areas of the city, and this is also where the poorest people live.

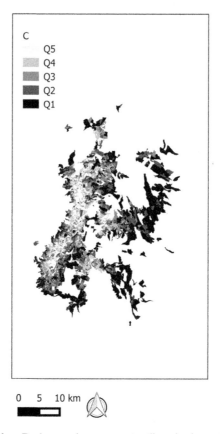

Fig. 6 The disparity index. Dark areas have a greater disparity between need and supply.

An estimate of the level of equity can be gained by comparing the population of census areas in the most and least favorable quintiles of the disparity index. In Quito, 429,000 people or 21% of the population are located in the most favorable group (Quintile 5 in Fig. 6). Not only are many in this group the best served by public transport, as the least deprived group, they are most likely to have access to private vehicles. In the least favorable quintile (Quintile 1 in Fig. 6), there are 375,000 people or 18% of the population. In these areas, individual residents are suffering from a lack of public transport.

We should note that we are dealing with aggregate data and so even in areas with a high level of deprivation and transport need, we do not know if *every* individual is suffering equally from transport inequities (e.g., despite their relative poverty, some people in these areas might own motorbikes or even cars). The disparity index therefore shows the *implied* inequity at an area-based level. This use of aggregate data provides a useful starting point for further investigation of transport inequity as it is experienced by individuals (e.g., as a starting point for bespoke surveys in the most deprived areas).

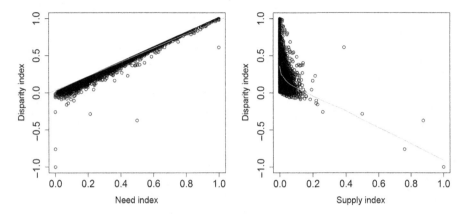

Fig. 7 The relationship between the disparity index and its components.

As discussed earlier the most deprived areas receive on average a poorer supply of public transport than the least deprived areas. In an equitable situation, the situation would be exactly opposite: deprived areas would experience better public transport supply than well-off areas. Over half of the areas within Quintile 1 of Fig. 6 (645 out of 1121) are in the highest quintile on the need index (most deprived) and have no supply of public transport at all.

Fig. 7 suggests that as deprivation increases the disparity index increases, as may be expected. The graph of supply index versus disparity index firstly illustrates that relatively few census areas have high quality public transit services. The disparity index rises rapidly where the transport supply approaches zero. Graphs and correlations do not *explain* the situation experienced by individuals, however they generate questions such as: Does even a small amount of public transport availability considerably reduce the disparity index and address inequity? Further questions such as this could be investigated by targeted further individual needs analysis particularly in areas with a high disparity index (see further reading for some suggestions).

4   Policy relevance

The presented disparity index offers a spatial approach to measuring transport equity and illustrates how policymakers can compile a simple spatial indicator of inequities in public transport supply using openly available secondary data sources. This spatial indicator is useful to policymakers because it makes it easier to think about the real geography of real communities and the issues faced by real people where they live in the city. It is somewhat less abstract than discussing "the poor" without any context of who they are and where they live. This approach is also useful in that it could be used as an initial stage for further deeper investigations. In our case study city, the approach is recommended as a starting point to assess the effectiveness of the BRT system. Although public transport provision in Quito has improved overall over the past

20 years, the equity benchmark provided through the application of our disparity index analysis seems to suggest that, in the case of Quito at least, there still exists substantial transport inequity. The question remains whether, if implemented differently and with more attention to socio-spatial inequities in the city, the outcome of the BRT could have been more equitable.

This question was investigated with policymakers, initially as an academic study (see Guzman et al., 2016), but the findings are now being practically applied to reflect upon and develop future transport policy in Ecuador. For example, one outcome of our study has been that the Ecuadorian Transport Ministry has submitted a proposal to adopt an equity approach to the future planning of public transport provision for the whole country.

To summarize, the benefits of this method to practitioners are as follows:

- The index is not excessively complex. It can be estimated by city planners, and practitioners. This method is "accessible" beyond the ivory tower of the academic expert.
- The principles of the methods have been demonstrated in other Latin American contexts (see Section 5). It is not simply an approach from the Global North being foisted, untested, upon the Global South.
- The methodology uses data that are available to local governments and practitioners and in many cases the data required is also genuinely "open data."

It is important to note that this should not be the only type of analysis for assessing transport equity. Mapping quantitative data provides a useful visualization of the situation at the small-area level and may be a useful starting point for a more detailed examination at the micro-scale of individual behaviors and experiences: examples of other similar approaches are given in the Further reading section.

5   Further reading

The disparity index approach was first used in Hobart, Australia to evidence the existing gap between provision of public transport and the need for affordable public transport at the zonal level. It was further developed for use in Melbourne (see Currie, 2004; Currie, 2010).

In the Latin American context, Jaramillo et al. (2012) used the same approach in Cali, Colombia. The variables and the weightings used by them (Jaramillo et al., 2012, Table 3 on p. 347) are more suitable for a developing country. Note that the data available and the case study context determine which data should be used and whether weighting is necessary.

The chapter by Fransen and Farber (this volume) illustrates techniques to analyze accessibility at the individual level, although note that the comprehensive individual data used in their case study may not always be available, particularly in developing world contexts. In this case, should individualized estimates be required, a spatial microsimulation-based approach to accessibility may be used (see, e.g., Philips et al., 2017).

Further steps should also consider qualitative and mixed methods analyses which provide more detailed investigation of the needs of people. An example of a mixed methods approach to social assessment for transport schemes can be found in Lucas et al. (2016).

It can also be of value to examine the governance processes underpinning transport strategies in a fuller examination of (in)equity (see, e.g., Guzman et al., 2016).

References

BRT Centre of Excellence, E., IEA, SIBRT. 2017. *BRTdata* [Online]. Available: http:/www. brtdata.org [Accessed 20 July 2017].

Currie, G., 2004. Gap analysis of public transport needs: measuring spatial distribution of public transport needs and identifying gaps in the quality of public transport provision. Transp. Res. Rec. J. Transp. Res. Board 1895, 137–146. https://doi.org/10.3141/1895-18.

Currie, G., 2010. Quantifying spatial gaps in public transport supply based on social needs. J. Transp. Geogr. 18, 31–41. https://doi.org/10.1016/j.jtrangeo.2008.12.002.

Guzman, A., Philips, I., Lucas, K., Marsden, G., 2016. Power relations in the development of bus rapid transit in Quito, Ecuador [WWW Document]. Transp. Res. Procedia. URL, http:/eprints.whiterose.ac.uk/105691/.

IBD data, http:/www.undp.org.lb/programme/pro-poor/poverty/povertyinlebanon/molc/meth odological/C/basicsneed.htm.

Jaramillo, C., Lizárraga, C., Grindlay, A.L., 2012. Spatial disparity in transport social needs and public transport provision in Santiago de Cali (Colombia). J. Transp. Geogr. 24, 340–357. https://doi.org/10.1016/j.jtrangeo.2012.04.014.

Lucas, K., Philips, I., Nellthorp, J., Laird, J., Reardon, L., Verlinghieri, E., 2016. Social Assessment of Section 3 of the A465 Heads of the Valleys Road: Brynmawr to Tredegar. Leeds, UK. http:/www.its.leeds.ac.uk/research/featured-projects/social-impacts/. (Accessed 5/5/2014 2014).

METRO-DE-QUITO, 2011. Metro de Quito [Online]. Available: http://www.metrodequito. gob.ec/metrohome.php?c=43.

National Statistics Office of Ecuador, http:/app.sni.gob.ec/sni-link/sni/Portal%20SNI% 202014/ESTADISTICA/Reportes/indicadores_pnbv/fichas/26.pdf.

Philips, I., Clarke, G.P., Watling, D., 2017. A fine grained hybrid spatial microsimulation technique for generating detailed synthetic individuals from multiple data sources: an application to walking and cycling. Int. J. Microsimulat. 10, 167–200. http:/www.microsimulation.org/IJM/V10_1/IJM_2017_10_1_6.pdf.

Measuring the influence of social capital and personal networks on transport disadvantage

Juan Antonio Carrasco, Karen Lucas

1 Introduction

The objective of this chapter is to present a mixed-methods approach to study the interplay between transport disadvantage and the maintenance of people's social networks and the formation and maintenance of network capital (social support). It an empirical case study application about how the role of transport in the formation and maintenance of social networks, as well as in the formation and activation of network capital. The term network capital is a phrase commonly used by John Urry and others in the *mobilities* literature to describe people's ability to appropriate travel-related resources (see Further reading section).

In our study, we understand transport equity from the perspective of people's ability to regularly access their social contacts, together with the emotional and material resources they can gain from these social support networks. In the case study, we compare the access of people with low and high incomes and in high-density and low-density areas to determine whether their access to social support differs according to their socio-spatial differences. We take the position that the people who cannot access social support due to a lack of network capital suffer from transport inequity because it negatively affects their social welfare (see Further reading section for more on this).

With this objective, we present a method on how to measure transport equity which incorporates people's activity disadvantage, transport disadvantage and accessibility, as well as the relationship between these three dimensions and people's personal network characteristics. The method was applied in the City of Concepcion in Chile.

2 Methodology: A mixed methods approach

2.1 Overview

A mixed method approach was used to explore the relationship between people's transport disadvantage and their social networks.

The methodology consists of two steps: first, gathering people's social networks and network capital data, and second, calculating activity and transport disadvantage

Measuring Transport Equity. https://doi.org/10.1016/B978-0-12-814818-1.00015-9

indexes (TDIs). For each respondent, information is gathered into six dimensions: (i) family and sociodemographic questions; (ii) mobility and history of home locations; (iii) communication and transport modes; (iv) income; (v) transport barriers, life experience, and health status; and (vi) personal networks.

The information about people's personal networks was collected through a *name generator technique* which served to calculate people' social capital in space. Each respondent completed a name generator and name interpreter module used to elicit their personal network members (called 'alters'). The criteria to define these social contacts is the same as elaborated in the past by Carrasco et al. (2008), which defined *close alters* to those "people with whom you discuss important matters with, or regularly keep in touch with, or they are there? for you if you need help." *Somewhat close alters*, in turn, consisted of "more than just casual acquaintances, but not very close."

This "closeness" approach defines two aspects in the instrument: (i) it measures the strength of the tie and (ii) it defines the physical "boundary" of the social. In other words, the criteria of closeness defines the overall scope of a personal support network, both in its strength of ties and geographical range. The available spatial information about the respondents and their personal networks included home, work, and previous home locations of the ego's; home location of the alters of that particular ego; the most frequent interaction place between the ego and each alter; and spatial locations from the time-use data.

After eliciting the members of each respondent's social networks, the instrument considered explicit questions regarding the types of social support that they received from each of their alters of social contacts. A set of subjective indexes is then developed to measure the respondent's perceived barriers to perform activities and travel for three different activity types (health, recreation, and shopping). Table 1 ennumerates the different social support dimensions that were gathered in the instrument.

In step two, these two sets of information (personal networks and perceived barriers) are used to develop *activity and TDIs* that are described in the following section. In addition, further analysis on the respondent's *personal networks spatial patterns*, including the spatiality of the social support resources embedded in it can be developed to understand people's access to their social contacts. Finally, the personal network index and the activity and transport index are combined in order to quantitatively describe the relationship between transport/activity disadvantage and the social capital and personal network dimensions. Further discussion on these indexes is presented in the following subsection.

To complement this quantitative analysis, a qualitative methodology was used to explore more in-depth the challenges that various age groups are facing in their everyday mobility experiences. These narrative interviews are not reported in this chapter, but it is a useful technique for providing in-depth understandings of how people use their personal support networks, and how they cope (or become excluded) when they cannot access them. This 'rich' information cannot easily be elicited using a quantitative survey tool.

2.2   Activity disadvantage index and TDI

The key indicators that link social networks with transport equity are the activity disadvantage index (ADI) and TDI, each of which measures the perceived difficulties or barriers that people feel they face when attempting to perform three specific activity types: health, socializing and recreation, and shopping, and personal business. The ADI identifies barriers or difficulties related with the activity location itself, the TDI focuses on the barriers or difficulties related with the transportation system. These self-perceived barriers are collected as dichotomous questions that try to capture the different dimensions that can constitute as constraints for people to perform their activities.

Table 2 presents the key definitions used in the indexes developed in the analysis of transport and activity disadvantage indicators.

These definitions are used to link the three activity types, seven activity disadvantage indicators, and seven transport disadvantage indicators, leading to a total potential score of 42 (2 x 3 x 7 indicators) for each respondent.

Once these indicators are calculated, the ADI and TDI were developed (see Table 3). The calculation of those indexes is based on the number of times a barrier was experienced by the respondent. Consequently, the values for those indexes vary between 0 and 7, with 0 representing not disadvantaged, and 7 representing very disadvantaged. Afterwards, those ADIs and TDIs are combined to result in an overall ADI (ADI_all) and TDI (TDI_all). These are simply the sum of the other three activity-specific indexes, resulting in a score between 0 and 21. The higher the score, the more barriers or constraints people experience and thus the more disadvantaged they are.

Table 1 Social support categories and dimensions

Category	Social support dimensions
Emotional	Information and advice on important matters
	Talking about the day
Practical	Helping when ill
	Helping with the children
	Taking care of the house, car or goods when you are away
Financial	Small money loans
Transport	Lift to work
	Lift to go shopping
	Lift to health facilities or education
	Lift to leisure
	Lift in emergency cases
Informational	Information and advice on new job opportunities

Table 2 Activity disadvantage index and transport disadvantage index

Activity disadvantage index (ADI)
Places with difficult physical access (the place is considered difficult to reach by the respondent) Knowledge of activity availability (health, recreation, and shopping) (the availability of facilities to perform the activities is not unknown by the respondent) Activity cost (the cost of undertaking an activity at the destination is a barrier to performing the activity) Knowledge of the activity supply characteristics (the facilities where the activity could be performed are unknown to the respondent) Capability to perform activities (physical and cognitive) (the respondent feels they have cognitive and/or physical problem, which prevent them performing the activity) Fear and safety (the respondent feels their personal security and/or safety is undermined, which is a barrier to performing the activity) Quality of service (the quality of the activity facilities is perceived as a barrier to the respondent performing the activity)
Transport disadvantage index (TDI)
Vehicle (private car ownership) (the respondent has a problem accessing a car) Cost (of public transport fares) (the public transport cost is an issue for the respondent) Time (travel time, frequency, and availability during night or weekends is a barrier for the respondent to use it) Supply (transport services may not exist or are unknown by the respondent) Capability to use transport (physical and cognitive) (the respondent feels they have cognitive and/or physical disability preventing their use of transport) Fear and safety (the respondents feel security and/or safety in the transportation system is a barrier to its use) Level of service (transport mode) (the respondent feels the quality of the service of the transport service prevent their use of it)

Table 3 Overview of the activity and transport disadvantage indexes

Index name	Description
ADI_health	Activity Disadvantage Index for health facilities
ADI_recrea	Activity Disadvantage Index for recreation facilities
ADI_shopping	Activity Disadvantage Index for shopping facilities
ADI_all	Overall Activity Disadvantage Index
TDI_health	Transport Disadvantage Index for health facilities
TDI_recrea	Transport Disadvantage Index for recreation facilities
TDI_shopping	Transport Disadvantage Index for shopping facilities
TDI_all	Overall Transport Disadvantage Index

2.3 Accessibility to social networks and social support

A series of quantitative indicators to measure people's *social network spatiality* can be developed for each alter or social contact, as shown in Table 4. These indicators include the distance with respect to each alter, and their type of social bonding.

Table 4 Overview of spatial personal network indicators

Personal network distance
HA: distance between the home location of the ego and the home location of the alter
LE: distance between the home location of the ego and the location of most frequent visiting
Type of alter (it separates bonding alters (family and neighbors) with bridging alters (co-workers and friends)
BON: only bonding alters (immediate family, extended family, neighbours)
BRI: only bridging alters (people from organizations, work/classmates, other friends)
ALL: bonding and bridging alters
Attractiveness measure (combination of social support types and frequency of interaction, or the diversity of those types)
A1: 1*frequency of visit (baseline)
AE: emotional support (yes/no)*frequency of visit
AF: financial support (yes/no)*frequency of visit
AT: transport support (yes/no)*frequency of visit
AI: informational support (yes/no)*frequency of visit
AD: diversity of support types (0 to 5)
ADF: diversity of support types (0 to 5)*frequency of visit

The personal network spatial location was calculated using the network distance between the home location of the ego and (1) the home location of each alter or (2) the location of most frequent interaction with each alter. For the initial calculations, a linear distance is used.

In addition, a series of *social support accessibility indicators* were developed to measure the respondent's personal network spatial location and social support. Different accessibility indicators were then calculated in order to have an ego's space-based accessibility to the social network and thus to the social support the egos receives from their networks. Overall, each indicator consisted of calculating the sum of social contacts that were reachable by each respondent, weighted by their distance, using a specific selection criteria. The selection criteria consisted on all the alters, each alter who give a specific social support type (Table 1), and the sum of alters giving any supporting types.

This accessibility index was calculated for all the alters of a particular ego as well as for his bonding and bridging alters, where bonding alters are defined as family and neighbors, and bridging alters are defined as workmates, people from organizations, and friends.

3 Case study: Barriers in Concepción, Chile

The quantitative analysis methods we applied to a dataset of 241 people living in the City of Concepción, Chile. The City of Concepción is the second largest urban area in Chile, with a population of 1.1 million, being served by a reasonably well-developed public transport and car infrastructure system. The data were gathered in a quadrant of neighborhoods combining two dimensions: low and high income, and high and low proximity to the city's CBD: (i) Agüita de la Perdiz (low income, close to the city's center); (ii) Barrio la Virgen (high income, close to the city center); (iii) Santa Sabina (low income, far from the city's center); and (iv) San Sebastián (high income, far from the city's center). This data collection design was the key to determining whether transport inequity was also aligned with social and spatial inequities across the city.

The fieldwork effort was based on in-depth interviews with local residents of the two low-income areas previously surveyed (Agüita de la Perdiz and Santa Sabina), whereby respondents of the Part 1 quantitative survey were invited to take part in the Part 2 qualitative interviews. In all, 35 individuals were selected to represent various age groups: young (18–40 years old), mature (51–65 years old), and older (over 65 years old); gender; education levels; employment status; ownership of automobile; possession of driving license; household composition; communication tools usage; and among other factors.

Due to personal availabilities, 18 in-depth interviews were successfully carried out and the interviewees included nine from Agüita de la Perdiz (three young, three mature, and three older) and nine (three young, three mature, and three older) from Santa Sabina, among which four females and five males were in each neighborhood.

3.1   Findings of the combined activity and transport disadvantage index (ATDI)

3.1.1   ADI characterization

The descriptive statistics for the seven activity disadvantage indicators are given in Table 4 for the health purpose. The same indicators were calculated for recreation and shopping facilities, obtaining similar trends. Since the values for the seven indicators are restricted to 0 or 1, the mean gives the percentage of people who answered 1 on the question. For all the questions, except for the knowledge of activity presence, zero equals "yes," and thus indicates an experienced disadvantage. The results show that almost all people know where health facilities are present. The same observation can be made for the other kinds of purposes (i.e., education and shopping).

The mean values of the other indicators vary between 70% and 85%, and overall between 15% and 25% of the people indicate one or more disadvantage barrier with respect to certain facilities (see example in Table 5). According to the results, the most repeated barrier to perform activities was the cost of performing health-related activities (i.e., the cost of a health appointment or medicines).

Fig. 1 presents the descriptive statistics for the overall ADIs calculated for health, recreation, shopping, and overall activities. Theoretically, the values of the first three ADIs can vary between 0 and 7; the overall ADI can vary between 0 and 21. In general, most of the individuals have a low score ADI (e.g., 75% of the individuals have a score of 2 or smaller on recreation). The average score for the overall ADI is 3.10. Most individuals either do not experience any disadvantage or have only experienced one kind of activity disadvantage. In fact, three outcome categories can be distinguished based on the results: individuals having virtually no disadvantage (scores between 1 and 3), individuals with hardly any disadvantages (between 4 and 7),

Table 5 Example of descriptive statistics for the activity disadvantage indicators for health facilities

	Are the health activities physically present? (1 = Yes)	Do you know where health facilities are present? (1 = Yes)	Is the cost of the health facilities a barrier? (1 = No)	Is the knowledge of activity supply to health facilities a barrier? (1 = No)	Is your physical capability a barrier to health facilities? (1 = No)	Is your fear a barrier to health facilities? (1 = No)	Is the level of service a barrier to health facilities? (1 = No)
Mean	0.87	0.98	0.79	0.83	0.89	0.85	0.84
Std. Deviation	0.34	0.13	0.41	0.34	0.31	0.35	0.37

and individuals with a substantial level of disadvantage (overall ADI score of more than 7), which roughly represent one-third of the sample each.

From an equity perspective, the previous results suggest that, although a high proportion of the respondents acknowledge few barriers to participate in activities, there is a non-negligible proportion of people that recognizes at least one barrier, while a few of them identify the majority of the barriers surveyed in the instrument. Then, although the barriers explored in the survey are not experienced by a majority of the respondents, from a policy perspective, there is a segment of the population that requires a stronger intervention.

The histograms presented in Fig. 1 complement the previous discussion. The majority of individuals identify at least one barrier to perform each activity type, with a non-negligible share of the sample experimenting the majority of them. This trend is somewhat similar for all activity types, although people identify less barriers for health than for the other activities. For the case of the overall ADI, it is interesting to see the long tail of people who experience an important number of barriers.

3.1.2 TDI characterization

Similarly to the activities, the results of the descriptive statistics for the seven transport disadvantage indicators were calculated for health, recreation, and shopping purposes. Table 5 shows the results for health as an illustration. The same remarks apply to the mean count as for the activity disadvantage indicators. The knowledge and private vehicle ownership factors are the two exceptions for which a zero equals "no" and one equals "yes."

For the three activity types, the mean for the 'time and scheduling' indicator is rather low (41%, 38%, and 45%, respectively). Thus, approximately 60% indicates the time and scheduling of transport as a barrier to going to a particular facility. On the other hand, for the recreation and shopping activities, 92% and 91%, respectively, indicate that the level of service of the transport is not a barrier, probably because they are at walking distance to these activities. In that regard, better schedules and hours of operations seem to be the only widespread barrier for the respondents.

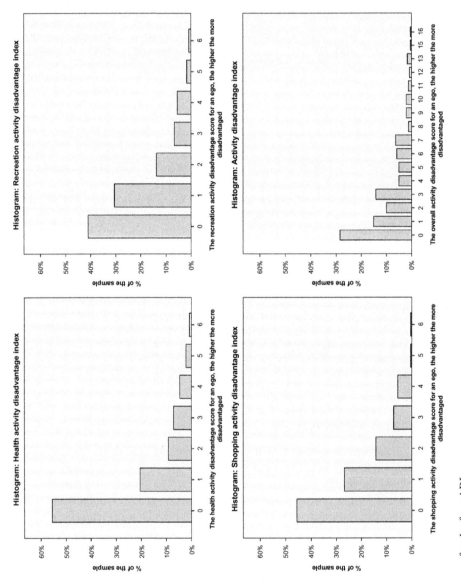

Fig. 1 Histogram for the four ADIs.

In addition, it is interesting to note that, although a high proportion of the respondents do not have a car available (around 36%), which is higher than the share of people that recognize transport barriers, with the exception of the already discussed time and scheduling. In other words, the lack of car does not necessary constitute a reason to perceive having a transport barrier.

Analogous to the ADIs, the three activity TDIs can have possible values between 0 and 7 so that the overall TDI possible score will be between 0 and 21. The minimum resulting values from the analysis were 0, and the maximum values were 7, 6, and 7 for health, recreation, and shopping, and the overall TDI was 18. Respondents that reported zero transport barriers were only 1/8 of the total, which an important result, considering that half of them correspond to medium- to high-income groups.

3.1.3   Transport and ADIs comparison

Comparing the means for the ADIs and TDIs, the TDIs have a limited higher score (approximately 2 for the activities and 6 for the overall to 1 and 3) as presented in Fig. 2. The histograms for the three activity TDIs, presented in Fig. 3, do not have the same logarithmic curve as those of the ADIs. From an equity perspective, TDIs were stronger than ADIs, base on the number of barriers that the respondents reported. Then, transport disadvantage seems to be more widely spread than activity disadvantage. In addition, there is a very important portion of people who experience more than half of the transport barriers, which illustrates the need to focus on a broader range of aspects within the transport provision, compared with activity-related aspects. Finally, equally to the ADIs, similar trends between health, recreation, and shopping activities, suggests that transport-related barriers occur across the different activity types; in other words, they need to be tackled independently of the trip purpose.

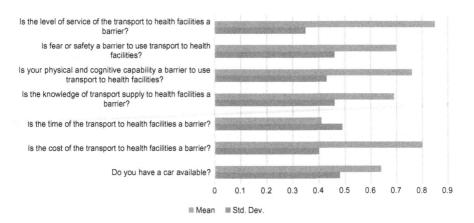

Fig. 2 Mean and standard deviation for the transport disadvantage indicators for health facilities.

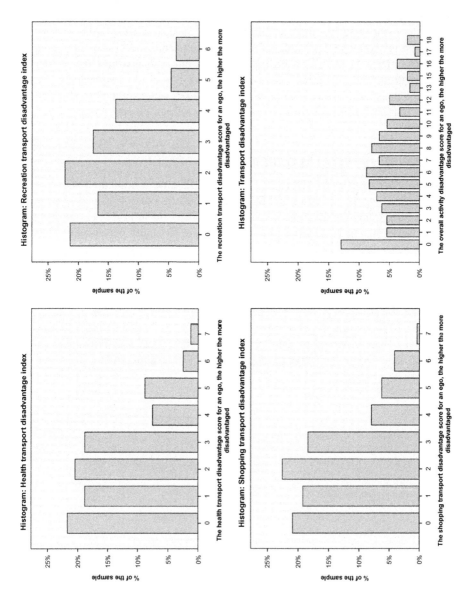

Fig. 3 Histograms for the four TDIs.

3.2   Social network characteristics

The next stage of the analysis was used to determine how these transport disadvantages and barriers to activity relate with people's social support networks, as they could compensate for ADI and TDI barriers.

3.2.1   Types of social support

Five types of support from alters to egos were identified in the dataset. The descriptive statistics for those five categories individually are presented in Table 5. On average, 36% of the alters give emotional support to his ego. Only 14% and 15%, respectively, give egos financial support or information about new job opportunities. An alter gives in average one type of support to the ego (with a standard deviation of 1.35).

3.2.2   Frequency of interactions

On average, an alter meets the ego 37 times a year, thus approximately once each 10 days. Fig. 5 gives more insight into the distribution of the visit frequency with a strong representation of the 'once a week' category. The high prevalence of frequent contacts underscores the importance for people of being capable of contacting their alters, that is, having an appropriate accessibility to their social contacts, both temporally (i.e., having enough time to socialize with others), and spatially (i.e., having the transport means for social encountering).

3.3   Accessibility indexes

Before going into more detail in the analysis of the accessibility indexes for the respondent's personal networks, some descriptive statistics were calculated with the available dataset.

3.3.1   Distances

Figs. 4, 5, 6, and 7 present the statistical descriptives of the distances between ego's home locations and each alter's home location and most frequent place of interaction, only considering social contacts at 100 km or less, which represent more than 85% of the alters considered in this analysis (only national locations). Similarly to the results from previous literature, personal network distance patterns tend to have a distance decay effect, that is, a declining probability of having a social contact for longer distances. On the other hand, there is a small cluster at long distances (at the interurban scale), denoting those contacts that are emotionally important for the egos to be maintained even if they live at longer distances.

3.3.2   Descriptive statistics

Using the definitions from Table 1, and the social network data, we developed indexes that take into account the respondent's accessibility to certain portions of their social network. A selection of these indicators is displayed in Table 5. For example,

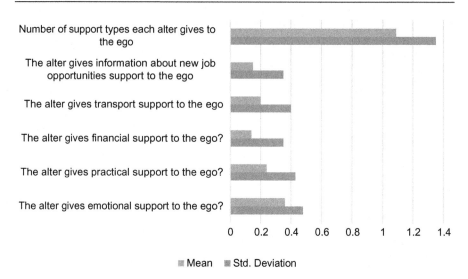

Fig. 4 Mean and standard deviation of the support types and the diversity of support an alter receives.

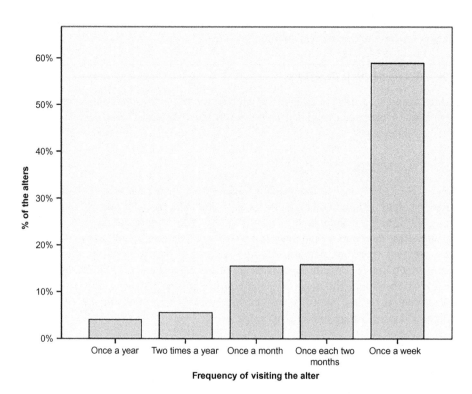

Fig. 5 Histogram of the face-to-face visit frequency between egos and alters.

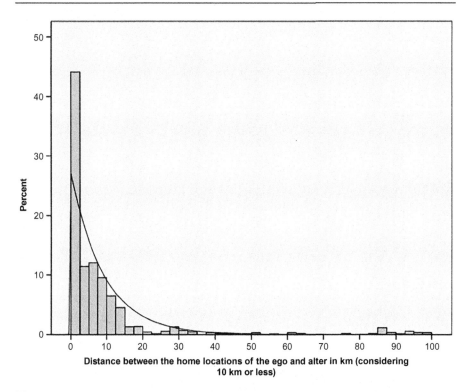

Fig. 6 Frequency graph of the distance (km) between each respondent and social contact home locations.

AI_LE_AE_ALL_sum indicates: accessibility indexes (AI) measured by the distance between the ego's home and their most frequent place of interaction with each alter (LE), for those alters that provide emotional support (AE), for all kinds of alters regardless whether they are bonding or bridging (ALL).

For all of the selected accessibility indexes, the mean index value is higher for the distance to the alter's home location (HA) than for the distance to the most frequent visiting location (LE) is used. This result remarks that people's access to social support depends heavily on their daily activities, where the place of most frequent interaction with their alters takes place. In other words, social network home locations—which tend to be more distant—are less important than the places of most frequent interaction in order to understand people's accessibility to social capital.

A second interesting result is that people's personal support networks (AE) have a higher geographical coverage with respect to financial support (AF), which suggests people have more interactions and travel longer distances to the alters that provide them with financial help compared with other elements of social support.

Finally, the overall indicators (AD and ADF) suggest that people have more interactions with their local neighborhood networks in terms of proximity; for example, the average travel distance of an alter who provides support is less than 1 km (901.06 m).

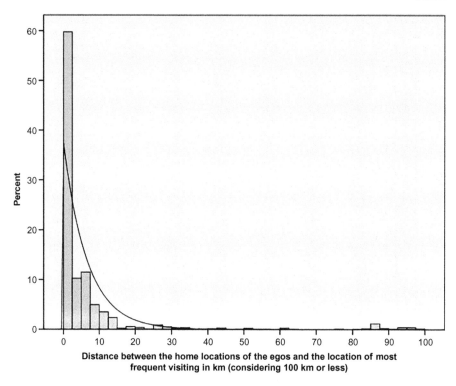

Fig. 7 Frequency graph of the distance (km) between each respondent's home location and the location of most frequent visit.

4 Policy relevance

The quantitative analysis presented in this chapter involves the development of transport and ADIs which incorporate people's self-perceived barriers to perform their health, recreation, and shopping activities. These barriers are classified in dimensions directly related with (a) the activities themselves and (b) the transport dimensions. The results indicate that, although a majority of the respondents have a high level of knowledge on where to undertake the specific activities, a relevant portion of them (10%–20%) perceive barriers to perform their activities, many of which are related to transport equity issues. The key barriers here are associated with high travel costs and the timing and scheduling of the transportation system and these transport-related barriers occur across the different activity types (health, education, and shopping). Simply put, lower-income people with less travel resources are less able to perform these activities generally, they also live in places where the public transport system is perceived to be less suited to their travel needs for reaching these activities, and are unable to overcome these travel barriers because they have less access to private transport.

The analysis on the respondents' social networks suggest that, despite the widespread geographic distribution of social contacts, proximity still plays an important role in the number of interactions with respondent's personal networks, as well as the nature of the social support they seek. Interactions linked to bridging networks tend to be spread physically further away from the respondent's home locations than their bonding networks. This is important from a social equity perspective because the ability to establish bridging networks is an important factor in being able to find and maintain employment and financial support.

5 Further reading

There is an extensive literature on transport disadvantage that can be traced back for more than two decades (see Lucas, 2012 for an overview of this literature). John Urry's work on the role of network capital in creating and overcoming mobility inequalities (2017) has helped to shape our understanding of how to measure this type of capital in this chapter. We would also refer the reader to Schwanen et al. (2015) for a further discussion of how lack of access to social networks can lead to reduced social capital and, overtime, social exclusion, which is recognized in the literatures as one aspect of social disadvantage.

Although using a different methodology, the work by Jirón (2010) employs some of the concepts of transport and activity barriers used in this chapter. The personal network eliciting technique follows the work by Carrasco et al. (2008), and the social capital and social support concepts are discussed more in depth in Carrasco and Cid-Aguayo (2012). Studies relating accessibility and transport disadvantage in the Latin American context are scarce; an exception are Bocarejo and Oviedo (2012) and Jaramillo et al. (2012).

Acknowledgments

We would like to thank our research collaborators for the study on which this chapter is based: Dr Tim Schwanen and Shuaishuai He from the Transport Studies Unit, University of Oxford; Berdien de Roo and Alexander de Wit from the Ghent University; and Daniel Sandoval from the Centro de Desarrollo Urbano Sustentable (CEDEUS), Chile. We would also like to recognize the European Marie Curie International Researcher Study Exchange Scheme as the primary funders of the project.

References

Bocarejo, P., Oviedo, R., 2012. Transport accessibility and social inequities: A tool for identification of mobility needs and evaluation of transport investments. J. Transp. Geogr. 24, 142–154.
Carrasco, J.A., Cid-Aguayo, B., 2012. Network capital, social networks, and travel: An empirical illustration from Concepción, Chile. Environ. Plann. A 44 (5), 1066–1084.
Carrasco, J.A., Hogan, B., Wellman, B., Miller, E.J., 2008. Collecting social network data to study social activity-travel behaviour: An egocentric approach. Environ. Plann. B 35 (6), 961–980.

Jaramillo, C., Lizarraga, C., Grindlay, A., 2012. Spatial disparity in transport social needs and public transport provision in Santiago de Cali (Colombia). J. Transp. Geogr. 24, 340–357.

Jirón, P., 2010. Mobile borders in urban daily mobility practices in Santiago de Chile. Int. Polit. Sociol. 4 (1), 66–79.

Lucas, K., 2012. Transport and social exclusion: Where are we now? Transp. Policy 20, 105–113.

Schwanen, T., Lucas, K., Akyelken, N., Solsona, D., Carrasco, J.A., Neutens, T., 2015. Rethinking the links between social exclusion and transport disadvantage through the lens of social capital. Transport. Res. Part A 74, 123–135.

Using a capability approach-based survey for reducing equity gaps in transport appraisal: Application in Santiago de Chile

16

Beatriz Mella Lira

1 Introduction

1.1 The capability approach

This chapter recognizes the shortcomings of transport project appraisal based on cost-benefit analysis and its emphasis on journey time savings. It thus seeks to expand the criteria on which the merits of projects are assessed. To this end, the theoretical approach adopted is the capability approach (CA), initially developed by Amartya Sen. CA is radical in the way it analyzes the development, opportunities, and capabilities of the individual. Although it is a broad conceptual and theoretical framework, it does not necessarily refer directly to application in the transport context.

First, it is important to clarify that the central concepts considered for this approach are "functionings and capabilities." Functionings, according to Sen, are the "various things a person may value doing and being"—the achieved actions by the person that s/he manages to do or to be. In transportation, this could be interpreted as the actual travel that allows a person to participate in their daily activities. Capabilities, in turn, represent the various combinations of doings and beings (functionings) that a person can feasibly achieve, and is thus largely synonymous with their freedoms and opportunities.

Initially, understanding the functionings is fundamental for determining what the real capabilities (opportunities and freedoms) of a person to achieve those functionings are. Therefore, functionings are crucial elements in the evaluation of capabilities. An example of how functionings are limited by transport is if a person decides not to travel to her personal activities because s/he cannot afford transportation, or because travel time does not allow him/her to carry out those activities. The assessment of his/her capabilities requires an assessment of the range of relevant opportunities, given the person's characteristics (so, for instance, taken as given a person's skills or income level while defining his/her range of capabilities). Thus, even if these parameters do not change, the evaluation of her capabilities is likely to be broader and closer to the real opportunities that s/he can reach. From this example, three elements can be distinguished: functionings, capabilities, and the gap between them.

Measuring Transport Equity. https://doi.org/10.1016/B978-0-12-814818-1.00016-0

Considering these definitions, the CA allows extending the range of the usual parameters used to assess transport projects, moving beyond profitability, or utility. Furthermore, the advantage of having both concepts of functionings and capabilities is the different types of information they reveal and the independence they give in their use. However, the measurement of capabilities is the most challenging aspect for the operationalization and use of CA in transport—that is, it is difficult to assess what the real opportunities for travel are, or what the real opportunities of access to activities are.

How can we understand transport equity through the lens of the CA? Another important concept proposed in CA is effective freedom, the capability to *choose*. An example of this, specifically in the case of the provision of public transport, is the option for people to take or not to take the public transit bus network because, in the case of Santiago, the bus network is quite homogeneous in terms of its users, so most high- and low-income people can access it. The difference is that for one group taking the bus is a matter of choice, while for another group this is the only feasible alternative to travel over larger distances. Having valuable options for people is relevant in this case.

Not only may people with low income experience a deprivation of capabilities, people with reduced mobility or mobility impairments are typically also in a position of disadvantage. For them, accessing the public buses could be even more complicated compared to people without mobility impairments, and it could even mean for them to reduce their trips up to the point of becoming immobile. For both groups, the lack of freedom to choose what is valuable can lead to a capability deprivation, persisting, and aggravating the original condition.

Now, even if people could freely choose the transport mode that best suits their needs, not everyone has the ability to convert the advantages of mobility into valuable functionings. In the framework of the CA, this is called "conversion factors." For example, having economic resources allows people to obtain certain goods. In transportation, improving the access to certain modes does not necessarily imply that people can reach valuable opportunities. Hence, it is unclear how valuable such transport decisions would be to them.

Achieving transport equity through the enhancement of capabilities means that people are able to perform the activities that fulfill their lives, irrespective that activities vary across groups, segments, and individuals. It also means having a minimum degree of respect for people's dignity. The use of any available transport mode should not act to the detriment of the quality of life of other people, for example, as a result of traffic pollution or pedestrian accidents. The level of accessibility to goods and services should not be a barrier for people to convert those resources into something valuable for them. For example, some brief results shown later on in this chapter show gender barriers in the use of public transport, since it does not live up to the requirements of use and activities of women, turning public transport into a barrier rather than an enabler for women. The CA assesses people's quality of life so that various dimensions can be incorporated.

The CA framework is based on the real opportunities for people to achieve what they value and want to be (or do). This framework has a strong link with the concepts of freedom and opportunities, which is fundamental in considering the benefits people derive from the existence and use of mobility infrastructures and services. This is different from an approach based on the needs, satisfaction, happiness, or subjective well-being of a person, which are some concepts that have been employed in the assessment of transport systems, both in the literature and in some chapters in this book. The radical and comprehensive perspective of evaluating the benefits and burdens on the individual is something that the CA has in common with these approaches—which go beyond the evaluation of the "net present value" or "benefit–cost ratio" of transport projects. This chapter, therefore, provides an alternative to the mainstream evaluation approach, by providing a coherent logic of the measurement of functionings and capabilities, and the presentation of an application in Santiago de Chile.

1.2   Santiago as case study

The Chilean economy has had a sustained and stable increase from the 1990s onwards. However, and despite being one of the currently most robust economies in Latin America, the income distribution is one of the most unequal of all countries of the Organization for Cooperation and Economic Development (OECD). The 1% of the richest people in Chile owns 30.5% of the national Gross Domestic Product (GDP), contrasting with countries as Sweden where the 1% wealthiest own a 9.1%, and in Spain where the number is 10.4%. Even compared to the United States (21%), Chile is more unequal.

The problems of income distribution have affected the way land uses have been distributed within the metropolitan region of Santiago de Chile. The history recognizing the processes of distribution of land uses, housing and residential provision, work places, trade locations, and industries goes back much further in the years, at the beginning of the 1970s. These spatial inequalities have led to economic, social, and environmental cultural outcomes that have run counter to the sustainable transport policies which are attempting to provide accessibility for the whole city. Over the years, not only the need to travel, but also journey times and travel distances have increased as a consequence of social inequalities reflected in increased housing prices in central and well-connected areas, combined with a lack of land-use incentives to (re)locate productive activities away from the center and with a deficient implementation and operation of the mass public transport system, the Transantiago. Both users of private and public transport have been affected in terms of travel efficiency and journey times, but especially in terms of their daily travel experience and quality of life. As consequence, the capital (as well as other cities in the country) has had a significant increase in car ownership due to the lack of incentives for using public transport—together with large incentives for money loans for vehicle purchases. Since 2008, the possession of motorized vehicles for private purposes has increased on average by 5.5% per year in the Metropolitan Region of Santiago. At the national level, this trend is similar, with an average increase of 6.6% per year (see Fig. 1).

Existing inequities of income distribution and opportunities seem to be accentuated by long travel distances and the inconveniences of not having a public transport

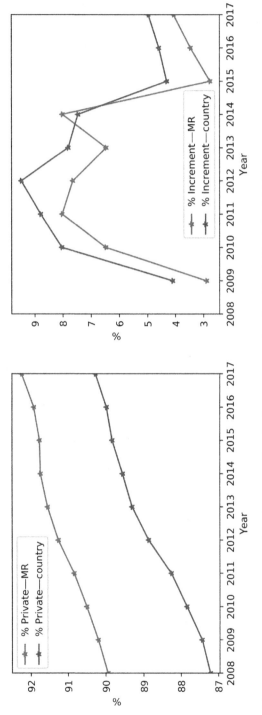

Fig. 1 Total motorised private vehicles in Metropolitan Region (*orange*) and national level (*blue*), 2008–2017.
Source: Own production based on National Statistics Institute (INE), 2017.

system adequate enough to cover the demands of distance, comfort, and flexibility of use. This situation of wealth distribution and transport modal choice has resulted in an unfair transport system that is particularly affecting the most vulnerable sector of population. Just as an example, the highest percentages of low-income families per household are located in the south-west extension area (38%), south (27.7%), and western (26%) area of the metropolitan region. These areas have a high daily usage of public transport (close to 60%) and very low percentage of car ownership and usage, compared to wealthiest areas in the East, where 57% of households have a high household income. According to the Origin Destination Survey of 2012, the longest trips reported in Santiago are made by public transport. On the other hand, the households that spend more time on trips are located in municipalities of the south, south-west, and northern areas—they coincide with municipalities located at the city edges, which have poor road infrastructure and poor public transport services.

2   Methodology: A capability-based quantitative sampling

The CA can help here to set-up a framework and methodology that considers a wider range of factors than what is common in transport planning as practiced in many countries around the world. CA can provide a more rich understanding of the transport situation of people as well as their perceptions, especially regarding their (accessibility or mobility) opportunities and their level of freedoms.

In this case, the CA was operationalized through a dedicated survey design. The core of the survey consisted of the identification of different user profiles, based among others on their primary transport mode. A pilot survey was important to define the spatial component of the sampling for representing a wider diversity of people. As Santiago has a strong territorial component of urban segregation, the sampling places were defined with the attempt of getting the most variety of income segments. The definition of the areas was based according to the information of the Census data from 2002. The pilot was also helpful to understand the extent of information that could be collected through a survey tool and the problems on each specific area of study.

2.1   Survey design

The first sketch of the survey took the categories defined by Martha Nussbaum (Nussbaum, 2011) in her central human capabilities list. This list of factors was used for defining the real opportunities of users when considering their individual perspective on transport participation and access, in order to understand their real capability. The capabilities then covered journey experience and access to activities associated with well-being, organized in seven categories:

1. health, physical, and mental integrity,
2. senses, imaginations, and thoughts,
3. reasoning and planning,
4. social interaction,
5. natural environment and sustainability,

6. information, and
7. travel to work and to other activities.

The categories first proposed by Nussbaum (2011) were "translated" into possible indicators for transport. For example, when considering the categories of life, health, and integrity proposed by Nussbaum, the possible application in transport planning could correspond with concepts as stress, physical activity, perception of air pollution while traveling, physical and psychological security levels (safety and security), accidents, noise, and crashes. Some of these elements have been previously addressed in transport research. However, the novelty of incorporating these factors relies on the assessment of the users' perceptions on how these factors affect the way they perceive their travel opportunities.

2.2 Data collection

The final questionnaire consisted of 65 questions, and the survey was conducted in Santiago during the months of November and December 2016. A quota sampling method was used for gathering the information at the city level, allowing for representativeness according to the Santiago Pre-Census of 2012. An equal gender representation and proportion of inhabitants per area was chosen. The survey was carried out in centers of activity with dense provision of offices, services, and educational centers. These subcentralities have different characteristics in regard to the built environment—it is assumed that these spatial factors will have an impact on the survey results. Examples of street sections and differences in the built environment (housing, roads, pedestrian space, and among others) can be seen in Fig. 2.

In the first part of the survey, participants were asked about basic sociodemographic data, such as the commune of residence, gender, age, disabilities, level of education, current occupation, income, and main and secondary transport mode for commuting. In the second part, the questionnaire asked about the modes that people associate with emotive and instrumental positive concepts of commuting, as well as the levels of overall satisfaction with the trips. The third part related to the aspects of reasoning and planning of the commuting or regular trips; assessment of the access to job opportunities; the reliance on public transport for commuting and frequently performed activities; and level of transport options and quality of life affected from access to transportation. The fourth part considered the aspects of social interaction with other people while performing trips; assessed the presence of other people and raised questions about feelings of being discriminated while traveling. The fifth part considered concepts related to nature and sustainability, asking about the consideration of switching modes when raining; access to sustainable transport modes and willingness to pay for more access to sustainable modes. The sixth part raised questions about access to information and modal interchanges when performing regular trips; waiting, transfers, and travel times; aspects that make transfers more difficult; and access to technological tools facilitating making decisions over daily trips. The seventh part assessed the built environment, considering transport infrastructure for private vehicles, public transport, and cycling infrastructure (see Fig. 2).

Fig. 2 Streets sections showing differences in the built environment, for the municipalities in which the survey was carried out. In descending order: (1) Providencia, (2) Nunoa, (3) Macul, (4) La Florida, and (5) Puente Alto.
Reproduced from Google Maps.

Table 1 Categories of the survey considering transferability of concepts from the central human capabilities list

1. Basic socioeconomic and sociodemographic data, as well as factors of self-assessed physical and mental integrity	For example, commune of residence; gender, age, disabilities, level of education; current occupation, income; main and secondary transport mode for commuting; levels of stress, levels of air pollution; crowdedness
2. Associations between primary transport mode and emotive/instrumental concepts while commuting (or performing main activity)	For example, freedom, insecurity, functionality, enjoyment, affordability, poverty, safety, value of time, unpunctuality, congestion, efficiency, luxury, environmental care, health, social interaction, comfort, happiness, status
3. Reasoning and planning for commuting and/or regular trips	For example, assessment of access to job opportunities; reliance on public transport for commuting; frequency; activities; access to transportation and life quality
4. Social interaction with other people while commuting or doing regular trips	For example, assessment of the level of interaction; importance of other people while traveling; feelings of discrimination
5. Nature and sustainability	For example, variability depending on weather; access to sustainable transport modes; willingness to pay for more access to sustainable modes
6. Information	For example, access to information and modal interchanges; waiting, transfers and travel times; difficulties when transferring; access to technological online tools
7. Built environment	For example, considering transport infrastructure for private vehicles, public transport and cycling infrastructure
8. Productive activities and commuting	For example, questions related to commuting and productive trips; possibilities of getting a good employment; assessment of current available opportunities; satisfaction with job; travel times and expenditure

The eighth and final part considered questions related to commuting and productive trips; level of access and possibilities of employment; travel times and expenditure. All concepts transferred from the central human capabilities list and reinterpreted for a transport discussion (Table 1).

Perception questions use a Likert scale with five points from bad to good (1 to 5). Categorical variables were analyzed through absolute and relative frequencies for the descriptive sociodemographic analysis. In total, 451 persons validly completed the survey, where 31% of the respondents are car users, 60% are public transport users, and 9% are active travel users. The following table shows a descriptive analysis by gender and primary transport mode. Fisher p-values indicate the significances for both gender and main transport mode. On gender, the main significances relate to income, occupation, and education, positioning men in all those variables "above" women. Women tend to earn lower wages have more precarious work positions and have less education than men. The survey analysis, from different domains and considering different criteria, shows that women are located in a position of disadvantage. Considering the differences between modes, private transport users (mostly car users—95%) tend to show higher advantages in terms of income, education, and occupation, when considering sociodemographic variables.

One of the most complex issues of measuring subjective factors of public and private transport users has to do with the objectivation of the individual perceptions for purposes of quantitative research and statistical data analysis. For example, one of the survey questions was looking for an assessment of the physical characteristics and available facilities close to the respondents' home location. This question that seemingly could be easily answered was more difficult to assess for the users living in low-income areas, as they simply did not have the physical infrastructure to be assessed. For instance, bus shelters, cycle lanes or bike sharing system, green public spaces, recreational, cultural, and sporty facilities were some of the examples difficult to assess by people living in low-income or deprived areas in light of the complete absence of these facilities in their local area.

Another reflection after sampling is how research can provide an objective source of information despite evaluating subjectivities from different individuals. Opposite to what happened in the first case, some interviewees living in the same area assessed the same existent infrastructure in a completely (even contradictory) way. Statistical analysis can help here, by aggregating the values obtained in order to create a more "objective" result. However, when doing so, the perceptions of the majority are often taken to represent those of the whole sample, and so mask the perceptions of the underlying minority responses. When discussing "less subjective matters" as personal or individual perceptions, overlooking of these minority perceptions factors could directly affect particular disadvantaged groups. For example, when assessing the state of the public realm in a particular municipality, the results may show a reasonable average on the evaluation, disregarding the minority of places in which the public realm could be critical for the development of a certain community or group.

The measurement and differentiation of the capabilities and functionings is a big challenge of using the capabilities approach. In the first part of the chapter, the importance of functionings to understand the capabilities of a person was pointed out. This led toward a reflection on the way of assessing the functionings-capabilities gap, with an alternative possibility of measuring "weighted functionings." This means considering the assessment of certain factors (taken from the transferability of the human capabilities list above), based on the levels of functionings, but weighted according to the levels of importance that the person attributes to that factor. The quantification of weighted functionings also allows looking at the level of inequalities that must be addressed by transport policy and practice. This is especially relevant in cases, for instance, in which the level of expectations of performing certain activity goes beyond the realized functionings. When having expectations on using a sport or leisure facility, without being able to access them, the value of functionings will be lower than the capabilities (as they represent "doings" and "beings" that a person can feasibly achieve). This is even more critical in sectors of the city or segments of society in which the capabilities of people are reduced as a consequence of the lack of facilities, reducing their opportunities to participate in these activities. When such facilities are present, the reduction in capabilities could be explained, for example, with a person with a high workload and long travel distances not having enough time to perform sport or leisure activities. These conditions, exacerbated by the (poor) quality of the transport system and related journey times, might have the effect of decreasing this person's opportunities and therefore, her capabilities.

The various ways of interpreting the differences between functionings and capabilities led into a specific way of discussing the gap. For this purpose, two ways for assessing the distance between functionings and capabilities have been defined in the survey.

The first way of measurement considers the assessment of the current status of a particular aspect (functionings) but assuming that people in these areas expect to have the greatest possible welfare. For example, in the case of evaluation of facilities close to home, people can assess the status and adequacy of educational facilities on a scale of 1–5 ("very bad" to "very good"), but as researcher we assume that the maximum expected (capabilities) is obtained for people who answer "very good." An example of this type of question could be: "How would you assess the space for pedestrian on the sidewalks, close to your home location?" ($1 =$ very bad and $5 =$ very good). This question assumes that reaching the maximum level of assessment would be preferable for people, so the question allows distinguishing between groups just based on this evaluation. The higher the score persons give to their status, the closer they are to reaching their personal capabilities.

The question does not directly ask respondents to report on their (perceived) capabilities, but only asks them to make a statement regarding the realized assessment of their functionings. This first type of questions was combined with a second type, asking about the level of importance of a particular facility. In this case, the definition of the levels of importance for that criteria helps to define the main relevant attributes for a particular group or segment. An example of such a question is: "How important is for you to improve sidewalks?" ($1 =$ less important and very important). The answer to this question allows weighting of the factors assessed. This measurement has been defined as "weighted functionings," as it combines the assessment of actual activities or facilities weighted according to the priority given to them.

A second way of measuring the functioning-capability gap is by the relative difference in people's perceptions regarding a particular variable. This alternative does not assume that the maximum would be desirable for the person, and yet asking the level of importance provides a more accurate way of discussing the weighting of that variable. This could be used especially for questions related to subjective perceptions of people about their trips, feelings, emotions, and experiences. For example: "How do you assess the level of proximity to other transport users that you experience on your usual trips?" (1 = bad and 5 = very good). Compared to the first question above, this one does not necessarily assume that the maximum level would be preferable or important for people, so the analysis relies on the second question: "How important is it for you to be close to other transport users while traveling?" (1 = not important and 5 = very important). The definition of the level of importance that that person attributes to this aspect helps to define the maximum value for which the gap between functionings and capabilities will be measured.

Unlike the first measurement method, the second compares the variables in relation to an estimated maximum. This is different from the first type of question as we cannot assume a maximum or minimum level of assessment of this factor, as the users' perceptions will vary according to their preferences. We can assume people will want a "very good" bus stop shelter, but we cannot assume they will want a low or high level of closeness to people. The difference indicates how distant are the expectations of the person vs what they can actually achieve the realization of that activity.

These two approaches have also been applied for assessing the levels of importance of performing productive or leisure activities; questions regarding willingness or preferences about transport modes; perceptions regarding transport expenditure; or aspects related regular travel experience. The difference in the use of a capability-based approach compared to more mainstream surveys into these issues is the nature of the questions, exploring the things people value doing or being that help them achieve higher levels of freedom in their lives.

3 Application of the measurement

The survey was conducted face-to-face in offices and working places, private and public open spaces, school facilities (parents), and in residential areas (door-to-door). In total, 451 surveys were validly completed. The nature of the survey and the number of questions allowed the creation of an extensive database. Here, we only present one issue as an example of the application of the CA. We focus on people's proximity to other transport users, with specific emphasis on the role of gender, in demonstrating the inequities of transport provision in this respect. The assessment of the situation was compared to the levels of importance attributed to that factor, showing the relative difference of people's perceptions on one particular factor. As the maximum (very good) level is relative to the person, the level of importance declared by the interviewee allows weighting that variable.

Proximity to other transport users (closeness) refers to the perception of likeliness of people of having social interaction with other people (around him or her) while traveling. Associations between crowdedness and negative health outcomes have been documented before, thus the factor here explores the differences between modes and individual's characteristics. This is a subjective measure that did not imply in the question a positive or negative consideration of the factor.

The question refers to the assessment of the user's perception on the physical distance or the value of the presence of other people while commuting. In cases of private vehicles, the lack of other users could be experienced as positive, given the nature of driving a private vehicle (although people may also experience boredom and loneliness in a private vehicle). However, in the case of public transport, this relationship is more complex as it could depend on the level of crowdedness.

Fig. 3 shows the results of proximity to other transport users compared by primary transport mode. Public transport users give the lowest assessment to the proximity to others. A total of 44% of public transport users score a low level of functionings, with similar trends in the weighted functionings—or the relative importance they attribute to this factor.

Data show that females from medium- and low-income segments indicate a lower level of functionings but are more likely to declare a higher level of importance to this factor. This may be explained by females often having longer trips and tending to feel more vulnerable or discouraged by the physical conditions of interaction with other passengers. As a matter of context, it is important to note that Chile, particularly Santiago, has a serious problem of street sexual harassment, which is well evidenced in public transportation but is not yet massively unveiled. This is possibly one of the aspects that more strongly justify the addition of "proximity to other users" as a relevant element to be considered in transport equity appraisal, since it can seriously affect the mental health of people, especially women. In terms of gender, this factor shows significant differences by gender between assessed and weighted functionings. The high scores correspond to women (72% female vs 60% male). Journey times (Fig. 4) are also significant (at the <0.01 level).

Fig. 4 shows the proximity to other users compared by journey times. The longer the trip, the worse is the evaluation of the proximity factor to other users. This becomes even more critical when this evaluation is weighted with the level of importance. The curve of the image on the right (Table 2) better reflects the differences between users with shorter travel times (20 min) and trips of >60 min.

Proximity to other users is mainly defined by transport mode, where public transport users have a more negative score, suggesting a lower achieved level of functioning. The metro system in Santiago has historically had a better evaluation in terms of levels of service compared to the bus fleet. However, at present, both modes of public transport score poorly in terms of the level of crowdedness. In Santiago, this condition is manifested mostly in central areas (such as Santiago Centro, Providencia, or along the corridor of the central business district area) and some catchment hubs in the most peripheral areas—usually converging at a particular metro station. The problem is again more significant for people who make longer journeys and live further away from the city center, showing significant gaps of inequality between transport users in poorer peripheral areas when compared with their richer inner city counterparts.

4   Policy relevance

The social impacts of transport systems and projects are poorly assessed in almost all contexts internationally. As a result, the disadvantaged groups gain the poorest travel experiences and access to activities in cities, impacting on their life experiences. Distributional issues are often overlooked as project appraisal focuses on economic

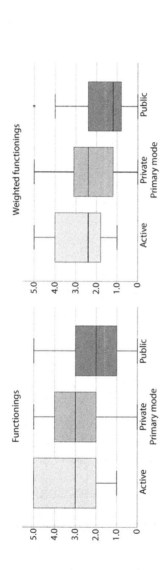

Fig. 3 Box plots showing the distribution of functionings (*left*) and weighted functionings (*right*) for the factor of proximity to other users compared by primary transport mode. The boxes represent the distribution of the 25th–75th percentile. *Bottom* and *top* horizontal lines represent the maximum and minimum values. In the *left*, active and private users have assessed a higher level of functionings than public transport users. In the *right* (weighted functionings), the distribution of data represents a significant amount of responses showing that public transport has a lower assessment when considering the levels of importance.

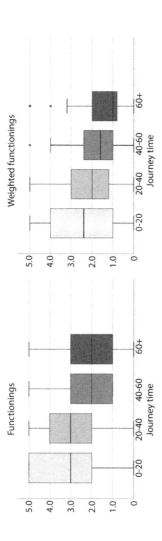

Fig. 4 Proximity to other users compared by journey times. Functioning total values *(left)* and weighted functioning values *(right)*.

Table 2 Chi-square test by primary mode and journey time, for proximity to other transport users (functionings and weighted functionings)

	Mode				Journey time				
	Private	Public	Active	Chi-square	0–20	20–40	40–60	60+	Chi-square
	31.0%	**59.9%**	**9.1%**		**20.4%**	**22.8%**	**25.1%**	**29.5%**	
Functionings									
High	33.6%	17.8%	48.8%	<0.01	42.4%	31.1%	19.5%	13.5%	<0.01
Neutral	31.4%	18.5%	22.0%		22.8%	24.3%	24.8%	20.3%	
Low	32.1%	62.2%	29.3%		32.6%	42.7%	54.9%	63.9%	
Weighted functionings									
High	65.0%	65.6%	75.6%	0.28	72.8%	71.8%	67.3%	56.4%	0.15
Neutral	23.6%	20.0%	24.4%		18.5%	22.3%	20.4%	24.8%	
Low	10.0%	12.6%	0.0%		6.5%	5.8%	11.5%	15.8%	

efficiency goals. The use of the CA in transport allows us to explore social impacts regarding the opportunities for travel, activity participation, and well-being. These impacts are related to actual travel, actual activity participation, and actual levels of well-being. This may seem a subtle distinction but is important if we are to consider improving levels of public transport accessibility and using this accessibility more effectively for producing advantages.

The CA, through the distinction between capabilities and functionings, might be used to determine existing levels of equity in terms of what the individuals wish to do and what they are actually able to perform. As presented at the beginning of the chapter, capabilities represent the various combinations of doings and beings (functionings) that a person can feasibly achieve. The analysis based on weighted functionings brings the measurement of capabilities closer, as the levels of importance that people attribute to their functionings relates to what a person would define in the range of her freedoms and opportunities.

However, the significance given to the individual level, considering for instance the importance of a freedom and personal subjective elements, can also be an important criticism of the CA. In transport, as well as other public goods, there is often a need to trade-off personal considerations with the idea of "a common good," so, when transferring these CA concepts to collective solutions, policy targets should consider personal abilities and individual assets but mostly they should also *be explicit* concerning how they affect different people's opportunities—especially the most disadvantaged groups.

How can the measurement of CA help to understand the capabilities achievement (or lack of it) in the case of Santiago? The case study has examined the CA through an evaluative and nonnormative framework. This has been the reason for raising the issues of the current inadequacy of transport project appraisal and its indicators. Although the chapter has not shown in depth the survey results, it reveals a real lack of opportunities for the most disadvantaged groups as low-income people, public transport users, and women. In these three groups, the methodology applied allows understanding of how difficult it is for these groups to transform the limited available transport resources into capabilities in comparison with the most advantaged groups. The possibility for more individuals to transform available transport resources to match their own personal travel needs may result greater accessibility to certain goods and services, and can also enhance their quality of life, increasing their opportunities of employment and social participation, and satisfy their physical and economic needs.

Sociodemographics factors showed in this chapter are all associated with lower scores in the case of low-income groups. There are clear social equity issues here—the current transport systems are disadvantaging low-income groups and neighborhoods in Santiago, and indeed in many other contexts in the Global South. The low-income areas often suffer from locational disadvantages, being on the edge of the urban metropolitan area, and are served very poorly by public transport networks. This results in the lower-income groups perceiving their capabilities and well-being more negatively, particularly when using public transport as the primary mode and traveling for longer journey times.

There are important issues by gender; females using public transport score poorly across the health indicators. Thus, policy and projects should aim especially at this group, improving access and journey conditions. The journey experience on public transport is very different by gender and needs much closer attention—with projects directly developed for improving the experience of female users. However, a more arduous analysis of gender has also remained a point that would require more attention in future research. It has been found that women are more disadvantages with respect to men (considering the capability factors explored). This is also the group that makes the most trips, both in number and diverse nature. The perceptions of women, and the subgroups accorded to the different transport modes, can be complemented with the activities they carry out. Research requires even more analysis in this regard.

The analysis aimed to consider a broader range of multidimensional transport-related impacts than usually found in social impact assessment. It uses the concept of functionings to foster discussion on service levels and journey experience, also considering the users' priority given to factors through the weighted functionings. The value of performing this analysis in the context of Santiago is significant, with most of the previous research carried out in the Global North, and with better economic and social indexes than those currently existing in the Chilean society.

The extent to which transport systems impact on people's capabilities and opportunities in life, and how this may be improved, can be the subject of further research. Other issues can also be explored, examining different evaluations of capability, beyond weighted functionings. For example, individual decision making and agency, considering relationships with the built environment (built form, public realm, and climate) and access to jobs. The current discussion points toward the development of transport policies and projects, which more thoroughly consider the range of social, well-being, and health impacts. Further evaluative research can lead us to a more comprehensive understanding of how transport projects have impacts on well-being.

5   Further reading

Readers interested in possible philosophical underpinnings for transport appraisal should consider reading Rawls (1971) for a wider framework on social justice. Rawls argued that we should promote the interests of the most disadvantaged in the society. Even though at the level of society these principles have a direct applicability, the theory of Rawls has not been well used in transport planning. Amarta Sen provides the basic background for the capabilities approach (Sen, 1985, 1999, 2009). Martha Nussbaum has attempted to operationalize the use of capabilities through the central human capabilities list (Nussbaum, 2011).

For further reading on the application to the transport domain, see, for example, Beyazit (2011) who synthesize social justice and transport literature in terms of equal rights, freedom, capabilities, opportunities, and choices. She also explores a methodology for engaging CA with existing methods for considering social justice norms in transport. For a broader definition of the translation of capabilities and functionings into transport, as well as the definition of the survey categories used in this chapter, see

Hickman et al. (2017). Martens (2016) provides an approach to distributive justice, specifically exploring accessibility as a capability. For more on capabilities in transport, see Cao et al. (2018), Uteng (2006), or Ryan et al. (2015). Pereira et al. (2017) also reviews key theories of justice (utilitarianism, libertarianism, intuitionism, Rawls' egalitarianism, and CA), evaluating their insights when applied to the transport domain.

For a nontransport-related analysis, see Comim et al. (2008) and Robeyns (2003, 2009), for a discussion on the multidimensional aspects of the well-being, capabilities and functionings, conversion factors, and agency—especially on assessing gender inequality in the Western societies. Gendered mobilities have also been discussed by and in Kronlid (2008).

References

Beyazit, E., 2011. Evaluating social justice in transport: lessons to be learned from the capability approach. Transp. Rev. 31 (1), 117–134.

Cao, M., Cao, M., Zhang, Y., Zhang, Y., Li, S., Hickman, R., 2018. Using different approaches to evaluate individual social equity in transport. In: Hickman, R., Mella Lira, B., Givoni, M., Geurs, K. (Eds.), Transport and Spatial Equity. Edward Elgar, Cheltenham.

Comim, F., Qizilbash, M., Alkire, S. (Eds.), 2008. The Capability Approach: Concepts, Measures and Applications. Cambridge University Press, Cambridge.

Hickman, R., Cao, M., Mella Lira, B., Fillone, A., Bienvenido Biona, J., 2017. Understanding capabilities, functionings and travel in high and low income neighbourhoods in Manila. Soc. Incl. 5 (4), 161–174.

Kronlid, D., 2008. Mobility as capability. In: Uteng, T.P., Cresswell, T. (Eds.), Gendered Mobilities. Routledge, pp. 5–34.

Martens, K., 2016. Transport justice: designing fair transportation systems. Routledge, London.

Nussbaum, M.C., 2011. Creating Capabilities. Harvard University Press, Cambridge, MA.

Pereira, R.H., Schwanen, T., Banister, D., 2017. Distributive justice and equity in transportation. Transp. Rev. 37 (2), 170–191.

Rawls, J., 1971. A Theory of Justice. Belknap Press/Harvard University Press, Cambridge.

Robeyns, I., 2003. Sen's capability approach and gender inequality: selecting relevant capabilities. Fem. Econ. 9 (2–3), 61–92.

Robeyns, I., 2009. Capabilities and theories of justice. In: Debating Global Society: Reach and Limits of the Capability Approach. Feltrinelli, Milan, pp. 61–68.

Ryan, J., Wretstrand, A., Schmidt, S.M., 2015. Exploring public transport as an element of older persons' mobility: a capability approach perspective. J. Transp. Geogr. 48, 105–114.

Sen, A., 1985. Commodities and Capabilities. Elsevier Science Pub. Co, Amsterdam; New York: North-Holland; New York: Sole distributors for the U.S.A. and Canada.

Sen, A., 1999. Development as Freedom. Oxford University Press, Oxford.

Sen, A., 2009. The Idea of Justice. Penguin, London.

Uteng, T.P., 2006. Mobility: discourses from the non-western immigrant groups in Norway. Mobilities 1 (3), 437–464.

A behavioral framework for needs-based transport assessment

17

Floridea Di Ciommo, Francesc Magrinyà, Gianni Rondinella, Yoram Shiftan

1 Introduction

Within the framework of equity in transport, this chapter provides an overview of the rationale for using a needs-satisfaction approach for transport planning assessment. It begins by presenting the main concepts and aims that have governed the transport planning process during the last decades: mobility and accessibility. Subsequently, a transition to a wider framework such as the proposed needs-satisfaction approach will be developed.

In the current literature, various approaches have been proposed to estimate transport benefits using traditional cost benefit analysis (CBA), which is mainly based on measuring journey time savings. However, the adoption of the travel time savings as the main criteria for assessing the benefits of transport planning policies has facilitated the construction of infrastructures that largely facilitate increased mobility and hypermobility, rather than delivering improved accessibility to destinations.

Relevant studies have shown that an adequate transport system is essential to the fulfillment of key human needs, including safety and security in health, employment, and social stability. Especially low-income households may experience some difficulties in travel, in part because excessive transport costs may compromise other household expenditures (health, education, quality of food). Failing to meet key human needs may result in physical, social, geographical, and economic social exclusion.

The current transport system seems particularly suited to facilitate mobility to employment during peak hours, while serving other off-peak and social travel needs less well, such as "mobility of caring" (i.e., trips' purposes related with foods shop, health centers, accompanying somebody). For example, many women's travel patterns are characterized by multiple and short trips, often made by walking. Yet, most transport investments tend to flow to costly mobility projects that enhance road capacity and increase the speed of cars, and improvements which may be benefiting men much more than women.

The advantage of accessibility indicators is to embed several characteristics of the transport-land use system in one indicator. By doing so, these indicators can provide a comprehensive assessment of the accessibility "service" received by the population. However, the accessibility approach retains the key idea that a trip is most relevant because it connects A to B and has also traditionally focused mostly on accessibility to work over other activities.

Measuring Transport Equity. https://doi.org/10.1016/B978-0-12-814818-1.00017-2

Trip chaining (i.e., visiting a number of destinations in one round trip) and accessibility to a set of activities covering a variety of needs beyond employment (i.e., accompanying children/elders, daily shops, health-care, visiting friends, and family) is still largely a "black-box" within accessibility analysis. Widely used accessibility measures, like cumulative opportunity measures, provide little insight into the question whether personal mobility needs are being met or not. More advanced accessibility indicators may also have their disadvantages, precisely because of how they are calculated: they tend to be a sum of overall accessibility to various destinations, with the results that the full *diversity* of individual people's accessibility needs may get lost in the aggregation. Therefore, one of the main objectives of this chapter is to define a complementary index for use alongside mainstream accessibility approaches to reveal the diversity of people's unmet (or poorly satisfied) travel needs. In other words, the objective of the needs-satisfaction approach is to highlight the differences between different people's needs instead of aggregating them.

People's travel to participate in activities, as well as travel itself, is driven by a set of subjective needs, such as existence needs (i.e., exercise, health, safety and security, multi-tasking during travel, travel independence), relatedness (i.e., togetherness, caregiving, norms, and social climate), and personal growth (i.e., self-esteem, competitiveness, self-identity, fitness). We posit that transport planners will be able to plan better transport systems if they understand the link between activities and the underlying personal needs. Needs can be best satisfied when they are first clearly identified at the individual level.

The major challenge of the needs-satisfaction approach is, therefore, how to identify personal mobility needs. While substantial progress has been made in the literature on how to assess basic needs, this remains a major issue in practice and is even more complicated when such basic needs have to be translated to transport needs. It is therefore necessary to define an ad hoc methodology for identifying needs in the terms of mobility. In this chapter, we propose a methodology that makes use of survey information on people's satisfaction or dissatisfaction with their current travel resources and their actual travel experiences as a basis for identifying the level of need satisfaction.

We assume that transport needs are poorly fulfilled when people are dissatisfied with their travel outcomes. We therefore propose to expand traditional travel surveys with questions about people's satisfaction with their travel experience. We have adopted this approach as part of the Barcelona metropolitan area (BMA) travel survey. The key advantage of this needs-satisfaction approach compared with equity assessments using place-based measures of accessibility is that different population groups are no longer considered as passive subjects waiting for a fair distribution of transport resources to be delivered, but are able to directly express their unmet travel needs (for which they require improved transport policies and additional resources) through the survey instrument.

2 Methodology: The needs-satisfaction approach

2.1 Approach

The core of our needs-satisfaction analysis encompasses two concepts: the notion of *travel time thresholds* and the notion of *travel satisfaction*.

As is common in travel behavior research, travel time represents the time it takes a traveler to reach a given activity. In our approach, we distinguish between different trip types based on trip purpose and between different sets of trips based on trip purpose, origin and destination combination, and transport mode. For each set of trips, we calculate s travel time threshold based on the average or median travel time for that particular set of trips, based on the understanding that people's willingness to travel will vary by activity type, for different origin-destinations combination, and for different transport modes.

People's travel satisfaction encompasses people's subjective assessment of a trip's characteristics. We measure satisfaction using a Likert scale, ranging from "very satisfied" to "very dissatisfied." We make a distinction between people who are (very) unsatisfied with their trip and those who indicate to be (very) satisfied with their trip. Here, we are only interested in people's satisfaction with their travel time, as this is perhaps the most important dimension of any trip.

We identify unmet, or poorly satisfied, travel needs by positioning each person's trips vis-à-vis the travel time threshold and the level of satisfaction (Table 1). A person's trip can belong to one of four categories: (1) trip is *shorter* than the travel time threshold and the user is satisfied with the travel time; (2) trip is *shorter* than the travel time threshold but the user is *not* satisfied with the travel time; (3) trip is *longer* than the travel time threshold but the user is satisfied with the travel time; and (4) trip is *longer* than the travel time threshold but the user is *not* satisfied with the travel time. Each of these trip categories is represented by the respective quadrants in Table 1.

We consider only trips that belong to the last category to represent the unmet, or poorly satisfied, travel needs. The persons that make these trips are not well-served by the existing transport system. The larger this group of people, and the more of their trips that belong to this category, the larger the inequity embodied by the transport system. These people are entitled to additional transport resources (e.g., quicker bus services, more direct walking routes, less waiting time at traffic lights) to improve their situation.

Based on the classification of trips we calculate the inaccessibility index (IA index). The IA index represents the share of a particular trip type that is not adequately served. More precisely, it represents the ratio between the trips that are not served well (all trips positioned in Quadrant 4 in Table 1) and the trips that are served reasonably well (all trips positioned in Quadrants 1-3 in Table 1). An IA value of zero implies that all people can reach desired destinations within the defined travel time threshold

Table 1 Classification of trips based on travel time threshold and satisfaction level; trips in category 4 represent unmet, or poorly satisfied, needs

		Level of satisfaction	
		satisfied	unsatisfied
Travel time threshold	Below (faster trip)	1	2
	Above (slower trip)	3	4

(Quadrant 1 and 2) or are satisfied with their trip in spite of a long travel time (Quadrant 3). The higher the IA score, the more people experience travel times above the threshold and express dissatisfaction with their travel times.

2.2 Data requirements and analysis

The proposed needs-satisfaction analysis can be carried out based on data collected through an extended travel behavior survey. In addition to regular data on respondents' trip making, this extended survey should collect data of people's satisfaction with each of the trips they made. This requires the expansion of the typical travel survey with questions about satisfaction with particular trip dimensions, in particular regarding people's satisfaction with their trip travel time. Data on satisfaction can be obtained by adding questions using a Likert scale with answering categories ranging from "very satisfied" to "very dissatisfied."

Based on these data, the needs-satisfaction methodology proceeds through five key steps:

1. Identify trip types and trip sets based on origin-destination combination, trip purpose and transport mode, and register the (distribution of) travel times associated with each trip sets based on a travel survey.
2. Determine the travel time threshold for each trip set based on the average or median travel time for the trip set (see further explanation).
3. Identify respondents' satisfaction with travel time for each trip. Make a distinction between trips with whom respondents are satisfied and trips with whom they are not.
4. Based on (2) and (3), determine for each trip to which of the four quadrants in Table 1 it belongs.
5. Estimate the inaccessibility score (IA score) per zone, for each trip set and for all trips originating in a zone, based on the categorization of trips in step (4).

Taken together, these steps allow us to identify the population groups with unmet, or poorly satisfied, needs: groups that experience travel times above the preset travel time threshold for one or more trip types and are dissatisfied with these travel times. The reasons why specific needs may not be met should then be investigated, taking into account the type of activity (i.e., work, study, daily shopping, occasional purchases, medical care and visits to family and friends, accompanying children/dependent others) and trip attribute levels about which respondents have expressed dissatisfaction (i.e., travel times).

For a formal specification of our impedance measure, we refer to the reader Di Ciommo and Lucas (2014).

3 The case-study implementation in the Barcelona Metropolitan Area

The needs-satisfaction approach proposed in this chapter aims to provide policymakers with a comprehensive assessment of the current transport system and to demonstrate the extent to which it satisfies the elicited needs of people to access their daily activities. We apply the needs-satisfaction approach here in a case study for the Barcelona metropolitan region. More specifically, we have implemented our approach to four "poverty corridors" located in the BMA. These corridors were identified according to three criteria: (i) income level, (ii) demographic profile of the population, and (iii) level of public and private transport service.

3.1 Step 1 of the needs-satisfaction approach

The initial step of the needs-satisfaction approach involves the identification of relevant study area (Fig. 1). In this case, we have focused on "poverty corridors" in the Barcelona metropolitan region.

The BMA is a territorial entity made up of Barcelona and 35 neighboring municipalities. In 2016, it has a population of 3,226,600 inhabitants in an area of 636 km^2. The identified poverty corridors occupy more than 30% of the area of the BMA and are home to about 40% of the metropolitan population outside of Barcelona city. The largest corridor is the N150, covering Cerdanyola del Vallès with its 29.6 km^2 and a population density of 12,000 persons/km^2, while the R4 (i.e., Llobregat corridor) is the most compact part, where Hospitalet de Llobregat is the city with the highest population density of 29,800 persons/km^2.

The poverty corridors are defined by their sociodemographic characteristics. It is here where poverty is concentrated and policymakers would like to act. The average income level in these corridors is between 21% and 30% lower than in the city of Barcelona, while people in need of "caring" mobility (i.e., trips for health-care, for being accompanied, to be visited) are between 45% and 55%. The needs-satisfaction approach helps policymakers to select the poverty corridor where the transport problem is bigger.

3.2 Step 2: Defining trip typology and estimation of travel time threshold

From the travel behavior survey a sample of 39,952 trips was selected. This sample included all trips made by people living in the selected poverty corridors, who have expressed their satisfaction in respect to their recurring or potential mode of transport. These trips were categorized into trip types and trip sets, based on travel purpose, origin-destination combination, and transport mode. For each trip set, the following steps were conducted:

(a) Identifying all trips belonging to a particular trip set as determined by travel purpose, origin-destination combination, and transport mode.
(b) Calculating the mean, median, and standard deviation of the variable "trip duration" for each trip set.
(c) Determining the travel time threshold for each trip set. The travel time threshold is equal to the mean, when the coefficient of variation is smaller or equal to 0.2 (the coefficient of variation equals the standard deviation divided by the mean). When the coefficient of variation is larger than 0.2, the travel time threshold is equal to the median. We adopt this statistical rule for selecting the mean or the median, so that the travel time threshold is a reasonable representation of the "average" situation experienced by the respondents that have made a particular type of trip.

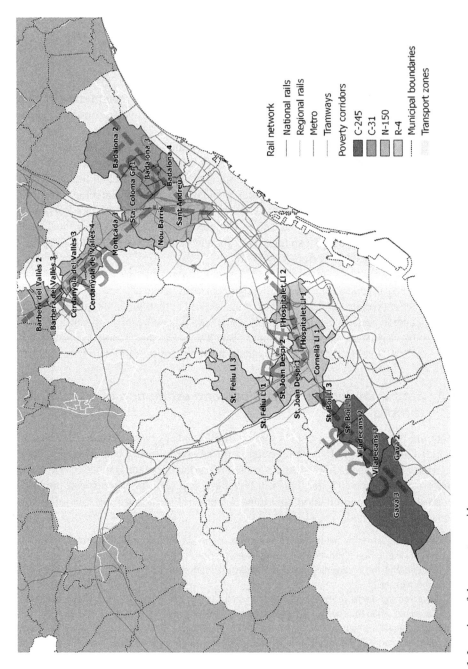

Fig. 1 Location of the poverty corridors.

The result of these three steps is a travel time threshold for each of the trip sets observed in the four poverty corridors (a total of 4135 trip sets encompassing the total number of 39,952 trips observed in the travel survey as originating in the four corridors).

3.3 Step 3: Identification of population groups with poorly satisfied needs

The third step aims to identify the population groups to which transport policy interventions should be directed primarily to reduce their risk of social exclusion and increase their quality of life. Generally speaking, the needs-satisfaction approach can assist to detect the corridor and population groups which are most poorly served by the existing transport system. Table 2 shows that both corridors N150 and C31 contain the weakest population in terms of socioeconomic profile. However, when we analyze the extent to which the population's transport needs are being fulfilled, N150 corridor shows the highest level of poorly satisfied travel needs.

An analysis by gender and employment situation suggests that the transport needs of women, students, and retired and unemployed people are well less catered for, in particular in the N150 corridor. In the other three corridors, especially the travel needs of students are poorly covered (Table 3).

When the IA score (Table 2, column 4) is used to estimate the amount and the percentage of population in need of improved accessibility, we observe differences between the four poverty corridors. The N150 corridor shows the highest percentage (17%), while the percentage for the other three corridors lies between 6.7% and 8.5%. This shows that the pattern of transport poverty is different from the pattern socioeconomic poverty and that corridors with similar socioeconomic compositions may have quite different rates of transport poverty (Table 4).

Analyzing the results behind Tables 3 and 4 we conclude that:

(a) A substantial share of the population living in corridor N150 experiences unmet travel needs. This is related to the long travel distances and people's time constraints for carrying out multiple tasks, including caring, studying, and work activities (e.g., to take care of daily food purchases or to gain access to the work or study place).

Table 2 Socioeconomic characteristics of the selected poverty corridors

Corridor	Total Population	Unemployed	People in need of mobility caring	Migrants	Young people with Low Education
N-150	356.831	30%	45%–50%	20%–30%	20%–25%
R-4	338.995	15%–20%	50%–55%	30%–40%	10%–15%
C-31	248.728	30%	45%–50%	30%–40%	20%–25%
C-245	109.107	20%–25%	45%–50%	20%–30%	15%–20%

Source: own elaboration.

Table 3 Needs detector: inaccessibility scores within the selected poverty corridors

Corridor/employment status	Female	Male	IA score
C-245	*0.07*	*0.07*	*0.07*
Unemployed	0.05	0.05	0.05
Workers	0.04	0.04	0.04
Student	0.15	0.14	0.14
Retired	0.05	0.05	0.05
Housewives	0.04		0.04
C-31	*0.08*	*0.09*	*0.09*
Unemployed	0.06	0.07	0.06
Workers	0.05	0.05	0.05
Student	0.16	0.17	0.17
Retired	0.08	0.06	0.07
Housewives	0.07		0.07
N-150	*0.17*	*0.17*	*0.17*
Unemployed	0.18	0.17	0.17
Workers	0.16	0.14	0.15
Student	0.20	0.20	0.20
Retired	0.18	0.19	0.19
Housewives	0.10	0.02	0.10
R-4	*0.07*	*0.07*	*0.07*
Unemployed	0.05	0.05	0.05
Workers	0.04	0.04	0.04
Student	0.14	0.13	0.14
Retired	0.05	0.05	0.05
Housewives	0.05	0.01	0.05
Total	*0.09*	*0.09*	*0.09*

Higher scores are highlighted.
Source: own elaboration.

Table 4 Population in need of mobility solutions corridor by corridor

Corridor	Area (m²)	Population	Population in need	% of Population in need	
N-150	**29.6**	**356.831**	**60.652**	**17.0%**	
R-4	31.7	338.995	23.085	6.8%	
C-31	22.1	248.728	21.257	8.6%	
C-245	27.5	109.107	7.316	6.7%	
Total	110.9	1.053.661	155.927	10.7%	

Source: own elaboration.

(b) The opposite seems to be the case for poverty corridors of R4, C31, and C245. Here, especially students experience unmet mobility needs mainly in relation to travel with a study purpose, which is reflected in the lower IA scores for these corridors than the N150 corridor.

(c) The results show that especially students experience unmet mobility needs across all four corridors.

Our needs-satisfaction approach could be generalized and adopted by policymakers for: (1) identifying needs that people cannot meet because of limitations in the transport system; (2) exploring the attributes of trips with particular purposes (e. g., work, leisure, health, daily food purchases, visits to relatives, and friends); and (3) exploring how these trips could be improved through the transport planning policies.

Following this needs-satisfaction approach, this chapter shows that a lower degree of satisfaction is associated with a higher travel time threshold mean. Such an observation is in line with expectations, but it only becomes possible to determine this if travel surveys include an additional section on respondents' satisfaction with various dimensions of their trips. This simple addition to standard travel surveys makes it possible to implement our proposed needs-satisfaction approach. This novel approach allows policymakers to have a better understanding of where and how to target transport investment and services improvement to improve social equity outcomes.

In the Barcelona case study, the analysis show that corridors of poverty with similar socioeconomic background reveal different needs in terms of mobility and that transport poverty can be independent from socioeconomic poverty. Women, and in particular housewives, experience more problems regarding unmet or poorly satisfied travel needs (Table 4), suggesting that policymakers need to adopt a gender perspective to understand why women experience a higher inaccessibility score and how their accessibility and satisfaction with travel can be improved.

4 Policy relevance

The results of this study have showed that our needs-satisfaction approach can be an effective tool for assessing the current transport situation experienced by different population groups and geographical areas of the city. It could also be used in "before/after" studies to evaluate the extent to which different transport interventions serve to meet people's identified needs and enhance their satisfaction with travel.

In particular, this methodology achieves six main objectives:

1. Provide the opportunity for specific population groups to express their needs by simply answering the satisfaction questionnaire and revealing their travel time.
2. Investigate the reasons why specific needs in transport may not be met through knowing the groups of population in needs of mobility solutions.
3. Show that transport poverty is different and sometimes independent from socioeconomic poverty and that it should be treated separately.
4. Allow prioritizing investments in transport for improving metropolitan bus and rail networks.

5. Adjust specific improvements for the accessibility poor corridor by meeting needs of people and rights to a transport system.
6. Orient the location of the investments in education and health equipment behind considering the inaccessibility index of different groups of people vs. socioeconomic CBA.

The Strategic Planning and Transport departments of the BMA will be using the results of our analysis to (re)orient their transport investment based on what people are revealing in terms of their needs.

5   Further reading

The needs-satisfaction approach developed here and the related inaccessibility index to reveal the unmet needs of different population groups is fully developed in Di Ciommo (2018). There is a growing body of literature on transport equity assessment, which has informed our approach and that can be traced back to around 6 years (Lucas and Jones, 2012; Di Ciommo and Lucas, 2014). Similarly, the concept of using a needs-satisfaction approach to understand the links between equity and transport planning provides a promising avenue for research both empirically and theoretically (Currie, 2004; Currie and Senbergs, 2007). Litman (2017) has shown that the transport system is perceived as an essential for key human needs in terms of safety and security in health, employment, and social stability, particularly among low-income households.

Existing approaches to assess transport interventions do not directly address (travel) needs. This is partly because transport needs are difficult to identify. Consequently, various "proxies" to capture social benefits of transport have been developed over the last few years. Among them, the most widely used are most probably those base on the accessibility concept (Geurs and Van Wee, 2004; Farber et al., 2014; Martens, 2015). The disadvantage of accessibility-based indicators is that they are estimated as a sum and average of various elements (i.e., space and time), where the diversity of in terms of people's needs is lost or at least remains hidden. Yet, some others have made progress in the measurement of needs. Arentze and Timmermans (2009) estimate poorly served needs for transport based on low levels of satisfaction. Along the same, Bláfoss Ingvardson et al. (2018) identify needs in terms of mobility, based on the fact that satisfaction or dissatisfaction is a criterion for revealing when needs are met or not.

References

Bláfoss Ingvardson, J., Kaplan, S., de Abreu e Silva, J., Di Ciommo, F., Shiftan, Y., Nielsen, O. A, 2018. Existence, relatedness and growth needs as mediators between mode choice and travel satisfaction: evidence from Denmark. Transportation. https:/doi.org/10.1007/s11116-018-9886-3.
Currie, G., 2004. Gap analysis of public transport needs: measuring spatial distribution of public transport needs and identifying gaps in the quality of public transport provision. Transp. Res. Rec.: J. Transp. Res. Board 1895, 137–146.

Currie, G., Senbergs, Z., 2007. Identifying spatial gaps in public transport provision for socially disadvantaged Australians: the Melbourne'Needs-Gap'Study.

Di Ciommo, F., Lucas, K., 2014. Evaluating the equity effects of road-pricing in the European urban context–The Madrid Metropolitan Area. Appl. Geogr. 54, 74–82.

Di Ciommo, F., 2018. How the Inaccessibility Index can improve transport planning and investment? International Transport Forum – OECD.

Lucas, K., Jones, P., 2012. Social impacts and equity issues in transport: an introduction. J. Transp. Geogr. 21, 1–3.

Arentze, T.A., Timmermans, H.J., 2009. A need-based model of multi-day, multi-person activity generation. Transport. Res. B: Methodol. 43 (2), 251–265.

Farber, S., Morang, M.Z., Widener, M.J., 2014. Temporal variability in transit-based accessibility to supermarkets. Appl. Geogr. 53, 149–159.

Geurs, K.T., Van Wee, B., 2004. Accessibility evaluation of land-use and transport strategies: review and research directions. J. Transp. Geogr. 12 (2), 127–140.

Litman, T., 2017. Transportation affordability. Transportation 250, 360–1560.

Martens, K., 2015. Accessibility and potential mobility as a guide for policy action. Transp. Res. Rec.: J. Transp. Res. Board 2499, 18–24.

Assessing the equity impacts of a transportation investment program

18

Alex Karner, Aaron Golub

1 Introduction

Transportation planning and programming are two fundamentally different but intimately related activities. Transportation plans typically establish a vision for long-term (20–30-year horizon) infrastructure development and often include a simulation of impacts relative to existing conditions or a no-build future scenario. Transportation investment programs, on the other hand, implement the plan in the near-term, attaching funding to specific projects. While a plan may remain simply a plan, a program is much more likely to result in the implementation of real transportation infrastructure.

When considering questions of transportation equity, concerning the fair distribution of the benefits and burdens of transportation investments, analyses of both the plan and the program are relevant. In practice, equity analyses of plans are much more common, but transportation justice advocates have increasingly argued for analyses focused on short-term (e.g., a 4- or 5-year horizon) impacts. Investment programs contain information about the precise locations of projects, making them an ideal data source with which to conduct this type of analysis.

One problem that must be avoided when analyzing investment programs is the assumption that proximity to transportation infrastructure is beneficial. This is only sometimes the case; roadway proximity in particular is a double-edged sword. On the one hand, roadway and interchange proximity is likely to be associated with enhanced accessibility to destinations. On the other, proximity brings exposure to air pollution, noise, and visual blight. Furthermore, automobile ownership and therefore the derived benefits of capacity improvements are not equitably distributed across demographic groups. For the equity analysis of an investment program to be considered meaningful, its results must reflect the lived experiences of those expected to be affected by each of the projects in the program.

The purpose of this chapter is to develop and test a replicable method that can be used to assess the equity impacts of a transportation investment program. To that end, we present an analysis using a dataset of proposed projects taken from the Delaware Valley Regional Planning Commission (DVRPC), a regional transportation planning organization in the greater Philadelphia area in Pennsylvania and New Jersey in the United States.

Measuring Transport Equity. https://doi.org/10.1016/B978-0-12-814818-1.00018-4

We adopt an equity standard for the identification of potentially unjust projects that simultaneously considers benefits and burdens. For highway capacity expansions, a project is considered unjust if carless households are generally located closer to the new road than households with automobiles available. For public transit expansions, a project is considered unjust if carless households are located further from the improvement than households with automobiles available. In both cases, projects with greater differences between the two population groups will be considered more or less just, depending on which is closer or further for a given project. The goal is to develop a meaningful approach that recognizes not all proximity is beneficial for all populations. The findings will be of interest to transportation planners and practitioners seeking to analyze the equity impacts of transportation investment programs or individual projects.

2 The United States context: Civil rights, environmental justice, and regional planning

The United States provides a unique example of relatively strong legal and institutional frameworks for conducting transportation equity assessments. These derive from specific laws, like Title VI of the 1964 Civil Rights Act, and executive actions like President Clinton's 1994 Executive Order 12898 on environmental justice. These measures define protected populations (e.g., racial/ethnic minority groups, low-income people) and require that they receive a fair share of the benefits of public investments while not being disproportionately burdened by them. Equity analyses—assessments of fairness and disproportionality—are usually conducted using quantitative data on demographics and transportation system performance. In most cases, completing any equity analysis is considered sufficient for legal compliance, whether the results truly reflect the experiences of populations likely to benefit from, or be burdened by, a plan or project. In the early 2010s, the US Federal Transit Administration released two documents intending to eliminate ambiguity from certain types of equity assessments, but their recommended methods have also been subject to criticism.

For the purposes of this chapter, metropolitan planning organizations (MPOs) are particularly relevant. According to federal law, urbanized areas that exceed a population of 50,000 must define and identify an MPO in order to receive federal funds. An MPO's jurisdiction is generally defined by commute patterns and encompasses multiple different city and county governments.

MPOs undertake a planning process that is performance-based, multimodal, and includes the development of a metropolitan transportation plan (MTP) and transportation improvement program (TIP). The MTP's horizon must be at least 20 years in the future, and short- and long-range actions must be included to drive toward a truly safe and multimodal transportation system. MPOs must use the best available knowledge regarding forecast population and land use, but they are free to develop additional scenarios that represent different future investment or land use patterns. Other requirements relate to those who must be consulted during MTP development, financial constraint, and other specific elements to include in the plan (e.g., infrastructure design concepts, the contribution of public transit to meeting regional goals, specific performance measure, etc.).

The TIP covers a period of at least 4 years and is continuously updated. It should also be consistent with the priorities embodied in the MTP. Federal regulations require coordination between the MPO, public transit agencies, and the relevant state department of transportation. In general, all projects (capital and noncapital) proposed for federal funding during the TIP period must be listed, but certain project types are exempted from inclusion (e.g., planning and research activities, emergency relief, among others). Importantly, while the specific US legal context of civil rights and environmental justice is unique, the particular manner in which transportation planning and programming unfolds is not. The methods described in this chapter can be used by any planning agency charged with implementing individual projects or entire investment programs with access to appropriate data. Multiyear transportation investment programs are common in many regions and countries around the world.

3 Approach and methodology

3.1 Assessing the benefits and burdens of transportation infrastructure

Transportation investment programs and similar lists of infrastructure investments with associated funding sources provide information about projects likely to be built in the near-term. Here, we propose a transportation justice analysis of these programs with a focus on assessing the effects of capacity-increasing highway and public transit projects. These types of projects hold the greatest potential to affect generalized travel costs and thus to influence route and mode choice. New highway infrastructure and new users will create burdens for nearby residents resulting from increased exposure to vehicle traffic and associated air pollution, noise, and vibration. The benefits of the same infrastructure will be widely dispersed among the population of drivers that use the facility.

Similarly, some public transit capacity expansions will increase burdens related to visual intrusion, air pollution (depending on fuel), noise, and vibration. Other public transit capacity expansions may be much more benign, including those that seek to reduce travel time and increase reliability by more easily moving passengers through stations, streamlining fare payment systems, or upgrading vehicles to facilitate all-door boarding. Those who do not regularly use the public transit system mostly derive secondary benefits associated with transit's congestion mitigating effects, reductions in environmental externalities, and increases in real estate value.

Our approach to the equity assessment of transportation investment programs involves simultaneously considering benefits and burdens and making several simplifying assumptions. Specifically, we assume that households with automobiles available are the only populations that derive benefits from highway capacity expansions and carless households are the only populations that derive benefits from public transit capacity expansions. Care must be taken when assessing public transit projects in this way, as not all may benefit carless households. Park-and-ride station construction or added parking capacity, for example, could both be considered capacity expanding but are not likely to benefit carless households directly. Only those projects that increase capacity on the types of transit services that carless households are likely to use should be assessed when that population group is defined as the beneficiary. Wherever possible, locations of transit stops and stations should be used instead of lines or routes since people can only access public transit at specific locations.

Each of these assumptions could easily be relaxed to include different population groups. For example, low-income households that own a vehicle may still derive substantial benefit from new investments in local transit frequency. On the other hand, high-income households are likely to benefit disproportionately from new commuter-oriented rail service. Different project types could also be evaluated. Regardless of the population or project type selected, a clear beneficiary group must be identified that can be separated from the rest of the population.

We assume further that both benefit and burden are inversely related to distance from the improvement—as distance increases, both benefit and burden decrease. Admittedly, the use of distance to measure benefits is imprecise; travelers who reside far from a project derive a benefit if they use the facility. On the other hand, nearby residents are more likely to use proximate facilities more often.

Considering only these two groups (automobile-owning and carless households), we propose that a project is just if the median distance from a project to the benefitting population is less than the median distance from a project to the other group. The possible categorial outcomes from the assessment process are summarized in Table 1. Of course, the analysis of an individual project will result in empirical measures of precisely how much closer one group is than the other. Consider two possible outcomes for a highway-capacity-expanding project: (1) median distance from the project is 250 m for carless households and 300 m for all other households and (2) median distance from the project is 250 m for carless households and 1000 m for all other households. While both outcomes would be considered unjust by our criterion, the second outcome is clearly *more* unjust than the first. In practice, agencies should work with affected population groups to determine appropriate thresholds or differences that would be deemed unacceptable.

3.2 Required data

The proposed method is most easily implemented in a geographic information system (GIS) environment. Data are required on the spatial location and attributes (e.g., project type) of proposed transportation infrastructure investments as well as the

Table 1 Equity assessment outcomes under different scenarios

Project type	Automobile-available households closer	Carless households closer
Highway capacity expansion	*Just*	*Unjust*
Public transit capacity expansion	*Unjust*	*Just*

concentration of population groups that might benefit from or be burdened by the proposed infrastructure. Transportation planning agencies regularly produce such spatial data when preparing their multiyear investment proposals, yet these data may not be available publicly. Demographic information, including counts of population groups summarized at small levels of geography are routinely produced by national governments in the Global North as part of census and related data collection efforts. We document the application of our proposed methods using data drawn from a region in the northeast United States.

4 Application

4.1 Case study area

The case study area for this work is the greater Philadelphia region in the United States, specifically the area that falls under the jurisdiction of the DVRPC, the region's MPO. The DVRPC was chosen because of the public availability of spatial data on a set of transport investments. Basic racial/ethnic demographics for the region are shown in Fig. 1. People of color tend to be concentrated in relatively small geographic areas and only achieve high demographic proportions within certain parts of the city of Philadelphia. Notably, patterns of segregation are strong and there is very little middle-ground; areas have either high proportions of white residents or high proportions of people of color.

4.2 Data sources

Spatial information about the location of proposed transportation projects and their attributes were taken from the DVRPC; the agency maintains this information on their open data portal (http:/www.dvrpc.org/Mapping/Data/). Nine categories are used by DVRPC to describe projects, as shown in Table 2. Projects are represented either as lines or points and there is often substantial duplication. For example, all highway capacity expansions that are represented as lines are also represented as points, but the converse is not true. Transportation system management (also known as intelligent transportation system) projects, for example, are represented as points, since those projects typically affect a single intersection or bottleneck location. Projects represented as both lines and points include roadway widenings, extensions, and new connectors. The point was typically located at the center of its associated line. Substantial care was taken to ensure that duplicates were removed and that each unique project was only included once in the final dataset. In general, lines were assumed to take precedence over points, as they represent the full spatial extent of a project.

Table 2 illustrates the total value of projects in each category as well as the count of unique project identification numbers in the assembled spatial datasets. Consistent with other regions in the United States, in terms of total numbers of projects, DVRPC's project list emphasizes maintenance and rehabilitation of existing infrastructure and transportation efficiency improvements (e.g., interchange improvements

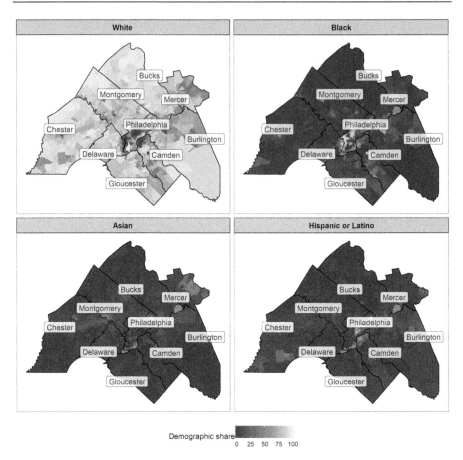

Fig. 1 Nine-county Delaware Valley Regional Planning Commission regional context, illustrating demographic proportions at the census tract level.
Source: 2011–2015 American Community Survey, 5-year estimates.

and intelligent transportation systems) as opposed to the construction of new highway or transit capacity (e.g., entirely new lanes or new fixed guideways). Certain categories, like transit improvements, are associated with particularly high costs per project (approximately $68 million each, on average).

Counts of households with automobiles available and carless households were taken from the 2011–2015 American Community Survey (ACS) 5-year estimates at the census tract level. Census tracts are spatial units that vary in area but typically delineate more-or-less cohesive neighborhoods. Populations contained within tracts range from approximately 1200 to 8000. The ACS replaced the "long form" that was previously used to collect detailed demographic information during US decennial censuses. Its small-area counts are generated by aggregating the results taken from samples that are collected continuously over multiple years. The 5-year estimates represent an average count over a 5-year period.

Table 2 Summary of all DVRPC TIP project costs (2017–2020 for Pennsylvania and 2016–2019 for New Jersey) by project type

	Number of projects	Total costs ($1,000)	Proportion of total costs	Average cost per project ($1,000)
Bridge Repair/ Replacement	127	$2,470,878	39.4%	$19,456
Intersection/ Interchange Improvements	88	$921,481	14.7%	$10,471
Signal/ITS Improvements	73	$78,632	1.3%	$1,077
Roadway Rehabilitation	55	$633,637	10.1%	$11,521
Bicycle/Pedestrian Improvement	34	$61,125	1.0%	$1,798
Roadway New Capacity	29	$723,721	11.5%	$24,956
Transit Improvements	20	$1,354,631	21.6%	$67,732
Streetscape	9	$28,694	0.5%	$3,188
Other	3	$3,912	0.1%	$1,304
Total	**438**	**$6,276,711**	**100%**	**$14,330**

4.3 Constructing required distance measures

Our approach to assessing the median distance to transportation improvements involves the creation of a continuous surface of residential population by converting tract-level counts of carless and automobile-owning households into points, where each point represents a household. Specifically, for each tract, we create a set of points randomly distributed within the tract so that the total number of points equals the number of households according to the ACS counts. Within ESRI's ArcGIS, the "Create Random Points" geoprocessing tool can be used for this purpose. The open-source QGIS has a similar tool available called "random points inside polygons."

Once the layers representing each population group as points are created, we calculate distances between each capacity-expanding project and each point. This distance matrix facilitates the creation of a distribution of carless and automobile-available households proximate to each capacity-expanding project. "Kernel density plots" can then be constructed for all households located within a predefined distance of individual projects to assess the empirical distribution of distance from the project for each population group. Throughout our case study, we employ 2 km as the relevant impact area. The kernel density is a smoothed histogram, suitable when an underlying variable is continuous. A histogram requires the analyst to set an appropriate column width (or "bin size") into which to place counts. The use of kernel density eliminates this step. An additional advantage of its use is that the area under the curve between

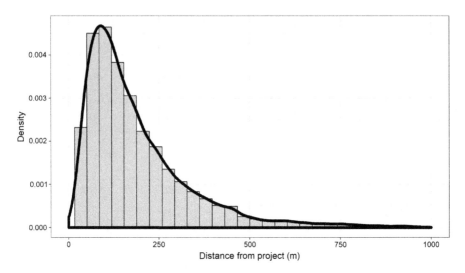

Fig. 2 Comparison of a histogram and kernel density plot prepared using simulated data on distance from road for a hypothetical transportation project. The histogram is shown in grey bars and the kernel density plot is the thick black line.

two points on the x-axis can be interpreted as the population share residing within that distance range. The greater the area, the greater the population share. A comparison of the two types of plots is shown in Fig. 2. The 1000 data points underlying the figure were generated by sampling from a hypothetical lognormal distribution with mean, median, and standard deviation of distance from the project of approximately 200, 150, and 160 m, respectively.

Once distributions like those shown in Fig. 2 are created for each group of interest and each project, they can be assessed visually for disparities (i.e., to determine whether one group is located relatively more closely to a project relative to the other) and characteristics of the distributions can be compared. One way to assess the relative proximity of each group to a project is to compare measures of central tendency for each of their distributions. To determine which group is closer to each project we first calculate a median for each distribution and population group. We then calculate the difference between median distances for carless households and households with automobiles available. If the result is negative, carless households are located closer to the project (unjust for highway capacity expansion and just for public transit capacity expansion). If the result is positive, automobile-owning households are located closer to the project (just for highway capacity expansion and unjust for public transit capacity expansion).

4.4   Results for highway capacity expansions

The distance-based analysis results for a subset of three DVRPC highway-capacity-expanding projects are summarized in Fig. 3. We are showing only a subset of project-level results that represent the full range of possible outcomes resulting from a visual

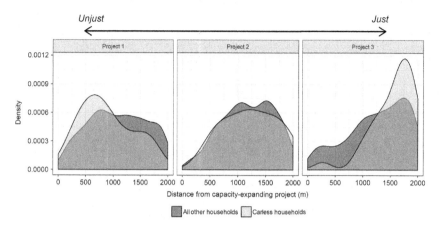

Fig. 3 Kernel density plots of population residing within 2 km of three different highway capacity expanding projects. The projects are ordered left to right from least to most just.

assessment of kernel density plots. They include a parkway reconstruction and extension (Project 1), a state route extension (Project 2), and a new connector (Project 3). The results could easily be extended to include one figure per capacity-expanding project.

Arranged from left to right, the projects shift from being least to most just. Project 1 has carless households concentrated relatively closer to the project than all other households, meeting our criterion for an unjust project because the population benefitting from the project is located relatively further away than the population that will derive less benefit but will still face substantial burdens. Project 2 shows very little difference in the spatial distribution of households close to the project. Additional analysis would be required in this case to determine precisely which group was located closer to or further from the project. The kernel density plot for Project 3 shows that carless households are located relatively far from the project and automobile-owning households are located relatively close to it. In this case the distribution of benefits and burdens is likely to be well-aligned and the project can be considered just by our criterion.

Visual assessments of the distributions can be limiting; it is difficult to draw conclusions based solely on them. The differences in project proximity for Project 2, for example, are not discernable from the plot. Further, these differences may or may not be judged to be substantively important when viewed in the context of an entire investment program. Such details will have to be worked out in the context of an actual planning process with input from affected populations.

Fig. 4 summarizes the difference in median distance from the project for each highway-capacity-expanding project in the investment program to facilitate more precise quantitative assessment. Only those 19 projects represented as lines in the DVRPC database are shown to ease interpretation of the figure. There are an additional 10 projects represented only as points in the database; those are not included here.

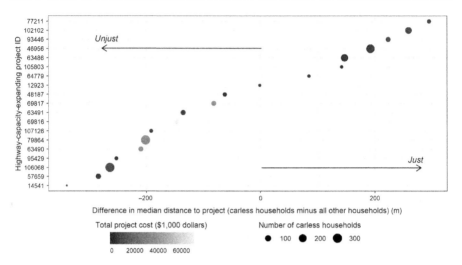

Fig. 4 Difference in median distance to project (carless households minus all other households) for highway-capacity-expanding projects, total project cost (color), and number of carless households located within 2 km (point size). Arrows in the figure illustrate those projects that are unjust (where carless households are closer to the project than all other households) and those that are just (where carless households are located further from the project than all other households).

Each plotted point in Fig. 4 presents the median distance from each project for carless households minus the median distance for all other households. Arrows in the figure indicate unjust and just projects. Negative values on the x-axis imply, for that project, that carless households tend to be located closer than all other households and thus are likely to face a heavier burden from the project once implemented. This result meets our criterion for injustice. Positive values imply the opposite: that households more likely to drive are located closer to the project. The benefits and burdens arising from that project are more likely to fall upon the same population group and the project can be considered just. As illustrated in Fig. 4, a spectrum of outcomes is possible. Those projects located further to the left (negative) or right (positive) can be considered worse or better from a justice perspective than those located closer to zero. Again, in the context of an actual planning process, the magnitude of difference deemed substantive will have to be determined. For instance, there may be a threshold of negative difference further which a project must be redesigned or mitigated.

Because not all projects have equal impacts, Fig. 4 adds two dimensions, showing the total value of each project as well as the total number of carless households located within 2 km. More costly projects may be associated with greater potential impacts, as they are likely to take longer to complete or involve greater degrees of capacity expansion. On the other hand, low numbers of affected carless households are less likely to be of concern. Project numbers are included in Fig. 4 to illustrate how this method can be used to rapidly diagnose potentially problematic projects included in an investment program. The costliest project (project ID 69816) involves an expansion of

Pennsylvania State Route 322 from two lanes to four over a 4-km segment, along with a litany of related intersection and signalization changes. One of the least costly projects is 95429, which involves an 85-m roadway extension. Both affect relatively few numbers of carless households, as indicated by the size of the plotted points.

Fig. 4 clearly shows that the costliest projects are concentrated among those that are most unjust (plotting in negative values on the x-axis) while demonstrating high variation in the number of affected carless households. Project 79864, for example, has a moderate cost but affects the greatest number of carless households among all 19 projects. It includes the construction of new lanes, a roadway extension, and interchange improvements over a 1.6-km segment. It is also part of a larger project that was broken into several distinct pieces to facilitate construction management. It is possible that a full accounting of this project's equity impacts would require unifying the component projects so that they can be considered as a single effort.

In general, the results demonstrate that substantial resources are being allocated to roadway capacity expanding projects likely to impose burdens on those unable to take advantage of a project's benefits. Many of these projects also affect relatively high numbers of carless households. In these cases, even small differences in median project distance might be deemed unjust because the impacts are likely to be so great.

4.5   Results for public transit capacity expansions

The application of this method is not limited to highway capacity expansions. In principle, it can be applied to any other project type for which a beneficiary group can be identified. Fig. 5 summarizes a subset of kernel density plots for three public transit capacity expansions. These projects are considered just if carless households are located closer to them than households without automobiles available. They include substantial station upgrades aimed in part at facilitating pedestrian access (Project A), a new light rail transit line (Project B), and a new intermodal transportation center (Project C). Projects A and C use the station as the reference point for calculating proximity, while Project B uses the transit line due to limited information about station locations.

Across all public transit capacity expansions, carless households were generally more proximate to projects than automobile-owning households. This result suggests either that planning agencies are targeting transit improvements to locations where carless households are concentrated or that carless households are located relatively closer to public transit infrastructure in general. Further analysis would be required to determine the extent to which these two factors are at work in this case.

One limitation of this analysis is that carless households are not the only beneficiaries of transit improvements. Automobile-owning households might reduce their vehicle holdings or use public transit more as its level of service improves. Upgraded stations or new service might also affect mode choice for particular trips. This is especially relevant for low-income households experiencing forced car ownership. The benefits of reducing transportation expenditures for these populations could be substantial when considered as a share of their total income. The purpose of Fig. 5 is to demonstrate how our method's logic could be applied to a different project type.

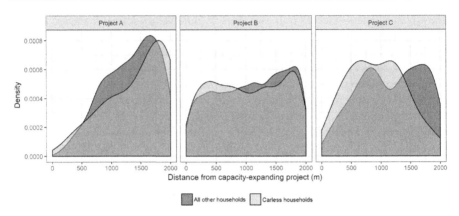

Fig. 5 Kernel density plots of population residing within 2 km of three different public transit capacity expanding projects. The projects are ordered left to right from least to most just.

5 Policy relevance

Transportation plans and investment programs are both important for future infrastructure development. The plan sets long-range goals and visions and the investment program associates funding sources with projects to realize the plan in the near-term. Both must be assessed for their performance on equity outcomes.

In this chapter, we have proposed one method that can be used to conduct an equity analysis of proposed transportation investments. It requires the identification of a beneficiary group for each project type. For highway capacity expansions, this group is assumed to be households with automobiles available. Such expansions are likely to result in increased traffic volumes and thus increased emissions, noise, vibration, and health-related impacts that will fall heavily on nearby populations. But proximity can also be construed as a benefit, in terms of reduced travel times and changes in accessibility. Performance measures should recognize and speak to this dual nature of transportation improvements. Accordingly, the method developed here compares the spatial distribution of households residing within 2 km of each proposed project, stratified by automobile ownership. This method shows clear differences in project-level performance that are potentially compounded by the value of each project.

The project-level analyses undertaken here improve upon the equity analysis results that are often presented by agencies that consist of a single answer: equitable or inequitable. By examining multiple dimensions of project-level impacts, they confront the analyst and the public with many individual outputs that must be carefully assessed and synthesized for their substantive significance. Simply because a disparity is found for a single project does not mean that it is in need of mitigation. It is possible that the overwhelming number of projects in an investment program is deemed just, so a single outlier is insignificant. The offending project may also meet other social goals, such as emissions mitigation, and be deemed beneficial even though it is unjust based on our criterion. The appropriate standard in these instances will need to be worked out within the context of a meaningful public involvement strategy. It is also possible that the project is relatively small in scope or affects a small population, so its impacts will also be low.

Conversely, some results (large disparities, large affected population, and large project costs) could indicate a real problem in potential violation of the principles of transportation justice that warrant a complete redesign or elimination of a particular project. A redesign could involve a change in the project alignment, scope (number of lanes, spatial extent), or the development of mitigations (e.g., vegetative barriers, landscaping, noise barriers). The elimination of a project from an investment program could be warranted in extreme cases but would depend upon the specific project, planning process, and input from the public. Once an alignment is decided upon, however, it will likely be difficult to change. If the investment program stage is judged to be too far along to make meaningful changes to a project, agencies should implement the method we propose (as well as other equity analyses) further upstream in the decision-making process, for example when project alternatives are being proposed. There is nothing about the proposed methods that limit them to an analysis of an entire investment program; they could also be applied to single projects and their alternatives.

Importantly, the method developed here is within reach of the analytical capabilities of typical transportation planning agencies in the United States and beyond. A prerequisite for the analysis is the existence of spatial data describing the locations of proposed investments, as well as data on households and their key characteristics. Once those are available, a GIS is all that is required to perform the analysis. Open-source alternatives to commercial GIS software are rapidly becoming available and can be used for this purpose. Continued experimentation, iteration, and public feedback is likely to be necessary to arrive at more meaningful transportation equity measures and metrics than are currently available. The method presented here is offered as one step in that direction.

6   Further reading

Analyses of transportation investment programs are relatively uncommon in both the academic literature and professional practice. Existing examples from practice tend to focus on the benefits conferred by transportation projects to nearby populations, rather than their burdens (e.g., MTC, 2016; PSRC, 2016; RISPP, 2016, pp. 61–70).

In contrast, academic studies have focused on the burdens of transportation infrastructure without simultaneously considering the benefits they may derive from them (Schweitzer and Valenzuela, 2004). For example, Chakraborty et al. (1999) examined the air pollution and noise impacts expected to result from changes to an urban arterial in Iowa using a buffer analysis combined with simulation models. A later study assessed potential equity impacts associated with two capacity-expanding highway projects by examining population shares within several buffer zones of the projects to those outside (Chakraborty, 2006). These measures did not consider that burdens decrease as distance from the project increases and they relied on polygon intersection to identify areas of impact rather than more spatially refined measures.

Klein (2007) conducted an analysis very similar to that reported here in that he sought to advance beyond typical agency practices for investment program analysis. Specifically, he applied GIS approaches to examine the spatial concentration of the financial investments embodied in the Pennsylvania portion of the DVRPC investment program in the late 2000s. An absence of appropriate comparison groups and a focus on benefits limited that analysis, as did an assumption that every dollar of TIP investment confers an equal benefit on the nearby population.

Acknowledgments

We thank the editors for their thoughtful comments and suggestions. They undoubtedly strengthened the chapter. Any remaining errors are the responsibility of the authors.

References

Chakraborty, J., 2006. Evaluating the environmental justice impacts of transportation improvement projects in the US. Transportation Research Part D: Transport and Environment 11 (5), 315–323.

Chakraborty, J., Schweitzer, L.A., Forkenbrock, D.J., 1999. Using GIS to assess the environmental justice consequences of transportation system changes. Transactions in GIS 3 (3), 239–258.

Klein, N., 2007. Spatial methodology for assessing distribution of transportation project impacts with environmental justice framework. Transportation Research Record: Journal of the Transportation Research Board 2013, 46–53.

MTC, 2016. Draft 2017 TIP Investment Analysis. Metropolitan Transportation Commission, San Francisco, CA.

PSRC, 2016. Environmental Justice and Social Equity Analysis for the Draft 2017–2020 Regional Transportation Improvement Program. Puget Sound Regional Council, Seattle, WA.

RISPP, 2016. State of Rhode Island Transportation Improvement Program. Rhode Island Statewide Planning Program, Providence, RI.

Schweitzer, L., Valenzuela, A., 2004. Environmental Injustice and Transportation: The Claims and the Evidence. Journal of Planning Literature 18 (4), 383–398.

Part Five

Closure

Conclusions

19

Karen Lucas, Karel Martens

In this edited collection, we have brought together some of the key contemporary approaches for measuring transport equity, offering a variety of perspectives and definitions of what equity might look like and which populations groups might need to be given special attention. In doing so, as editors, we have attempted to keep an open mind about exactly how to determine what is equitable. This is partly in recognition that what is needed to determine this can vary greatly in different geographical contexts, as well as according to different local social, cultural, and political norms. It is anyway our view that there is *no single definitive right or wrong way to establish equity or what is deemed to be fair.*

Certainly, there appears to be a prevalent policy understanding and rhetoric that all human beings deserve to have 'the right to life' and that there are some basic needs which have to be met in order for them to survive. There is also a general recognition that some social groups are more vulnerable than others. There is broad agreement that children, the elderly, and people with disabilities are particularly vulnerable. Also recognized in some, but certainly not all countries, is that women (especially in the Global South) and ethnic and faith minorities maybe more at risk than other population groups. Overwhelmingly, underpinning all of these social divisions is the issue of poverty and class distinctions, which still remain as the key determinant of social disadvantage in every country of the world, and inequities in mobility, accessibility, and transport can certainly have a marked effect on this in many cases.

Despite these common acceptances, it is not always the case in practice that every society provides for all basic needs or human rights, such as food, water, shelter, education, health care, and so forth. Indeed, many people across the world are denied the basic resources they need to live in dignity or even to survive. When compared to these more fundamental injustices, unfairly distributed transport resources may seem to become quite a trivial matter. However, the authors of this book are united in their belief that in the modern world where some form of *transportation is almost always needed* to facilitate access to goods and services, transport itself can become a basic human need in terms of its intervening accessibility function.

Part 1 of the book has sought to identify a range of key issues that are associated with transport (in)equity and to provide an overarching framework for measuring them.

A key issue for Part 2 following from these introductory chapters was then to determine whether the main social benefit of transport is deemed to be mobility itself or the associated accessibility that this mobility provides. General opinion on this matter is divided, and much of mainstream transport policy still largely focuses on speeding up journey times and improving the travel experience (albeit often not for all people). In contrast, the methodologies presented in Part 2 of this book focus their attention more

Measuring Transport Equity. https://doi.org/10.1016/B978-0-12-814818-1.00019-6

on evaluation of the *accessibility function* of mobility in terms of people's opportunity and ability to reach a range of destinations. The identification of equity or fairness in these methodologies is usually addressed through either the implicit or explicit suggestion that everyone should have an *equal opportunity* to, or a *minimal level* of, access a set of key activity destinations in their vicinity, such as employment, education and training centers, healthcare services, shops, and so forth. They use measures such as journey times to destinations, distances, costs, safety as impedance values within their analyses to compare the accessibility of different groups and areas. Fairness is most often judged against a locally normalized average travel time (e.g., such as 30 min to a hospital) and/or based on the empirical evidence of this from bespoke travel surveys. Some of the more sophisticated approaches in this category also consider impedance factors such as people's travel time budgets and activity spaces as constraints to accessibility.

In Part 3 of the book, the authors have been more concerned with the *adverse effects or burdens of the transport system* itself, and how these impacts are unevenly distributed across different population sectors and/or comparative geographical locations. The two impacts they have identified as of key concern in this respect are traffic injuries/fatalities and exposure to traffic-related air pollutants. However, the list could also include exposure to noise, loss of green space, severance, or any other negative externality of transport which affects human health and well-being. The measure of equity here is certainly *not* based on an idea that everyone should have an equal opportunity to be exposed to such health hazards, but rather that they should be designed out of the transport system, and/or that people should not be physically located in areas where they are exposed beyond an acceptable level, whether at home, work, or school. There is an additional equity issue to be considered, however, in that some population groups are more vulnerable to these impacts that others, such as children, older and disabled people, as well as poorer households who tend to walk more and also live near busy road, and so are more exposed to these externalities. This understanding challenges the use of standards for negative impacts such as air and noise pollution, as such standards ignore the wide variety of actual exposures resulting from variations in people's travel behaviors. The increasing evidence that both air and noise pollution lead to thousands of premature deaths in virtually every major city suggests that more research on the equity impacts of existing norms and standards is certainly called for.

Part 4 of the book has primarily focused on measuring the social outcomes and consequences of transport inequalities, such as for health and well-being, the maintenance of social capital, social cohesion, and social exclusion. In some chapters, these social outcome measures have been used as descriptors of people's lived experiences of transport, in which case they might be measured in single snapshots in time and/or following changes to the transport or land-use system (e.g., the introduction or loss of services or infrastructures). In other cases, the social outcomes can be seen as both positive and negative dynamic processes, in which case these assessment are used to track to the changing condition of people's lives (e.g., through the various life stages or in response to wider influencing factors such as changes to the structure of the economy, physical environment, governance, or both). Here, the combined use of both qualitative and quantitative methods is particularly important for establishing people's perceptions and experiences of transport and how this relates to their participative capacities and choice constraints, as a couple of the chapters have demonstrated. However, the book does not majorly consider the important use of qualitative data in the measurement of transport equity. This is less because these methods are not useful in the assessment of transport equity but more because to give them the full attention they deserve is outside the scope of this book.

From an overview of the book, we can conclude that transport equity is a burgeoning field both within the academic and policy domains and there is an increasing proliferation of approaches. In the assessment of mobility and accessibility, the methodologies are quite advanced and, in some cases, can be highly complex. Similarly, as the spatial datasets and computational capacities have improved, there has been considerable progress in the measurement of the burdens and risks of transport in terms of human exposure to noise, air pollutants, and safety risks. How to relate different levels and concentrations of exposure to people's physical and mental health outcomes is less certain, although great strides have been made in monitoring these outcomes in public health spheres in the recent years. There is also now much greater communication and interaction between local transport and health professionals, as an awareness of the problems of traffic pollution and safety has been raised on the international stage by the World Health Organization and other global campaign organizations.

Measurement of the other social outcomes that are more broadly associated with transport provision, such as economic and social participation, well-being, social inclusion, and quality of life, is generally less well evolved within the academic domain and also thereby less recognized by policymakers. The six illustrative chapters in Part 4 of the book offer some novel ways in which these wider societal considerations can and have been measured in relation to transport. All of these methodologies are a long way from what is currently being done in practice to assess the positive and negatives contributions of transport to these wider social outcomes. Many of these narratives of social well-being, human capital, social integration, inclusion, and cohesion have been recognized in a general sense within the transport policies of numerous countries. Their specific measurement in the context of the assessment of transport equity, or even in the assessment of transport investments at the aggregate level, is not so prevalent or well defined, and so this space is wide open for further experimentation and research.

It will be evident to the experts in this field that some of the more mainstream approaches to measuring the distribution of people's travel behaviors have not been included within the book. We are referring here, amongst others, to mainstream travel behavior surveys that provide a deep understanding of the variety in travel behaviors of different social groups, as well as sometimes to the large revealed disparities in the number, length, and duration of trips and uses of different transport modes across differently positioned population groups. We have not included these approaches partly because we felt that the measurements and methodological techniques used are already well described elsewhere, and so we aimed rather to highlight the less-traditional approaches that maybe less familiar to the reader. However, we have also not included them because these techniques do not usually *directly* seek to address the issue of transport inequity of itself, but only describe the distributions across different social groups so as to predict the future direction of their behaviors, either overtime or in response to an intervention. From the perspective of mainstream transport planning, these differences are typically seen as 'a given' rather than as an issue requiring normative assessment and directed interventions. We are not suggesting that these methods could not be used to measure equity if used for that specific intention, but most generally this is not what they are currently used for within the transport community and certain adaptations would need to be made in order for them to be useful in this capacity.

There are other missing contributions that do directly measure transport equity in novel and innovative ways, and we can only apologize to you for their absence. In some cases, the authors were invited to join us but could not due to conflicting time pressures, or because of restrictive copyright rules, which prevented them from reproducing their work. We have directed you to some of these additional methodologies in the Further Reading sections at the end of each of the chapters and we have also included additional references to our own recent work in this area at the end of this concluding chapter. In this way, we hope that you will see our book as a stepping stone in your further exploration of this important and engaging topic of transport equity, how to identify and measure it. Ultimately, we urge you to join us in the quest to make the transport sector fairer and more socially inclusive, so that everyone in the society has an equal chance to thrive through the transport systems we build and operate, now and for the future generations yet to come.

Further reading

For those who are interested in reading more about some of the basic principles behind transport equity and the rationale behind why we have developed this book in the way that we have, you can refer to the book chapter by Martens and Lucas (2018).

Two useful perspectives on the conceptualization of transport inequality and transport justice are Martens' book on Transport Justice (Martens, 2017) and Banister's on Inequality in Transport (Banister, 2018).

For wider reading and supporting materials to support the measurement of transport equity within policy decision making, please refer to publications from the EU COST Action on Transport Equity Assessment, which can be found at http:/teacost.eu/.

References

Banister, D., 2018. Inequality in Transport. Alexandrine Press, Oxfordshire.
Martens, K., 2017. Transport Justice: Developing Fair Transport Systems. Routledge, New York.
Martens, K., Lucas, K., 2018. Perspectives on transport and social justice. Chapter 26, In: Craig, G. (Ed.), Handbook on Global Social Justice. Edward Elgar Publishing Inc., UK.

Index

Note: Page numbers followed by *f* indicate figures and *t* indicate tables.

Printed in the United States
By Bookmasters